Women of the New Mexico Frontier

1846-1912

Women of the New Mexico Frontier

1846-1912

Cheryl J. Foote

University of New Mexico Press
Albuquerque

ISBN-13: 978-0-8263-3755-9
ISBN-10: 0-8263-3755-4

Library of Congress Cataloging-in-Publication Data

Foote, Cheryl J., 1947–
  Women of the New Mexico frontier, 1846–1912 / Cheryl J. Foote.
      p. cm.
  Originally published: Niwot, Colo. : University Press of Colorado, c1990.
  "Chapter 5 of this book was first published in the Fall 1982 issue of Journal
of Presbyterian History"—Verso t.p.
  Includes bibliographical references and index.
  ISBN 0-8263-3755-4 (pbk. : alk. paper)
  1. Women pioneers—New Mexico—History. 2. New Mexico—History—1848–
3. Frontier and pioneer life—New Mexico. I. Title.
  F801.F56 2005
  978.9'04—dc22
                    2004028726

Chapter 5 of this book was first published in the Fall 1982 issue of
Journal of Presbyterian History–Verso t.p.

Chapter 4 was first published in the April 1990 issue of *New Mexico
Historical Review.*

To Bill, Jeremy, and Jennifer

Contents

New Introduction to the 2005 Edition

"Women were an important part of the frontier experience,"[1] historian Sandra L. Myres noted in 1982, as scholars of the American West had begun to mine the rich ore of women's history in the region. Still, she cautioned, many authors wrote about western women based on sources men had written *about* women rather than on the "treasure trove"[2] of women's writings in archives, libraries, and private collections across the country. As Myres, Julie Roy Jeffrey, and Lillian Schlissel tapped into this vein,[3] they inspired others to join them in using women's voices to tell a new version of western American history.

Women of the New Mexico Frontier, 1846–1912 resulted from my search for New Mexican women's writings. Despite New Mexico's long history, women authored few documents during the Spanish Colonial (1598–1821) or Mexican periods (1821–1846). Although they gave testimony in court cases, made wills, conveyed land, conducted businesses, and withstood investigations by the Inquisition, most women were unable to write so that traditional historical sources such as diaries, letters, and memoirs are not available until the period after 1846, when the United States conquered the region. After the American occupation a number of literate women gave voice to women's presence in the territory. Susan Magoffin's *Down the Santa Fe Trail and Into Mexico*, Marian Russell's *Land of Enchantment*, and Agnes Morley Cleaveland's *No Life for a Lady* became southwestern classics. Several army wives also described their adventures in New Mexico, and by the mid-twentieth century Fabiola Cabeza de Baca's *We Fed Them Cactus* and Cleofas Jaramillo's *Romance of a Little Village Girl* furnished a much needed Hispana perspective.[4]

Even as I savored these, I wondered about other women who might have come to New Mexico. I wanted to know about their lives and about the American Southwest as they saw it. What expectations did they bring with them, and did New Mexico shatter or fulfill those? Did living in a remote and foreign landscape, in close contact with peoples of other languages, religion, culture, and history, reshape the newcomers' attitudes, or confirm their suspicions of cultural superiority? And, as the documentary evidence revealed that many of those women who wrote about New Mexico lived here only a short time, what happened to them when they left? Despite their brief residence in the territory, did they have any lasting effect on New Mexico's development? Most of all, I wanted to hear their voices speak through the scattered documents they left behind and to share their stories with general readers as well as scholars.

To my delight, I found an array of sources ranging from letters and diaries to military records, missionary reports, short stories, and scientific studies. Most, however, were fragmentary accounts of women's lives. Rather than produce an edited collection of their writings, as interesting as they were, I resolved instead to learn as much as I could about the authors. Whenever I could, I wanted to continue their stories to provide a more comprehensive view of their lives. Eventually, I found that collective biographies about early missionary women and army wives fit better with their more limited sources. In other cases, more abundant materials allowed me to write the biographies of women whose New Mexican experiences profoundly influenced their lives, whether they stayed in the area or merely passed through. As I learned more about them as individuals, I also concluded that these Anglo American women contributed to the Americanization of the territory in significant respects. If I were rewriting their stories today, I would emphasize that theme more seriously and also try to analyze the effects of that Americanization upon the original residents of the territory. In addition, because I based my study on documents that women wrote themselves, Hispanas and Native Americans appear in the work only through the eyes of the American women who intended them to adapt to the new political regime and the culture that came with it. If I were to rewrite the book today, I would try to include more about these original settlers of the region. Fortunately, other scholars have done so.

In the twenty years since I commenced the research for this book, the field of women's history has exploded. Many newer works focus less on letting women's sources speak for themselves and more on studying women through the prism of race, class, and gender. Similarly, the very concept of the American frontier, implicitly positive toward American westward expansion and Anglo-centric, has been challenged and replaced with "the new western history," which considers instead the harmful effects of American conquest and colonization on the West.[5]

Numerous historians, influenced by the ideas of the new western history, offer a broader analysis of New Mexican history that includes important information about Hispanas and Native American women. For example, Ramon A. Gutierrez's *When Jesus Came, the Corn Mothers Went Away: Marriage, Sexuality, and Power in New Mexico, 1500–1846* resulted from extensive research into the Spanish and Mexican Archives of New Mexico and into ethnographical literature about the Pueblos. *Captives and Cousins: Slavery, Kinship, and Community in the Southwest Borderlands* by James F. Brooks is a monumental work of scholarship based on some of the same sources that strips away myths about the slave trade between Native peoples and Hispanic settlers. The Spanish and Mexican archives, wills, judicial proceedings, and census records are the basis for Deena J. Gonzalez's *Refusing the Favor: The Spanish–Mexican Women of Santa Fe, 1820–1880*. Sarah Deutsch made extensive use of Protestant missionary records and other sources for *No Separate Refuge: Culture, Class, and Gender on an Anglo-Hispanic Frontier in the American Southwest*. These two works consider the disruptive and negative consequences of the American conquest for Hispanas in the region. Hispanas also receive attention in more traditional histories like Nasario Garcia's collection of oral histories, *Comadres: Hispanic Women of the Rio Puerco Valley*, in which Hispanas recount their own stories. And a fine article by Janet Lecompte provides new information about Gertrudes Barceló (Doña

Tules), the best-known, though often romanticized, Hispana in New Mexican history.[6]

Other important works discuss Protestant mission work and cross-cultural interactions between Anglos, Hispanos, and Native Americans in the Southwest. Susan Yohn, *A Contest of Faith: Missionary Women and Pluralism in the American Southwest* specifically evaluates the efforts and results of women in the mission field, while Mark A. Banker's *Presbyterian Missions and Cultural Interactions in the Far Southwest 1850–1950* considers the Presbyterian experiment more broadly. Although the Roman Catholic Sisters of Loretto and Sisters of Charity deserve more scholarly attention, new works have not appeared about their cross-cultural experiences. However, a reprinted edition of Sister Blandina Segale's *At the End of the Santa Fe Trail*, with an informative foreword by Marc Simmons and an afterword by Anne M. Butler that places the Sisters of Charity in New Mexico in broader national context, is recommended. Sandra Schackel also discusses cross-cultural exchanges in her significant volume *Social Housekeepers: Women Shaping Public Policy in New Mexico 1920–1940*, which details changing roles for women and the development of social welfare programs for the state. Moreover, though African American women's history in New Mexico remains largely untold, Schackel's book discusses African American women's work in the women's club movement of the early twentieth century.[7]

Finally, additional accounts by and about Anglo American women have been published in the last two decades. Sharon Niederman's *A Quilt of Words: Women's Diaries, Letters, & Original Accounts of Life in the Southwest, 1860–1960* is an edited collection of the writings of fifteen women, and *Mary Donoho: New First Lady of the Santa Fe Trail* by Marian Meyer reveals new information about Anglo American women in New Mexico before 1846. Leslie Poling-Kempes brings a scholarly eye to a western legend in *The Harvey Girls: Women Who Opened the West*. Finally, LaVerne Hanners's *Girl on a Pony* opens a window to cattle ranching in northeastern New Mexico between World War I and World War II, and *Pie Town*

Woman, by Joan Myers, brings to life the endurance and resiliency of settlers in west central New Mexico during the Depression.[8] Two women whose stories appear in the present volume have also spurred additional research. Leo and Bonita Oliva are editing Katie Bowen's letters for publication, while Darlis Miller is at work on a full-length biography of Matilda Coxe Stevenson.

As these publications indicate, women were active participants in New Mexico's past, and their experiences, whether tragic, interesting, inspiring, or shocking, add greatly to our understanding of New Mexico's history. Hopefully, the sources I uncovered will inspire others to dig deeper into still more aspects of women's history. I am pleased that the University of New Mexico Press is making available again *Women of the New Mexico Frontier, 1846–1912,* so that readers may continue to vicariously experience life in territorial New Mexico through the pens of military wives and missionaries, authors, and scientists. Forgotten no longer, their stories reveal the extraordinary diversity of New Mexico's history.

1. Sandra L. Myres, *Westering Women and the Frontier Experience, 1800–1915* (Albuquerque: University of New Mexico Press, 1982), xv.
2. Myres, *Westering Women,* xvii.
3. Myres, *Westering Women* and Myres, ed., *Ho for California! Women's Overland Diaries from the Huntington Library* (San Marino, California: Huntington Library, 1980); Julie Roy Jeffrey, *Frontier Women: The Trans-Mississippi West, 1840–1880* (New York: Hill and Wang, 1979); Lillian Schlissel, *Women's Diaries of the Westward Journey* (New York: Schocken Books, 1982).
4. Susan Magoffin, *Down the Santa Fe Trail and Into Mexico* (1926; reprint ed., Lincoln: University of Nebraska, 1982); Marian Russell, *Land of Enchantment* (1954; reprint ed., Albuquerque: University of New Mexico Press, 1981); Agnes Morley Cleaveland, *No Life for a Lady* (1941; reprint ed., Lincoln: University of Nebraska Press, 1977); Fabiola Cabeza de Baca, *We Fed Them Cactus* (Albuquerque: University of New Mexico Press, 1954); Cleofas M. Jaramillo, *Romance of a Little Village Girl* (1955; reprint ed., Albuquerque: University of New Mexico Press, 2000).

5. See, for example, Patricia Nelson Limerick, *A Legacy of Conquest: The Unbroken Past of the American West* (New York: W.W. Norton & Co., 1987).

6. Ramon A. Gutierrez, *When Jesus Came, the Corn Mothers Went Away: Marriage, Sexuality, and Power in New Mexico, 1500–1846* (Stanford, California: Stanford University Press, 1991); James Brooks, *Captives and Cousins: Slavery, Kinship, and Community in the Southwest Borderlands* (Chapel Hill: University of North Carolina Press, 2002); Deena J. Gonzalez, *Refusing the Favor: The Spanish-Mexican Women of Santa Fe 1820–1880* (New York: Oxford University Press, 1999); Sarah Deutsch, *No Separate Refuge: Culture, Class, and Gender on an Anglo-Hispanic Frontier in the American Southwest* (New York: Oxford University Press, 1987); Nasario Garcia, ed. *Comadres: Hispanic Women of the Rio Puerco Valley* (Albuquerque: University of New Mexico Press, 1997); Janet Lecompte, "La Tules: The Ultimate New Mexican Woman," in *By Grit and Grace,* edited by Glenda Riley and Richard W. Etulain (Golden, Colorado: Fulcrum Press, 1997).

7. Susan M. Yohn, *Missionary Women and Pluralism in the American Southwest* (Ithaca: Cornell University Press, 1995); Mark Banker, *Presbyterian Missions and Cultural Interactions in the Far Southwest, 1850–1950* (Urbana: University of Illinois Press, 1993); Blandina Segale, *At the End of the Santa Fe Trail* (1932; reprint ed., Albuquerque: University of New Mexico Press, 1999); Sandra Schackel, *Social Housekeepers: Women Shaping Public Policy in New Mexico, 1920–1940* (Albuquerque: University of New Mexico Press, 1992).

8. Sharon Niederman, *A Quilt of Words: Women's Diaries, Letters, and Original Accounts of Life in the Southwest, 1860–1960* (Boulder: Johnson Press, 1988); Marian Meyer, *Mary Donoho: New First Lady of the Santa Fe Trail* (Santa Fe: Ancient City Press, 1991); Leslie Poling Kempes, *The Harvey Girls: Women Who Opened the West* (New York: Paragon House, 1989); La Verne Hanners, *Girl on a Pony* (Norman: University of Oklahoma Press, 1994); Joan Myers, *Pie Town Woman: The Hard Life and Good Times of a New Mexico Homesteader* (Albuquerque: University of New Mexico Press, 2001).

Acknowledgments

During the course of this study, I was blessed with the kindness and assistance of many people. I particularly wish to thank Donald C. Cutter, professor emeritus at the University of New Mexico, who urged me to pursue advanced historical studies, and Richard N. Ellis, at Ft. Lewis College, who advised and encouraged me throughout this project. Richard Etulain, John Kessell, and Ferenc Szasz at the University of New Mexico also offered many useful suggestions. I am most grateful to the Sandia Foundation, trustees of the estate of Dorothy Woodward, late professor of history at the University of New Mexico. The generous Dorothy Woodward fellowship I received helped with the expenses incurred during this study.

At the National Archives and the National Anthropological Archives, staff members provided helpful and reliable service. Librarians at the Bancroft Library similarly proved courteous and attentive to my requests for information by mail. Especially generous with her time was Sibylle Zemitis at the California State Library, who provided me with numerous photocopies and other information from collections there. Closer to home, Sherry Smith (formerly with the State Records Center and Archives) and the staff of the Special Collections Department at the University of New Mexico Library, particularly Mary Blumenthal, were most gracious with their assistance. At the Menaul Historical Library, Carolyn Atkins and Dorothy Stevenson extended every courtesy and their expertise on Presbyterian mission work in the Southwest. Similarly, Betty Danielson, church historian of First Baptist Church in Albuquerque, shared with me with copies of correspondence, church reports, and photographs of early Baptist missionaries in the state. Nancy Brown at the *New Mexico Historical Review* cheerfully and promptly answered innumerable requests for information.

Miss Gwladys Bowen, Mrs. Jeanne McIntosh, Mrs. Roy Blake, and the late S. Omar Barker patiently answered my many questions about their relatives and friends whose stories are presented herein. I also thank Donald Dreesen, whose knowledge of the genealogy of Albuquerque families led me to Mrs. McIntosh.

My appreciation goes to the *New Mexico Historical Review* for permission to use the chapter on Josephine Clifford, which appeared in the April 1990 issue.

Finally, I thank my husband Bill, particularly for his professional advice for chapter four, and my children Jeremy and Jennifer for their forbearance and encouragement.

Introduction

In 1846, an eighteen-year-old bride from Kentucky became the first Anglo-American woman to describe her travels through New Mexico.[1] With her husband, Samuel, Susan Magoffin arrived in Santa Fe on the heels of Stephen Watts Kearny and the Army of the West. Her eyewitness account of the U.S. conquest of the Mexican province, first published in 1926 as *Down the Santa Fe Trail and into Mexico,* has become a southwestern classic. As Magoffin described, the military acquisition of the region proceeded quickly and encountered little resistance. Integrating the new territory and its inhabitants into the U.S. political system, however, proved slower and more difficult. New Mexico (which included the present-day state of Arizona until 1863) was organized as a territory in 1850, but it did not achieve statehood until 1912.

During this lengthy territorial period, many Anglo women participated in the process of Americanizing the region, and some of them, like Susan Magoffin, left written records about their experiences in this remote area. Most Americans of the mid-nineteenth century knew little about the lands that officially became part of the United States under the Treaty of Guadalupe-Hidalgo of 1848. Still, the acquisition of the area later to become the states of California, Nevada, Utah, Colorado, New Mexico, and Arizona fulfilled many aspects of Manifest Destiny, including the conviction that the United States was divinely intended to stretch from the Atlantic to the Pacific. In addition to territorial goals, the annexation of California furthered U.S. commercial interests. Control of the ports on the west coast protected U.S. trade, and the discovery of gold in 1848 multiplied the area's economic importance to the growing nation. Commerce was a powerful motive for acquiring New Mexico as well, not only as a route to the Pacific but also because of the lucrative Santa Fe trade.

After a long history as an isolated frontier province of Spain and then Mexico, New Mexico became an eager market for U.S. goods when the Mexican republic relaxed trade restrictions in 1821. Merchants brought their wares westward along the Santa Fe Trail, and by the mid-1840s the Santa Fe trade had grown to such proportions that its protection became a matter of particular concern for the U.S. government during the Mexican War.[2] In the decades following annexation, New Mexico grew in economic potential — cattle ranching expanded and mineral wealth was discovered; in addition, it lay on the routes for transcontinental railroads. New Mexico's economic development, however, proceeded at a much slower pace than California's, and the territory's large area (nearly 122,000 square miles in the present-day state of New Mexico) and arid climate presented the government with special problems. Among them were maintaining communication and transportation across vast distances where water supplies were sparse. Aridity also meant that settlement depended more on water available for irrigation than on the simple existence of unowned land.

Even more perplexing to the Anglo newcomers were the people they encountered already living in the American Southwest. The smallest groups, numerically speaking, were the nomadic Apaches and Navajos, who swept across the mesas and plains to attack settlers and travelers. The Apaches particularly remained a threat to much of New Mexico until the late nineteenth century. For nearly fifty years the U.S. Army battled to subdue the hostiles, to protect settlers and miners, and to keep lines of communication and transportation open.

In addition to these nomadic peoples, about 55,000 Hispanic New Mexicans lived in small settlements throughout the province when the area became part of the United States in 1846. Some 10,000 Pueblo Indians also resided in their communities clustered near the central Rio Grande valley. Three hundred years before, the autonomy of the Pueblos had been challenged when Spanish explorers claimed the region for their sovereign, and the first Spanish settlement was established in 1598, north of present-day Santa Fe. Although the Europeans failed to find great riches in the area, Spain maintained the colony for the next two centuries, first as a mission field (to bring Christianity to the Pueblos) and later as a buffer colony to protect the rich silver mines of Mexico's central plateau from attacks by Indians or other European interests. The province became part of Mexico when the viceroyalty of New Spain won independence from Spain and became the republic of Mexico in 1821.

On this northern frontier, most Hispanics and Pueblos lived in small scattered settlements, practiced subsistence agriculture, and grazed herds of cattle and sheep. A few families became involved in commerce, but industry and the professions were almost unknown before the Americans entered the region. Few New Mexicans spoke English, nearly all were Roman Catholics (the Pueblos having converted at least nominally, though they also maintained their traditional religion), and most could neither read nor write. No colleges, universities, or public schools existed in the province; private schools were scanty and sporadic at best. But to the consternation of most Anglo observers, these New Mexicans were suddenly U.S. citizens.

Most newcomers to the territory agreed that New Mexicans, because of their illiteracy and unfamiliarity with English, were ill-suited to partake of the blessings of democracy. Unanimity of opinion ended there, however. The question of political participation for New Mexicans revolved around the question of statehood. Many opposed early statehood for the territory, some because of a true conviction that Hispanics and Indians needed education and an understanding of American culture before they could appropriately participate in the democratic process. They supported territorial status because it meant the U.S. government would appoint most officials instead of providing for their election by the local populace. Other Americans sought territorial office as a means of lining their pockets at the expense of Hispanics and Native Americans, and these unscrupulous politicians and their friends often led the fight against statehood. U.S. merchants and Hispanic leaders, though, pushed vigorously for the home rule that statehood would provide. The struggle over this political question persisted for more than sixty years, but the process of instilling American values, customs, and culture into New Mexicans began soon after the military conquest of the area.[3]

Two institutions — the Protestant churches and the U.S. government — played key roles in this process. By the mid-nineteenth century, the United States was in the midst of what one historian has called the Protestant Crusade,[4] and the Hispanic and native American residents of the Southwest provided a new focus for missionary zeal. As well-meaning Protestants saw it, the ignorance, poverty, and moral laxity of the New Mexican population resulted from the influence of the Catholic church. They proposed to establish schools to alleviate the problem of ignorance and churches to bring a "truer" message of Christianity to the populace. The churches often worked toward this goal hand in hand with the government. In fact, under the "peace policy" of Ulysses S. Grant, the Bureau of Indian Affairs (BIA) turned the problem of educating and assimilating the American Indians over to the churches (including the Roman Catholic church).

Other agencies of the federal government influenced the process of Americanization in New Mexico during the territorial period. The army first conquered, then provided military rule for the region between 1846 and 1850. For the next forty years, the army established and maintained routes for transportation and communication and protected New Mexicans from the raids of nomadic Indians. During the Civil War, Union troops thwarted a Confederate plan to annex New Mexico, which would then have provided a base for Southern campaigns to seize the goldfields of Colorado and the Pacific Coast.

Another government agency that became important in the Southwest was the Bureau of Ethnology (later the Bureau of American Ethnology — BAE) of the Smithsonian Institution. By the 1870s, humanitarians, church leaders, and officials of the BIA had agreed that earlier policies of extermination and removal of Native Americans should be replaced by one of assimiliation. Accordingly, various denominations established schools and churches on reservations and attempted to "Americanize" indigenous populations, which were expected not only to learn new ways but also to abandon their traditional lifestyles and beliefs. Because scientists who supported the goal of assimilation at the same time understood that the program would doom the original American Indian cultures, the BAE dispatched anthropologists and ethnologists to the West to record the vanishing traditions and customs.

Representatives of both church and government in New Mexico included Anglo women, some of whom left written accounts about their lives there. Their stories reveal considerable variety in their experiences, not surprising in an area recognized for its geographical, ethnic, and historical diversity. Scholars have studied many aspects of this diversity, but until recently have overlooked the contributions that women made to the region. In the past decade, however, historians, anthropologists, and investigators from other disciplines have produced a prodigious amount of research about women in the West.[5] Some of this material, to be sure, has examined southwestern women,[6] but as one author noted recently, the Southwest remains "relatively neglected in regional studies" compared with other parts of the country.[7] This vast scholarship about western women has yet to be incorporated into a synthetic overview of western history, in part because gaps in the literature remain.[8]

This work profiles women who came to the Southwest between 1846 and 1912. Their stories fill in some of the gaps in the history of western women and provide a sample for comparison with that of women in other areas of the country. Based on diaries, letters, memoirs, and other literary sources, including newspaper articles and short stories, as well as on official documents such as census returns and pension records, this book recounts the experiences of women on the New Mexico frontier largely in their own words, using their own punctuation and spelling.

The first chapter presents the stories of women married to Protestant ministers who came to New Mexico between 1846 and 1890. The writings that Harriett Shaw, Martha Roberts, and numerous other missionary wives left provide an intimate view not only of their commitment to serve as full partners with their husbands in converting American Indian and Hispanic residents of the territory but also of their preoccupations with daily domestic duties and family concerns. Often, childless missionary wives enjoyed considerable success in their vocations, while those with families found that the exigencies of making a home and raising children precluded full participation in missionary work.

Chapter Two explores the lives of women married to army officers who came to the territory before the Civil War. Although many army wives' writings about the postwar army have recently been reprinted, few women's descriptions of garrison life in the antebellum period are available. The letters and diary of two women stationed at New Mexican posts in the 1850s reveal that, like their later compatriots, early army wives in the West confronted new peoples and situations with courage, humor, and adaptability.

The army frontier is again the setting for the third and fourth portraits. Chapter Three tells of Ellen Williams, who served as a laundress and nurse with a Colorado regiment during the Civil War. Although many women married to officers wrote memoirs and reminiscences about their military association, few working-class women produced accounts of their army experiences. In her book *Three Years and a Half in the Army, or History of the Second Colorados,* Ellen Williams offers a rare, female perspective on New Mexico during the Civil War — a glimpse of working women's participation in the frontier army and enlisted men's family lives.

Still another aspect of life in the frontier military emerges from the story of Josephine Clifford, told in Chapter Four. Mrs. Clifford, who came to New Mexico in 1866, spent several harrowing months as an abused wife before she summoned the courage to leave her husband (an officer in the Third Cavalry) and embark on a new life as a local-color writer in California. Her account paints a graphic picture of domestic violence on the frontier. In contrast to missionary wives and other army women who often confined their activities and interests to the domestic sphere, Josephine Clifford became self-supporting through a fulfilling career in the West.

A satisfying career in the West also awaited Alice Blake, whose lengthy service as a mission teacher in Hispanic villages in New Mexico is the subject of Chapter Five. Although missionary wives were often frustrated in the mission field, single women found that mission work gave them new opportunities on the frontier. Many of these women devoted their lives to this endeavor; Alice Blake, for example, spent more than forty years (1888–1931) in missionary service, providing education and health care to rural Hispanics. In the process, these mission teachers and the people they served achieved a rare level of intercultural cooperation and appreciation.

Intercultural relations also dominated the career of Matilda Coxe Stevenson. Chapter Six discusses her life and work as an ethnologist among the Zuni and Zia people of New Mexico from 1879 to 1915. In the late nineteenth century, anthropologists believed that women's traditional concern with domestic and familial issues suited them to conduct ethnological investigations among women of other cultures, and in her early studies Mrs. Stevenson dutifully examined women and children in indigenous societies. After her husband's death, however, Matilda Coxe Stevenson expanded her scientific inquiries into a variety of other subjects, including religion, mythology, and botany of the Pueblos. For Stevenson and other women, anthropology offered a new career option in the American West.

Clearly, although they remained a minority, Anglo women in territorial New Mexico participated in a wide range of activities. The stories of these New Mexican pioneers illustrate their varied experiences and add another dimension to our understanding of the region's diverse history. Home and family remained the primary sphere of interest for missionary and army wives, yet their lives on the frontier exposed them to other cultures and required of them unusual levels of innovation and adaptation within the domestic environment. Other women abandoned traditional female roles as wives and mothers and found new careers in the West. Ordinary women met extraordinary challenges, as well as the demands of daily life, with determination and courage.

Women of the New Mexico Frontier
1846–1912

CHAPTER ONE

"A Faithful and Efficient Helpmate"

Missionary Wives in New Mexico

"I hope I shall be enabled to perform my duties faithfully to my husband and my Lord . . . that I may prove a blessing instead of a curse to my dear husband and to the world." In these words to her mother, Harriett Bidwell Shaw encapsulated the aspirations of missionary wives who accompanied their husbands to New Mexico following the U.S. occupation of the territory in 1846. Throughout the first half of the nineteenth century, Protestant denominations had dispatched missionaries around the globe to spread the Protestant gospel; now, a similar opportunity lay within the continental boundaries of the United States. Residents of the new territory, which was almost as remote and unfamiliar to the average citizen as were mission fields in Africa and Polynesia, included not only "heathens" but also Hispanics whose religion was Roman Catholic, which Protestants considered little better than paganism.

In the first decade following U.S. annexation, Baptists, Methodists, and Presbyterians sent missionaries to New Mexico to establish churches and schools in the territory. Missionaries failed to make significant inroads into the Hispanic or native American communities, however, and, for the most part, these denominations abandoned the area during the Civil War. Somewhat ironically, in the very years that Protestant efforts began, New Mexico's first bishop, Jean Baptiste Lamy, undertook a program to revitalize the Catholic church and to open schools. Lamy's efforts continued during and after the war, and Protestants renewed their interest in the territory in the postwar years. Under President Ulysses Grant's "peace policy," Protestant denominations recommended candidates for appointments as Indian agents, and missionaries frequently held positions as teachers, doctors, and matrons on American Indian reservations. Thus, throughout the territorial period, Protestant missionary couples played a significant role in the area's religious development.[1]

Despite denominational differences, Anglo women who came to New Mexico as wives of missionaries between 1849 and 1880 shared ideals, concerns, and experiences and (fortunately for the historian) left written accounts about life on this frontier. These documents are particularly useful because they not only describe missionary life but also provide the intimate details about the daily lives of women and families in the territory that are unavailable in most other sources for the period. These materials indicate that whereas missionary wives shared many concerns and events with other Anglo women in the area, some of their expectations and ideals regarding their own participation in this frontier experience were unique.[2]

Among women in the West, according to one historian, "the missionary wife was doubtless the one with the highest religious and cultural purposes and the highest standards."[3] Indeed, missionary wives of the nineteenth century shared the prevalent ideology of middle-class white women, which enjoined women to be pure, pious, submissive, and domestic. Domesticity required more than a knowledge of housewifery; women centered attention on their families and assumed

responsibility for the spiritual and emotional well-being of
family members. While a woman's life focused on the home,
her moral influence expanded her sphere to include religious
activities, and the education of young children also merged
into a woman's duty, consistent with expressed ideals. By
bringing the Christian gospel to the "heathen," the missionary wife exercised her religious and moral duty and served as
an example of a proper Christian female. Her responsibility
extended to training women of other cultures in the domestic
arts and to teaching native children in mission schools.[4]

Simply trying to establish a home that met New England
standards of domesticity was a challenge to the frontier
housewife. Women responded with ingenuity to the task of
creating a homelike environment, learning to substitute for
or do without the familiar trappings of civilization. Their
responses, depending on temperamental differences, varied
from humorous acceptance of the situation to resignation or
bitterness. For the missionary wife, however, recreating a
suitable home formed only part of her duty. She also assumed
the extra-domestic role of teacher and co-missionary with her
husband. As her family grew, the demands of her roles as wife
and mother often made it impossible for her to meet obligations as teacher and missionary. For some women, abandon-
ing their expected vocation as teacher was frustrating and
disappointing; others surrendered it with relief. But a wife's
inability to fulfill her missionary duties (in addition to her
wifely tasks) meant that her husband took on additional
tasks and sought assistants in the work. Thus, what missionary couples had perceived as a joint venture in which
they would labor together (although with distinct duties)
often reverted to established patterns of separate spheres of
activity.[5]

Indeed, administrators, ministers, and missionaries, as
well as the wives themselves, from the beginning stressed the
importance of women in the missionary endeavor and made it

clear that single men were not much of an asset in this regard. Hiram W. Read, the first Protestant missionary in the Southwest, with his wife, Alzina, arrived in Santa Fe in 1849. Read soon wrote to the American Baptist Home Mission Society requesting additional missionaries for New Mexico. He asked the church to send *"married* men (unmarried ones would be useless) of good physical and mental endowments" able to endure "a long, toilsome, and somewhat dangerous journey to the field, and its privations and difficulties when there." Further, he cautioned, these men and "their wives should be people of good sense and possess tact and talent sufficient to conduct elementary schools and enter upon that work as their principal employment" and should "all possess undoubted piety, good biblical knowledge, and be influenced by the true missionary spirit."[6] Several decades later, at a conference of missionary societies held in 1870, a speaker expressed a similar sentiment, noting that if Indian agents and employees were married men, "the influence of their wives and daughters would be beneficial to the Indians." Because Native American women were "shy and timid," he went on, they "have but little to say to any except women, and consequently the presence of white women among them will be of immense advantage." And, he concluded, "if you can commence the work of civilization among the women, the civilization of the whole tribe will rapidly follow."[7]

Women, then, came to the mission fields not as excess baggage, but as co-workers. Clearly, missionary wives in New Mexico considered themselves and their husbands partners in this venture. "We feel an increasing confidence that God's own hand has pointed us . . . to this portion of his vineyard," wrote Alzina Read, and her husband affirmed the joint nature of their undertaking, noting that "in all New Mexico there are but two missionaries — a minister and his wife."[8] Other women echoed the Reads, affirming that "we came . . .

Alzina Read. She and her husband Hiram were the first Protestant missionaries to New Mexico. *Courtesy of Betty Danielson.*

as teachers and missionaries" and referring to their tasks as "our work."[9]

Nevertheless, New Mexican missionary wives (in contrast to missionary wives on other frontiers) still saw themselves as wives first and missionaries second. For example, Harriett Shaw wrote to her mother upon leaving for New Mexico, "I feel a peace in going where my dear husband will feel he is doing good . . . for he could never be contented here." Similarly, in a brief reminiscence Harriett Ladd wrote for her children, she described the missionary work she and her husband undertook as the "story of your dear papa," adding, "I must tell you with what pride and thankfulness I write of him."[10]

Like their husbands, missionary wives were embued with zeal to save souls but were often dismayed when they encountered the physical bodies these souls inhabited. Alzina Read, for example, spent a Saturday morning passing out tracts to Hispanics in Santa Fe and commented that many of those who came were "filthy in the extreme." But, she continued, although they were "as verily heathen as earth contains," she tried to overlook "their present wretchedness" by remembering that they all had "immortal souls." Similarly, when Harriett Shaw encountered Navajos at Fort Defiance, where her husband served as both army chaplain and missionary, she described Indians as "a half clad filthy set of creatures called human beings" but recalled that "they have souls as well as we." While most Anglos initially made disparaging remarks about Hispanics and American Indians, few worried about their own reactions or considered the intrinsic value of the groups they maligned. But for these missionaries, remarking on the souls of the territory's residents was not merely pious rhetoric; rather, it underscored the missionaries' commitment and affirmed their purpose and presence in the Southwest.[11]

Nearly all missionary wives reacted unfavorably when they first encountered Hispanics and American Indians, for they found little to admire in their cultures. Religious differences further widened the gap, particularly between Anglos and Hispanics who clung to Catholicism. Harriett Shaw, for example, never overcame her prejudices toward Hispanics who remained Catholics, although she commented more favorably about those who converted. Yet as these missionaries came to know individual members of Hispanic and native American societies, they slowly began to reassess their original evaluations. Individual temperaments played an important part in these intercultural impressions as well. Whereas many missionaries encountered hostility from local Catholic priests, Taylor and Mary Ealy reported that the priest at Anton Chico welcomed them and urged them to stay. Affection characterized some relationships between natives and missionaries: When Samuel and Catherine Gorman left Laguna to live in Santa Fe, for example, many of the Lagunas wept, and J. M. Shields reported that native women at Jemez grieved over the death of his wife, Emily. Missionaries in turn became fond of the people they lived among. Mrs. J. D. Perkins, teaching Navajo children at Fort Defiance, reported, "We are becoming so much attached to our pupils we shall find it hard to leave them."[12]

Despite initial misgivings about native populations, Protestant missionaries quickly set out to fulfill their ministry. In this work, missionary husbands (usually ordained ministers) undertook the task of preaching. Wives could not preach nor perform marriages, baptisms, or burials, but they assisted in other ways. During worship services they played hymns on organs or melodeons and led singing, read the Bible at public gatherings, distributed tracts, and helped establish and taught Sunday schools. An important part of their ministry consisted of calling on other women in hopes of establishing friendships that might lead to conversion.[13]

To the missionaries' surprise, however, most of the native populace did not long for schools and thirst for the gospel as these Anglos had expected they would. Protestants encountered not only indifference among these peoples but, in many locations, active opposition from Catholic priests. Harriett Shaw, who attempted to establish schools for girls in Albuquerque and Peralta, indignantly noted that Protestants could only hope to succeed in their educational endeavors by avoiding religious topics. "We must keep away from religion, or lose our scholars," she complained. But Protestants expected education would go hand in hand with conversion and would not abandon religious subjects. "To be obliged to educate Catholics and passively let them remain so is not our calling," Mrs. Shaw declared emphatically.[14]

Often, in addition to indifference and Catholic opposition, missionaries faced other obstacles, including language. Many learned Spanish, but Native American languages presented a greater problem, for they had never been written down. Although missionaries conscientiously attempted to learn the languages, they rarely achieved much success. Cultural differences, too, made it difficult for the missionaries to secure pupils who regularly attended classes. Susan Gates Perea (whose husband, José Ynez Perea, converted to Presbyterianism and became an evangelist) struggled to maintain regular hours at her school in Corrales. Because her Hispanic scholars paid little attention to the time, they came too early or too late. As a remedy, her husband requested a "steamboat sized" bell to call her students to class. Missionaries to the Navajos found that the Navajos' nomadic lifestyles made children's school attendance irregular, and Indians and Hispanics often considered education for girls unnecessary. Despite these limitations, however, Protestants attempted to establish educational institutions wherever they thought such facilities had even a remote chance of success.[15]

Sometimes missionaries found that their schools could serve one population even if they had originally intended to attract another. For example, the Reverend Lewis Smith and his wife established a school in Santa Fe in 1852, hoping that Hispanic children would attend. But when it became apparent that Hispanics would not send their children, the school continued to teach pupils from the garrison at Fort Marcy. Similarly, when James and Matilda Roberts arrived at Taos pueblo to found a school, the Taos people vehemently opposed the enterprise. Nearby Hispanics, however, expressed interest in a school, so the Roberts turned their attention to the small Hispanic communities of the valley. And when J. M. Shields, missionary teacher at Jemez pueblo, saw that his school for American Indian students was more successful than his missionary efforts, he hoped to transfer his ministry and educational efforts to adjacent Hispanic villages.[16]

Whether these Protestant schools drew Hispanic, Anglo, or American Indian pupils, missionary couples assumed that wives would teach; mission boards and the government Indian Service held similar expectations. Indeed, many of the wives of missionaries in New Mexico had previous experience as teachers, and a number had some college education.[17] Rarely, however, did the subjects they taught extend beyond the elementary level. In addition to such basics as reading and writing, missionary wives taught domestic arts, including sewing, knitting, and cooking, to female pupils. Frequently, students boarded with the family of the missionary, an arrangement that added to the wife's responsibilities. Her domestic environment suffered further disarray when classes took place in the family's home. Harriett Ladd recounted that when her husband, H. O. Ladd, started a school in Santa Fe (rather grandiosely named "the University of New Mexico"), her family lived in a six-room adobe house with a parlor "quite prettily fitted up." As part of the new enterprise, however, four of the rooms — "the pleasantest, largest, and most sunny" — became schoolrooms, and the Ladds, with their four children, occupied the remaining space.[18]

Like the Ladds, most missionaries encountered inadequate provisions for living quarters as well as classrooms at some time during their stays in New Mexico. When Samuel and Catherine Gorman arrived at Laguna in 1852, they rented lodging in the pueblo, but the small adobe rooms and the persistence of vermin made the quarters unsatisfactory. Soon Gorman built a large stone house slightly removed from the pueblo, and part of the new building served as classrooms for the school. Other missionaries also found it necessary to build suitable houses for their families. Taylor and Mary Ealy lived for a time in Zuni in 1878, but fearing that the "damp rooms" in the pueblo represented a health hazard to their young children, Ealy began building a house for his family that could also provide classroom space for the school. At the same time, J. M. Shields undertook a similar project at Jemez pueblo.[19]

Accustomed to homes of brick, stone, or wood, missionary wives, like other newcomers to the territory, marveled at adobe buildings. "I would like to bring a mud house to the states as a curiosity," Harriett Shaw wrote to her sister. The major drawback of adobe dwellings became obvious during rain or snow storms: They leaked. During a storm in Santa Fe, Harriett Ladd awoke to find drops of water falling "on the rug — on the piano — then on the mattresses and . . . on the faces of my sleeping children." After several successive rainy nights, the Ladd family moved to other lodgings. Other missionary families, however, found that, with significant modifications, adobe buildings could provide adequate shelter.[20] At Fort Defiance, the Shaws installed spouts on the roof of their "mud house" to carry off the water, with satisfactory results. "The rain poured in streams," Harriett reported to her sister, but the "house did not leak, so you see we can build houses of mud and keep dry." Other improvements also helped to bring these abodes closer to the ideal that Anglo women cherished. They considered windows "quite a necessity," for instance, but found that in these native dwellings more than one window to a room constituted a "luxury." When Harriett Shaw's family moved to Socorro and purchased a home in 1857, she planned changes for the building, including the installation of more windows as well as the addition of three rooms. She also hired carpenters to build a fireplace flanked by shelves and cupboards in the dining room, declaring that when the house was thus "altered and Americanized [it] will be the pleasantest I have ever seen in this country."[21] Another modified adobe furnished a "very pleasant and liveable" domicile for James and Martha Roberts and their children when they moved to the Taos valley in 1873. In some of the rooms, James installed wooden floors, while his wife covered the remaining dirt floors with "good hand woven Ohio rag carpet." The Roberts also added another eastern touch to their home, planting a lawn in the patio, where a large cottonwood provided shade.[22]

Even after missionaries solved the immediate dilemma of establishing a suitable residence and classroom facilities and had attracted students to their schools, a host of other problems waited to challenge their efforts. A common vexation involved a scarcity of supplies, not only for family use but also for educational and religious endeavors. Many items were unavailable in the territory; others carried prices missionaries could ill-afford to pay. When Harriett Shaw's husband accepted a call to New Mexico, she visited relatives of Mr. and Mrs. Lewis Smith, who had gone to the territory a few months earlier, to learn what to take to the mission field. When Mrs. Shaw arrived in Santa Fe, however, she found that despite her precautions she lacked many items she considered necessities. "I very much regret that I did not bring my flat irons," she lamented and added, "Had we known we might have brought many other things for our comfort. . . .

We are very sorry we did not bring more as everything is so enormously expensive here."[23]

These exorbitant prices resulted from the high cost of freighting goods across the prairies. Later, families learned to take items most difficult to replace and make whatever else they needed when they reached their destinations. When John Menaul was assigned to the Navajo mission at Fort Defiance, for example, James Roberts advised him what to bring. "We have tableware for your use," he wrote, but "no bedding. I have made all my own furniture except a bureau I brought along." Roberts went on to recommend that Menaul bring "a good washing machine and a first-class wringer" because "washing is the hardest thing to get done here."[24]

Missionaries in the area also petitioned churches, mission boards, and ladies' auxiliaries to send Bibles and tracts, instructional materials for schools, and other supplies for their students. For example, in 1878, Mary and Taylor Ealy arrived in Lincoln, New Mexico, where they established a Sunday school. Soon Mrs. Ealy wrote to the superintendent of missions to request supplies, noting that "we have scarcely any books. Bibles are very scarce, and also music books." Later, at Zuni, she found that lack of supplies hampered her efforts to teach domestic arts. "I have been trying to teach some of the little girls to sew, but find I have no sewing implements," she advised the superintendent. "If you are sending anything soon, please send some needles, thimbles, knitting needles, etc."[25]

Often pupils came to school inadequately or improperly clad, and missionary wives tried to provide these children with clothing and toilet articles. Sewing and knitting garments for students added one more chore to the seemingly endless list of duties that made up "woman's work." To help clothe these pupils, mission women solicited "missionary barrels" of garments from women's church societies and used their own funds to purchase sewing machines to speed up the work. "We have two . . . Mexican girls in our family attending school," Elizabeth Annin of Las Vegas wrote the superintendent of missions, and, in response to his query about a missionary barrel, she replied, "We need one. Our salary is small, . . . and we clothe the two Mexican girls."[26]

Mrs. Annin also referred to another common problem for missionaries. Most ministers to the territory found their salaries insufficient even when supplemented by mission barrels, and they relied on the generosity of their converts or bolstered their incomes in other ways. Many Baptist missionaries who received salaries from the American Baptist Home Mission Society, for example, soon found that with the high prices in the territory, their funds were inadequate. To augment his income, Samuel Gorman opened a store at Laguna, and J. M. Shaw and Frederick Tolhurst accepted appointments as army chaplains. Later, Shaw started a freighting business, and his wife made and sold butter and cheese.[27]

Missionaries who came to the territory following the Civil War fared little better, whether home mission boards, boards of foreign missions, women's auxiliaries, or the government Indian Service paid their salaries. Although these clergymen intended to minister to the spiritual needs of the mixed populace, they also expected to provide for the temporal necessities of their families. "God's Word says that the man who does not provide for his own household is worse than an Infidel," John Menaul testily reminded the secretary of the Presbyterian Mission Board. "It is about time that the Church and the Board should accept the truth, that missionaries are men, not angels or even prophets fed by ravens."[28]

Inadequate salaries meant psychological stress and physical hardships for missionary families, yet they remained determined to carry out their endeavors. "We were completely disheartened without money," Mary Ealy wrote after she and her husband left Lincoln, New Mexico, but the couple agreed to go to Zuni because "[we] would like nothing better than to instruct those Indians." Harriett Ladd expressed similar sentiments when her husband gave up his salaried position at the Santa Fe Academy to establish a new school. In this new undertaking, the family's only financial support came from the tuition pupils paid to attend the new institution, and the Ladds existed for several weeks on oatmeal, bread, and butter because they could not pay the butcher $3 they owed. Furniture was also in short supply, and the Ladd children slept on mattresses on the floor until a rat infestation forced them to sleep on the school tables. "God alone knows the agony" of those years, Mrs. Ladd recalled, for "we concealed our poverty and privations as well as we could." But despite these sacrifices, the family resolved that "so long as there was any work for our Master for us to do, we would not give up."[29]

To ease financial hardships, missionary wives made significant economic contributions to their families and to general mission efforts. They provided emotional support in times of financial stress and frugally tended family resources. In addition, they furnished domestic services, including cooking and preparing food, laundering, and sewing, that male missionaries would otherwise have had to hire. Some missionary wives received no compensation for teaching, but their services made it unnecessary to hire salaried teachers. The salaries other women earned enabled couples to accept positions that a single salary would have precluded.

Apparently, few of these missionary wives or their husbands realized the enormity of the task they planned to undertake. Within a short while, however, women recognized how taxing domestic duties on the frontier could be, particularly without good hired help. "Neither Mrs. M[enaul] nor any other woman can leave her home and children to teach school without much inconvenience and expense," John Menaul complained when the Presbyterian Mission Board suggested that Mrs. Menaul forgo her salary. In fact, Mrs.

Menaul was able to teach only because her husband's sister lived with the family, "performing Mrs. Menaul's housework."[30]

Some missionary wives who were childless enjoyed distinguished careers as teachers. Emily Harwood, for example, helped her husband, the Reverend Thomas Harwood, establish the Harwood School for Girls in Albuquerque and provided maternal care to the boarding students. Amanda McFarland, following the death of her husband, David (who established the first Presbyterian church in Santa Fe), spent many years as a mission teacher in Alaska. In contrast, Alzina Read, whose only child died before the Reads came to New Mexico, abandoned a teaching career in New Mexico because of ill health.[31]

Several other women with children had to relinquish teaching duties, in part or altogether, because of family demands. Susan Gates, who taught at Zuni with Taylor and Mary Ealy, married José Ynes Perea, and together the newlyweds set forth for missionary work at Corrales. Less than a year later, however, Perea wrote to the superintendent of missions that his wife would be unable to continue teaching the school they had opened. "She has all the housework to do, the child to nurse, and the school to teach," he commented, adding that she "feels the school is too much for her." Isabelle Shields continued to teach at Jemez after the birth of her first child and even during her second pregnancy, although she also had two stepsons to care for. She finally quit teaching three months before her second son was born, to the regret of the Indian agent in charge of the school. "We have lost one of our very best teachers," he reported. Martha Roberts also found that caring for three children under the age of four made it difficult to fulfill teaching responsibilities. When a single woman hired as a teacher suggested that she care for the children and Mrs. Roberts resume teaching, the harried mother quickly agreed, since she enjoyed school duties. In contrast, Harriett Shaw was only too glad to abandon her efforts at teaching when she became pregnant with her first child.[32]

In fact, childbearing and childrearing occupied the attentions of most missionary wives during their stays in New Mexico. For example, Catherine Gorman, who came to the territory in 1852 with two children, gave birth to two sons during her ten years there. Her contemporary, Harriett Shaw, who arrived in 1851, bore two boys and two girls before her death in 1862 (three of the births occurred in the territory, the fourth in New York during Mrs. Shaw's visit home). And in the fourteen years Martha Roberts lived in New Mexico (1868–1882), she welcomed six children into her family (a seventh was born later in California).[33]

At least ten missionary wives bore children while living in New Mexico; and despite popular notions about the rigors of childbirth and infant mortality on the frontier, none of these mothers or their infants died during the birth process or immediately thereafter. Like other women of the period, missionary wives accepted childbirth as a predictable occurrence, but they often awaited the event — particularly the birth of their first child — with apprehension. Although Harriett Shaw expected a "good physician" to attend her at her first confinement, she confessed that "I do dread what I must pass through," especially when "no dear mother or sister can be with me." Martha Roberts, however, worried that she lived too far from a doctor to count on his services. Her husband journeyed from Fort Defiance to Santa Fe for instructions, which the doctor willingly provided, but at the crucial moment "Mr. Roberts grew so nervous and terrified as to be rendered absolutely useless," and his wife delivered the baby herself.[34] Similarly, at the birth of his first child, John Milton Shaw intended to provide emotional support for his wife, but she later reported, he "stood over me in such agony that I forgot my own" and "his groans and tears affected me more than my own sufferings." By the time the couple's fourth child arrived, though, Shaw had become accustomed to the birth process and attended his wife in the absence of a physician. Taylor Ealy, a medical doctor as well as a missionary, served as attendant to his wife at the birth of their son Albert, and J. M. Shields, also an M.D., likely delivered the children born to him and his wife, Isabelle.[35]

Although material about intimate details of women's lives is scarce, evidence suggests that missionary wives did not avail themselves of contraceptives, which became increasingly available in the second half of the nineteenth century. Married to doctors, Mary Ealy and Isabelle Shields might have had greater access to information about birth control than other women, but they apparently did not attempt to limit their families: Mary Ealy had seven children, and Isabelle Shields eight, her last when she was forty-five (similarly, Martha Roberts gave birth to her seventh child at the age of forty-seven). Harriett Shaw, whose letters to her mother and sister are remarkably frank about pregnancy and childbirth, almost certainly knew nothing about means to prevent conception. Her only comment on the subject followed the birth of her second child, when she wrote to her mother about other women who were having babies. "You must think this a fruitful country and so it seems to be," she noted, adding, "I think I shall get out of it as soon as possible."[36]

Even if missionary couples wished to limit the number of children they had, these parents clearly enjoyed and took pride in their families. As their schedules permitted, husbands played with and cared for their sons and daughters, but the primary duties of childcare fell to missionary mothers. In some instances, the arrival of children presented missionary couples with an intriguing paradox. If children transformed couples into that prized unit, the family, the responsibilities of caring for these children often challenged family unity, bringing about both physical and psychological separations between the parents. With children to tend, missionary wives stayed at home while their husbands frequently traveled to carry out their work. For example, Samuel Gorman often made trips to Santa Fe and other locations in the territory, but his wife, Catherine, left her home at Laguna only three times in seven years (and on only one of those excursions was she absent overnight). John Milton Shaw also found it necessary to be gone from home a great deal. "Well, as usual, husband is on a travelling tour and expects to be gone 3 or 4 weeks," Harriett Shaw reported to her sister on one such occasion; "I stay alone with my little ones."[37]

Wives were not the only ones who found this situation stressful, as Taylor Ealy's letter to the superintendent of missions reveals. Expressing hope that an assistant teacher would be sent to Zuni, Ealy commented, "I am obliged to be away sometime; then it is very unpleasant to leave Mrs. Ealy alone." And James Roberts tried to convince the secretary of the Presbyterian Mission Board to send another missionary to him at Fort Defiance. "If you had to travel over this country *alone* leaving your wife *more* alone among savages," he complained, "you would not think of sending [only] one."[38]

Husbands' absences accentuated the loneliness of missionary women who found themselves geographically distant from friends and family and culturally isolated from the American Indians and Hispanics they had come to live among. Before Harriett Shaw left New York for New Mexico, she enjoyed a very close relationship with her mother, sister, and brothers, and she missed them intensely throughout her years in the territory. Although her friendships with other Anglo women in Albuquerque were comforting, when she and her husband moved to Fort Defiance in early 1853, Mrs. Shaw found "not a solitary female to come and look upon me in my loneliness," and she confided to her sister that "my dear husband [is] my only friend here." Eighteen months later, however, Mrs. Shaw rejoiced at the news that the Reverend and Mrs. Frederick Tolhurst, accompanied by Mrs. Tolhurst's sister, would soon arrive at Fort Defiance. Sharing her excitement in a letter to her mother, Mrs. Shaw wrote: "Only think, mother . . . to have *two christian females* to associate with in our own house. Oh it is a blessing greater than I deserve."[39]

Separation from friends and family also heightened missionaries' awareness of mortality, which accounted, at least in part, for their preoccupation with issues of sickness and health. Missionary letters often include the phrase "if I am spared" or a similar sentiment indicating a recognition that death might occur swiftly and indiscriminately. Although enormous advances in medicine took place in the nineteenth century — among them, the introduction of anesthetics and a gradual acceptance of Joseph Lister's germ theory — diseases such as tuberculosis, smallpox, influenza, cholera, yellow fever, diphtheria, and typhoid continued to challenge even the most enlightened physicians of the period. Without antibiotics to combat infection, respiratory complaints often developed into pneumonia, and minor cuts could lead to blood poisoning, with fatal results. Common medical remedies for a variety of ailments employed powerful purgatives and emetics that weakened the system and may have increased susceptibility to disease. Poor nutrition also played a role in general debilitation and resulted in diseases such as scurvy and pyorrhea.[40]

During their years in New Mexico, most missionary wives added nursing to other domestic duties as their husbands and children suffered from a variety of illnesses. When they lived in Taos, Martha Roberts's husband and children contracted smallpox, although vaccination was available even in New Mexico decades earlier. Harriett Shaw, for example, had her children vaccinated in 1861 when an epidemic threatened in Socorro. More frequently, other ailments (particularly colds and other respiratory diseases and intestinal disorders variously identified as diarrhea, dysentery, and worms) plagued missionary families. Even as they administered remedies (of dubious value in many cases), mothers worried about the cause of their children's complaints and hoped to find ways to prevent recurrences. Mary Ealy's daughters suffered from colds and severe coughs brought on, she believed, by the dampness of their living quarters. Harriett Shaw blamed herself for her daughter Lillie's illness because she had weaned the child at the age of nineteen months. Mary Ealy and Isabelle Shields turned to their physician husbands for advice and care, but other women sought assistance from more distant sources. When Martha Roberts's children displayed symptoms of a disease she could not identify, she took them to Ohio, where a trusted family doctor recommended treatment.

Harriett Shaw placed greater confidence in herbal remedies than in the medications — largely calomel (mercurous chloride) and mercury — that the post physician at Fort Defiance regularly prescribed.[41] Like many women of the period, she relied on catnip tea, which acted as a mild laxative, to protect her infants' health and grew her own supply from seeds sent by her relatives in the East. They also supplied numerous other ingredients for home remedies, including chamomile to relieve infant colic. (Hispanic women of New Mexico also used chamomile, locally available as *manzanillo*, for the same purpose, but Mrs. Shaw apparently never sought their medical advice.)[42]

At least some missionary families also clung to a preference for familiar foods, even when these were unobtainable in New Mexico. Whenever possible, they grew vegetables and fruits or purchased such items as melons, peaches, plums, beets, carrots, and potatoes from local farmers. Meat and bread frequently formed the mainstay of their diets, however, and there is no indication that missionary wives introduced their families to native foods such as tortillas, pinto beans, or chiles. These newcomers particularly missed potatoes, which often were unavailable or very expensive in the territory. When fresh fruits and vegetables disappeared from family diets, wives tried to compensate. Martha Roberts bought canned tomatoes and made huge quantities of plum marmalade to assure her children (who suffered from scurvy) of a reliable supply of fruit throughout the winter. (Unfortunately, because cooking destroys some of the vitamin C found in foods, her efforts were not totally successful.) Harriett Shaw dosed her family with herbal cathartics and tonics and other medicinal preparations. When she began to lose teeth as a result of deteriorating gums, she attempted to arrest the process by bathing her mouth with "tincture of peruvian bark & myrrh, and . . . burnt alum & charcoal." (Sadly, these remedies, too, proved ineffective.)[43]

Mothers not only worried about their children's health but also fretted about how to obtain suitable instruction for their children. Missionary families valued education and often feared that living in New Mexico meant their children would be deprived of educational opportunities. When Mrs. J. D. Perkins and her husband were assigned to Fort Defiance, she expressed concern about her son Willie's education in a letter to the superintendent of missions. "What about Willie? His tender years and prospective future will hardly admit of our isolating him from all society. We would not teach him for lack of time, and we could not afford now to send him East." In fact, sending children to schools in the East seemed, to many parents, the best solution to the problem. After living at Laguna for three years, Catherine and Samuel Gorman sent their daughter Mary (then thirteen) to Hamilton, New York. J. M. Shields also sent his sons by his first and second marriages to eastern schools, and Harriett Shaw recognized that she might need to part with her children to secure their education. Thoughts of such a separation distressed her, however, and she commented to her sister, "I don't know as I have the fortitude to send them among strangers alone."[44]

Missionary families in New Mexico faced separations of another kind as well. As they bade farewell to loved ones and friends in the East, they realized that they might never see them again. Although ill, Harriett Ladd accompanied her husband to Santa Fe but left three of her children with friends and relatives in several New England states. She found it "very hard indeed to leave . . . dearly prized children" but believed that the parting was even harder for her daughter Lillie, who faced the "possibility of losing her mother" before the family could be reunited. The probability that her mother, an invalid, would die before Harriett Shaw could return home similarly haunted her. Neither Harriett Ladd nor Susannah Bidwell (Mrs. Shaw's mother) died as their children feared, but death visited other missionary families in New Mexico. Children were particularly vulnerable, and mothers knew that their best efforts to protect them might not be sufficient. "While we love him [her son George] dearly we know he is only lent us for a season," Harriett Shaw wrote to her family, "but our home would be indeed desolate without him." Luckily, Mrs. Shaw's fears that her son might fall victim to some childhood complaint were groundless, but several other missionary wives were not as fortunate. Alzina Read's only child, a daughter, died before the Reads came to the territory; Amanda McFarland and Mary Ealy lost infant sons during their years in New Mexico. And although Isabelle Shields gave birth to eight children, only five lived past the age of ten.[45]

Other wives became widows during missionary service. Amanda McFarland's husband died of tuberculosis after they left New Mexico, and the death of James Roberts (who had continued his missionary work in Anaheim, California) left his wife, Martha, with seven children to support. Upon her husband's death, Mrs. A. H. Donaldson had three young daughters to care for and reluctantly abandoned her missionary work at Fort Defiance. "I know I shall get along some way," she wrote the superintendent of missions, "but none but God knows all the trying circumstances . . . [and] he is the only one who can help me."[46]

Nor did death spare missionary wives. Soon after Harriett Shaw arrived in the territory, she wrote to her mother that Ann Eliza Nicholson, wife of a Methodist minister, was not expected to live more than a few weeks longer because "the climate and want of care after confinement has brought her to the verge of the grave." Mrs. Shaw went on to reveal that Mrs. Nicholson "like the rest of us feels a dread of being buried in this horrible country." In later years Harriett Shaw feared her own death would leave her children without maternal care;[47] as she confided to her mother and sister during one of her pregnancies, "the thought of leaving my little ones to the cold charities of the world rendered me very nervous so that I had but little courage or strength."[48] Indeed, the fate she dreaded awaited Harriett Shaw as well as Catherine Gorman, both of whom died in 1862. Mrs. Gorman died of illness at Santa Fe, and Harriett Shaw suffered an attack of appendicitis at her home in Socorro while her husband was away on business. Ten days after Mrs. Shaw's illness began, Shaw returned home to find his house closed up and his children in the care of a neighbor; his "faithful and devoted wife" had been interred five days before. Typhoid fever complicated by pneumonia claimed the life of Emily Shields at Jemez in 1878 despite the efforts of her husband, an M.D. "I will try and trust God and not let the broodings of dispare [sic] come over me," her husband assured the superintendent of missions, "but the tears are blinding my eyes and the way seems difficult so much more than ever."[49]

Yet no matter how much they mourned their deceased spouses, missionaries often remarried. Shields had already lost his first wife, Elizabeth, a decade before Emily died, and after Emily's death he married a third time; ironically, his new wife, Isabelle, also died of typhoid pneumonia in 1900. Hiram Read, whose missionary work took him to Arizona, married again following the death of his wife, Alzina, in 1864, and Samuel Gorman, whose missionary career continued in Mexico, married twice more. J. M. Shaw also married three times; after Harriett's death, he sent to New York for her sister Cornelia, and they married in Socorro in 1866. When Cornelia died soon after, Shaw took a local Hispanic woman for his third wife. John Menaul was a widower before he married Charity Ann Gaston, as was José Ynez Perea at the time of his marriage to Susan Gates.

Remarriage seemed essential for men who wished to continue their mission work. The death of a missionary wife was not only tragic for her family but also threatened the entire missionary endeavor. On the day his wife died, J. M. Shields wrote to the superintendent of missions, "There is so much needs to be done here and Mrs. Shields worked too hard, but how shall we do without her God only knows." Several weeks later, he requested assistance from the mission board, saying, "There should be help sent to the Jemes Mission, for . . . I have too much to do here, and the care of my little family also. I am not lazy, not a bit. But I know I cannot do all the work that should be done." Because the board did not immediately appoint an assistant, Shields made inquiries of his own. He approached Mrs. M. E. Griffith, a widow teaching a small Presbyterian mission school for Hispanic children in Santa Fe. She agreed to come to Jemez as teacher and housekeeper, if the board approved.[50]

Before the Presbyterian Mission Board had time to decide, however, Benjamin M. Thomas, Indian agent for the Pueblo Agency, intervened. He forbade Mrs. Griffith to proceed to Jemez because he feared her presence "would create a scandal." This action infuriated the bereaved missionary, who emphatically reminded the superintendent of missions, "It is female help we want here." But, he noted bitterly, such help apparently could "not come in any shape except as my wife without danger of scandal." Without a likely matrimonial candidate, Shields resolved to carry on his work alone.[51] But the mission board had other plans, and initiated efforts to recruit two unmarried women to go to Jemez as teachers, the president of the board expressing the hope that "Shields will want to marry one of them." He instructed Sheldon Jackson, superintendent of missions, to visit Shields and "tell him he *must have a wife and cannot get along without one.*" The president further emphasized the pragmatic nature of these arrangements when he concluded, "'Business is Business' and we and he must face the facts."[52]

During the spring of 1879, a relative of Shields who was a minister in Pennsylvania assisted in recruiting the teachers for Jemez, and by May the plan was implemented. One of the women was Lora Shields, cousin of J. M. Shields; the other was Isabelle Leech. The well-meaning relative confidently assured the superintendent of missions that he had made a wise selection. "Miss Leech is not engaged, . . . and she will fill the bill as teacher." He also predicted that the desired marriage would take place, and he was right. Isabelle Leech arrived at Jemez on June 18, 1879, and in a letter six weeks later J. M. Shields announced their plans to marry. "Miss Leech and I expect to get married, she seems to be very well qualified for the work here, and . . . will do all in her power to advance the master's interest here," he confided and continued, "I think she will be a faithful and efficient helpmate and I have great reason to thank God and be encouraged to persevere longer in the difficult work at Jemes."[53]

"A faithful and efficient helpmate" was indeed the type of partner missionaries sought to share their work on the frontier. Husbands, churches, and women themselves enthusiastically proclaimed that a missionary wife would further the

causes of Christianity and civilization. In tending to the domestic needs of her family, she would also provide a model of
Christian womanhood. By example and instruction, she
would introduce the highest ideals of American culture to all
she encountered.

The prevalent ideology of the nineteenth century shaped
and reinforced these expectations. On the frontier, though,
these ideals were sharply tested. Dismayed to find that the
people they came to uplift were often hostile or indifferent,
and subjected to rigorous living conditions, illness, and loss of
loved ones, these women doggedly endeavored to recreate the
proper domestic environment in the wilderness. Although
they held fast to their Christian faith, missionary wives were
not immune to fear, discouragement, and loneliness. Yet they
rarely abandoned a commitment to the mission they chose or
the values they espoused.

The role of missionary wife appeared to offer women an
opportunity to expand their influence beyond the immediate
domestic sphere, but in fact the exigencies of family life on
the frontier severely limited women's ability to explore this
possibility. Emotionally and ideologically tied to family responsibilities, missionary wives responded first to family
needs. But their participation in other aspects of mission
efforts, though limited, revealed that women could play a
significant role therein. In the late nineteenth and early
twentieth centuries, missionary work offered single women
an alternative to domesticity, and many chose careers in
teaching and health care. This expansion in women's roles
resulted, in part, from the experiences of missionary wives in
the West.

CHAPTER TWO

"I Will Make My Letters as Interesting as Possible"

Army Wives in the Southwest, 1850–1855

Wherever Anglo women of the nineteenth century traveled, they commemorated their journeys in letters, diaries, journals, and memoirs. Many women's writings about the West described the trek across the continent to California or Oregon. Other than these chroniclers of the overland trails, however, no group of women who participated in the frontier experience left a greater written record of their adventures than women who married army officers and accompanied them to various posts throughout the West. While many army wives did not intend their correspondence for public perusal, others wrote their reminiscences for publication. Few of these published works received much critical acclaim or widespread popularity when they originally appeared, yet they (in addition to the unpublished materials) have become invaluable to historians seeking to illuminate the social history of frontier forts and women's roles in the West.

Several recent studies, based on examinations of these women's sources and other pertinent materials, provide a fairly complete picture of the roles and experiences of women married to officers in the period from 1865 to 1900, yet the lives of army officers' wives in the West before the Civil War remain somewhat obscure. So do those of women married to enlisted men throughout the period of western expansion. In addition, not all officers' wives had the good fortune to marry upright and protective husbands whose attentions and affection mitigated harsh frontier conditions.[1]

Many of the army women who authored accounts of their military adventures spent a portion of their army "careers" in New Mexico, and not a few considered their time in the territory among the most pleasant of their western experiences.[2] Most of these accounts deal with the post–Civil War period (only Lydia Spencer Lane and Marian Russell describe army life before 1865), and, with the exception of Eveline Alexander's diary, all were written years after the events took place. Certainly their value as accurate portrayals of frontier life is not diminished by that lapse of time, particularly when historians employ these writings as impressionistic representations rather than as strict factual accounts. Still, as Marian Russell noted when she dictated her recollections, in retrospect "the big things seem little and the little things seem big."[3]

Thus, even though letters and a diary two women wrote between 1850 and 1853 from forts in New Mexico reveal no startling contrasts between the experiences of army wives in the antebellum period and those in the postwar years, these documents offer an opportunity to examine the lives of officers' wives in the Southwest during the early territorial period. They also indicate the significance of daily events and concerns that Anna Maria Morris and Katie Bowen mention in letters and diary entries. Because the two wrote about the same period and, for six months, from the same place, differences in writing style and in personality emerge, a reminder that temperament and talent also affected women's word portraits of their western ventures.[4]

Despite their individual personalities and traits, however, Mrs. Bowen and Mrs. Morris shared many characteristics with other women married to army officers. For example, they came from comfortable middle- or upper-class eastern backgrounds. Anna Maria Morris, the daughter of a surgeon major of the army, was born in New Jersey. Her husband, named for his illustrious forebear, Gouverneur Morris (one of the writers of the Constitution), belonged to a prominent family in New York. Isaac Bowen, another New Yorker (though with a less prestigious pedigree), met his bride, Katie Cary, during a tour of duty in eastern Maine, close to the Canadian border.[5]

Moreover, these military wives, like most other literate women of their class in nineteenth-century America, espoused the ideology of "true womanhood." Their lives centered on husbands, home, and family. Although many women married to officers chose to remain in the East with their families during their husbands' tours of duty in the West, others went along. Some refused to endure a separation from husbands they loved; others undoubtedly believed it their duty to accompany their spouses to the uncivilized regions of the continent in order to recreate a suitable domestic environment and to preserve the unity of the family. Indeed, affection and a sense of duty, in combination with a yearning for unusual experiences or adventure, prompted a number of army wives to follow their husbands west. Katie Bowen and Anna Maria Morris may be included in this group of enthusiastic pioneers. Certainly these women could have chosen to stay in the East, for both came from large and affectionate families; instead, they elected to make the westward journey and to share their husbands' lives in New Mexico territory.[6]

During their years in the Southwest, Mrs. Bowen and Mrs. Morris wrote numerous letters home to parents, siblings, and friends. In addition, Mrs. Morris kept a daily journal that she continued after her return to New York. These documents not only describe daily events at forts throughout New Mexico but also provide substantial insight into the characters of the women who wrote them. Katie Bowen emerges as dutiful daughter, devoted and doting mother, and proud and supportive wife. Daily hardships failed to dampen the good humor of this bouyant, lively young woman. Similarly, Anna Maria Morris maintained a fond relationship with her parents and a deep affection for her husband. More reserved than Katie Bowen, Mrs. Morris suffered from ill health during much of her stay in New Mexico, yet she complained very little about conditions she encountered.[7]

Neither Mrs. Bowen nor Mrs. Morris intended their accounts for publication, but they wrote with a sense that their participation on the frontier would seem perilous and adventurous to loved ones left behind who would share the letters and journals. If they often found daily life repetitive and monotonous, they attempted to keep their narratives entertaining. "Every day is alike and nothing to make a journal interesting," Mrs. Morris noted during her trip across the prairie, just as from Fort Union Katie Bowen wrote that "one day is very much like another here" but assured her parents, "I will make my letters as interesting as possible."[8]

In 1850 Anna Maria Morris, who was thirty-six when her journey began, traveled with her husband, Major Gouverneur Morris, and a military train along the Santa Fe Trail to Santa Fe, where Morris was assigned to duty at Fort Marcy. In August of the following year, Captain Isaac Bowen and his wife, Katie, twenty-three years old, reached their destination of Fort Union, a new post under construction one hundred miles northeast of the territorial capital. Echoing numerous other Anglo visitors to the region, Mrs. Morris and Mrs. Bowen reacted similarly to the Hispanic villages they encountered. "The town [Las Vegas] looks very much like a brick yard," Mrs. Morris observed, and Katie Bowen informed her parents that "Mexican towns very much resemble large

Anna Maria Morris, age 22. *Reprinted with the permission of the New Jersey Historical Society. Courtesy of the Special Collections Department, University of Virginia Library.*

brick yards." Katie, however, responded more favorably to the geography around Fort Union than Anna Maria Morris did to Santa Fe. "This point . . . is well adapted, plenty of water, abundance of wood and to all appearances a fertile valley, with mountains on two sides," Mrs. Bowen reported enthusiastically. Mrs. Morris, however, expressed disappointment in her new place of residence. "It is the most miserable squalid looking place I ever beheld," she mourned. "The houses are mud, the fences are mud, the churches & courts are mud, in fact it is *all* mud."[9]

Although anxious to set up housekeeping, neither Anna Maria Morris nor Katie Bowen found permanent quarters awaiting them on their arrival in the territory. Mrs. Morris stayed in rented lodgings until the military reassigned numerous personnel; finally, after a month and a half, the Morrises selected quarters and Mrs. Morris began to establish a home-like atmosphere. The Bowens passed their first months in New Mexico in three tents, waiting for their quarters to be built. Although Katie at first assured her mother that "we do not find our tents at all uncomfortable," she wrote to her parents two months later that "we have been fortunate enough to get into quarters and . . . we find it vastly preferable to tents [because] we escape the constant dust if nothing more."[10]

Although the Bowen residence was only partially completed when the couple moved in, they enjoyed the good fortune of remaining in the same house for two years, the length of their stay at Fort Union. Late in 1853, the Bowens moved to Albuquerque and later to Santa Fe before their return to the East. In fact, frequent relocations commonly occurred in the military. During her three years in the Southwest, for example, Anna Maria Morris moved numerous times. In July 1851, Major Morris was ordered from Santa Fe to El Paso, and his wife confided to her journal, "I am very low spirited about going to El Paso — I fear the climate & heat." When she arrived, however, she found the "place is better looking than I supposed." In any event, her stay at El Paso was brief, for within a short while her husband was ordered to establish Fort Fillmore near Mesilla and Fort Webster close to the Santa Rita copper mines, in the vicinity of present-day Silver City. Mrs. Morris spent brief periods at each of these posts until her husband took command of Fort

Union in December 1852, where they remained until June 1853, when they returned east.[11]

Securing permanent (or semipermanent) housing was merely the first trial army wives faced in their efforts to create homes in the wilderness. In many cases the quarters they had eagerly waited for turned out to be unsatisfactory in several respects. Although some army wives found their lodgings too small, Katie Bowen had no complaints on that account. At Fort Union, she reported, "the rooms are well arranged and are large and very high." But the dwelling, constructed of timber and adobe, had its drawbacks. During New Mexico's frequent dust storms, dirt swirled into living quarters, and after one such storm, Katie found "my bedroom carpet was so covered that the colors could not be distinguished." The roofs, built of logs covered with earth, also presented problems. "I was in hopes the house was clean for the summer," Mrs. Bowen wrote, "but so much dirt scattered through the logs that I will be obliged to take up carpets."[12] Moreover, adobe dwellings leaked during rainstorms, as Anna Maria Morris discovered when she returned from a shopping trip: "We found Mrs. Sibley's rooms and two of mine in a wretched condition from the rain," she noted. On another occasion, she reported, "It rained very hard last night and my parlor wall is pretty well streaked with mud this morning."[13] In drier weather, the structures posed another hazard: "Now we are secure against wet, though I feel rather timid respecting fire," Katie Bowen wrote to her parents. And her worries were not ill-founded, for Anna Maria Morris lost "a nice gingham dress . . .[and] and other things" when the chimney in her house caught fire and spread to the clothesline.[14]

Despite these irritations, army wives set about making their quarters comfortable and inviting. They laid carpet on rough wooden or dirt floors and hung curtains at the windows. Although some women brought furniture with them, the high price of transportation, coupled with the likelihood

Katie and Isaac Bowen. *Courtesy of Gwladys Bowen.*

that goods might be damaged in transit, contributed to the
practice of "selling off" one's household items when leaving
the territory.[15] Thus, women purchased articles from families
who had been reassigned or improvised in setting up their
households. Katie Bowen was particularly proud of her abil-

ity to furnish her home frugally; noting that one of the other wives at Fort Union "went into the extravagance of buying nice furniture," Katie assured her parents that she would "be equally comfortable with my homemade lounges and benches. Isaac had frames of two easy chairs made at Leavenworth and I shall take some of my extra pillows and cover them with turkey red and find them charming."[16]

In addition to furnishing quarters, army women were occupied with numerous other domestic duties. Officers' wives relied on servants to perform some of these household tasks, and often had difficulty securing adequate help in their new homes. To solve this problem, some women employed enlisted men (known as "strikers") or their wives, but others brought domestic help with them. In the antebellum years, most of these domestic servants were black slaves.[17] Katie Bowen took Margaret, a black slave, with her to New Mexico, and a young black woman, Louisa (likely also a slave), accompanied Anna Maria Morris on her travels throughout the Southwest. Frequently, military women complained that their servants quickly succumbed to the romantic overtures of enlisted men and married, leaving domestic service. For Louisa and Margaret, their slave status precluded such a choice, and they remained with their mistresses during their western tours. Katie Bowen worried, however, that Margaret might form a liaison with a slave another military family owned, and she declared, "I will not allow our girl to associate with the black." And, although no evidence suggests that Louisa married during her stay in New Mexico, she gave birth to a son named Carlos a year after her arrival in the territory.[18]

Even with the assistance domestic servants provided, army wives maintained numerous housekeeping responsibilities, including food preparation. For the most part, women found the foodstuffs available to them at forts in New Mexico greatly exceeded the selection in other western locations.[19]

They enjoyed the post gardens and facilities for keeping livestock that assured a supply of fresh vegetables (for at least
part of the year), eggs, and dairy products, and they also
purchased fresh produce from nearby Hispanic settlements.
Servants did most of the cooking while their mistresses supervised and kept a close eye on supplies. Wives also prepared special treats, such as mincemeat and cakes, and
preserved seasonal foodstuffs for later consumption. Katie
Bowen and Anna Maria Morris praised the fresh fruits available in New Mexico and made jellies and jams of raspberries,
plums, quinces, and grapes, as well as brandied peaches. In
preparing these delicacies, officers' wives may have been reluctant to entrust such rare and expensive items as sugar
and fruit to servants' hands. Katie Bowen confided to her
mother that "all the husbands cry out about making jelly
with sugar at twenty cents a pound," but, she continued, "I
sweetened the mincemeat with molasses to pay for it." Another activity that wives rarely entrusted to servants was
butter-making, an enterprise they believed required considerable skill. Frugality and experience, however, were not the
only reasons officers' wives carried out these tasks. They also
derived considerable satisfaction from creating such delicacies and proudly recorded their accomplishments. "All of us
ladies have had a great time making plum jelly to see who
would succeed best," Katie Bowen declared on one occasion,
adding that although "I never made jelly before . . . [I] never
will be beat at anything."[20]

Another domestic duty that army wives retained was
needlework. As in the preparation of foods, some types of
stitchery, such as embroidery, served as a means for artistic
expression. But, more often, army wives sewed practical garments for themselves and other family members (including
servants). Sewing and mending, in fact, took up a large portion of the women's time. Although husbands wore uniforms,
wives kept these in repair and furnished such items as shirt

fronts, nightshirts, and undergarments.[21] Children, too, kept their mothers occupied. "I am nearly all the time busy making clothes for Willie [her son]," Katie Bowen commented. "He wears out and outgrows a great deal." Anna Maria Morris, though childless during her years in New Mexico, employed her needle in making garments for children of other families. Children grew quickly, but that was not the only reason they continually required new clothing. Mrs. Bowen noticed that in New Mexico, hard water, coupled with vigorous laundering practices, took a toll on fabric. "There is something in the water that rots clothes faster than I ever saw before," she noted and went on, "one set wears out as soon and sometimes before I have another ready."[22]

Women found that the absence of dressmakers required them to make or modify their own apparel as well, and they found it difficult to keep up with fashions in the East. Soon after she arrived at Fort Union, Katie Bowen announced her intentions to furnish herself with stylish garb during her western stay so that she would "not be quite behind the age" when she returned home. In fact, she commented to her mother, "all the ladies here dress very prettily and from outward appearance you would not imagine we were so far from fashion and civilization."[23] Some of these women, however, had been in the territory only a little longer than Mrs. Bowen. Within two years, she acknowledged that, despite her original intention to maintain a fashionable wardrobe, during her years on the frontier she had become unfamiliar with new trends. When a friend sent her "some queer looking patterns" featuring "bishop sleeves and big collars," Katie expressed misgivings about these styles and admitted that "nice dresses are out of place here." Her daily garb on the frontier consisted of "calico wrappers." Still, she concluded, "I suppose that fashion must be regarded" and confessed that she expected "to look like 'fossil remains' when I get home after being shut out from the dress circle so long."[24]

In addition to concerns about food and clothing, wives' responsibilities included childbearing and childrearing. Pregnancy did not prevent women from accompanying their husbands to western posts; for example, Mrs. Langdon Easton, who traveled with Anna Maria Morris across the plains, gave birth to a daughter two days after she reached Santa Fe. Katie Bowen, who arrived at Fort Union in August 1851, was also pregnant on the overland trip, for her son William arrived in January 1852. Other families added children during their stay in the West, and this experience formed bonds between women at frontier posts. Writing to her mother about Mrs. Sibley, her neighbor at Fort Union, whose son was born two months after William Bowen, Katie Bowen commented, "We will have a great many feelings in common after a few months." Katie also assured her mother that in addition to the services of a doctor to attend her at her confinement, she could rely on "the attention of a good many friends who always offer services." Later, after she and Mrs. Sibley had produced sons, Katie humorously related that "the *staff* is increasing. Capt. Shoemaker . . . has a daughter, or rather his wife has, and Mrs. Carleton will furnish a dragoon sometime in June. So you see we will each have a care and when we gather together will be a musical set."[25]

Most of the women Anna Maria Morris and Katie Bowen knew during their tenure in New Mexico could depend upon a doctor's attendance at the births of their babies, although other army wives in the West often lacked such care. With or without a physician, certain rituals surrounded the birth process. For example, the services of a woman (either a hired assistant or a family friend) to attend to the mother and to care for the baby for the first weeks of its life was deemed essential. Katie Bowen secured a woman married to an enlisted man at the post to care for mother and baby for nearly three weeks. In addition, women remained confined to their beds for a specified period after the birth; although Katie reported she had an easy delivery and no "bad feeling of any sort, not even a headache," she remained in bed for ten days "to be on the prudent side." Other proscriptions concerned diet, and Mrs. Bowen observed that women who refused to observe conventional practices "suffered the penalty of waywardness." At birth, the son of her neighbor, Mrs. Sibley, resembled "a picked bird, large bones, but no flesh," which Katie believed resulted from the mother's decision to starve herself "so to have an easy time." To add to Mrs. Bowen's consternation, her neighbor ate rich foods (including hot rolls and broiled duck!) too soon after the birth and as a result was "mending slowly." Mrs. Sibley's ill health prevented her from successfully nursing her child, and another officer's wife suckled the infant for a time; later, the wife of an enlisted man was hired as wet nurse. Mrs. Sibley and her baby survived the ordeal, but other women died in childbirth and from its complications. Less than two weeks after she arrived in Santa Fe, Anna Maria Morris sat in attendance at the death bed of her friend, Mrs. Easton, who had given birth to a daughter two days after completing the overland journey.[26]

Even if infants survived birth, numerous perils threatened their growth to adulthood. Many diseases, most commonly colds and diarrheas, attacked children, and even minor ailments led to complications and death.[27] Before the Bowens came to New Mexico, their young daughter died of pneumonia, and Katie was well aware that tragedy could again strike the family. Fortunately, neither of their two children born in New Mexico experienced serious illnesses, although both suffered from colic. Katie took every precaution to assure that they remained "hearty and strong as . . . young antelope," relying particularly on catnip (which she grew herself) as "a medicine for all baby ailings."[28] Moreover, since smallpox was common in the territory, Katie insisted that her infant son be vaccinated. Despite the threat of smallpox, Mrs. Bowen, like other army wives, believed that New

Mexico's climate afforded health benefits not available in eastern cities. "In no country or place have I known as much health as here," she advised her mother. "Children seem to thrive."[29]

Even though mothers in New Mexico did not fear such scourges as yellow fever, accidents incapacitated or killed children and adults alike. On one occasion, Katie reported to her mother that "Willie got a bad fall on the back of his head . . . which made him look very badly for an hour," though he suffered no permanent harm from the injury. Another family at Fort Union was not so fortunate when two boys, aged eight and six, were thrown from a hay wagon as the mules drawing it bolted. The elder child "was cut badly on the back of the head and had his front teeth broken," and the younger child died from internal injuries. Adults also were victims of accidents. Isaac Bowen was severely bruised when thrown from his horse. Katie sustained a more serious injury when she tripped in a drainage canal and fractured her leg in several places. Although she received prompt medical attention (which included immobilizing the leg and suspending it in traction from the ceiling), the limb never healed properly, and the injury troubled Katie for the rest of her life.[30]

Despite the many responsibilities and concerns that surrounded childrearing, army wives clearly enjoyed their children. "A better child never lived," Katie Bowen said of her son Willie, and her letters home are filled with references to his cutting teeth, attempts to crawl and walk, and other milestones that parents treasure. In one letter, for example, she boasted that he had "learned a great many tricks, squealing for the little pig that can't get over the stile and tossing patty cakes in the oven."[31] Although Anna Maria Morris had no children of her own, she took pleasure in the child of her servant, Louisa. "My little darky was one year old yesterday," she noted in her journal, and in another entry she wrote, "Carlos is 21 months old today."[32]

Katie Bowen rejoiced that her husband shared her pride in their son and enjoyed caring for the child. "He is the happiest man you ever saw when playing horse and cutting capers with the boy," she wrote her parents. Moreover, Isaac often took the child to his office, which Katie found gave her "time for a great many things." Indeed, the Bowens's attitude toward parenting and their marital relationship provide a good example of what one historian of the nineteenth-century family in the United States has termed a "companionate" marriage. Such relationships rested on mutual affection, trust, and respect rather than on patriarchal domination and came to represent the ideal marriage and family life. Yet many families fell short of this goal. Katie's letters indicate that other officers did not necessarily emulate Isaac's behavior as a father and a husband. She was quick to criticize her neighbor's husband as "not a man that can assist a woman at all and will poke about his office all day instead of being at home to relieve her of that baby for an hour." Later, she surmised that her neighbor "sometimes wishes that her husband were a little *younger* to help her in taking care of his own productions." Katie also appreciated Isaac's devoted attention when he presided as chief nurse after Katie broke her leg. She wrote her mother that "it is a great comfort to have one's husband perform all these attentions and minister to one's wants." Her friend, Mrs. Sibley (whose husband had twice been widowed), meanwhile, seemed doomed to "lead a slave's life instead of being an *old man's darling.*"[33]

While wives devoted much of their attention to husbands and children, they also maintained and established other rewarding relationships to combat the loneliness and isolation they sometimes felt. Family ties in the East remained very important, despite the miles that separated army wives from parents, siblings, and friends, and these women spent many hours writing letters home. Mail was eagerly awaited, and the lapse of time between deliveries seemed inordinately long to women hoping to hear from loved ones. "A month today since our last mail," Anna Maria Morris noted dispiritedly in her journal on one occasion; ten days later, however, she rejoiced that "plenty of letters" had arrived. Letters were also welcomed by homesick wives when their husbands' duties required them to be absent from the post. "I am lonely and low spirited," Mrs. Morris confided to her journal on several occasions when her husband was gone. Katie Bowen acknowledged similar feelings but found that she was "a great deal more contented when I am busy than when I have a plenty of time on my hands."[34]

Besides simply keeping busy to combat loneliness, army wives also sought the companionship of other women in similar circumstances and formed close friendships at frontier forts. Although some wives found themselves at remote posts where few women of their station lived, Katie Bowen and Anna Maria Morris usually enjoyed the good fortune to have other officers' wives nearby. "You would like the social way we are living," Katie informed her mother, adding that she and her neighbors "are always sewing and run into each others' rooms every day." Besides spending hours companionably engaged in household activities with other wives, the women regularly received calls from officers at the garrison. Moreover, guests at the post needed to be fed and entertained, and army wives hosted dinners, dances, card parties, and other social gatherings, often at short notice. Holidays, such as Christmas, New Year's, Valentine's Day, or the Fourth of July, provided excuses for more elaborate festivities. For their first Christmas at Fort Union, Katie and Isaac Bowen gave a party for all the officers and families at the post. The menu included "a roast of pig, a saddle of venison . . . , a fillet of veal and cold roast fowls with jellies and all the fixins'," as well as mincemeat pies, blancmange, and fruitcake. Proud of her success in presenting her guests with such an elegant repast, Katie assured her mother that "we can live if we try."[35]

Not all women at frontier forts attended such lavish entertainments. Although officers' wives apparently did not socialize with women of lower economic and social classes, such as enlisted men's wives and laundresses, they interacted with them in other ways. For example, women married to enlisted men sometimes worked for the ladies of the garrison. After the birth of Katie Bowen's son, she employed a machinist's wife to care for her. "She would not take a dime in money," Katie declared, "but I shall be able to pay her in more ways than one, in milk, butter and little presents of all sorts acceptable at this post." And upon her arrival at Fort Webster, Anna Maria Morris gratefully accepted the dinner and accommodations that a sergeant's wife offered. Officers' wives in turn helped these enlisted men's wives on occasion, as when Mrs. Morris and her friends provided a layette for the baby of "Mrs. Murphy, a camp woman," cutting and sewing the garments themselves.[36]

Although married to enlisted men, the women that Mrs. Morris and Mrs. Bowen employed or assisted apparently were "respectable" women, while others who accompanied the troops had broken the bounds of respectability and worked as prostitutes. Anna Maria Morris's reaction to known prostitutes is particularly intriguing and puzzling. Her disparaging references to "so-called laundresses" (reflecting her awareness that they provided soldiers with more than clean clothes) indicate some contempt for these women, a sentiment that might well be expected from an officer's wife with an upper-class background. Her comment likely also indicates a distinction between bona fide laundresses and those who sought to hide their true profession under that title. More interesting, however, are her matter-of-fact remarks about "the Great Western," Sarah Bowman, a well-known prostitute of the El Paso area. Mrs. Morris noted the order of their march to Fort Webster, with "the company headed by the 'Great Western'" and the Morris's carriage immediately following. Several weeks after the party reached its destination, Anna Maria Morris again mentioned Mrs. Bowman. "The 'Western' Mrs. Bowman is going with the party to Calafornia. In the evening I commenced a quilted skirt for her little orphan girl." (Mrs. Bowman had adopted a child whose parents had died on the way to California.)[37]

Unfortunately, Mrs. Morris's comments raise more questions than they answer about respectable women's responses to prostitution and prostitutes. Nor does Katie Bowen's single reference to the subject prove much more enlightening. When the commander of Fort Union ordered a raid on a nearby area in an effort to recover stolen military property, Katie reported that "all the shanties and grogeries around this post . . . have been burned down," and added that, when the buildings were fired, "[M]exican women scattered like sheep from all the places." Two of the prostitutes were taken into military custody, held in the post guardhouse, and publicly punished, an event that Mrs. Bowen undoubtedly witnessed or heard about, though she made no further reference to the incident in her letters home. Perhaps she hesitated to discuss such a subject with her aged parents.[38]

Somewhat easier to discern are the attitudes Katie Bowen and Anna Maria Morris held toward non-Anglos they met during their western sojourns. Mrs. Bowen and Mrs. Morris came into more frequent contact with Hispanics than with American Indians and, like many other Anglo visitors to the territory, found some Hispanic customs amusing, others displeasing or revolting. For example, Anna Maria Morris mentioned that a room she occupied in Santa Fe contained "nineteen looking glasses," and Katie Bowen reported that Hispanics used "glasses for ornaments, as we hang pictures, halfway to the ceiling, and never use them to dress by." Both ladies also observed Hispanic religious celebrations (St. Mary's Day and St. John's Day, as well as Holy Week), and Mrs. Morris witnessed an infant's funeral. All of these observances seemed pagan and incomprehensible to these army women. "It was a ridiculous sight," Katie wrote, "but no one could have the heart to laugh at what they deem religious." Moreover, lack of hygenic practices among the indigenous population bothered the ladies. En route to Albuquerque from Santa Fe, Mrs. Morris stayed overnight with a Hispanic family at Algodones. Although she did not protest that supper consisted of chile, she was shaken to see it served in a "dirty tin wash-basin."[39]

Mrs. Morris and Mrs. Bowen did not always display such ethnocentricism, however. Both praised Hispanic handiworks, for example. Anna Maria Morris admitted that she "particularly admire[d]" the small corner fireplaces in adobe residences and also found Hispanic silverwork exceptionally fine. Katie Bowen noted that "Mexican women sew beautifully" and considered their embroidery so lovely that she endeavored to learn it soon after her arrival in the Southwest. These army wives also remarked favorably on Hispanic hospitality and generosity, and Mrs. Morris took lessons in Spanish during her years in the territory.[40]

Although these women no doubt retained numerous prejudices about Hispanics as a people (Katie Bowen, for example, refused to allow her son to be vaccinated against smallpox until the doctor assured her that he had taken the active matter from the child of a U.S. clergyman in Santa Fe), personal acquaintance began to erode these preconceptions. Hispanic women's admiration of Mrs. Bowen's son, for example, changed some of her attitudes. "Dona Morca, a very respectable woman," sent a baby gift, Katie reported; later she took her child to a nearby settlement (Barclay's Fort), where she "thought he would be smothered with kisses and squeezes." His admirers, she added, "are very kind hearted." Most of the Hispanics Mrs. Morris and Mrs. Bowen met likely belonged to upper-class Hispanic families, and many had married U.S. citizens. Anna Maria Morris found several of these women "pretty and intelligent" and during her stay in El Paso became close friends with two of these "Mexican ladies," Mrs. Hart and Mrs. Magoffin, sister-in-law to the husband of Susan Magoffin.[41]

Like women on other frontiers, Katie Bowen and Anna Maria Morris were also ambivalent toward American Indians, their feelings differing according to the groups they met and the circumstances surrounding their encounters. These women had relatively little contact with the natives of New Mexico, nor did they evince interest in the native culture or view American Indians as possible candidates for missionization, as army wives of a later period often did.[42] For the most part, Mrs. Morris and Mrs. Bowen saw them as part of the landscape on their travels in the West, a perspective that is somewhat remarkable in light of an event that took place shortly before they came to the territory. In October 1849 Apaches attacked a family named White on the Santa Fe Trail and took Mrs. White, her daughter, and a servant as captives. When a rescue party pursued these Apaches, the captors killed Mrs. White. Anna Maria Morris knew this story, as she mentioned passing the site of the "White tragedy," and doubtless Mrs. Bowen had also heard the story before she came west.[43]

Apparently, neither Anna Maria Morris nor Katie Bowen regarded Native Americans as particularly hostile or threatening. Katie Bowen acknowledged that "the mail route is always more or less infested with Indians" but advised her parents not to "let any rumors of Indians distress you for they are much exaggerated. Men get killed, tis true, traveling in the lower country, but it is through their own imprudence. The Apaches seem friendly enough in this part of the country and hunt over these mountains without giving any trouble." When a party of Apaches wandered into the fort to beg, Katie reported the incident with more humor than fear. "They are the most frightful beings that the sun ever shown upon. Some

of their red faces seem to be a foot broad through the cheeks."
When the Indians looked in the windows, one little girl was
frightened, but "Willie thought them a great curiosity" because, Katie concluded, "they look savage enough for canni-
bals."[44]

Although Anglos often gawked at American Indians, the
natives also found Anglos fascinating. When Anna Maria
Morris and her husband stopped overnight at Isleta, she
reported that Isletas gathered "about the carriage to look at
me." She was not frightened, however, and added that "as I
knew I was a perfect novelty to them I endured it patiently."
In another situation, she (appropriately) became more fearful. Early in 1852, when Apaches raided the southern portion
of the territory, she confessed in her journal, "I am afraid to
go to the Copper Mines," where her husband had been sent to
establish Fort Webster. When the situation improved later
that year, she joined her husband; with peace restored, she no
longer feared the Apaches and reported that "the Indians
were in again to-day. The Maj. bought me two nice baskets of
the chief's daughter."[45] Ambivalent attitudes toward Native
Americans also appear in later writings of army wives on
other frontiers, many of their experiences paralleling those of
Anna Maria Morris and Katie Bowen.

Neither woman returned to serve another tour in the
West. In June 1853 Mrs. Morris left New Mexico and with her
husband returned home to New York where, in 1855, she
gave birth to a son. She continued to make entries into her
journal, and these reflect the activities of an upper-class
woman in New York, visiting friends, shopping, attending
church, and overseeing domestic concerns. She died in New
York on May 6, 1861.[46] Katie Bowen also left Fort Union in
1853, but she spent another two years in Albuquerque and
Santa Fe before she and her husband returned east. Before
the couple left New Mexico, Katie wrote to her mother that
they hoped to return to the Southwest for Isaac's next tour of

duty because "it seems as though I would rather stay in a healthy country for ever than go to a climate like New Orleans — how dreadful the scourge [yellow fever] has been." Her words seem strangely prophetic, for Isaac Bowen's next assignment sent them to Louisiana, where Katie gave birth to two additional sons. There, in October 1858, yellow fever struck again, and claimed as its victims Katie, Isaac, and their infant son Robert.[47]

Even though Katie Bowen and Anna Maria Morris did not participate in frontier events in New Mexico following the Civil War, their writings reveal remarkable similarities between the pre- and postwar experiences of officers' wives. Their contemporary observations corroborate Lydia Spencer Lane's reminiscences about garrison life in the antebellum period. These army wives struggled to create homes in the wilderness, and with considerable innovation, courage, and good humor, they succeeded. Moreover, their success set a precedent for army wives of the next several decades. During her stay at El Paso and Fort Fillmore, for example, Anna Maria Morris became friends with Mrs. John Wilkins, another army wife, with whom she shared numerous experiences. Years later, in Arizona, Martha Summerhayes met Mrs. Wilkins, who provided an example in practical matters and in decorum for the younger woman to follow. Summerhayes affectionately recalled Mrs. Wilkins as "the best type of the older army woman." Katie Bowen and Anna Maria Morris, too, merited such praise.[48]

CHAPTER THREE

"You Did as Much for the U.S. as Any Soldier"

Ellen Williams, Army Laundress and Nurse

In letters, diaries, and reminiscences, ladies married to army officers provided revealing descriptions about their lives with the frontier army, yet these genteel authors were only one group of women who accompanied military forces in the West during the nineteenth century. Because dependents of enlisted men, laundresses, and prostitutes left few written accounts of their army experiences, glimpses of their lives most often depend on comments of men in the ranks, official regulations and reports, and references officers and their wives made to these women of a different social level. This scattered material provides a partial and contradictory view of these historically voiceless women; scholars have debated, for example, whether laundresses — usually married to enlisted men — embodied female virtues or exemplified female depravity. Moreover, these sources focus upon the women's military service and rarely reveal much about their earlier or later years. Although the contributions women made to the army in the West are belatedly receiving recognition, the largest sections of their lives remain obscure.[1]

Somewhat paradoxically, the opportunity to examine the life of one of these women arises from an event by no means ordinary for working-class women. Ellen Williams, who served as laundress and nurse in the West during the Civil War, would probably be indistinguishable from her contemporaries had she not written a book about the conflict, entitled *Three Years and a Half in the Army, or History of the Second Colorados*. The narrow focus of the work limits its appeal among military historians, and the volume has little literary merit. Her book, however, appears to be the only extant memoir written by the wife of an enlisted man in the West during the Civil War period; as such, it provides a rare view of women's participation in the frontier army. Aside from her military affiliation, Ellen Williams shared throughout her life numerous experiences with other working-class women. A scrutiny of her life, then, may also reveal influences that shaped the lives of countless anonymous women in the West.[2]

In some respects, Ellen Williams's military career differed from that of many army laundresses; her services in the military lasted only forty months, and her husband, a volunteer, never served in the regular army. In other regards, however, her background, experiences, and later life probably more closely approximate those of other women married to enlisted men. As immigrants to the United States, she and her husband struggled for financial stability; although they left the army near the close of the Civil War, Mrs. Williams's washtub remained an important source of family income.

Born in England in 1828, Ellen Barber accompanied her parents to the United States in 1851. On board the vessel carrying them to the new land, she met Charles Williams, a young widower from Wales, and by the time they docked in Philadelphia, the couple had decided to marry. Charles traveled around the area seeking employment, and when he had secured a job in Bordentown, New Jersey, he returned to Philadelphia, where he and Ellen married in August 1851. A

Ellen Williams.

decade later, with two small sons, the Williams family had moved westward across the continent to the goldfields of Colorado. In the mining camps, Charles Williams plied his trade as a carpenter and, like countless others, hoped to strike it rich. But the Civil War interrupted his plans and those of his colleagues; in October 1861, as Ellen Williams recalled, these "hardy miners" exchanged "'Pick and Shovel' for the 'Sword and Bayonet.'" Charles Williams enlisted in an independent company (later Company A of the Second Colorado Cavalry) as a bugler, and his wife offered her services as company laundress.[3]

In accordance with military regulation, Captain James Ford approved Mrs. Williams's appointment as laundress, which entitled her to receive rations as well as wages collected from the enlisted men and officers whose clothing she maintained. He also secured her services as nurse, although he admitted that he lacked the authority to make an official appointment in that capacity. In December 1861, independent Companies A and B were mustered into service and proceeded to Fort Garland in southern Colorado. Union forces in New Mexico, under the command of General E.R.S. Canby, prepared to defend the territory from a Confederate invasion, and Company B of the independent volunteers hurried south to reinforce Union troops. Shortly thereafter, Company A received orders to advance to Santa Fe and set forth from the garrison at Fort Garland early in February 1862. This midwinter march was a chilling introduction to military hardships not only for dependents traveling with the army but for soldiers as well.[4]

The company marched forth with rations for ten days, expecting to receive additional supplies when they reached Santa Fe. Severe snow storms and icy roads slowed their progress, however, and the journey lasted nearly a month. Intense cold and hunger marked the trek, and Mrs. Williams declared that crossing the mountains of southern Colorado and northern New Mexico in winter made "Napoleon's march across the Alps . . . sink into insignificance" by comparison. Although three ox-drawn wagons had been allocated to convey women, children, and supplies to their destination, rough terrain and low temperatures made riding impossible. Mrs. Williams walked most of the way, assisting her elder son, while soldiers took turns carrying her baby. She worried particularly that the children might freeze and took care to place them between her and her husband when they bedded down for the night. Fortunately, neither Ellen Williams nor her children suffered lasting effects from their privations en route to New Mexico. Because of inadequate footwear, though, Charles Williams was plagued by severe pains in his legs and feet, the result of rheumatism that would trouble him for the rest of his life.[5]

At last the company reached Santa Fe, where food and better shelter awaited them. Almost immediately, however, the unit received orders to march from the territorial capital to Fort Union, about one hundred miles to the northeast. While Company A battled the elements in the mountain passes of New Mexico, Union and Confederate forces clashed at Valverde, south of Socorro, on February 21, 1862. Union forces under Canby remained in possession of Fort Craig, near the site of the battle, but Confederate troops marched north hoping to capture Fort Union, the major supply depot of the region. The volunteers from Colorado hastened eastward to thwart Confederate plans, while Ellen Williams and other dependents were ordered to remain in Santa Fe. This, she recalled, was "the most trying time for me." She had accompanied the army hoping "to be with or near my husband" and for the first time she feared "what the war might bring to me."[6]

Hastily, Williams secured lodgings near the plaza for his wife and sons and brought in foodstuffs from army stores to sustain the family in his absence. Then, in a few hours, he rejoined his comrades. From the door of her new home, Ellen Williams watched them go, engulfed, as she wrote, by "a sense of loneliness . . . such as I never felt before." Afraid for her husband's safety, she also realized that she was "hundreds of miles from home and kindred, among a nation of people whose language I could not understand."[7]

Mrs. Williams, like numerous other Anglos who visited New Mexico, found little to admire there. "The general condition of the country," she noted, was "scarcely a step above barbarism." Her first observations of the populace seemed to confirm her fears. When ordered to withdraw from Santa Fe, the commissary officer sold as many government supplies as he could, then discarded the remainder into the street to prevent their falling into Confederate hands. Immediately, local residents — "all Mexicans . . . but one"— rushed into the plaza hoping to obtain some of the spoils. "Such a charge as they made on the provisions was scarcely ever witnessed by mortal eye," Mrs. Williams remembered. These discards were not the only attractions; the "motley crew" also descended upon a nearby house that Union troops had abandoned and "tore therefrom everything made of either wood, iron or glass . . . like so many famishing wolves."[8]

A more substantial threat, however, dispelled the possibility of mob rule. Confederate troops occupied Santa Fe in early March, and members of the rebel army began confiscating foodstuffs from Union dependents. Determined not to lose her meager supplies, Ellen Williams enlisted the aid of her eldest son in hiding them. "[We] dug a long shaped hole in the ground at the back of the house," she recalled, and "there we placed our sack of flour and other stores, covering them up carefully and scattered ashes and dry dirt over the place to hide the fresh digging." Another army wife took advantage of her social position to stop the thievery; Mrs. Ford, wife of the company commander, appealed to the Confederate commanding officer, an old acquaintance, and he chivalrously "put a stop to such doings."[9]

The relief that these army women felt was of short duration, for they worried about their husbands and "feared the worst" as another confrontation between Federal and Confederate forces appeared likely. Soon, though, Mrs. Williams received reassurance of her husband's well-being. Captain Ford dispatched him to Santa Fe with letters for Mrs. Ford, who had taken ill. Because Confederate troops in the territorial capital took Williams prisoner, he escaped the battles of Apache Canyon and Pigeon's Ranch during the last week of March 1862. With the destruction of the rebel supply train in these engagements, Confederate hopes to seize Fort Union died, and the Southern army began its retreat down the Rio Grande valley. Williams, restored to liberty, was temporarily assigned to another unit to await the arrival of his company in the capital. By late April, the Stars and Stripes again flew above the plaza in Santa Fe, and Ellen Williams commemorated the event in a flowery poem published in the *Santa Fe Gazette*.[10]

The retreating Confederates, unable to transport their wounded southward, entrusted them to the care of the victorious Union army and the women of Santa Fe. Even while Southern forces held the city and prepared for battle, Louisa Canby, wife of the Union commander, readied the capital to receive the inevitable casualties of the conflict. Mrs. Williams recalled that Mrs. Canby "urged all loyal women to help" to care for the wounded, whether they wore Union blue or Confederate gray, and the *Santa Fe Gazette* reported that the women of Santa Fe complied with her request. "The sick and wounded Texans in the hospital in this city" received care worthy of the "highest commendation," the newspaper noted, adding that "in health the invalids were regarded as enemies; in sickness and suffering they were administered to with a kindness that might have been shown to friends." Nor were these accolades partisan hyperbole; Confederate wounded later recalled that "noble lady Mrs. Canby" and the attentive care they received in the territorial capital.[11]

Mrs. Williams, who had acted as company nurse en route to New Mexico, probably assisted in caring for the injured in Santa Fe. While Company A proceeded southward in pursuit of the retreating Confederates and was stationed for several months at Fort Craig, Charles Williams remained on temporary assignment in Santa Fe. Although assured of her husband's safety, Ellen Williams's experience with the horrible "wounds and sufferings" led her to wonder, "When will such carnage pass from view?" Her lament, published in the *Santa Fe Gazette,* reflected a nonpartisan concern for those injured and killed, as well as sympathy for bereaved families on both sides of the "fratracidal war."[12]

On another occasion, however, she expressed partisan patriotic fervor. During the chaotic early months of 1862, Confederate troops and local residents had damaged or destroyed numerous buildings, corrals, and other structures on military property. On temporary assignment in the capital, Charles Williams employed his carpentry skills to repair and replace these damaged edifices and completed a new flagpole for the military plaza in time for the Fourth of July celebration. The *Santa Fe Gazette* duly reported on the festivities, noting that the highlight took place when "the national flag was run up the beautiful staff . . . one hundred and twenty feet above the ground. . . . As the banner ascended beautifully unfurled by the gentle breeze that prevailed enthusiastic cheers broke forth from the surrounding throng." In honor of the event, Ellen Williams composed another poem, reminding loyal citizens that they had seen "the traitors succumb in their rebel disgrace" and could now pay homage to "our own glorious emblem, the flag of the free."[13]

By mid-July, the last Confederate forces had left New Mexico, and for several months Companies A and B of the

Colorado Volunteers remained on garrison duty in Santa Fe. In the fall, these troops moved to Fort Union to shore up defenses in anticipation of a rumored invasion from west Texas. Company A encamped in Coyote Canyon, about five miles from the fort, and Mrs. Williams continued to care for ill and wounded soldiers in the command. When the invasion failed to materialize, the troops again performed normal garrison duties until early in 1863, when they received orders to return to their home state of Colorado. Ellen Williams dreaded the prospect of another midwinter journey through the mountains, but to her surprise "it was a quiet march with only the fun of camping out thrown in." Indeed, most members of the company enjoyed the experience, and Mrs. Williams observed that "the sick out-door patients I cared for improved every day."[14]

Upon their arrival at Fort Lyons, Colorado, most of the volunteers received orders to proceed to Kansas. Charles Williams, however, was suffering from severe rheumatic pains in his legs and feet and was reassigned to Company F, composed of ailing soldiers, which remained for a time in camp. In November 1863, these troops followed their comrades into Kansas, a journey that was as terrible as the march through the snow-packed passes of northern New Mexico. After more than six weeks on the road, the column camped east of Salina, Kansas, and Mrs. Williams and her family yielded to the temptation of visiting a nearby hostelry, where they "partook of a hotel dinner." Later, she recalled that the meal cost twenty-five cents, "a great extravagance for a poor soldier after living in the snow on hard tack and beans so long." A few days later, the troops arrived at Fort Riley, Kansas, but their stay there — "a great treat" — was brief, and they resumed the march through eastern Kansas. Although the army passed numerous houses during the trek, most of the citizenry remained indifferent to their sufferings. Mrs. Williams and other women asked for overnight lodgings on many occasions, but their requests were rarely met, and she remembered that "no one appeared to pity us poor women and children out in that inclement weather." The men of the company provided whatever comfort they could, but Ellen Williams admitted that "the fatigue of setting tent, packing and unpacking . . . was telling heavily upon my health."[15]

When the column arrived in Kansas City early in 1864, the Second and Third Colorado Regiments combined to form the Second Colorado Cavalry. For the remainder of the year, the new unit patrolled eastern Kansas and western Missouri in pursuit of "bushwhackers" and other Confederate sympathizers, and frequent skirmishes took place. Charles Williams's company was stationed at Hickman's Mill, Missouri (about sixteen miles from Kansas City), for about seven months; during that period, Mrs. Williams continued (as she had on the march) to perform her duties as laundress and nurse. Although there was no regimental hospital, a temporary facility at Hickman's Mill served as such, and, in the absence of a doctor, Ellen Williams assisted the hospital steward in caring for ill and injured soldiers. Union troops abandoned this post, however, when ordered to repel a Confederate advance on Kansas City. Despite orders that forbade women from traveling with the troops on this occasion, Mrs. Williams appealed to the regimental commander, who instructed her to "go along" because he expected the men would require her care. Union forces successfully quelled Price's raid (named after Major General Sterling Price, who commanded the Confederate troops), and the Second Colorado Cavalry proceeded to Fort Leavenworth to await further orders.[16]

Most of the volunteers in Companies A and B of the regiment had enlisted for three years, so their commitment to the army was nearly over. Accordingly, they were mustered out at Fort Leavenworth on December 21, 1864; the Williams's military service had ended, and "bidding farewell to their comrades," Charles and Ellen Williams went to southern Iowa. There they settled in the small community of Lewisburg, near members of Ellen's family. Later, Charles's daughter, Mary Jane (from his first marriage), and her husband joined them. After the numerous hardships of the previous forty months, they hoped that the return to civilian life marked the end of hard times.[17]

Military experiences, however, continued to influence Charles and Ellen Williams in later years. As a result of the rheumatism he had contracted during his army service, Charles became increasingly incapacitated. With her husband unable to perform heavy work, Ellen Williams again turned to her washtub to supplement the family income. By 1880, Charles Williams's health had deteriorated so much that he applied for and received a veteran's pension of $4 per month for total disability. Throughout these years the couple continued to correspond with their former comrades in arms and maintained a proud interest in the record of the Second Colorado Cavalry. Eventually, Ellen Williams decided to commemorate the regiment's contributions to the Union cause and compiled material for a book. Although she doubtless hoped to receive some financial reward for her efforts, it is likely that her main motivation was to "give to the Soldiers of Colorado a record which shall impart pleasure to themselves, their families and friends."[18]

Perhaps Mrs. Williams had seen Ovando Hollister's book about the First Colorado Volunteers, published in 1863, and hoped to ensure that the Second Colorado Volunteers received equal credit for their service. In any event, Ellen Williams did not write her book as many army wives did, either as an autobiographical account of her experiences or as a testimonial to the courage and character of her husband. Indeed, the Williams family appears in disappointingly few references throughout the narrative, although Mrs. Williams included several poems that she and her husband wrote to commemorate various occasions. Most of her personal reactions to army life occur in the early parts of the story, which mention her stay in New Mexico and her journey through Kansas to Missouri. Although she drew heavily on her own recollections and those of her husband, she augmented them with letters elicited from other members of the regiment and, in at least one instance, used material from the *Soldier's Letter,* a newspaper of the Second Colorado Cavalry published at Fort Riley, Kansas, during 1864 and 1865.[19]

Mrs. Williams faithfully chronicled the trials and travels of the Second Colorados, but her style is convoluted rather than lively, and her digressions make the narrative difficult to follow. What clearly emerges, however, is Mrs. Williams's conviction that she, no less than her husband and his comrades, was part of the regiment. Other women who wrote about their army experiences expressed similar sentiments, though few to the extent of Ellen Williams. In fact, her use of "we" in describing troop deployment often obscures her own whereabouts. Perhaps because of the volume's shortcomings, Mrs. Williams had it privately printed in 1885, probably financing the cost of the project by subscriptions to former colleagues.[20]

Apparently the book did little to boost the family's precarious financial status, which continued to decline. A fire destroyed the couple's home, and although insurance covered their debts, Mrs. Williams reported that they "stood in the open air without bed or board." Moreover, in 1888, Charles Williams began to suffer from epileptic seizures, possibly brought on by a stroke, and required almost constant attention from his wife or other relatives. They turned to their son Owen for assistance and for a time made their home with him and his wife in southern Colorado. Wary of charity, even from her son, Ellen Williams attempted to continue working as a laundress to support herself, but her advancing age made these efforts difficult. Charles's monthly pension increased to $24, but even this sum was inadequate for the couple's needs.

When an act of Congress of August 5, 1892, made Civil War nurses eligible for pensions, Ellen Williams attempted to secure this compensation.[21] Her first application was denied, but on June 5, 1893, she again applied from Cripple Creek, Colorado, stating that she was no longer able to "earn a support" because of "disability and age." The wheels of bureaucracy ground slowly, and it soon became apparent that despite Ellen Williams's devoted service to the men in her care, she held no legal status to entitle her to a pension. The case dragged on for eighteen months, with Mrs. Williams struggling to comply with each demand the Pension Office made. An initial query to the surgeon general's office revealed no record of Ellen Williams; additional records that listed payments had never been properly filed with the Treasury Department. In lieu of these documents, the Pension Office requested a statement from the officer who appointed her as nurse and certification that she had spent at least six months serving in this capacity. With some difficulty, Mrs. Williams located one of the officers who had known her at Hickman's Mill and who attested that she had indeed performed the services in question. That failed to satisfy the Pension Office, however, which demanded proof from Mrs. Williams that she had, in fact, been officially appointed to the post. Dispirited, she responded, "I cannot give the evidence the law demands," adding, "I sadly fear all my hard labor goes for naught."[22] She went on to note that her "labor was performed almost entirely in camp and field" rather than in a regular hospital setting and admitted that, when she agreed to serve as nurse, the company commander advised her that he had no authority to appoint her. He assured her, however, that if the opportunity arose, he would see her officially appointed, and she accepted his promise. "I marched hundreds of miles through snow and storm," Mrs. Williams related, "and when I saw a soldier whose hands were bitten with frost or limbs drawn and aching with rheumatism or pain I did not stop to ask if I was appointed." Instead, she went on, "I did my best to try to relieve pain wherever found" and the unit's officers "sanctioned my efforts and even sought my aid themselves."

Officials at the Pension Office, moved perhaps by her eloquence and honesty, referred the case to the surgeon general's office, but Ellen Williams's plight carried little weight there. In his memo to the Pension Office, the surgeon general recommended that her claim be rejected because she had never been appointed "by competent authority." Moreover, he pompously noted, Mrs. Williams had traveled with the troops in violation of "General Orders No. 31, War Department, A.G.O., June 9, 1861," which "directed that 'women nurses will not reside in the camps, nor accompany regiments on a march.'" On the basis of his remarks, the Pension Office denied Mrs. Williams's claim in January 1895.

"I tried so long to live without aid," Ellen Williams commented, but now she and her husband became increasingly dependent upon their son. In April 1897, Charles Williams died in Cañon City, Colorado, and, without his pension, Ellen had no further income. Within a few weeks, she applied for a widow's pension but once again encountered difficulty with the bureaucracy at the Pension Office. This time, officials insisted upon proof of her marriage, as well as statements from doctors who had attended her husband. Although she was able to secure an affidavit from the physician who cared for her husband during his final illness, the Bureau of Health in Philadelphia advised her that no records of marriages had been kept before 1860. As she could not provide affidavits from those who had witnessed the ceremony, in desperation she sent her original marriage certificate to the Pension Office, hoping that it would serve as proof. "I am left destitute," she implored. Finally, more than a year after her husband's death, the Pension Office granted her a widow's pension of

$12 per month — half of what her husband had received at the time he died.

For the next twenty years, Ellen Williams depended on the charity of her son and on her widowed stepdaughter for a place to live. On Mary Jane's farm in Iowa, the two women raised vegetables for their own use and sold the excess but otherwise relied on Mrs. Williams's widow's pension for support. On several occasions, she sought assistance to pursue her claim for a nurse's pension. Neighbors, as well as Iowa's congressional delegation, wrote to the Pension Office on her behalf, but the agency remained firm in its denial. Despite her disappointment that the government denied her right to compensation for her work, Mrs. Williams continued to believe that her services to the sick had been valuable, and she knew that she had their appreciation. "If kind words and wishes would furnish the needs of life, I should have abundance," she declared. By 1916, Mrs. Williams had returned to her son Owen's home in Alamosa, Colorado, where she lived until her death on April 24, 1920.[23]

Like countless other women throughout the country, Ellen Williams spent her final years bereft of home and husband and dependent upon the grudging benevolence of the federal government and the charity of relatives. Many of these women lived, worked, and died known only to friends and family, but others participated in events that extended their circle of acquaintance. While these incidents rarely resulted in wealth or fame, these women experienced a sense of satisfaction from the contributions they made, and others recognized and appreciated their efforts. Ellen Williams, for example, nursed the men of Company A of the Second Colorado Volunteers throughout the Civil War. If the federal government refused to acknowledge her labors, her patients remembered her care. "You did as much for the U.S. as any soldier," one trooper reminded her, and another recalled that she "served her full time as well as the rest of us."[24] No doubt other women, who left few records of their frontier experiences, received similar recognition from those whose lives they touched. The contributions of these working-class women helped to shape the history of the American West.

CHAPTER FOUR

"My Husband Was a Madman and a Murderer"

Josephine Clifford, Army Wife, Writer, and Conservationist

I was living, day and night, in sunlight or darkness, in a state of terror, fear, and suspence, such as cannot be described. In the midst of apparent safety and protection, death stared me constantly in the face — not the swift, sudden death that the Indian's arrow or the ball of an assassin grants, but the slow tortures with which the cunning of the maniac puts its victim to the rack; for my husband was a madman and a murderer, and I was given, helpless and without defence, into his hands.[1]

Such a dramatic passage, one would suspect, might open a Gothic romance or a Hollywood screenplay; few would guess that it comes instead from an autobiography of an army officer's wife on the New Mexico frontier. Josephine Clifford's account of her experiences in the Southwest provides insight into aspects of frontier military life — including unhappy marriages, domestic violence, and alcoholism — that the memoirs and diaries of most other officers' wives barely men-

tion. On less sensational subjects, such as camp life, social
functions, or housekeeping arrangements, Clifford's perceptions differ little from those of her contemporaries Frances
Boyd, Lydia Spencer Lane, Marian Russell, Eveline Alexander, and Alice Baldwin. But in addition to her frank discussion of a terrifying and unforgettable marriage, Josephine
Clifford's descriptions of the southwestern landscape, flora,
and fauna and her precise depiction of the enlisted soldier set
her writings apart from others of the genre. What is more,
Clifford's sketches of army life in Arizona and New Mexico
number among the earliest of such women's writings to be
published.[2]

Indeed, many army wives committed their western experiences to paper. Some wrote letters and diaries not intended
for publication; others published memoirs at the urging of
family members or to commemorate their husbands' careers.
But Josephine Clifford turned to writing as a career that
would make her self-supporting. Between 1869 and her death
in 1920, she wrote short stories (in the local-color tradition of
Bret Harte), autobiographical sketches, travelogues, and articles calling for conservation of natural resources. Clifford's
work appeared in *Overland Monthly, Lakeside Monthly, Californian, Out West,* and other regional and national magazines, as well as in California newspapers. Eventually, many
of her stories formed three volumes of her collected works.
Clifford's choice of career was not unusual, for increasing
numbers of female authors entered the literary market in the
second half of the nineteenth century. As one student of this
trend has noted, a career as a writer gave women an opportunity to achieve "an independent income . . . [and] friends
outside the family circle." And though Clifford certainly appreciated her earnings, perhaps even more she valued the
friends she made during her early years as a writer. These
numbered among California's most notable literary figures of

the nineteenth century and included Bret Harte, Charles Warren Stoddard, Ambrose Bierce, and Ina Coolbrith.[3]

Clifford's association with this group of authors and the variety of her writings have tended to obscure her identity as an army wife. Adding to the confusion, her three books contain seemingly random collections of short stories set in the Southwest (most on military posts), in California (which lack an army setting but may include military personnel), and in Germany, and autobiographical essays. Indeed, at first glance, because some of these autobiographical sketches are presented as fiction, they are difficult to distinguish from the fictional stories. But unraveled, separated, and placed into the chronological order they lacked in publication (using official military records as corroboration), these sketches provide a remarkably intimate view of Clifford's marriage to an army officer and other details of her life at military posts throughout the Southwest.[4]

While Josephine Clifford wrote more candidly than other officers' wives about her husband's alcoholism and abuse, her marriage was by no means the only unhappy marital relationship in the frontier army. Teresa Vielé, who rarely mentioned her husband in a book about army life in Texas, later divorced him and went to live abroad. Similarly, Mrs. D. Dyer divorced her husband, whose fondness for alcohol and other women she alluded to in her own account of army life. Either intentionally or unconsciously, other wives, too, revealed in their writings dissatisfaction or disappointment with their chosen mates.[5]

Although the incidence of infidelity, alcoholism, domestic violence, incest, insanity, and other family problems in the nineteenth-century army would be impossible to quantify, research indicates that these problems existed both on military posts and in mainstream society of the period. Because of the intimate nature of these issues, references in published reminiscences tend to be fragmented and vague, whereas the franker comments in diaries and letters rarely reveal the outcomes of the incidents. Fortunately, official records can often provide additional details. Thus, Josephine Clifford's story, as it emerges from her own recollections and from military records, may represent one of the most complete accounts of family discord in the frontier army.[6]

A journey to the unknown Southwest intimidated many women, but Josephine Clifford eagerly awaited this new adventure. Born in a castle in Prussia in 1838, Josephine Woempner accompanied her parents when they emigrated to the United States in 1846. Her father ardently believed it would be a land of opportunity and freedom for his three sons and two daughters, and he even hoped to buy "poor black slaves" from "their cruel masters" and help them to settle on land he purchased near St. Louis, Missouri. As his daughter recalled, however, he lacked the financial resources to make this dream a reality before he died in 1854. Josephine and her younger sister attended convent schools in St. Louis, where they continued to live with their widowed mother. An older brother, George, went to seek his fortune in California.[7]

During the Civil War, Josephine met James Clifford, then a captain with the First Missouri Cavalry, and fell in love with the charming, blue-eyed Irishman. Clifford, who became a U.S. citizen in 1856, had served as an enlisted man in the Second Dragoons and the First Cavalry at various southwestern posts before the war. The couple probably married in St. Louis in November 1863. Josephine continued to reside there until the fall of 1864, when she and Clifford traveled to Washington, D.C., where he expected to be mustered out of the service. Clifford, honorably discharged in January 1865, spent the following fifteen months in pursuit of a commission in the regular army. Josephine, meanwhile, worked as a postal clerk in the dead letter office in Washington, D.C.[8]

In March 1866, Clifford received his appointment as a lieutenant in the Third Cavalry. The couple went first to

Josephine Clifford. *Reprinted with permission from the California State Library, Sacramento, California.*

Carlisle Barracks, Pennsylvania, then to Fort Leavenworth, Kansas, to travel with the Fifth Infantry to New Mexico, where Clifford could join his regiment. Another member of the party was Lydia Spencer Lane, making her fifth trip across the plains. In her memoirs, Lane wrote that she suspected the "uninitiated" found the trip "exceedingly wearisome," and perhaps some of the others wives did. Josephine Clifford, though she admitted that she often tired of sitting in her carriage, remembered that the march had "something grand about it at the same time — a forest of bayonets in front of us, an endless train of wagons behind us, moving silently through the solemn wilds; hosts of red-winged blackbirds fluttering along with us, the rarer blue-jay flying haughtily over their heads."[9]

In fact, Josephine recalled several particularly pleasant aspects of the trip to Fort Union, New Mexico. The variety of landscapes she passed through, for example, relieved the tedium of the journey, for "there was always something to see; the prairie-flowers were so dazzingly colored some days, or the rock lay in such odd strata." She also rejoiced that she had hired as cook an experienced "old army woman" who knew what supplies to bring along and how to prepare meals on the trail. Mrs. Clifford also befriended a lonely German recruit, who devoted his off-duty hours to waiting on the Cliffords.

More than anything else, however, Josephine delighted in the horse she acquired at Fort Leavenworth for the trip west. From her childhood, she had loved pets and at various times owned dogs, horses, chickens, and even a squirrel. Later, at Fort Union, she temporarily adopted a mink named Max. But Toby, a beautiful white horse, became her special favorite, and the animal returned her devotion. Toby kept the entire camp entertained with his antics, as he refused to remain corralled with the other horses and wandered freely in search of Mrs. Clifford's tent. More than amusement, more than transportation, Toby represented a staunch friend. "There was something human in his affection for me," Josephine recalled. "Many a time did he stand beside me while I poured all my trouble and my fears into his ear."[10]

Other army wives, particularly those who, like Clifford, had no children, shared her fondness for animals. In her diary, for example, Eveline Alexander frequently mentioned her dog, Fanny, and her litter of puppies, and Frances Roe disobeyed her husband Fayette's orders to leave behind her greyhound puppy, Hal, when Fayette was transferred to another post. But Josephine's deep affection for Toby perhaps also reflected her loneliness. Although her writings indicate no sense of estrangement from the other officers and their families, years later another member of the party recalled that "Clifford was not highly regarded by the other officers. He was tolerated only. His record as an enlisted man was known to be bad and the other officers ostracized him." And, this acquaintance continued, although she remembered Josephine as "a refined ladylike woman . . . Clifford showed evidence of dissipation & he was rough in his demeanor." Moreover, "he drank constantly."[11]

If Clifford failed to impress favorably his comrades on the trail, his behavior after his arrival at Fort Union in August 1866 did nothing to enhance his reputation. Charged with stealing a hat from the quartermaster's stores, Clifford appeared before a court-martial, which placed him under arrest pending the decision of a higher authority.[12] In fact, Clifford remained under arrest on a variety of charges for most of the twenty-three months he spent in New Mexico as an officer of the Third Cavalry, antagonizing fellow officers and flaunting authority as the opportunity arose. Josephine related one incident that occurred at Albuquerque as the couple traveled with the troops to Fort Bayard in the southwestern part of the territory. Although all officers and troopers had received orders not to enter Albuquerque en route to their new destinations, Clifford determined to visit the village, and Josephine went along, hoping to secure supplies at the quartermaster's store. But as the couple arrived, she reported, they "were somewhat startled to see the colonel's light carriage" and decided to beat "a hasty retreat." The colonel had already seen the lieutenant and his wife, however, and demanded to know if Clifford had forgotten the commanding general's orders. Far from being humble or embarrassed, Clifford coolly responded that he was "not aware that any exception had been made in favor of the colonel," and, Josephine went on, "for the rest of the day . . . [we were] invisible to the colonel's official eye."[13]

Despite Clifford's problems with military authorities, Josephine continued to find aspects of the journey enjoyable, as she responded enthusiastically to new places and customs. If at first she saw only "mud hovels . . . [and] hard clay and cheerless sand" in New Mexican villages, she found that "the whole place somehow look[ed] different" after she discovered "the tips of the pomegranate tree peering curiously over the high mud wall[s] enclosing . . . neat *adobe*[s] with well-cultivated garden[s]" and met the hospitable and generous Hispanics who inhabited these dwellings. At Albuquerque she wondered, "Could [an] artist with brush and pencil create anything more perfect than the gentle rise away off there, over which houses and vineyards are scattered, and which climbs up steeper and higher, till the faintest shadow of a passing cloud seems resting on the blue-green peak?"[14]

The command continued south along the Rio Grande, passing through Socorro and Fort Craig, and then entered the *Jornada del Muerto,* which Josephine described as a "horrible stretch of ninety-five miles of desert land." They then passed through Fort Selden on the way to Fort Cummings, where Josephine experienced her first fear of American Indians. The week before she arrived, Apaches had killed two men traveling from Fort Bayard to Fort Cummings, and

she recalled she had never seen "a larger number of memen-
tos of Indian hostility."[15] Despite her fears, the last leg of the
journey passed peacefully, and in late August the Cliffords
arrived at Fort Bayard, near present-day Silver City. As it
happened, no fort yet existed. One of the responsibilities
assigned to the men stationed there was construction of the
facility; their other duty was to protect miners and settlers in
the area from Apaches. Josephine, the only officer's wife in
camp, appreciated the attentions of officers and enlisted men,
who proffered such luxuries as sugar and coffee from their
own rations. Soon after her arrival in camp, she explored the
surrounding countryside, riding sidesaddle on Toby with an
armed escort to various mines and the nearby community of
Piños Altos. On these excursions, the variety of New Mexico's
landscape continued to interest her. "New beauty surprised
us every little while: sometimes it was a little silver rivulet,
running over the most beautiful ferns; then a group of trees
and red-berried shrubs; and again, a clump of rare flowers,"
she remembered.[16]

Yet the beauty of the countryside, the pleasant excursions, and the kindness of the men at the fort could not erase
Josephine's growing awareness that her husband's behavior
had become increasingly abnormal. Since their arrival in
New Mexico, he had continued to drink heavily, but, more
significantly, he also began to exhibit symptoms of paranoia.
Clifford had, in fact, something to hide, and the likelihood
existed that someone in the army might know what he hoped
would remain secret. But Clifford translated that real possibility into a paranoid fantasy; soon after they reached Fort
Bayard, he confessed to Josephine that he had killed a man
in Texas a number of years before. Moreover, he had decided
that military authorities recently had traced him to Fort
Bayard and would soon arrive to bring him to justice. To
Josephine's horror, he alternated between the belief that Jo-

sephine had informed the authorities and the conviction that she might serve to aid him in an escape.[17]

Clifford, with some ease, made his wife a prisoner. As he remained under arrest, he received no assigned duties, and his free time allowed him to keep his wife under close surveillance. Forbidden by Clifford to visit Toby or to ride without her husband, Josephine's only contact with the rest of the camp came through the enlisted men who served as the couple's cook and orderly. To the casual observer, Clifford's reluctance to allow his wife to ride without him seemed sensible, for the threat of Apache attacks continued. Moreover, Josephine's reclusiveness also had a plausible explanation, since the only other woman in camp was the company laundress, and the social distance between them might have influenced their lack of congeniality. But Clifford's mistreatment of his wife extended far beyond confinement, and for a period of more than six months, Josephine suffered tremendous physical and emotional abuse.

The more Clifford drank, the more abusive he became, and he frequently threatened to kill his wife. On several occasions, he nearly strangled her. On others, he amused himself with a form of Russian roulette — with the muzzle of his pistol aimed not at his own head, but at Josephine's. As she recalled, "he would hold the revolver pressed close against my temple and let that horrid 'click-click' sound in my ears till I was fairly numb with terror." He varied these threats with others, at times menacing Josephine with a hatchet he told her he would use to cut her into small pieces to roast over the fire. And he particularly delighted in reminding her that even if she screamed for help, he could carry out his threats before anyone could rush to her aid. Yet at other times he made elaborate plans to escape his supposed pursuers, and these plans centered on Josephine's compliance and assistance.[18]

Lieutenant James A. Clifford. *Courtesy of Jeanne McIntosh.*

In later years, Josephine confessed that she could not completely understand her own response to this terrifying situation. In fact, Josephine's responses to her ordeal are strikingly similar to the behavior of other victims of wife abuse. For several months, Josephine remembered, she lived in a "dazed, unresisting state," which she likened to paralysis. A variety of emotions, particularly pride and fear (that, in retrospect, seemed "ridiculous") contributed to her inability to seek help. She knew that family and close friends lived too far away to assist her and at the same time felt the "natural reluctance of a wife to disclose her wretchedness to strangers." Then, too, miles of difficult terrain separated Fort Bayard from other communities, and she feared that her husband might injure or kill anyone who tried to aid her, as he repeatedly threatened to do.[19]

So instead of making plans to end to her ordeal, Josephine tried to hide the distressing events from her orderly and cook and infrequent visitors to the Clifford home. When Clifford's violence left marks on her neck, for example, she tied a strip of flannel around her throat, pretending to employ a remedy for a cold. Meanwhile, Clifford began to chafe at his enforced inactivity, and, in his deranged condition, suspected that his commanding officer and other members of the garrison were conspiring to keep him under arrest until proper authorities arrived to try him for murder. Early in January 1867, he requested a pass so that he could visit Santa Fe and demand redress and reinstatement to duty from General James Carleton, but the commanding officer of the fort denied this and subsequent requests. At last Clifford decided that Josephine must go in his stead and seek "redress and protection" for her spouse. "Redress and protection for *him!*" Josephine later recalled. "The bitter irony and humor of the thing was not lost upon me even in the abject state of mind I was then in."[20]

Nonetheless, Josephine quickly acquiesced to the plan because she realized that in it lay a chance for escape. She also learned that her efforts to conceal Clifford's mistreatment had fooled few at the post. Already, the commissary clerk had severely limited Clifford's rations of whisky from the military stores. Now, the post commander willingly granted Josephine's request for transportation and an escort to Santa Fe because, she related, "something of the true condition of affairs at our quarters had become known to him through our orderly and the cook." So on a cold morning in late January 1867, Josephine set out for the territorial capital and, perhaps, freedom from her insane spouse. Yet she felt no elation, but instead found herself strangely ambivalent about her flight. Clifford had refused to allow her to take Toby, and she feared that he would harm the animal if she failed to return. Indeed, her orderly acknowledged that Clifford relied on Josephine's love for Toby to bring her back to Fort Bayard and had vowed to beat and starve the horse if she escaped.

But Clifford employed weapons more subtle than mere fear and coercion to assure that his wife would return. The night before she left, he preyed upon her continuing love for him and her grief at the changes he had undergone since their marriage. Begging forgiveness for his past actions, Clifford assured Josephine that he loved her and promised to reform, demonstrating a common cycle of abuse and repentance that frequently occurs in abusive marriages. In spite of herself, his wife, like other abused women, found these "parting appeals and promises" moving. As she later explained, "women . . . are the most foolish, unaccountable, soft-hearted idiots in creation." During the first part of her journey, then, Josephine intended to return to her tormentor.[21]

Her initial resolve to return to Clifford evaporated, however, as her journey continued. Still, she determined not to reveal the true nature of her trip to officers at the various posts she passed through, partly from pride and partly because she feared that someone might send a message to her husband. But her orderly made sure that the commanders at Forts Cummings, Selden, McCrae, and Craig recognized Mrs. Clifford's need for haste, and they eagerly assisted her. Indeed, the sympathy and support that members of these garrisons and their wives offered strengthened Josephine's decision to escape, as she became aware that no one condoned Clifford's behavior or thought her wifely duties should include living with a murderous lunatic. Yet even as her hopes of escape increased, so too did her conviction that Clifford would realize that he had unwittingly given her an opportunity to leave him. Josephine further believed that once he decided he must follow her, he would pursue her even if the commander at Fort Bayard denied his requests for leave. Her worst fears came true at the small community of San Antonio, south of Socorro.

As she and her escort prepared to depart for Albuquerque, her orderly noticed a rider rapidly approaching the settlement. Almost without looking, Josephine knew who it was, and she remembered that "the sight of *this* horseman turned my heart to stone, and paralyzed every nerve of my body." As she had feared, Clifford had realized that his wife would never return. He recklessly deserted his post at Fort Bayard and avoided other military establishments as he covered one hundred and fifty miles within twenty-four hours, stopping for neither rest nor food. To add to Josephine's distress, he accomplished this madman's feat on her beloved Toby. The horse "was trembling in every limb," she later painfully related, "but when he spied me a low whinny struck my ear, and he moved forward a step to reach my side. I rushed toward him, but before I could reach him he had tottered and fallen at my very feet, with a deep, almost human groan." Moments later, Toby died as she cradled his head in her lap.[22]

As Josephine's grief and horror gave way to numbness, Clifford informed her of his plans to proceed to Santa Fe and demanded that she corroborate his story of persecution at the hands of his commanding officer. Again he overwhelmed his wife with "protestations of affection, repentence, and reform." This time she gave no credence to these promises but believed that he would not hesitate to carry out his threats to kill her and anyone who might come to her aid. On the journey to Santa Fe, Clifford refused to allow his wife out of his sight, and when they arrived in the territorial capital, he locked her in a room at the inn as he went to report to General Carleton.

But news of Josephine's plight had reached the general's ear, and he enlisted the help of several other officers and their wives to assist Josephine in escaping from her husband. Clifford, however, seemed aware of their designs and craftily refused to leave his wife's side or to allow her to visit with the ladies. Josephine, for her part, could not sufficiently overcome her fear and despair to take advantage of this unexpected opportunity. As she later related, her behavior confused the kind people who had come to her aid. "Not a word or a sign from me told them that I wanted their help, and how could they interfere without or against my wish and desire?" When she met them again, she remembered that "they blamed me for the passive submission." Yet, she went on, "that was easy enough said, but they had never stood in my shoes."[23]

General Carleton himself was reluctant to interfere in a private matter between husband and wife, behavior that may seem unfeeling but that closely parallels the conduct of law enforcement officials who avoid involvement in domestic disputes. No doubt in an effort to spare Mrs. Clifford further distress, General Carleton assured the lieutenant that he would consider Clifford's claims of persecution. Meanwhile, he ordered Clifford to return to Fort Bayard and consider himself under arrest again. In reality, of course, Carleton added desertion to charges pending against Clifford that a court-martial set for the spring would address. And while he took no steps to incarcerate Clifford, Carleton characterized the lieutenant as "a very bad man," and he added, "His wife is to be pitied."[24]

As the Cliffords left Santa Fe to return to Fort Bayard in early February, Josephine recalled that she left "all hope behind." Indeed, the attentive and affectionate behavior Clifford had displayed in the territorial capital evaporated almost immediately. The couple's orderly, hoping to cheer Mrs. Clifford, made her the present of a dog he had secured in Santa Fe. She took comfort in the animal's companionship until, a short way along their journey, her husband decided to use the unfortunate creature as an object lesson to his wife. Seizing the dog, Clifford beat "the struggling animal's brains out" with the butt of his pistol, then calmly rubbed his hands clean in the sand of the road. As Josephine watched in "speechless horror," he turned to her and told her that he would not hesitate to dispatch her in a similar manner.[25]

Once back at Fort Bayard, Clifford's behavior showed no signs of improvement. Although the post commander demanded Clifford turn in his side arms, the lieutenant continued to terrorize his wife in other ways. He also persuaded a hapless member of the commissary to provide him with two gallons of whisky, and his subsequent drunken actions prompted the commander to place a guard at the Cliffords' tent. During this period, Josephine lapsed into despondency and no longer contemplated escape. For two months, she recalled, she almost hoped that Clifford would carry out his threats and kill her so that her sufferings might end.

But with spring came a new opportunity for her to attempt to flee. In mid-April, a court-martial convened at Fort Bayard to consider a number of cases, including Clifford's. During the proceedings, Clifford was expected to sit before the court, under guard, and thus he could no longer scrutinize his wife's every movement. Fear that she might again try to leave, coupled with the additional stress of the trial, led Clifford to risk resuming his abusive behavior even while the garrison included the additional officers who made up the court. One evening he entered his tent, dismissed the orderly, and waved a hatchet at his wife, ordering her to kneel down so that he could cut into her skull.

As she complied, she displayed no fear, and her husband decided to prolong her ordeal. Next, he threatened to throw her into the fire and in fact burned a number of her belongings as a prelude. In the process, he discovered whisky that Josephine had hidden and paused in his grisly work to consume about a quart. To his wife's surprise, the liquor seemed to calm him, and he fell asleep, keeping a hand on Josephine during his nap. Worn out from this terrifying experience, she also dozed. When she awoke, she saw "the sharp edge of the hatchet, and the maniac face" of Clifford "grinning fiendishly behind it" as he took aim to strike. Disconcerted to discover she had awakened, Clifford paused and eventually fell asleep again. But this incident, the culmination of months of torture, penetrated Josephine's lethargy and she vowed that should she "ever again see the light of day, . . . no fear, no pride should ever deter" her from escaping.[26]

In the morning, as soon as Clifford left for the court, Josephine, with the aid of her orderly and the rest of the garrison, made careful plans to leave in the early evening of April 19, 1867. As she departed, the post commander assured her that he had assigned a whole company to guard her husband. Then, bidding her farewell, he furnished her with a letter to the commanders of the posts she would pass. This missive advised these officers that "treatment of [Mrs. Clifford] . . . is reported *Brutal* and anything you can do to assist her in leaving the country will be endorsed as a just cause."[27]

As during her earlier attempt to leave her deranged husband, Josephine received compassion, support, and assistance on her journey northward. At Fort Union, she joined a military train en route to St. Louis under the command of General Andrew Alexander. Alexander's wife, Eveline, numbered among Josephine's companions on the trip east, and Josephine never forgot her kindness. Yet, as Josephine left the territory, she still feared that Clifford would somehow try to follow her; once again, she was right. This time, however, Josephine had eluded his grasp forever. After she arrived at St. Louis, she journeyed to California, where her brother and mother lived, and filed for a divorce, which was granted in April 1869.[28]

Clifford was determined to pursue his wife, even though he remained under arrest. Charges pending against him from his offenses at Fort Union had been dropped, but as Josephine left Fort Bayard, his trial there continued. This court-martial found him guilty of desertion, breach of arrest, and conduct unbecoming an officer and recommended that he be cashiered from the army. The court also agreed that Clifford's mental condition had deteriorated and suggested that he be assessed for insanity. Cagily, Clifford parleyed that decision into a medical leave, which he received within a week after his wife's departure. He hastened as far as Albuquerque, where he paused to confront members of the garrison there because they had helped Josephine. In a rage, he drew a gun on a superior officer and threatened to kill him. This rash act effectively halted Clifford's pursuit of his unfortunate spouse, as military officials turned the errant officer over to civil authorities, who tried Clifford on charges of assault. An army doctor who examined Clifford, however, pronounced him insane, and the case was dismissed. Next, Clifford turned his attention toward the verdict of the court-martial at Fort Bayard, discovering a legal loophole that overturned the sentence calling for his dismissal from the army. For a short time he was released from arrest and returned to duty at Fort Wingate in western New Mexico. Meanwhile, he correctly surmised that Josephine had fled to California to live with her mother, and he continued harrassing his wife by letter, alternating threats to kill her should he find her with pleas for her return.[29]

Military officials, however, had not yet finished with Clifford, and brought new charges against him relating to his assault on Lieutenant Colonel Duncan at Albuquerque. This court-martial found Clifford guilty, and members of the court called for his dismissal from the service and for incarceration in a federal penitentiary for five years. The case automatically proceeded to the secretary of war for review. In these proceedings, Clifford's closely guarded secret emerged; though he had successfully kept it from his wife, he could not hide it from his superior officers. Even before Josephine fled the territory in the spring of 1867, General Carleton had received letters from military officials asking him to investigate a matter relating to Clifford, and in the latter trial this new development and Clifford's treatment of Josephine formed part of the evidence against him.[30]

In fact, not one but two women had fallen sway to Clifford's charms and shared his life at frontier posts in New Mexico. Clifford — alcoholic, abusive, and periodically displaying symptoms of insanity — was also a bigamist. Because his first wife, Margaret, could neither read nor write, she left a much less detailed record of her life with Clifford than did Josephine. But from affidavits Margaret made when she applied for a pension as Clifford's widow and from other official records emerges the story of another army wife who experienced neglect, desertion, and destitution. Like Josephine's, Margaret's story illustrates an aspect of family life in the nineteenth-century army that seldom has been examined. And, although these two women never met, their life stories are interwoven because they married the same man.

At the age of twenty-two, Clifford had married his first wife, Margaret Dillon, in New Orleans in February 1851, under his real name, James Ingram. With his seventeen-year-old bride, he journeyed to Fort Leavenworth, Kansas, where he planned to join a wagon train bound for California. Inexplicably, however, he decided instead to enlist in the army, a plan he failed to discuss with Margaret; indeed, she remembered, she had no knowledge of his intent until "he approached my tent in soldier's clothes." He adopted the name Clifford because he needed an alias, he explained, telling Margaret the same story he would later relate to Josephine, that he had killed a man in Texas and fled from justice. Under the name of James Clifford, he joined the Second Dragoons as a private, and he and Margaret went westward to Fort Conrad, New Mexico, where their daughter, Emma, was born in November 1851. For the next several years, Clifford served at various posts in New Mexico, until he decided to leave the military in 1855. He received an honorable discharge at Fort Leavenworth, where the Cliffords added son William to their family.[31]

During the next three years, as Margaret later recalled, the family "wandered around considerable," living for a time in Philadelphia, and later in Brooklyn (where a second son, Oakleaf, joined the family in 1856). Eventually, Clifford reenlisted in the army, joining the First Cavalry in 1858 as a bugler, and the Cliffords returned with this unit to New Mexico. At the outbreak of the Civil War, Clifford applied for a commission in the First Missouri Cavalry, and the family returned to the St. Louis area with a fourth child, Annie, born at Fort Smith, Arkansas, in 1860. In all, Margaret bore nine children (five of whom died in infancy or soon after) during her marriage to Clifford.[32]

From 1861 until Clifford's departure for Washington late in 1864, Margaret and the children remained in the St. Louis area, where, as his regimental duties permitted, Clifford visited them. As Margaret later admitted, during this period friends advised her that Clifford carried on an affair with

Margaret Dillon Clifford. *Courtesy of Jeanne McIntosh.*

another woman. (The scanty evidence suggests, however, that this woman was not Josephine Woempner.) But she apparently knew nothing of his second, bigamous marriage to Josephine. Thus, Margaret had no reason to suspect, as she bade her husband farewell in the fall of 1864, that she would not see him again for more than five years. Clifford set out for Washington (with Josephine), and Margaret and the children returned to New Orleans, where Margaret had relatives.

During the first fifteen months of their separation, Clifford wrote often to Margaret and sent her money. In February 1866, he wrote her a tender missive recalling their wedding anniversary, sending love to the children, and assuring her that he expected to join the family shortly. But, in fact, Margaret received no additional news of her husband (or any money for her support) until he suddenly appeared at her home on Palm Sunday, 1870. For four trying years, Margaret depended on the charity of relatives and friends and the kindness of military officials to support herself and her children. As she recalled, General Philip Sheridan and other officers "were cognizant of the fact that my husband had deserted me & all were kind to me." They permitted her to draw rations from the quartermaster's department. In addition, Willie and Oakleaf "worked as messengers" for the army, while their mother "sewed for some of the officers."[33]

These kindly officers also investigated Clifford's whereabouts so that military authorities might compel him to support his family. Eventually, they traced him to New Mexico. Their letters detailing his neglect of Margaret and the children, combined with those of officers describing his cruel treatment of Josephine, formed part of the material that the secretary of war reviewed in Clifford's case. On the basis of these documents, the secretary questioned Clifford's sanity and ordered another examination to assess his mental condition. The post physician at Fort Wingate conducted this second evaluation, concluding that Clifford was "not insane," although he admitted that the officer possessed a "disposition naturally suspicious and revengeful" and that he might "be capable of acts of violence." Therefore, the secretary endorsed the recommendations of the court-martial, and Clifford was cashiered from the army on June 9, 1868. The sentence was reduced somewhat, however, so that he avoided incarceration.[34]

Not surprisingly, Clifford immediately requested a new trial, charging that he had been the victim of unfair legal proceedings and persecution. Ultimately, he petitioned President Grant to reappoint him as an officer; fortunately for the army, the chief executive declined to do so. By the spring of 1870, Clifford abandoned his quest for a military career and, no doubt in need of emotional solace, returned to New Orleans and the family he had abandoned five years before. Margaret's immediate reaction to her husband's reappearance is unrecorded, although she later maintained that she "forgave him for his neglect" and that from Clifford's return until his death their "relations were entirely amicable." Moreover, she recalled, "we never talked of his conduct[,] whereabouts[,] or business from '65 to '70."[35]

For about a year, Clifford worked for the police force in New Orleans but then became restless for the West. In June 1871, the family moved to Santa Fe, where Clifford sought employment with the quartermaster's department at Fort Marcy. The following year, he opened his own livery stable in the territorial capital, but his health began to fail. Afflicted with chronic dysentery, Clifford moved his family back to New Orleans in 1873, and Willie and Oakleaf supported their parents until Clifford died in 1874.

His widow never remarried. She returned to New Orleans briefly, then accompanied her son Oakleaf to the West again. For a time they lived in Colorado and in the mid-1880s returned to New Mexico. By 1890, Oakleaf had settled in Albuquerque with his family and owned a livery stable that

later grew into a taxi service. Margaret's health declined as
she approached the age of sixty, and in 1894 she applied for a
widow's pension, testifying that "I depend wholly upon my
son Oakleaf for support — for clothing food & shelter." After a
lengthy and complicated investigation, the Pension Office
granted Margaret's request, and she received a widow's pension until her death in Albuquerque in 1905.[36]

For Margaret, of course, such an application represented
a possibility for financial support in her old age; but to Josephine, Margaret's simple request brought embarrassment
and a resurgence of memories she had tried to exorcise for
nearly thirty years. As investigators for the Pension Office
proceeded with Margaret's claim, they learned about
Clifford's second marriage; eventually, they located Josephine, and traveled to Santa Cruz, California, to take her
deposition in the case. Not surprisingly, Josephine found the
procedure upsetting, as she knew nothing about Clifford's
earlier marriage to Margaret, testifying that Clifford "never
told me that he had been previously married." Josephine
knew that Clifford's prior marriage invalidated his marriage
to her, but, just as her husband had concealed his bigamy,
Josephine kept this information secret. Although she had
written explicitly about her ill-fated marriage, she had never
publicly disclosed her divorce from her abusive spouse, nor
would she ever reveal this further evidence of Clifford's per-
fidy.[37]

In the years since she had left Clifford, Josephine had not
been able to forget the terrifying and tragic events of her
marriage. Yet she did not lose her enthusiasm for the southwestern landscape and visited army friends in Arizona on
several occasions. She had established herself as a writer and
had made friends with some of California's literary elite.
Soon after she came to California, she met Bret Harte, editor
of the young *Overland Monthly* ("one of the best American
magazines" of the day), and became his editorial assistant.

Harte urged her to try her hand at writing about her experiences. She took his advice, and in December 1869 her first piece, a sketch about her employment in the postal service, entitled "Down Among the Dead Letters," appeared in Harte's magazine. During the next two decades she wrote additional sketches about her travels and life as an army wife; she also began to write numerous short stories that had western settings or German backdrops. Not only *Overland Monthly,* but also *Californian* (another California magazine), *Lakeside Monthly* (a regional periodical based in Chicago), and *Potter's American Monthly* regularly featured her work. In 1877 Josephine's first book, *Overland Tales,* appeared. Most of the twenty-one sketches and stories had been published previously in *Overland Monthly* or *Lakeside.* A second volume of her work, *"Another Juanita" and Other Stories,* followed in 1893, and a third collection, *"The Woman Who Lost Him" and Tales of the Army Frontier* appeared in 1913.[38]

Josephine's early association with Harte and the *Overland Monthly* was fortuituous not only for her writing career, but also for her personal happiness. She became friends with many of the other authors who wrote for the magazine, particularly Ina Coolbrith, later known as California's poet laureate. Indeed, aside from their chosen careers as writers and their association with the magazine, Josephine and Ina had a good deal else in common; most significantly, both had experienced unhappy marriages to abusive husbands who exhibited signs of mental illness, and both women terminated their marriages with divorce — a secret that each carefully guarded even though increasing numbers of wives in California divorced their husbands, particularly on the grounds of cruelty, between 1860 and 1890.[39]

Another of these friends was Anton Roman (owner first of the *Overland Monthly* and later of *Californian*), for whom Josephine may have felt a special kinship because he, too, was of German descent. She probably confided in him about her marriage to Clifford, for Roman seems to have made inquiries to ascertain her former husband's whereabouts. From Roman, in about 1880 or 1881, Josephine learned that Clifford was dead. As a Roman Catholic, she apparently had hestitated to consider remarriage after divorce; now, she felt free to marry again. In 1882, during a visit to friends in Arizona, she met Jackson McCrackin, a miner from South Carolina, and the couple married. Returning to Santa Cruz, California, they built a ranch in the nearby mountains that Josephine christened Monte Paraiso.[40]

At Monte Paraiso Josephine found her life closer to something like paradise than it had ever been. Happy in her second marriage, surrounded by beautiful countryside and a number of pets, she also kept in touch with her literary friends, particularly Ina Coolbrith and Ambrose Bierce, who lived nearby. Yet she had not forgotten her experiences with Clifford, although she had skillfully concealed her unhappy marriage and attendant details in her early autobiographical sketches. Not until Josephine learned of Clifford's death did she commit her most terrifying memories to print in "Toby" and "Flight: A Sequel to Toby," two stories that appeared in *Californian* in 1881 (and later in her second book, *"Another Juanita"*). Until the publication of these articles, Josephine had shared these events only with her family and a few intimate friends. And, indeed, these frank and vivid depictions so startled readers that most assumed the works were fiction — and sensational, lurid fiction at that — rather than accounts of a troubled, torturous relationship.[41]

In addition to these autobiographical articles, a number of Josephine's short stories include themes that derive from her own experiences. In "La Graciosa," "Her Red Hair," "Penitencia," and "That Ranch of His," for example, the heroine flees from a husband who has misused her, although few details of the mistreatment appear in the narrative. Nor are women in Clifford's stories incapable of treachery and deceit; in "An Episode of 'Fort Desolation'" (also published under the title "A Woman's Treachery"), "The Gentleman from Siskiyou," "Manuela," and "Her Name Was Sylvia," women are responsible for the evils that ultimately befall the male protagonists. Along similar lines, several of Josephine's stories feature star-crossed lovers who, for one reason or another, have been unwilling or unable to marry; when they meet again and realize that they have loved each other all along, usually the death of one (or both) prevents them from achieving happiness together. In fact, most love affairs in Josephine's writings do not end happily.[42]

That Josephine wrote of her own unhappy marriage in both fictional and autobiographical form underscores the long-lasting emotional impact of the events she chronicled. Writing about them no doubt allowed her some kind of catharsis, much as psychotherapy might provide today. But even as she incorporated these painful memories into her accounts, she did not neglect other themes. Her affection for animals clearly emerges from her stories and sketches, and her appreciation of natural beauty illuminates her writing, whether she describes the wild terrain of southwestern New Mexico or the peaceful setting of a California garden. Her characters — particularly women — are often complex and varied, her stories depicting women of various social classes, ranging from society matrons to army wives, schoolteachers, servants, and prostitutes. Hispanics and native Americans also frequently appear in her stories as fully developed characters, not demeaning stereotypes.

In her later life, other events shaped her writing. In 1899 a forest fire destroyed the McCrackins' mountain ranch, a personal tragedy that awakened Josephine to the threat not only fires but also human encroachment and greed posed to California's redwood forests. In 1900, she wrote an impassioned letter that launched a campaign to save these giant trees, and her efforts eventually led to the formation of a California state redwood park. Similar concern led her to organize a protective organization for California's endangered songbirds in 1901. For the rest of her life she supported various movements to conserve the natural resources of her adopted state and wrote numerous letters and articles to further these goals.[43]

After Jackson McCrackin died in 1904, Josephine became the society editor for the *Santa Cruz Sentinel*. Heavy debts in addition to the loss of Monte Paraiso forced Josephine, nearing seventy, to support herself again. She continued to write articles for *Overland Monthly, Out West,* and other magazines. Her third collection of stories and sketches was published in 1913, but financial need compelled Josephine to continue working even as she approached her eightieth birthday. "I have worked faithfully while I was able," she wrote to her friend Ina Coolbrith, "and I am still working when I am no longer able . . . principally for the few dollars it brings me." She died shortly after she reached the age of eighty-two, in December 1920.[44]

Although Josephine Clifford's name invariably appears in discussions of California's nineteenth-century literary figures, no serious study of her literary career has yet appeared. Josephine wrote for some of the best-known regional journals of her day, but she once confessed that in "matters literary, . . . genius alone counts, and I do not possess it." Recent scholars have agreed, maintaining that "Mrs. Clifford had little literary talent" and further asserting that her "plots and characterizations are melodramatic and repetitious."[45]

Perhaps her work deserves closer scrutiny, however, because her contemporaries appraised her contributions in more favorable terms. John Carmony, who purchased the *Overland Monthly* from Anton Roman, recalled, "I shall always look back to that period of my life as the brightest of my existence — in connection and close association with the stars of Californian literature — Joaquin Miller, Mark Twain, Bret Harte, Charles Warren Stoddard[,] Edward Sill, Ina Coolbrith, Josephine Clifford and many others." Ella Sterling Cummins Mighels, who wrote an early history of California's literary scene, noted that Josephine's "style is clear and vigorous, her plots vivid and original" and concluded that "no better work of the kind is to be found from any woman writer's pen in California." Moreover, Hubert Howe Bancroft praised her for her treatment of Hispanics as well as her "neat bits of character portrayal, . . . spirit of narration and smoothness of diction" and observed that "Josephine Clifford has been among the happiest contributors of short tales."[46]

From a castle in Prussia to the deserts of New Mexico to the mountains of California — Josephine Woempner Clifford McCrackin undoubtedly lived a varied and interesting life; moreover, her writings make it possible for the twentieth-century reader to glimpse something of those experiences. Her stark depictions of an unhappy marriage provide a picture of family life in the frontier army not often open to public scrutiny; her later literary career and efforts to promote conservation of natural resources are similarly noteworthy. As one of her admirers noted, hers is indeed "the romantic history of a remarkable woman."[47]

CHAPTER FIVE

"My Heart Was in the Work"

Alice Blake, Mission Teacher in the Southwest

"So often a seed sown in some wayside corner, or even cast on the wind, takes deepest root. And so I am trying to sow patiently in my little corner," Alice Blake confided in a quarterly report to her mission board. For more than forty years, Blake's "little corner," where she labored as a mission teacher, consisted of small Hispanic villages in northeastern New Mexico. During the decade following the Civil War, Protestant denominations (particularly Presbyterians and Methodists) renewed efforts to convert the territory's native peoples from Roman Catholicism, sending traditional missionary couples to the region. Reflecting a trend in worldwide missionary activity, increasing numbers of single women also came to the territory to participate in the Christianizing and civilizing programs of these churches.[1]

One aspect of civilization — education — dominated Protestant hopes and concerns for the region. As early missionaries realized that New Mexico was indeed a Catholic stronghold, they admitted that opportunities for converting adults seemed slim. But they shared the conviction of Sheldon Jackson, a notable Presbyterian missionary, that children were more likely candidates for missionary efforts and that education would pave the way for conversion. The establishment of mission schools, they believed, should accompany evangelization. In some areas, these institutions would provide the only opportunity for many children in northern New Mexican villages to receive an education, as no uniform system of public schools existed in the territory until 1891; in other locations, they would offer an alternative to schools that Roman Catholic clergy and nuns staffed.

Although missionaries in the field agreed on the importance of schools in New Mexican communities, the Presbyterian Board of Home Missions rejected Jackson's request to establish a system of mission schools in the territory. Undaunted, however, Jackson turned to another potential source of help: Presbyterian women. Throughout the late 1860s and 1870s, church women had formed various regional organizations to assist in the work of home missions. One of the first of these bodies was created in response to letters Eveline Alexander, an army wife stationed with her husband at Fort Union, New Mexico, wrote to her mother about the need for education among New Mexico's native peoples. This Santa Fe Mission Association pledged to pay the teacher's salary for a school for Hispanic students established in Santa Fe in 1867.[2]

Sheldon Jackson encouraged such groups to unite and devote their efforts to raising funds for home mission schools. Eventually his efforts led to the formation of the Woman's Executive Committee of Home Missions of the Presbyterian Church (later the Woman's Board of Home Missions). Women administered, staffed, and funded this body and served as teachers in its mission schools. Within five years of its founding, the Woman's Board had raised funds to support 175 teachers in 86 schools for Hispanics, American Indians, southern mountaineers, and Mormons, and eventually the Presbyterian Board of Home Missions transferred all home mission work among these "exceptional" peoples to the Woman's Board.[3]

In fact, Jackson's appeal to Presbyterian women fortuitously occurred during a period when women's involvement in religious activities rapidly escalated. Throughout the nineteenth century, middle- and upper-class women believed that their sphere of influence embraced religion and morality; piety represented one of the four cornerstones of the cult of domesticity. As women assumed responsibility for the moral and spiritual welfare of their families, they also became increasingly aware of their duty and capacity to extend their beliefs and blessings to others deemed less fortunate than they. "Woman's work for women" became a rallying cry in Protestant churches in the decades following the Civil War, as women across the United States formed volunteer organizations and made financial contributions toward missionary work. Other women married missionaries and accompanied their spouses to mission fields. Yet their experiences, like those of missionary wives in earlier years, indicated that married women might have too many other duties to teach effectively in mission schools. Thus, greater numbers of single women joined the missionary movement and traveled to Africa, the Orient, or the western United States.[4]

A career as missionary teacher not only offered single women a socially acceptable occupation, but also afforded them the opportunity to be leaders in the civilizing work of the churches on the frontier. Churches carefully scrutinized candidates for these positions, selecting teachers with religious commitment, good moral character, suitable education, and strong constitutions. Mission boards also hoped to keep these women in teaching positions and sometimes required that teachers agree not to marry for a specified period.[5] Although some women who came to New Mexico as mission teachers abandoned the occupation for a variety of reasons (including marriage), a number of others remained in the mission field for years. For them, mission work may have required a long-term commitment but was a rewarding vocation. In addition to their teaching duties, missionaries like Alice Blake, Alice Hyson, and Elizabeth Craig (to mention but three) became skilled administrators as they assisted in community development and acquired medical knowledge as they provided health care in their villages. Thus, if domestic duties kept many missionary wives from fully participating in these other activities, single women could better enjoy the expansion of women's roles that mission work on the frontier allowed.[6]

As women across the country responded to the requests of the Woman's Board for money, funds became available to open mission schools in New Mexico. Between 1881 and 1885, Presbyterians opened educational institutions in eighteen New Mexican communities, and by 1923 Presbyterians had established schools at fifty locations throughout the state. Many declined and eventually closed, particularly after the territory established a public school system. But others continued to provide educational opportunities for students in remote areas of the state into the mid-twentieth century.[7]

Among those who came to teach in the villages of northern New Mexico was Alice Alta Blake, who shared many characteristics with other mission teachers in the West. Her attitude, upbringing, and values reflected Protestant, middle-class America. And like other young women from a similar environment, she found herself poorly prepared to cope with the distinct cultural and religious traits of the people she came to instruct.[8] For more than forty years, Blake served as teacher, nurse, and community servant in Presbyterian missions in New Mexico. When her work began, she found herself among people whose poverty and ignorance repelled her, whose religious beliefs horrified her, and whose apparent lack of moral values made her believe that she could understand life in Sodom and Gomorrah.[9]

Alice Blake during her years of mission service. *Reprinted with permission from the Menaul Historical Library of the Southwest. Courtesy of Mrs. Ida Westwood and S. Omar Barker.*

Villagers in turn viewed Blake (and other missionaries) with suspicion and resentment. Gradually, however, tolerance, appreciation, and a lasting affection between Alice Blake and "her" people replaced these initial reactions. As the story of this transition traces Alice Blake's life and work and the birth and death of the New Mexican town of Trementina, it also provides a close-up view of the cross-cultural interaction brought about by Protestant missions in the Southwest. Alice Blake's experiences were by no means unique among the mission teachers. Indeed, when Blake wrote a history of the mission schools, she asked numerous other teachers for their impressions and memories and concluded that these women had shared a "universality of experiences."[10]

Allie, as her family knew her, was born in Okoboji, Iowa, on June 24, 1867, the eldest of seven children. Her father, Fletcher Blake, served a term in the Iowa State Legislature (1871–1872) but eventually migrated west as a result of poor health. The Blake family traveled first to Kansas, then settled for a time in Texas before relocating in 1881 near Las Vegas, New Mexico. In New Mexico's salubrious climate, Mr. Blake quickly regained his health and went on to serve in New Mexico's volunteer militia in a campaign against Geronimo.[11]

Alice remembered that her father's ancestors were New Englanders and Yankee values predominated in her home; presumably, these included thrift, practicality, a sense of duty, and a respect for education. In any event, Alice attended school in Kansas City and later spent a year at the Presbyterian Academy in Santa Fe. At that time, she became acquainted with several mission teachers and observed their commitment to the girls in their charge. Later, she attended Bethany College in Topeka, Kansas. By 1888, Alice had returned to the family home and taught school in Las Vegas. Simultaneously, she became active in the Presbyterian church, and considered becoming a mission teacher to southern blacks. But when a vacancy at a mission school closer to home occurred, Blake responded to her minister's request and accepted the post.[12]

In September 1889, the stocky young woman of average height, with rosy cheeks and sparkling eyes, set out for her new job at Rociada, New Mexico. For company, the twenty-two-year-old Blake took a fourteen-year-old neighbor girl. Fortunately, she also sallied forth armed with characteristic faith, energy, and determination, for she needed all these qualities in her new undertaking. One of the first obstacles she encountered was a linguistic one; despite several years of residence in New Mexico, Alice spoke almost no Spanish, and few people in her new community spoke English. Primitive living conditions presented another challenge, as did the hostility of many area residents to the new, Anglo, Protestant teacher.[13]

Alice Blake first reacted negatively to the "Mexicans" she had come to live among. Characterizing them as dirty and ignorant, she also considered them "so corrupt in their moral nature that they would scorch the soul of an angel."[14] But Protestant missionaries, despite their ethnocentrism, thought that education and conversion would "raise" the native populace to the level of Anglo-Americans. Whatever their sense of cultural and religious superiority, Alice Blake and other missionaries believed that Hispanic residents of New Mexico suffered no inherent, racially linked obstacle to advancement. Rather, Blake confidently maintained that mission work would succeed among these people precisely because they were "not by any means a primitive race."[15]

Alice Blake, like most Protestants, blamed the inferior condition of southwestern residents on the influence of the Roman Catholic church. New Mexico's Catholic church, Protestants charged, remained medieval in character because of the territory's isolation and its subservient parishioners reduced to poverty by priests who demanded excessive fees for performing baptisms, marriages, and burials. Moreover, missionaries asserted, these clerics suppressed Bible reading to keep the populace ignorant and submissive. In many areas, Catholic priests provided the only education available, which further extended their control over what Alice Blake called the "priest-ridden people."[16]

Nor did Protestants keep their vehement anti-Catholicism to themselves. Ministers and missionaries actively challenged their religious opponents in the schools and from the pulpits and in Spanish-language newspapers (the Presbyterian *El Anciano,* which *La Aurora* later replaced, and the Methodist *El Abogado Cristiano*) dedicated to advancing the "mission of Protestantism" by "carrying testimony of the truth."[17] The Catholic response appeared in the Jesuit *Revista Católica,* which often maintained a lofty tone that treated Protestants as a trivial nuisance. For example, at one point the *Revista* commented that "Protestantism among the Mexicans is a farce." On other occasions, however, both groups resorted to little more than name calling. After a particularly heated exchange, the Catholic periodical charged that "in all the world it would be difficult to find an adversary more loathsome and shamelessly vile" than *El Anciano.*[18]

Protestants, on the other hand, reserved their harshest criticism of Catholics for the activities of the Penitentes, a lay society whose members practiced extreme forms of penance through self-torture. Despite official condemnation from the hierarchy of the Catholic church, the society flourished in remote New Mexican communities, and their Lenten rites (which included self-flagellations and crucifixions) were morbidly fascinating to Protestant observers.[19]

In light of this cultural climate, Blake's fear and revulsion when she arrived at Rociada become more understandable. In 1889, in her first report from this community of about 350 people, she noted that most of the residents were

Penitentes whose "daily lives are at the mercy of the priest" and who "believe their souls to be." But Blake remained enthusiastically devoted to her task even as she witnessed the frightening Lenten rituals. Throughout her five years at Rociada, she determined that the educational intent of her mission was more important than she had once understood. If some Protestants jealously counted converts, Blake concluded that "we should be slow about filling our church rolls with names of people who did not understand what they are doing." Instead, she aimed primarily (through education) to "inculcate new moral standards, even a new interpretation of religious terms." Thus, although few converts joined the church, Blake believed that her mission program was succeeding. School enrollments steadily increased, and village residents formed a literary society to promote the learning of English and even hoped to establish a library.[20]

Numbers of converts, however, indicated success or failure to the Woman's Board, which closed the school at Rociada in 1894 and transferred Alice Blake to Buena Vista, a small community northeast of Las Vegas. The mission at Buena Vista boasted a school enrollment of fifty students and a church membership of thirty, and Blake found such prospects encouraging. Moreover, Buena Vista offered her an additional compensation in the form of an assistant, Margaret Laumbaugh. The two women became close friends, calling each other "*Hermana* [Sister] Blakey" and "*Hermana* Maggie." Although some unmarried women disliked being paired with other missionaries, Blake valued the companionship that made difficult living conditions easier. When Laumbaugh was transferred, Blake protested that this loss represented a greater hardship than living in a house with a roof "green with mould." The Woman's Board, however, had suffered financial problems as a result of the nationwide depression following the Panic of 1893, and they had removed Blake's assistant as an economic measure. Even such personnel cuts were insufficient, and although Buena Vista had demonstrated success as a mission field, the board closed the enterprise in 1897. Alice Blake found herself without a job, so she returned to Las Vegas and secured a position teaching fifth grade in the public schools.[21]

Within a year, however, Alice Blake returned to missionary work. Her new field, El Aguila (near Chaperito), southeast of Las Vegas on the Antonio Ortiz land grant, escaped closure during the cutbacks of the Woman's Board, not because of its excellent prospects, but because its funding rested on the generosity of a private benefactress, Frances Bray. When the elderly teacher at El Aguila retired in 1898, Blake eagerly stepped in as her replacement, declaring that "my heart was in the work." Her enthusiasm evaporated quickly, however, when she confronted people with "hearts . . . as sterile as the hills among which . . . [they] live." She believed that she worked harder — with fewer results — at El Aguila than at either Rociada or Buena Vista, but she resolved to carry on because the mission continued to be privately funded. Although Mrs. Bray died, her sister persuaded the women's society of the First Presbyterian Church in Morristown, New Jersey, to maintain the mission project. These women accepted the challenge and paid Alice Blake's salary during her years at El Aguila and later at Trementina. Bolstered by their support and aware that her efforts represented a tangible link for these women to mission work, Blake perservered. Once again, she attributed most of the difficulties she encountered to the influence of the Catholic church. The "moral consciousness" of the people, she wrote, had been "deadened with the opiate of Roman doctrine." But after two years of intense work with no notable success, even Alice Blake's energy and enthusiasm reached a nadir during the summer of 1900.[22]

Tired and discouraged, Blake closed the school for its annual summer recess and spent her vacation traveling in the Jemez and Santa Clara mountains to the west. There she was inspired to find that children who had attended the Presbyterian school in Santa Fe were speaking English, telling Bible stories, and reading the Bible to their parents. Moved by these signs of Protestant missionary success, Blake reaffirmed her commitment to the work and returned to El Aguila. In her next quarterly report, she declared that even if she spent three-fourths of her life in a remote, lonely place, her time would be well spent in helping Hispanics "to a higher place."[23]

But in spite of Blake's renewed dedication to the work at El Aguila, that mission closed a short time later, not from financial problems, but as a result of political and environmental concerns. Many residents of El Aguila and the neighboring community of Chaperito diverted the waters of the Gallinas River to irrigate their crops. But upstream, wool-washing enterprises and pickling plants polluted the water to such an extent that it could no longer be used for irrigation. In addition, the *ejidos* (common lands) of the Antonio Ortiz grant were closed to villagers who grazed livestock and gathered firewood there when the grant passed into the hands of Thomas B. Catron, whom Alice Blake called the "most noted land-grabber of the day."[24]

In response to these pressures, emigrants from El Aguila and Chaperito began moving into a homestead area to the east, along the Trementina arroyo. Other settlers from the grant, particularly from the small village of Los Valles, joined them. The well-established Presbyterian church from Los Valles also moved to the new settlement, but the community had no school. When El Aguila was nearly abandoned, Blake relocated the mission school to Trementina.[25] The most remote of all the missions Alice Blake served, Trementina lay about sixty miles southeast of Las Vegas on the open plains, in an area Blake called "the land below the mesas." The burgeoning settlement, forty miles from the railroad, had no

services or commercial enterprises and no telephone or tele-
graph links to the rest of the territory. The nearest post office,
at the Bell Ranch, required a journey of twenty-three miles.
Settlers of the area primarily farmed, raising beans, corn,
chile, and sorghum, which they made into molasses. The
sweet syrup became an important item in the region's barter
economy.[26]

Between 1901 and 1931, Alice Blake influenced the development of Trementina to such an extent that mission
teachers arriving in New Mexico in the 1920s considered her
a legendary figure. They called her "Moses," mistakenly believing that Blake, too, had led her people forth from bondage
to a land flowing with milk and honey (or, in this case,
molasses). In truth, of course, Blake followed her people, but
other aspects of her legend came nearer to fact.[27]

At Trementina, more than she had in her previous mission stations, Blake assumed responsibility for parts of community life other than teaching. To avoid severe periodic
floods from the Trementina arroyo, the new settlement grew
up about a mile from the stream. Because carrying water
from the arroyo to town was both arduous and time-consum-
ing, Blake planned and oversaw the digging of a well near the
new mission house. As village women congregated at the well
every day, they paused to chat and enjoy each other's company, a custom Blake somewhat romantically insisted reminded her of the women of Palestine. (Other missionaries in
the territory similarly compared native customs to those of
Biblical settings. Mary Stright, a teacher at Jemez pueblo,
noted that she visited a Pueblo woman and found her "grind-
ing corn, which they do by rubbing or crushing it between two
stones . . . I suppose like they did in the East in Bible times."
And Anna McKee, who taught at a mission school near Taos,
reported that the manner of threshing was "as they did in the
time of Abraham.")[28]

In addition to providing a well, Blake succeeded in securing a post office for Trementina, and, when no one else would accept the job of postmaster, she did. At the same time, Blake closely guarded the moral climate of the community she came to regard as hers. When a saloon opened a few miles from town, Blake immediately wrote to the territorial governor to protest that the presence of the establishment violated the law. When her first letter brought no immediate response, she impatiently wrote again, and her campaign eventually paid off when the saloon closed.[29]

Blake's involvement in community affairs did not replace her primary role as teacher. Within a few years after the school at Trementina was established, enrollment reached forty-nine students, who came from a forty-mile radius to attend. As enrollment continued to increase, an assistant teacher joined Blake, who assumed the role of school principal. Former pupils recalled her as a strict but kindly disciplinarian. Drawing on her years of experience, Blake presented sessions for other teachers at the annual Mission Teachers Institute usually held in Santa Fe or Albuquerque. She chose to share practical advice rather than lofty ideals, and her topics included "how to interest the boys while the girls are in sewing class" and "how to hold our pupils when they are desirous of leading a new life and their parents are not in sympathy with them."[30]

In addition to teaching, Blake (like other mission teachers) often conducted worship services when ministers could not visit the local church. Most residents of the town and the outlying areas joined the Presbyterian church because Trementina's remote location meant that it rarely received visits from Catholic priests. Blake grew to appreciate this isolation; religious polarization was minimized, and the town remained free of other detrimental influences from the rest of the world. Not only did the community appear as a "center of civilization," an oasis in the desert, more importantly, Blake believed, Trementina and her people were "a city set on a hill."[31]

Isolation also meant that residents of the village had only each other to turn to in times of need. As a result, in the process of working together to establish a new community, Blake and her Hispanic neighbors began to bridge the cultural gap that separated them. Blake became increasingly involved in ministering to what she called "the sundry bodily needs of the people" as she added nursing and midwifery to her other duties. Indeed, she found that providing assistance during illness or accidents was even more fulfilling than teaching, for it was "the greatest service in opening doors and hearts" to her missionary efforts.[32]

In the last three months of 1903, a major epidemic of diphtheria challenged Alice Blake's nursing abilities as it swept the town of Trementina and the surrounding countryside. Blake immediately appealed to Las Vegas for assistance, and two doctors came to the little village to bring antitoxin. But the heavy load of nursing fell to Blake, who eventually came down with the disease. In a heroic gesture, she refused her dose of antitoxin and directed it instead to a small child. Fortunately, she recovered quickly, and most of the fifty-six cases she nursed also survived.[33]

Blake emerged from this experience convinced that such emergencies, as well as the usual assortment of childbirths, accidents, "septic sore throats," tonsillitis, and snake bites, required more than dedication. To secure proper medical training, she spent her summer vacations of 1904 and 1905 at the University of Colorado at Boulder taking courses in nursing. She also decided that Trementina needed some sort of medical facility and began a ten-year crusade of badgering the mission board to supply necessary funding. Whenever the opportunity arose, Blake campaigned for her pet project. At an interdenominational conference of mission teachers held in Albuquerque during the summer of 1913, for example, she addressed the assembly on "the value of a knowledge of hygiene and medical practice for the mission teacher." The following spring, Blake journeyed to Chicago to serve as delegate to the annual national meeting of the Woman's Board. There, she described her most recent medical crisis, nursing typhoid patients at their homes. Without a proper medical facility, she emphasized, these patients' families suffered exposure to the disease. Her plea convinced delegates that "the need of medical attention and instruction in sanitation and hygiene is very great in the plazas of New Mexico," and at last Blake received approval and funds for the construction of a hospital in Trementina.[34]

Blake's interest in medical matters not only provided better health care for area residents but also brought her into closer and more frequent contact with the Hispanic settlers. The interaction was rewarding for both parties. As before, Blake's reports from Trementina continued to express hope that Protestant activity would improve the lot of the area's Hispanic residents, but her comments about the people and their customs became much more favorable and tolerant than her reactions in her early years of service. For example, Blake reminded readers of the Home Mission Monthly that Hispanics are "a people of inbred . . . courtesy, warm-hearted and hospitable, needing only to be known to be loved for many admirable qualities." Still, she observed, Anglo-Americans, including those in the churches, allowed "class feeling . . . [to stand] like a wall between all the natural demands of neighborly courtesy" and so discouraged Hispanic efforts to "hold their own as American citizens."[35]

The people of Trementina and surrounding regions returned Blake's affection and came to rely on her for help in many areas of their lives. Blake reported that her people called her "the mother of us all," and she came to feel so necessary to the town that she seemed "like a deserter" when she took her vacations. In fact, she noted, Trementina residents implored her not to take her annual holiday because they told her "the time is so long when you are gone." Such protestations contributed to Blake's sense that Trementina was indeed her home. In addition, her introduction of new customs such as a New-England style Thanksgiving celebration, heightened the sense of kinship as Hispanic residents gathered annually for a communal feast.[36]

By 1918, Blake had completed almost thirty years of missionary work. Her services as teacher were no longer required, for a public school had been established near Trementina by 1913. But she continued her medical work at her hospital and in the rural areas, administered the mission, and ran the post office from time to time. Whenever a need arose, Blake plunged into other areas of service. In 1918, for example, the Children's Bureau of the United States Department of Labor called for a weighing and measuring test of all children in the nation to be conducted by volunteers. The bureau intended to use such data to assess the status of children's health throughout the country and to provide preventive health care where necessary. Blake, excited by a new challenge, also believed that her knowledge of Spanish would be helpful in rural New Mexican communities. With the blessing of the mission board, she volunteered her time and took a preliminary training course at Santa Fe.[37] But her participation in this project ended abruptly when Blake was needed to nurse a co-worker who had fallen ill with pneumonia. Immediately thereafter, she received an urgent request from her family in Denver to come home. Several members of her family had fallen victim to the Spanish influenza that was sweeping the nation. When her family had recovered, Blake set out for Trementina. En route she passed through Las Vegas, where she found many former students and their families down with the same Spanish influenza; assured that the disease had not yet reached

Trementina, she agreed to remain in Las Vegas to assist during the crisis.

Blake's return to Trementina was again delayed when, at the height of the epidemic in Las Vegas, the matron of the East Las Vegas Hospital quit her job. The president of the institution appealed to Blake to assume the post temporarily, and she agreed. After four months in that position, Blake made a momentous decision. She wrote to the Board of Home Missions to resign her post at Trementina. In her letter of resignation, she admitted that her long stint of nursing had left her tired; for the first time, she felt her age, then past fifty. Several years before, she had suffered a serious illness, and she now feared that a return to the rigorous life at Trementina might cause another breakdown in her health. With regret, the board honored her request.[38]

But Alice Blake had not completed her work at Trementina. Within a year, inactivity bothered the vigorous missionary, and when the people of the village implored her to return, she eagerly accepted the opportunity. Again she took charge of projects designed to improve the quality of life for residents; for example, she convinced the men to build a laundry adjacent to the well at the mission for the women's convenience. And she resumed her medical work. Soon her familiar figure, clutching a black obstetrical bag as she stepped down from her Model-T Ford, reappeared throughout the countryside.[39]

Within a year after her return, however, her medical preeminence in the area was challenged. In 1919, New Mexico belatedly established a Board of Public Health, which required that all who dispensed medical care throughout the state meet certain qualifications for licensure. Blake could not meet the new requirements, but she refused to allow this technicality to deprive her people of her nursing skill. Undaunted, she took a correspondence course in nursing from New York University, went back to the University of Colorado

at Boulder for a course in bacteriology, and attended a Public
Health Institute in New York in 1921. Armed with a diploma
from the Public Health Service, she returned to New Mexico
just in time for the Thanksgiving celebration at
Trementina.[40]

For the next decade, Blake continued to provide medical
care to the region and to supervise community activities.
During the 1920s, village residents built a new church to
replace the old one that had burned several years before, and
church membership increased steadily. By the end of the
decade, the town boasted a community center complete with
electricity. The area no longer seemed so remote; politicians
even began to visit the village to solicit votes, and women of
Trementina took interest in topics of global importance and
studied such issues as "the merits of the League of Nations."[41] But lessening of isolation also made the community
more susceptible to national catastrophes. By the end of the
decade, people began to drift away from Trementina in search
of better jobs. Drought, ruined crops, and the Great Depression were formidable adversaries not even the indomitable
Alice Blake could overcome. Her work in the community was
nearly finished, and she planned to retire in 1931. In recognition of her long and dedicated service, the board granted her
a year's leave of absence with pay in 1930.

Characteristically, Blake spent that year involved in yet
another project. She traveled to most of the Presbyterian
missions in the state, conducting oral interviews and garner-
ing information for her proposed history of the Presbyterian
mission movement in New Mexico. But inevitably, the time
came for Alice Blake to retire. Reluctantly, she prepared to
leave Trementina, leaving lengthy and detailed instructions
for her successors, the Reverend Julian Duran and his wife,
Rosa. After delaying as long as possible, Blake finally bade
farewell to the little town that she had helped to build.

Alice Blake went to Wheat Ridge, Colorado, to live with her brother, Cecil, and sister, Helen. None of the three had ever married, and they devoted their time to gardening and raising chickens and dogs. And, for the first several years of her retirement, Blake worked on her history of the Presbyterian missions of New Mexico. But whatever other activities she pursued, Blake's abiding interest continued to be the people of Trementina and other communities she had served.[42]

The mission at Trementina closed in 1933, and by the following year the settlement became a virtual ghost town. Many former residents of the small community migrated north to work in the sugar beet fields of northern Colorado. They attended church at Jerome Park Mission in Denver, where the Reverend Alfonso Esquibel served as minister. Esquibel had known Alice Blake for many years, having met her when she tended to an accidental gunshot wound he had received. Later, she had encouraged Esquibel to continue his education at Menaul Presbyterian High School in Albuquerque. Esquibel's mission became a gathering place, and Alice Blake attended services not only to worship but also to see old friends. Former residents of Trementina hastened to the mission when they heard she might be present. In that manner, Blake maintained contact with many people she had lived and worked with at Trementina. For most of her retirement, she remained active and energetic. But in her late seventies, she suffered an incapacitating stroke. After several years as an invalid, she died at Wheat Ridge on November 19, 1950.[43] Several friends from her missionary days in New Mexico delivered eulogies at her funeral, and the Reverend Esquibel officiated.

Nearly forty years after her death, people who knew Alice Blake remembered her with great affection and respect, calling her the "Angel of Trementina."[44] In 1921, the Woman's Board of Home Missions created a pin to honor women who had dedicated their lives to serving others. Alice Blake was among the first group of fifteen recipients of the award, whose names, the board hoped, would be "indelibly recorded in the minds and hearts of Presbyterians" because of their lengthy and devoted ministries.[45]

But Alice Blake and other mission teachers deserve to be remembered for other contributions they made to the Southwest. Cultural conflict has had a long history in the area, and many Anglo-Americans not only denigrated Hispanic residents but robbed and cheated them as well. As might be expected, Hispanics responded with suspicion, distrust, and resentment. If Protestant mission teachers like Alice Blake came to the area laden with beliefs in their own ethnic and cultural superiority, they also brought a firm and sincere commitment to the Christian faith and an honest desire to serve. In many instances, these women found that mission service offered them expanded roles, allowing them opportunities to find personal fulfillment and to demonstrate their faith through good works. In the process, they began to break down the cultural barriers that separated them from the area's Hispanic residents. Mission teachers like Alice Blake came to value Hispanics for their own merits; Hispanics gradually began to trust these missionary women and benefited from their services. By working together, the two peoples learned to understand, appreciate, and respect each other.

CHAPTER SIX

"Every Moment is Golden for the Ethnologist"

Matilda Coxe Stevenson in New Mexico

For more than three hundred years, newcomers to the Southwest regarded indigenous residents as interesting (and sometimes frightening) features of an unfamiliar landscape. First Hispanics, then Anglos recorded their impressions of southwestern American Indians when they described the territory, and by the end of the third decade of U.S. occupation some observers developed plans for more formal and systematic study of these distinctive peoples. Under the auspices of the newly formed Bureau of Ethnology (later the Bureau of American Ethnology) of the Smithsonian Institution, parties of researchers journeyed to the Southwest to scrutinize aboriginal life and to collect native artifacts for preservation in museums. The first of these expeditions set out for the Zuni pueblo of New Mexico in the summer of 1879 with James Stevenson in charge. Other members of the party included Frank Hamilton Cushing, an ethnologist, and John Hillers, a photographer, as well as Stevenson's wife, Matilda, the region's first woman anthropologist. Between her introduction to the Southwest in 1879 and her death in 1915, Matilda

Coxe Stevenson devoted her life to studying the natives of New Mexico, and portions of her research still remain basic sources for scholars.

New Mexico's selection as a site for the bureau's initial survey resulted from the personal experiences of the bureau's first director, John Wesley Powell. For more than a decade before the BAE's creation in 1879, Powell explored much of the West as leader of one of four government geological surveys. He also collected ethnological material as the opportunity arose. To lead the first official ethnological expedition, Powell chose another explorer, James Stevenson, who had participated in a number of geological expeditions under the direction of Ferdinand Hayden and George Wheeler.[1]

Stevenson's orders directed him to obtain artifacts, to photograph and sketch aspects of native life, and to collect other information regarding religion, mythology, and customs that would contribute to a broader understanding of these aboriginal Americans.[2] As his wife later emphasized, gathering up "objects of interest, both ancient and modern," seemed important because "tourists and curiosity-seekers, fired with the desire for collecting, were effecting trades with the Indians, and many choice specimens were already crossing the seas."[3] But preserving relics figured only as part of the bureau's purpose. The prevalent ideology of the day maintained that American Indians faced extinction unless they progressed to a "higher" plane of civilization (embodied by Anglo America). Ethnological research, therefore, would not only provide a record of a culture that was fast disappearing but, more importantly, would also facilitate understanding of the country's indigenous residents. Based on this information, new programs to help the Native American "up" the ladder to "civilization" could then be implemented.[4] Embracing this philosophy, James and Matilda Stevenson enthusiastically began their work in the Southwest.

When they set out for New Mexico, the Stevensons had been married for seven years. James, born in Kentucky in 1840, had taught himself geology and ethnology as he participated in a variety of explorations throughout the 1860s and 1870s. In 1872, he married Matilda Coxe Evans. Tilly, as her friends and family knew her, was born in Texas in 1849, but her parents returned east soon after and took up residence in Washington, D.C. Matilda received her early education through governesses and at a private school in Philadelphia; later, she privately studied chemistry and mineralogy. After her marriage at the age of twenty-two, however, she abandoned these fields in favor of her husband's interests and learned ethnology while assisting him in writing up his notes.[5]

Although Matilda served in no official capacity on the Stevensons' southwestern expeditions for the BAE between 1879 and 1887, she continued to help her husband, particularly in preparing for publication catalogues of the artifacts collected during their earliest trips. The Stevensons remained at Zuni for six months (until the end of 1879), then traveled to most of the other New Mexican pueblos in 1880 and to the Hopi villages in 1881. The couple returned to Zuni in that year and again in 1882, when they also explored Cañon de Chelly and Rito de los Frijoles (now Bandelier National Monument). Matilda's continued participation in these activities set her apart from other women whose husbands engaged in anthropological work in New Mexico at the same time. Josephine Bandelier, for example, visited her husband, Adolph, occasionally while he conducted field studies, but ill health (and perhaps lack of inclination) prevented her from providing him with much assistance. Similarly, Emily Cushing, who married Frank in 1882 and went to live with him at Zuni, displayed little interest in his research.[6]

Matilda, however, fully shared her husband's interest in the work; moreover, she began to conduct her own studies soon after arriving in the field. By 1881, she had written a brief study entitled "Zuni and the Zunians," and in 1884 the BAE accepted her study on "The Religious Life of the Zuni Child" for inclusion in its *Fifth Annual Report.*[7] BAE director Powell noted that Mrs. Stevenson had focused her research upon the activities of Zuni women, and he observed that "no male investigator . . . can become acquainted with the peculiar beliefs and rituals among the women." Similar commendation of Matilda's work came from a prominent British anthropologist, Edwin B. Tylor, who visited the Stevensons at the New Mexican pueblo. In a speech to the Anthropological Society of Washington, Tylor praised Mrs. Stevenson's efforts and suggested that women be included in anthropological research to gather information about domestic life and women's roles in aboriginal societies.[8]

Gratified by this recognition of her work, Matilda Stevenson continued her studies of women and children, but she also believed that women could participate in ethnological work on other topics. She decided to found a society for women interested in the "development of the science of anthropology," and in 1885 she and others met in Washington to form the Women's Anthropological Society of America. The organization's original members also included another anthropologist whose early work focused upon women and children, Alice C. Fletcher. Matilda served as president of the group for the first three years and during that period delivered six papers on a variety of subjects, including the Hopi snake dances and Navajo sand paintings. Other members of the society spoke about equally diverse topics, ranging from a discussion of "Ceramic Art of the Pacific Coast" to a description of "Winter Life among the Winnebago Indians."[9]

As the topics of her speeches suggest, Matilda continued to work with her husband in the Southwest during a part of each year, and while the couple pursued collection of articles for the Smithsonian, they also conducted a broader range of

Matilda Coxe Stevenson as a young woman. *National Anthropological Archives, Smithsonian Institution, #86-11412.*

ethnological inquiry. In 1885, for example, the couple visited archaeological sites near Santa Clara pueblo (probably Puye cliff dwellings) and also spent some time among the Navajos, where Matilda, the BAE enthusiatically reported, "made complete sketches of the sand altars, masks, and other objects" used in the Yeibichai ceremony. These accompanied her husband's paper that appeared in the *Eighth Annual Report*.[10] In 1887, the Stevensons spent six weeks at Zia pueblo, where James made copious notes. Although he intended to return to the pueblo on other occasions to complete his research, he died in July 1888 of a heart ailment.[11]

The death of her husband marked a turning point in Matilda's career. Deprived of his companionship, she easily could have chosen to remain in the East. With her husband at her side in the remote areas they visited, Matilda had apparently felt little apprehension even when among an unreceptive populace. To return to the pueblos of New Mexico alone, even under government auspices, might have intimidated a woman less committed to her work or more strongly influenced by a society that expected women to be submissive, meek, and dependent upon men. Matilda Coxe Stevenson, however, was determined to complete the studies her husband had begun. In 1890, she joined the staff of the BAE as an ethnologist and traveled back to New Mexico at once.[12]

Matilda's decision to return to field studies reflected more than a commitment to complete her husband's unfinished work, although she unquestionably desired to insure that his contributions to science would not be overlooked. In addition, though, Matilda found in ethnological investigation a career consistent with her interests, abilities, and attitudes. She espoused the ultimate goal of the BAE, agreeing that "the prime requisite for improving the conditions of the Indian is familiarity with Indian thought and customs." But this long-term goal, though important, affected Matilda less, rather than more, as her work among the Native Americans

James Stevenson. *National Anthropological Archives, Smithsonian Institution,* *#76-13442.*

progressed. As Alice Fletcher, for example, became increasingly involved in political struggles to bring the indigenous populace closer to an ideal of white civilization, Matilda grew aware that changes in Native American society spelled doom for the old ways, and she resolved to record these disappearing remnants of aboriginal life. Nor did Matilda's interest in recording and preserving vast amounts of data devalue her contribution to anthropology or conflict with Powell's intent for BAE ethnologists. As one historian noted, "the generalizing savant stood apart from the mass of data-collectors . . . [and] the scientific enterprise was consequently divided into two classes of functions: the lower, preliminary work of exploration, observation, and collection; and the higher task of synthesis."[13]

Undoubtedly Mrs. Stevenson's escalating determination to capture as much of American Indian life as she could made her contributions to science richer and more complete than they might otherwise have been. But in combination with her forceful personality and strong convictions, this commitment to her task brought her into continual conflict with members of the communities she studied, other ethnologists, and many others she met during her career. Numerous writers, beginning with Cushing and others of Stevenson's contemporaries and continuing until the present, have criticized Matilda Coxe Stevenson's methods of securing data, which varied from personal observation and use of willing informants to intimidation, bribery, and threats. On several occasions, she even forced her way into kivas to observe secret religious rites. A recent biographer of Cushing noted that Matilda bought and "bullied" information; another student of Zuni charged that she threatened to call government troops to assist her when faced with Zuni opposition. Yet a closer examination reveals that other scholars have occasionally employed similar methods that appear, by present standards or later reflection, insensitive and exploitive. For example,

Cushing, for a time Matilda's contemporary at Zuni, initially forced himself onto a Zuni family and took advantage of their hospitality, and J. Walter Fewkes, an ethnologist who studied the Hopis, admitted that he had also entered a kiva uninvited and that he was "unceremoniously" removed. Twentieth-century anthropologists also relate that they employ a variety of strategies to obtain data. One woman who studied in Mexico recalled that "I bartered, cajoled, and wheedled or bluffed knowledge I didn't have in order to get more. At times I deliberately exaggerated or distorted facts . . . [and] sometimes I was petulant." Leslie A. White, who studied the pueblo of Zia some years after Stevenson completed her investigations there, remarked that he "always paid informants for their time." Indeed, Stevenson's personality as much as the methods she used probably generated a portion of the criticism directed against her.[14]

In fact, Mrs. Stevenson's willingness to use any means at her disposal to gather information reveals a great deal about her personality and her attitudes. Various writers have characterized Matilda as "strong-willed," "arrogant," "domineering," and "aggressive," and they could have added "stubborn" and "combative" to the list. In fairness, however, such a list should also include "tenacious," "dedicated," "courageous," and "thorough." Moreover, Matilda was an elitist. Throughout her life she revealed a sense of self-assurance based upon family background (her family held a position of prominence in Washington, D.C.), association with the Smithsonian, and her own achievements as well as those of her husband. She also placed a high value on intelligence. The Women's Anthropological Society, which she founded, sought for membership "thinking, intelligent women," and she once commented that "those possessing superior intelligence and a love for humanity, and only such, may lead our Indians from darkness into light." Her conviction that she represented a society culturally and intellectually superior to those she studied determined much of her behavior in the field.[15] If Matilda's tenacity and determination led her into conflicts, they also enabled her to collect most of the data she sought.

Although Matilda's fascination with Native American life and her commitment to describing it increased during her extended period of study, she never relinquished her intense ethnocentrism. When Frank Cushing, who accompanied the Stevensons on their first visit to Zuni, adopted native dress and moved in with a Zuni family to enhance his understanding of these people, Matilda considered his actions ludicrous, characterizing him as "the biggest fool and charlatan I ever knew." Much of the acrimony between the two ethnologists likely resulted from Matilda's sense that Cushing had forgotten that he belonged to a higher social order, an attitude that Taylor F. Ealy, missionary at Zuni, and an inspector in the Indian Service shared. Nor did Matilda confine her criticism to Cushing; in later years she wrote that another anthropologist, "a born gentleman . . . with a college education," had suffered difficulty in his work "ever since he married the Indian woman," and she went on to comment that such a situation was "always the case. Indians have no time for Americans who sink to their level." In general, she believed Anglos needed to recognize that American Indians, whom she likened to children, could "be controlled through kindness or firmness, as occasion requires." In this regard, Matilda probably more accurately portrayed predominant Anglo opinion than did Cushing; indeed, the reactions of Cushing's wife, Emily, to the Zunis indicate that she shared Matilda's attitudes, since Mrs. Cushing viewed them as childish nuisances.[16]

In addition to her personality, ethnocentrism, and dedication to her task, another factor — gender — influenced Matilda Stevenson's work among the Pueblos of New Mexico. Her early field work revealed her awareness that, as a woman, she had access to information unavailable to male ethnologists, and accordingly she studied women's work, food preparation, childbirth and childhood, as well as women's participation in Pueblo religion and medicine. But in addition to shaping Stevenson's initial ethnological inquiries, her gender affected relationships with peers and with the people she came to study. Perhaps some of the animosity that Cushing and another ethnologist, John Gregory Bourke, revealed toward Matilda related to her deviation from traditional gender roles; some of her character traits, including aggressiveness and arrogance, may have violated these Victorian men's expectations of female demeanor. On one occasion, for example, Bourke noted in his diary that he advised the residents at Zuni to ignore Mrs. Stevenson's comments that Cushing held no presidential appointment to the pueblo because "among us, women don't know much about what the G[reat]. F[ather]. is doing." As one historian has suggested, these conflicts about gender roles created "intense pressure" for Matilda and may have contributed to her overbearing behavior.[17]

Not surprisingly, the Zunis also initially considered Matilda's behavior inappropriate for a woman. As Bourke related, one of the most influential Zunis referred to Mrs. Stevenson as *la cacique mujer* — "the female chief" — and Bourke hastened to add that the Zuni used this term "in contempt." But, like women anthropologists of a later day, Matilda eventually found that once the natives became accustomed to her lack of conformity to their expectation of female roles, her gender proved less a hindrance than a help in permitting her access to a wide range of activities.[18]

Although Matilda undoubtedly appreciated the extended opportunities for ethnological research that her gender provided, it never superseded her sense that she was first, and foremost, an ethnologist. The brief history of the Women's Anthropological Society therefore explained the need for such an organization until "the time when science shall regard only the work, not the worker" and emphasized that members had "no desire to perpetuate a distinction of sex in science." Still, when the occasion demanded, Matilda successfully resorted to traditional feminine wiles to secure assistance; for example, a friend related that during one of the Stevensons' expeditions among the Navajos, workers deserted the party when they heard of impending Navajo hostilities. As the couple continued to excavate a ruin, two Navajos passed by, and Matilda offered them employment; they declined, insisting that they were en route to join other Navajos to "kill all Americans." Undaunted, her friend related, "Mrs. Stevenson — though knowing her action would have meant death to a man — laid her hand on the old man's arm and said smilingly, 'But you will come for me and help me,'" and he and his companion acquiesced.[19]

In other aspects of the female sphere, Matilda evinced little interest. Because she came from an upper-class family, she remained unfamiliar with many domestic tasks, and her later professional obligations, as other women anthropologists have noted, demanded time and energy that precluded performance of household duties. Matilda engaged help for domestic services and also, after her husband's death, often employed an assistant (whose salary the BAE paid) to perform many of the tasks she had carried out for her husband, including sketching and photographing.[20]

One such assistant, May Clark, accompanied Mrs. Stevenson on her first trip to the Southwest as principal investigator. In the spring of 1890, Matilda and Miss Clark arrived at Zia, New Mexico, to complete the study that James and Matilda had initiated in 1887. During the summer they lived in tents near the pueblo while Mrs. Stevenson pursued ethnological inquiry in the style that her husband had employed and that she would rely on for her researches at Zia, Zuni, and, later, other pueblos. First, of course, came direct observation, but she also needed informants to share secret and sacred information, as well as those who would guide her to shrines and other sites. Not surprisingly, with her elitist tendencies, Mrs. Stevenson did not waste time wooing a whole village; instead, she quickly discerned and sought out the people who were most likely to provide the information she desired and who might be most receptive to her goal of recording the vanishing segments of American Indian life. Next, she hammered home what became her common theme, that by assisting her in recording Pueblo customs and beliefs, these tribal members assured the survival of ancient traditions. At Zia, for example, she convinced the five men most knowledgeable about the pueblo's religion that "each shadow on the dial brings nearer to a close the lives of those upon whose minds are graven the traditions, mythology, and folklore as indelibly as are the pictographs and monochromes upon the rocky walls." As a result, these men served as her informants and permitted her access to a number of secret ceremonies and rites.[21]

Until the fall of 1890, Matilda carried out her studies at Zia, then returned to Washington, D.C., where she worked through the spring of 1891, combining the information she had obtained with the notes she and her husband had taken on their earlier trip. The resulting study, entitled simply "The Sia," appeared in the BAE's *Eleventh Annual Report*. Although Matilda initially intended the work to focus upon cosmogony and cults, the report details many other aspects of Zia life, including childbirth, pottery manufacture, and rites for the dead. She also began collecting plants for further study of native medicines.[22]

No doubt encouraged by her success at Zia, Stevenson decided to pursue additional work at Zuni that, in combination with material from her earlier sojourns there and her husband's notes, would furnish material for a study similar to "The Sia." Accordingly, in August 1891, she returned to Zuni, where she remained until March of the following year. She renewed old acquaintances and under the auspices of prominent priests and theurgists added considerably to her knowledge through observation of many religious and healing ceremonies. Later, Matilda reported that although she had witnessed changes in Zuni since her earlier visits, these alterations appeared minor compared with those she noticed on subsequent visits in 1896, 1902, and 1904. And while she continued to express concern about the disappearance of various aspects of indigenous culture, she deemed some of the changes decided improvements and noted that they resulted from elements of civilization — including window panes, candles, and lamps — that the Stevensons had introduced in 1879.

Although Matilda left no record of her initial impressions of Zuni, undoubtedly she reacted strongly to the lack of hygiene of the populace, for she imported soap and attempted to teach the Zunis to wash their clothing (even though she had little experience in performing such tasks) and presumably to bathe. This new practice apparently grew very slowly at first, according to comments other observers made about Zuni a few years later. Emily Cushing, for example, came to the settlement as a bride in 1882 and soon despised the residents for "their filthy ways." In that same year, an inspector of the Indian Service reported that the entire pueblo smelled bad, and another inspector who visited the pueblo in 1885 concurred with these evaluations, adding that he found the Zunis "the filthiest band of human beings on the face of the earth."[23]

Nonetheless, Mrs. Stevenson eventually reported that "a great change for the better" took place as Zunis followed the example of her first pupil, We'wha, and learned to launder their garments. We'wha, in fact, soon generated a thriving laundry business among members of the various expeditions and other Anglos in the area and, more importantly, became a close friend and informant of Stevenson. On one occasion, several Zunis, including We'wha, traveled to Washington, met President Arthur and other dignitaries, and stayed with the Stevensons as houseguests. In spite of their close association, Matilda did not discover for a number of years that her friend was not a woman, as We'wha's clothing and roles in Zuni life indicated, but a man who had adopted women's dress and identity (a not uncommon practice among the Zunis). Perhaps her own experiences in departing from proscribed gender roles influenced Matilda's reaction; in any event, she continued to regard We'wha as a woman and a valued friend.[24]

Other Zunis who became friends and informants of Mrs. Stevenson and who assisted her in research included Nai'uchi, a prominent priest and theurgist in the pueblo; Pedro Pino, who served for a time as governor of the pueblo; and other important individuals in the community. Under their auspices, she observed additional ceremonies, visited sacred shrines, and photographed and sketched religious symbols. While Zuni mythology and religion remained her primary subjects of inquiry, Matilda also collected artifacts for the Smithsonian and investigated numerous other aspects of pueblo life, as she had at Zia. Returning to Washington in the spring of 1892, she began to organize her copious notes for publication. More than a decade elapsed, however, before her massive compendium about the Zunis appeared in print.

In the intervening years, Matilda made three additional trips to the pueblo and from her notes prepared several articles that appeared in *American Anthropologist* and the *Proceedings of the American Association for the Advancement of Science*. In 1893 she helped to prepare the BAE's exhibit for the World's Columbian Exposition at Chicago, where she also served as a judge of the anthropological materials displayed at the event. She continued to work on the manuscript, despite several bouts of illness, and concluded that she lacked essential information to complete her research. Thus, in

1896, she returned to Zuni for another visit of six months and collected important amounts of new information. More significantly, she obtained sacred Zuni masks used in religious ceremonies. As she noted, "in 1879, no amount of money could have purchased a genuine Zuni mask" and added that she finally "succeeded in securing nine choice specimens" only because of her "long acquaintance with the priests and their attachment to her." In spite of this gratifying triumph, the trip brought her sadness as well, for, during her visit to the pueblo, We'wha died.[25]

Events surrounding We'wha's death also called to mind an aspect of Zuni life — witchcraft — that troubled Matilda Coxe Stevenson as well as other Anglo visitors to the pueblo, including Frank Cushing, missionaries, and Indian Service officials. Some members of the pueblo attributed We'wha's death to a spell cast by a woman We'wha had offended, although Mrs. Stevenson related that We'wha died from heart disease. But belief in sorcery and witches, firmly rooted in mythology and tradition, pervaded Zuni society, and these Indians (explaining misfortunes such as drought, crop failure, and illness as results of witchcraft) demanded the death of the witch responsible. Anglos, however, found the execution of innocent people on the basis of superstition abhorrent and on occasion employed various means to prevent it. In 1880, for example, Taylor F. Ealy, a Presbyterian missionary at Zuni, witnessed the witch trial of an elderly man and threatened to report the murder of the witch to the Indian agent if the Zunis carried out the sentence. But, as he later indicated, the priests merely waited until the agent had come and gone before secretly executing the witch.[26] Another observer, Frank Cushing, met with mixed success in dealing with similar situations. Once he pleaded for a more lenient sentence for an accused witch, and the pueblo council trying the case agreed. On another occasion, however, the ethnologist proved powerless. Like the missionary, he valiantly confronted the village priests and argued that the execution of a witch would bring the wrath of U.S. authorities upon the pueblo. But officials ignored these arguments and carried out the sentence of death in secrecy.[27]

Matilda Coxe Stevenson had heard about witchcraft accusations during her visits to Zuni before 1896. Indeed, in 1892 she became directly involved in two incidents. When she learned that the accused in the first case had been condemned to die, she related, "it seemed too terrible to believe," and she appealed to her friend Nai'uchi, prominent in the affair, for a milder punishment. He refused, and Matilda (like Cushing) threatened that the government would punish those responsible for the murder. Nai'uchi replied firmly that even if she turned informant, he must carry out his duty to his people and protect them from sorcerers. At last, in response to her continued pleas, he agreed to delay the hanging until the following day. Then, Matilda recalled, she found herself in a "delicate" position because although she knew "the man must be saved," she needed to avoid making "an enemy of a tried friend and one of the men most important . . . to her studies."[28]

Finally, Matilda arrived at a solution that reflected her courage as well as her determination to prevent the hanging. Reasoning that if Zuni superstition could condemn a witch, superstition could also save him, Matilda visited the accused, then "held a court of her own" and announced that "she had deprived the man of his power of sorcery." Somewhat to her surprise, tribal officials accepted her statements and released the witch. A while later, Matilda employed the same strategy, and in this case the accused testified that during a visit with the ethnologist, "I felt all my power of witchcraft was gone, not only for a little while, but for all time." As in the earlier incident, the witch went free, and Nai'uchi, Matilda reported, expressed the wish that she could continue to reside at Zuni and "rob all witches of their power to destroy." As historian Marc Simmons has suggested, had she remained at Zuni, the witchcraft craze at that pueblo might have ended much sooner.[29]

Instead, witchcraft continued to plague the Zunis. Several months after Matilda returned to Washington, she read accounts in eastern newspapers that the Zunis had executed two women as witches and troops from Fort Wingate had arrested several for the crime. Characteristically, Matilda immediately sought information from the secretary of war and the Department of Interior, and, when the officials admitted they had no information about the incidents, she wrote to L. Bradford Prince, the territorial governor of New Mexico. Although she termed Zuni belief in witchcraft "miserable superstitions," she also maintained that the Zunis sought to explain their loss of livestock, which really occurred because white men "robbed [the Zunis] on all sides." Moreover, she reminded the governor, these people, "believing as implicitly in witches as did our Puritan forefathers . . . hang [witches] as destroyers of life just as we condemn the criminal to capital punishment." She asked Prince to investigate and pleaded for leniency for the accused.[30]

Although the outcome of this case is unclear, initial government intervention failed to quell Zuni determination to punish sorcerers. The government acted in another witchcraft incident in 1894 and again in 1896. While Matilda resided in the pueblo during that year, the Zunis made no effort to punish the woman accused of bewitching We'wha, but after Stevenson departed, an elderly woman was tried and sentenced to die. On that occasion, George Wharton James, a visitor to the pueblo, helped to rescue the woman after she had been severely beaten. Meanwhile, the government had been apprised of the situation, and troops from Fort Wingate and Fort Apache arrived in time to save the accused. The soldiers arrested several Zunis, including Nai'uchi, whom they imprisoned in Albuquerque. One detachment of troops remained in the pueblo for several months thereafter as a precautionary measure. While Matilda had deplored such action in the earlier incident, Francis Leupp, a member of the Indian Rights Association, supported the move in this latest outbreak; obviously, he held Matilda's and Cushing's methods of dealing with witchcraft in contempt. In his report of 1897, Leupp complained that the Zunis had gone unpunished for "violations of the law of the land" for years, largely because they "have been so petted and pampered and coddled by a number of white persons of both sexes who have lived among them ostensibly in the interest of science, that they have come to consider themselves a little better than the whites." And as Leupp hoped, reports of witchcraft at Zuni diminished after the incarceration of prominent Zunis.[31]

If Matilda irritated Leupp because of her involvement in Zuni affairs, she frustrated John Wesley Powell, director of the BAE, because she failed to complete her manuscript about Zuni, even though her trip to New Mexico in 1896 had been to finish up research. Upon her return to Washington, Stevenson again became ill, and she worked on the Zuni project only intermittently during the next several years. She remained on the payroll of the BAE, however, possibly because Powell had held her husband in high esteem. Yet, although Powell regarded Matilda's work highly, he had no great liking for his friend's widow and grew increasingly annoyed at her inability to produce a manuscript for publication. (Frank Cushing, it might be noted, also failed to complete a monograph on his Zuni work, but Powell entertained no animosity toward his protégé.)

Finally, his patience exhausted and his health failing, the director decided to terminate Matilda's employment with the bureau and to secure her permission for the BAE to publish the completed portions of the Zuni study. Calling upon Mrs. Stevenson in early June 1901, Powell found her "suffering much depression," which the director believed accounted for

her ill health, as his daughter also suffered from "neurasthe-
nia." He hesitated to broach the subjects he had come to
discuss but made delicate suggestions about a furlough and
publication of the manuscript and recommended that she
"seek that rest and retirement from active life" — the BAE —
that would bring about a "restoration to health." To drive
home his points, Powell instructed his assistant, W. J.
McGee, to formalize these plans in a letter to Stevenson, then
prudently left Washington for a summer vacation.[32]

Despite Powell's careful and diplomatic approach, the
director's plans to remove his difficult employee from the
staff of the BAE provided just the tonic Matilda needed to
rouse her from depression and lethargy. Immediately after
she received notice that she had been "put on furlough without pay," she wrote to Powell in protest and refused him
permission to publish any portion of her manuscript. In addition, she sent a copy of her letter to the secretary of the
Smithsonian and threatened to "lay the matter before Congress" if necessary. As Powell knew, this, coming from Matilda, was no idle threat, and, indeed, as the dispute dragged
on, she enlisted Senator Henry Teller as her champion. Finally, the two parties reached an agreement that must have
been more satisfactory to Stevenson than it was to Powell:
Matilda agreed to be furloughed until the completion of the
manuscript (for which she was paid a lump sum of $500), but
she retained the right to return to the staff of the BAE
thereafter. Accordingly, she notified Powell in May 1902 to
send "some responsible person" to pick up the Zuni monograph and returned to the offices of the bureau a few days
later. In any event, Matilda did not trouble Powell much
longer, for he died in September 1902.[33]

Shortly after Matilda submitted her manuscript about
Zuni, she set out for another visit to the pueblo. Although the
massive work filled more than six hundred pages, its author
apologized for the "restricted account of many subjects that

are deserving of more extensive treatment" and noted that she expected to continue her studies of the pueblo. Her work at Zia and Zuni also convinced her that "a comparative study of the Pueblos" merited the attention of scholars like herself. Between July and November 1902, Stevenson resided at Zuni, gathering more information about the tribe and adding considerably to her collection of plants that the Zunis utilized for medicines, foods, and dyes. She also noticed a number of distressing changes in Zuni that had occurred since her previous visit in 1896. For example, the pueblo had virtually abandoned the production of traditional, excellent ceramics; instead, she noted, "large quantities of exceedingly poor pottery are made and sold to the traders for china and tin ware," which the Zunis used even in religious ceremonies. In view of this and similar evidence of vanishing traditions, Matilda reaffirmed her commitment to the task at hand, realizing "more fully each day, that every moment is golden for the ethnologist, for changes in the life of the Indian are becoming more rapid each year."[34]

Worried that the erosion of traditional art forms meant that the Zunis would soon forget the ancient symbolism employed in the decoration of these objects, Mrs. Stevenson devoted particular attention to "the religious symbolism embodied in the various arts" on her visits to Zuni in 1902 and 1904. During those trips she also collected numerous items, both ceremonial and utilitarian, to illustrate Zuni life for the Smithsonian's exhibition at the Louisiana Purchase Exposition in St. Louis. She spent 1905 in Washington, revising her massive work, "The Zuni," and adding to it material she had gleaned during her visits of 1902 and 1904; finally, in December 1905, the volume appeared.[35]

Early the following year, Matilda returned to New Mexico for further research. In her previous sojourn, in addition to studying the Zunis, she had visited the pueblos of Jemez, Zia, Cochiti, Santo Domingo, and Santa Clara, where she

photographed numerous ceremonials, as well as archaeological sites on the Pajarito plateau (now part of Bandelier National Monument) and the Puye cliff dwellings. These
experiences bolstered her earlier decision to make a comparative study of the pueblos, and she chose to begin at Taos,
confident that she could succeed where earlier students, including Adolph Bandelier, had failed. To her surprise, however, she encountered a good deal of hostility not only from
the Taos Indians but also from teachers and officials of the
Indian Service and other Anglos in the area, including one of
the founders of the Taos art colony, Bert Phillips.

Matilda blamed most of the opposition to her work on a
newspaper article that appeared immediately before she arrived in Taos, labeling the column "a creation of the reporter's
brain"; more likely, however, the article too accurately indicated Stevenson's real intent, particularly her interest in "the
practice of the priests, the religious ceremonials, the secret
societies," which aroused the ire of the natives and their
supporters. In spite of her cool reception, Matilda set up
camp near the pueblo and wrote to W. H. Holmes (who had
succeeded Powell as BAE director) with the request that
Holmes ask the commissioner of Indian Affairs (ironically,
Francis Leupp) to direct employees of the Indian Service and
the governor of Taos pueblo to cooperate. Meanwhile, she
recruited an elderly Taos Indian as informant and began
compiling material about the pueblo's language, religion, and
social structure.[36]

Although opposition to her work continued, Matilda refused to abandon the project. Instead, she went on with her
ethnological studies of Taos and also visited Picuris pueblo.
She found other aspects of her life in New Mexico interesting
and rewarding, including excursions into the mountains near
Taos where she picnicked "on the bank of the mountain
stream," enjoying "the beauties of nature." She also made
friends among the Hispanic residents of the community and

reported that they invited her to a Penitente *morada* (chapel), "a rare privilege for a white person." Like other Anglos, she found the ceremonies fascinating and frightening, remarking that "the whole ceremony was as weird as if it was performed by Indians."[37]

Matilda remained at Taos until the fall of 1906, when she reported improvement in her relations with the residents of the pueblo. "The head war chief," she noted, "has always been my warm friend," and other prominent residents had begun to realize the extent of Matilda's determination. In a report to Holmes, she related an incident that occurred on the feast day of San Geronimo, the patron saint of Taos pueblo. Matilda intended to photograph the ceremonies, although she admitted she "expected to have many battles in my efforts to secure pictures." Instead, she went on, "I had very little trouble"; although "two men called for revolvers," she continued to take pictures, and "the firearms did not come to light." And while the "assistant war chief," whom she termed "one of my bitterest opponents," repeatedly demanded that she stop her photography session, she added that "at the same time a twinkle in his eyes told me to go on. Perhaps he knew I would go on anyway."[38]

Nevertheless, Matilda eventually decided she might enjoy greater success in her comparative studies of the pueblos at a different location. In November 1906 and again in 1907, she visited Santa Clara pueblo and determined to locate permanently in the area of Española, New Mexico. This site offered several advantages; proximate to several pueblos (Santa Clara, San Ildefonso, San Juan, and Nambe), it was far enough from Taos that Matilda could proceed with her work unobserved, yet near enough for her informant to visit her as occasion demanded. Also, Matilda had hoped for some time to purchase a home in New Mexico, and she had made friends with the True family there. Mrs. Frances True, a widow, worked as a matron in the Indian Service school at

Santa Clara, where her daughter Clara taught school; another daughter, Lizzie Randall (also a widow), taught in a nearby pueblo school. Lonely and estranged from other Anglos in Taos, Matilda welcomed the friendship of the Trues, particularly Clara, and accepted her offer to purchase land that adjoined the True property between Santa Clara and San Ildefonso pueblos. Matilda authorized Clara to act as her agent in acquiring the property before she returned to Washington in the fall of 1907, intent on making plans for the next year's studies at Tuonyo (named for Black Mesa nearby) Ranch, as Stevenson called her new domain.

But the ranch near Black Mesa did not become the restful haven and home that Matilda had hoped. In selecting Clara True as a friend and representative, the ethnologist made one of the worst mistakes of her life. Between 1907 and her death in 1915, Matilda's association with the Trues was extremely costly — financially and emotionally — as well as disruptive to Stevenson's continuing studies of the pueblos of New Mexico. The True family apparently had a poor reputation in the area, despite their employment in the Indian Service. One official of that agency labeled Frances True "the vampire of this section" and added that "the woman is crazy." Another Indian Service employee, a victim of Clara's meddling in private affairs, called True "an unsexed female with a most vindictive mind." Moreover, Clara had proved that she could not be trusted with money. Indeed, at the very time that Matilda placed funds at the disposal of the Indian Service teacher, an investigation of True's failure to pay her debts was under way. In this case, True's superior remarked that he was all too familiar with her "irresponsibility financially and with property" and recommended her transfer from her autonomous position at Santa Clara to a boarding school in Banning, California, where she could be closely supervised. Before Clara departed for her new post, however, she completed the purchase of the property for Matilda as agreed, except that she craftily neglected to include several small parcels of land that enhanced the Trues' holdings when she transferred the deed to the rest of the property to Matilda's name.[39]

When Mrs. Stevenson arrived in New Mexico the following summer, she learned of Clara's swindle and faced additional problems with Clara's mother and sister about maintenance of the property and related issues. After a lengthy, expensive, and acrimonious legal struggle, Matilda emerged victorious, and the court ordered Clara to return the land she had essentially stolen from Stevenson. But Matilda's troubles with the Trues continued: They sent charges to the BAE alleging that Matilda had mishandled funds allocated for research. Although the allegations proved groundless, the experience humiliated and worried Stevenson. "I am distressed that such letters should be filed against me in the Institution which I have served for many years with all my heart," she wrote to Charles Walcott, secretary of the Smithsonian.[40]

The animosity between Matilda and her neighbors continued to smolder, particularly after Clara returned to New Mexico following a few years in California. The stress of this situation, combined with advancing age, declining health, and a growing reliance on alcohol, affected Mrs. Stevenson's work. She completed her study of Zuni plant use and submitted it for publication in the *Thirtieth Annual Report* but thereafter made little progress in preparing a manuscript based on her diligent research among the Tewa pueblos of Santa Clara, San Ildefonso, San Juan, and Nambe, and, to a more limited extent, the Tiwa pueblos of Taos and Picuris. Her discoveries, however, continued to stimulate her interest in comparisons among these peoples, and she began to contemplate studies that would take her into Mexico and even to Siberia to identify early influences on Pueblo culture and the subsequent dispersion of Pueblo traits.[41]

At the BAE, Stevenson's suggestions for more extensive research generated little enthusiasm; Frederick Webb Hodge, ethnologist-in-charge, reacted negatively to Matilda's requests for additional funds to finance her comparative studies. "To extend your work from Taos to Zuni . . . with nothing sufficiently intensive to afford the basis of a publication except in the indefinite future . . . would hardly be justified," he wrote, and instead suggested that she confine herself to studying "some special phase of the Tewa culture, in order that we may publish some results in the reasonably immediate future." Under his prodding, Matilda completed a manuscript on Pueblo dress (which was never published) and concentrated on the nearby Tewa pueblos. After several years, she submitted two brief reports on this work, which appeared in *Smithsonian Miscellaneous Collections* in 1913 and 1914.[42]

Undoubtedly Hodge soon regretted his earlier advice, for in concentrating on a particular facet of Tewa life, Matilda had delved deeply into a subject that for years had figured in Hispanic folklore of the region. Legends maintained that the Pueblo Indians confined to secret chambers rattlesnakes to whom they sacrified human infants. Whether Matilda was influenced by these stories is unclear, but she was not the first ethnologist to suggest that the Pueblos practiced human sacrifice. In 1881 at Zuni, Frank Cushing confided his suspicions to John Bourke. "Cushing emphatically asserted his belief that human sacrifices were still kept up, altho, in the deepest secrecy and at rare intervals," Bourke noted, and continued, "Cushing enjoined me not to mention this matter outside of my note-books, fearing to excite too much bitter comment."[43]

In any event, Stevenson conducted extensive interviews over a period of several years with informants from various Tewa pueblos and concluded that some pueblos periodically sacrificed women or female infants to rattlesnakes, which consumed the victims' flesh. Predictably, her brief description provoked heated controversy among naturalists, who argued that the reptiles could not perform such a feat, and, more significantly, perhaps, among outraged U.S. citizens, who demanded that Cato Sells, commissioner of Indian Affairs, put a stop to such practice. Hodge drew the brunt of these criticisms and demanded from Matilda further details and corroboration to protect the Smithsonian from appearing ridiculous. Eager to comply, Matilda furnished Hodge with more detailed and grisly descriptions of the rites that she believed would quell the objections of herpetologists and carefully summarized her methods of investigation to assure Hodge that she had weighed and evaluated her evidence objectively.[44]

Indeed, Matilda's calm, scholarly responses to Hodge's queries are particularly noteworthy because this criticism of her work came at a time when personal problems stemming from her acquaintance with the Trues again caused her a great deal of emotional distress. Clara True had returned to the area following a few years in California, but she had no intention of burying the hatchet with Matilda. Instead, as *mayordomo* (steward) of the San Ildefonso acequia, she cut off the water supply to Matilda's ranch; after another heated court battle, the judge ruled in Matilda's favor, but Clara refused to give up in her effort to drive the ethnologist away from the region and to discredit Stevenson into the bargain. For a second time, Clara and an associate filed a lengthy list of serious charges against Matilda with the BAE. As she had earlier, Clara charged Matilda with improper handling of government funds, but she also made a variety of other allegations of a more personal nature, including drunkenness, use of obscene language, and mistreatment of a child (apparently an Indian) who lived with Matilda for a time. Matilda, of course, vigorously denied all of these accusations, but, to her shock and embarrassment, Frederick Webb Hodge came from Washington to investigate the incident. That the bureau could take the incident seriously goaded Stevenson into action, and she filed a libel suit against her accusers.[45]

Hodge's thorough investigation brought a total vindication of Stevenson on all the charges; his inquiries, he noted, "resulted in testimony of Mrs. Stevenson's good name so strong" that he could only conclude that Clara and her friend had indeed acted on their expressed desire to "drive Mrs. Stevenson out of the country." He added, however, that he believed that some of the animosity toward Matilda stemmed from her "criticism of others" and the "extreme forcefulness of her character." That same forcefulness kept Matilda from dimissing the libel suit even after the official investigation ended. Yet Clara True had, in a sense, succeeded, for Stevenson suffered increasingly from bad health as she waited for the trial to begin. Finally, her physician and her attorney advised her to abandon the lawsuit because they feared that such a proceeding would "bring collapse, if not demise," and she left New Mexico in the spring of 1915 for Washington, where she hoped a lower altitude would benefit her heart.[46]

Despite these tribulations, Matilda remained committed to her work and after her return to the capital attempted to clarify her statements about the Tewa sacrifices. In addition, she advised Hodge that she felt "quite sure" that she would have a study on the Tewa "done and ready to turn over to the Bureau by the end of June." But Matilda did not complete the manuscript. She died at the home of relatives on June 24, 1915, and her voluminous work on the Tewa pueblos, like her notes on Taos, were never published. And, no doubt to Hodge's relief, the controversy about her story of human sacrifice among the Pueblos faded away.[47]

For more than three decades, Matilda Coxe Stevenson observed the natives of the Southwest, and some of her works still remain the standard sources for studies of these people. Subsequent anthropologists and historians have criticized many of Stevenson's attitudes and actions, which indeed re-flected her ethnocentrism and her conviction of cultural supe-riority. As several of these scholars suggest, she may bear responsibility for some of the animosity toward anthropolo-gists that presently exists among the Pueblos. Generally, however, assessments of her work have been more favorable than those of her personality and methodology. A. L. Kroeber, for example, attached more value to Matilda's thorough re-cording of details than he did to Cushing's brilliant and flam-boyant descriptions, and Leslie White, who followed in Stevenson's footsteps in studying Zia pueblo, believed that she was "both objective and sympathetic."[48]

Even those who criticize her ethnological work for vari-ous reasons stress the value of the contribution she made not only to anthropology but also to history in recording a disap-pearing way of life. Particularly important are her descrip-tions of women in Native American societies; Matilda's studies are valuable references for historians, who have only recently begun to examine the lives of these women. Steven-son also broke new ground for women in the West as a pioneer anthropologist. Even before she left New Mexico, another woman anthropologist, Barbara Freire-Marreco, had arrived to study at Santa Clara. And in 1915, the year of Matilda's death, Elsie Clews Parsons initiated her studies at Zuni, where Matilda's career as an ethnologist had begun thirty-six years before. In later years, Ruth Benedict, Ruth Bunzel, Dorothea Leighton, and numerous other women traveled to New Mexico to pursue anthropological investiga-tions.

Matilda Coxe Stevenson set out to record permanently the traditions and beliefs of native peoples, and she remained faithful to that task despite setbacks and frequent opposi-tion. And it appears that, whatever her other failings, she successfully fulfilled this objective. As one scholar has pointed out, Zunis themselves continue to employ her book as the authority on the proper conduct of ceremonials.[49] Matilda would have liked that.

CONCLUSION

"Women are Venturesome Creatures"

Matilda Coxe Stevenson's death in 1915 ended a career in southwestern anthropology that had spanned thirty-six years — more than half of New Mexico's territorial period. During that time, from 1846 to 1912, women influenced the cultural and social development of the territory.

One of the first Anglo women to visit the Southwest was Susan Magoffin, whose travels took her to the frontier — not only the geographic frontier of the young republic, but also to the frontier where cultures met. En route, she discovered her ability to withstand physical hardships; and as she encountered Hispanics and Indians, she found her attitudes challenged and her world view enlarged. Susan enjoyed these experiences and gained self-confidence from them. In her diary, Susan boasted that she had indeed demonstrated that "Women are venturesome creatures."[1]

As the Anglo occupation of New Mexico continued in the years following Susan's journey, other women proved her assertion correct. And, like Susan, as they ventured into unfamiliar landscapes and situations, they recorded their impressions in diaries, letters, and other literary forms. It is through these windows to the past that we share their accomplishments and disappointments, their daily concerns and exciting events. In a sense, the women whose stories are told in the preceding chapters were "Everywoman." They were not chosen systematically, but randomly and solely because they left sufficient literary sources to tell their stories. Many of the problems these women faced (financial difficulties, illness, death of loved ones) were common to other women in the nineteenth century and today. Nor were these southwestern women alone strong and resilient. Still, their participation in the events of westward expansion and settlement set them apart and required of them flexibility and courage.

Although their experiences in the Southwest varied considerably, they shared many attributes and attitudes. For example, they were literate; most came from middle-class backgrounds; most were born in the United States; and nearly all came to New Mexico as adult, married women. Also, these newcomers to New Mexico believed in the superiority of Anglo-American culture and values. Yet when these women lived in New Mexico, where Hispanics and Indians comprised the majority of the population, most Anglo women inevitably encountered members of these ethnic groups. The newcomers usually reacted negatively and disparagingly when they first met the peoples who had lived in the region for centuries. But after a longer acquaintance, their opinions often softened, though their biases usually prevented them from fully appreciating another culture. Still, in many instances these encounters were the first between women of the different cultures, and it is noteworthy that in fact some of these Anglo women made friends with Hispanics and Indians.

These Anglo women represented American institutions during a critical period in the history of the Southwest. Between 1846 and 1912, New Mexico underwent a transformation from a remote frontier province of the Mexican republic to the forty-seventh state in the Union. The women profiled in this volume were keenly aware of the significance of the events in which they participated, and they believed that their experiences and contributions were important. Army women like Katie Bowen and Anna Maria Morris considered that their efforts to maintain morale and to provide their families with a comfortable home enabled their husbands to perform better their assigned duties. As missionary wives, Harriett Shaw, Harriett Ladd, and other women served as support networks for their spouses and helped to introduce religious pluralism to the Southwest. Later, mission teachers brought education and health care to rural areas. To keep her family together during the Civil War, Ellen Williams accompanied her husband Charles during his tour of duty, and she nursed sick and wounded soldiers throughout the conflict. In later years, her wages from menial labor provided an important source of family income. Josephine Clifford's experiences as an army wife inspired stories she wrote for western magazines. And Matilda Coxe Stevenson recognized that her research among the Pueblos would provide a permanent record of a culture she feared was disappearing.

To be sure, most of these women met with setbacks or adversity along the way. Yet they discovered that they were more courageous and resourceful than they had imagined. Their southwestern experiences also made them redefine or recreate the identities that each had developed for herself. For some, a stronger sense of self occurred within the context of the family; for others, it emerged through a career.

In addition to filling in some of the gaps that remain in the scholarship of women in the Southwest, the experiences of the women in this volume provide a basis for comparison with those of other women in the West. But as Marian Russell remarked in her memoir *Land of Enchantment,* "it is in the little incidents of life that the interest of existence really lies, not in just the grand results."[2] The writings of the women portrayed in this work — from the lonely and home-

sick Harriett Shaw to the confident and forceful Matilda
Coxe Stevenson — allow us to share the little incidents in the
lives of these New Mexican pioneers.

Notes

Introduction
1. Susan Magoffin has long been considered the first Anglo-American woman to visit New Mexico. See Susan Shelby Magoffin, *Down the Santa Fe Trail and into Mexico*, ed. Stella M. Drumm (1926; reprint, New Haven, Conn.: Yale University Press, 1962). Recent research, however, indicates that Mary Donoho may hold the distinction of being the first Anglo woman in the territory. See Marian Meyer, "Mary Donoho: New First Lady on the Santa Fe Trail," *Wagon Track* (August 1987): 1. Meyer is completing a book about Mary Donoho.
2. Howard Roberts Lamar, *The Far Southwest, 1846–1912: A Territorial History* (New York: W. W. Norton, 1970), 57.
3. For a discussion of political struggles in territorial New Mexico, see Lamar, *The Far Southwest*, and Robert W. Larson, *New Mexico's Quest for Statehood, 1846–1912* (Albuquerque: University of New Mexico Press, 1968). See also Marc Simmons, *New Mexico: A Bicentennial History* (New York: W. W. Norton, 1977).
4. Ray A. Billington, *The Protestant Crusade, 1800–1860: A Study of the Origins of American Nativism* (1938; reprint, Chicago: Quadrangle Books, 1964).
5. Important studies about women in the West include Julie Roy Jeffrey, *Frontier Women: The Trans-Mississippi West, 1840–1880* (New York: Hill and Wang, 1979); Joan M. Jensen and Darlis A. Miller, "The Gentle Tamers Revisited: New Approaches to the History of Women in the American West," *Pacific Historical Review* 49 (May 1980): 173–214; Sandra Myres, *Westering Women and the Frontier Experience, 1800–1915* (Albuquerque: University of New Mexico Press, 1982); Glenda Riley, *Frontierswomen: The Iowa Experience* (Ames: Iowa State University Press, 1982); and Lillian Schlissel, *Women's Diaries of the Westward Journey* (New York: Schocken Books, 1982).
6. Recent regional works include Joan M. Jensen and Darlis A. Miller, eds., *New Mexico Women: Intercultural Perspectives* (Albuquerque: University of New Mexico Press, 1986); and Arlene Scadron, ed., *On Their Own: Widows and Widowhood in the American Southwest, 1848–1939* (Urbana: University of Illinois Press, 1988).
7. Scadron, *On Their Own*, x.
8. Susan Armitage, "Women and Men in Western History: A Stereoptical Vision," *Western Historical Quarterly* 16 (October 1985): 381–395.

Chapter One
1. Harriett Bidwell Shaw to Susannah Bidwell, November 10, 1850, typescript copies of Harriett Shaw's letters, 1850–1862, Dorothy Woodward Collection, State Records Center and Archives (SRCA), Santa Fe, N. Mex. (hereafter cited as HBS, Woodward Collection, SRCA). Ernest Stapleton, who used the letters as the basis for "The History of Baptist Missions in New Mexico, 1849–1866" (Master's thesis, University of New Mexico, 1954), is descended from John M. Shaw and his third wife. He donated copies of Harriett Shaw's letters to the SRCA. Harriett Shaw's letters to her mother, sister, and brother constitute the most complete record that an Anglo woman left of her experiences in New Mexico before the Civil War.

No comprehensive history of religion in New Mexico during the territorial period currently exists. Denominational histories include R. Douglas Brackenridge and Francisco O. Garcia-Treto, *Iglesia Presbiteriana: A History of Presbyterians and Mexican-Americans in the Southwest* (San Antonio, Tex.: Trinity University Press, 1974); Ruth K. Barber and Edith J. Agnew, *Sowers Went Forth: The Story of Presbyterian Missions in New Mexico and Southern Colorado* (Albuquerque, N. Mex.: Menaul Historical Library of the Southwest, 1981); Mark T. Banker, "They Made Haste Slowly: Presbyterian Mission Schools and Southwestern Pluralism" (Ph.D. diss., University of New Mexico, 1987); David Stratton, *The First Century of Baptists in New Mexico, 1849–1950* (Albuquerque: Woman's Missionary Union of New Mexico, 1954); Lewis A. Myers, *A History of New Mexico Baptists* (n.p., Baptist Convention of New Mexico, 1965); Stapleton, "History of Baptist Missions;" and Thomas Harwood, *History of New Mexico Spanish and English Missions of the Methodist Episcopal Church from 1850 to 1910 in Decades*, 2 vol. (Albuquerque, N. Mex.: El Abogado Press, 1908–1910).

The present study does not attempt to evaluate the reasons that missionary efforts often had little success. Discouraged by their failure among Hispanics and Native Americans in the years preceding the Civil War, Baptists in the postwar decades concentrated on founding churches among the growing Anglo population until very late in the nineteenth century. Methodists and Presbyterians, however, not only started churches for Anglo residents of the territory but also persisted in attempting to convert Hispanics. In addition, Presbyterians played an important part in missionary efforts to the American Indians as a part of Grant's "peace policy." For a general view of that subject, see Robert F. Berkhofer, Jr., *Salvation and the Savage: An Analysis of Protestant Missions and American Indian Response, 1787–1862* (1965; reprint, New York: Atheneum, 1972). A useful study of missionary endeavor in the Southwest is Michael J. Warner, "Protestant Missionary Work with the Navajo Indians from 1846 to 1912" (Ph.D. diss., University of New Mexico, 1977). Other denominations, including the Congregationalists, Episcopalians, and the Christian Reformed, also began missionary work in New Mexico following the Civil War.

2. Most of the material about missionary wives used in this study covers the period 1849 to 1880. After 1870, increasing numbers of single women came to the territory as mission teachers, and manuscript materials about their endeavors are also available. These women shared many experiences and expectations with missionary wives, but because important distinctions may be made, single mission teachers will be treated separately in Chapter Five.

3. Julie Roy Jeffrey, *Frontier Women: The Trans-Mississippi West, 1840–1880* (New York: Hill and Wang, 1979), 100.

4. See Barbara Welter, "The Cult of True Womanhood: 1820–1860," *American Quarterly* 18 (1966): 151–175; Nancy F. Cott, *The Bonds of Womanhood: "Woman's Sphere" in New England, 1780–1835* (New Haven, Conn.: Yale University Press, 1977); Barbara Welter, "'She Hath Done What She Could': Protestant Women's Missionary Careers in Nineteenth- Century America," in *Women in American Religion*, ed. Janet Wilson James (Philadelphia: University of Pennsylvania Press, 1980); Jeffrey, *Frontier Women*, 100–104; and Ann Douglas, *The Feminization of American Culture* (1977, reprint, New York: Avon, 1978).

5. The best discussion of missionary wives is Patricia Grimshaw, "'Christian Woman, Pious Wife, Faithful Mother, Devoted Missionary': Conflicts in Roles of

American Missionary Women in Nineteenth-Century Hawaii," *Feminist Studies* 9 (Fall 1983): 488–521. Grimshaw discusses the conflict that missionary wives in Hawaii faced between what they felt was their calling and what was their duty. See also Patricia V. Horner, "Mary Richardson Walker: The Shattered Dreams of a Missionary Woman," *Montana, the Magazine of Western History* 32 (Summer 1982): 20–31.

6. Letter of Hiram W. Read, no date, *Home Mission Record* (August 1850). Betty Danielson, church historian of First Baptist Church, Albuquerque, N. Mex., kindly furnished copies of the letters by and articles about New Mexico's early Baptist missionaries that appeared in the *Home Mission Record*. For additional information about the Reads, see Betty and Dale Danielson, "New Mexico's First Protestant Preacher," *Albuquerque Journal Impact Magazine* (June 30, 1981).

7. Speech of Samuel Janney of the Hicksite Friends, Conference with Missionary Societies, *Report of the Commissioner of Indian Affairs to the Secretary of the Interior for the Year 1871* (Washington, D.C.: Government Printing Office, 1872), 191.

8. Letter of Alzina Read, March 28, 1851, in *Home Mission Record* (July 1851); letter of Hiram W. Read, March 4, 1850, *Home Mission Record* (May 1850).

9. Mrs. M. E. Roberts to Sheldon Jackson, July 2, 1874, Sheldon Jackson Correspondence (SJC) of the Presbyterian Historical Society, reel 3, vol. 5, 447–449; and Mary Ealy, March 16, 1878, in *The Rocky Mountain Presbyterian*, quoted in Norman J. Bender, *Missionaries, Outlaws, and Indians: Taylor F. Ealy at Lincoln and Zuni, 1878–1881* (Albuquerque: University of New Mexico Press, 1984), 14.

10. See, for example, Horner, "Mary Richardson Walker," 22; HBS to "Dear Sister," June 2, 1851, HBS letters, Woodward Collection, SRCA; see also Mrs. Horatio Oliver Ladd, "History of the University of New Mexico for Our Children" (unpublished manuscript, Ladd Collection, University of New Mexico Library, Special Collections Department [UNM-SC]). Another item that a missionary wife wrote to honor her husband's memory (with little note of her own participation in the events) is Mrs. Lewis Smith, *Sermons of Rev. Lewis Smith with a Biographical Sketch of the Author* (Auburn, N.Y.: Wm. J. Moses, 1867).

11. Letter of Alzina Read, March 28, 1851, *Home Mission Record* (July 1851); and HBS to "My dear friends," June 11, 1853, HBS letters, Woodward Collection, SRCA. Missionaries have often been criticized for the ethnocentrism and cultural superiority they displayed. A close examination of their motives and ideals, however, results in a more favorable assessment. For sympathetic treatments of missionary endeavors, see Warner, "Protestant Missionary Work"; and Michael C. Coleman, "Not Race, but Grace: Presbyterian Missionaries and American Indians, 1837–1893," *Journal of American History* 67 (June 1980): 41–60. For an extensive discussion of Anglo women's reactions to Native Americans, see Glenda Riley, *Women and Indians on the Frontier, 1825–1915* (Albuquerque: University of New Mexico Press, 1984).

12. Mary Ealy to Jackson, September 14, 1878, SJC, reel 2, vol. 8, 238–239; Mrs. Samuel Gorman, "Reverend Samuel Gorman — Memorial," *Old Santa Fe* 1 (January 1914): 308–331; J. M. Shields letter, Sheldon Jackson Scrapbook, vols. 34, 36, 38, 39, Menaul Historical Library of the Southwest, Albuquerque, N. Mex.; Mrs. J. D. Perkins to Jackson, June 3, 1882, SJC, reel 3, vol. 12, 200–201.

13. Mary Ealy, cited in Bender, *Missionaries, Outlaws, and Indians,* 19, 48; HBS to "My Dear Mother and Sister," October 10, 1854, and November 7, 1860, HBS letters, Woodward Collection, SRCA; letter of Alzina Read, March 28, 1851, *Home Mission Record* (July 1851); letter of Alzina Read, October 29, 1852, *Home Mission Record* (January 1853).

14. HBS to "My Dear Mother," January 26, 1852, HBS letters, Woodward Collection, SRCA.

15. José Ynez Perea to Jackson, December 8, 1879, SJC, reel 2, vol. 9, 305–306; Warner, "Protestant Missionary Work," 115; Read, "Journal of Rev. H. W. Read," *Home Mission Record* (June 1851); Mary Ealy, quoted in Bender, *Missionaries, Outlaws, and Indians,* 105.

16. Mrs. Smith, *Rev. Lewis Smith,* 33; Mrs. M. E. Roberts to Jackson, July 2, 1874, SJC, reel 1, vol. 5, 447–448; J. M. Shields to Jackson, February 3, 1882, SJC, reel 3, vol. 12, 85–86.

17. Those with some teaching experience include Alzina Read, Catherine Gorman, Martha Roberts, Emily and Isabelle Shields, Mary Ealy, Charity Menaul, and Mrs. Perkins. Read, Shaw, Roberts, and Emily Harwood also attended college.

18. Ladd, "History of the University of New Mexico," 21. For the story of the first University of New Mexico (later the Ramona Indian School in Santa Fe), see Frank D. Reeve, "The Old University of New Mexico at Santa Fe," *New Mexico Historical Review* 8 (July 1933): 202–210.

19. Mrs. Gorman, "Samuel Gorman"; Mary Ealy to Jackson, November 18, 1878, quoted in Bender, *Missionaries, Outlaws, and Indians,* 90; J. M. Shields to Jackson, September 18, 1878, SJC, reel 2, vol. 8, 243–244.

20. HBS to "My dear sister," July 20, 1854, HBS letters, Woodward Collection, SRCA; Harriett Ladd, "The University of New Mexico," UNM-SC, 34.

21. Harriett Ladd, "The University of New Mexico," UNM-SC, 20; HBS to "Dear Mother, sister, and brothers," November 3, 1857; and HBS to "Dear friends," December 20, 1857, HBS letters, Woodward Collection, SRCA.

22. Mary Maude Roberts Mercereau, "Story of the Life of Some Home Missionaries in the Early Days," 5–6, James M. Roberts file, Menaul Historical Library of the Southwest, Albuquerque, N. Mex.

23. HBS to "Dear Sister," June 2, 1851, and HBS to "my dear dear Mother, Sister, and Brother," November 28, 1851, HBS letters, Woodward Collection, SRCA.

24. James M. Roberts to John Menaul, October 23, 1870, American Indian Correspondence: The Presbyterian Historical Society Collection of Missionaries' Letters, 1833–1893, box B, vol. 2, letter 211. Many women on the frontier agreed about the difficulty of laundering clothing; see Sandra Myres, *Westering Women and the Frontier Experience, 1800–1915* (Albuquerque: University of New Mexico Press, 1982), 151.

25. Mary Ealy to Jackson, July 9, 1878, quoted in Bender, *Missionaries, Outlaws, and Indians,* 49; and Mary Ealy to Jackson, November 18, 1878, SJC, reel 2, vol. 9, 18–19.

26. J. M. Shields to Jackson, November [no date], 1878, SJC, reel 2, vol. 8, 288–290; J. M. Shields to Jackson, March 24, 1882, SJC, reel 3, vol. 12, 120–123; J. M. Shields to Jackson, June 22, 1878, SJC, reel 2, vol. 8, 99–100; F.E.H. Haines to Jackson, October 24, 1881, SJC, reel 3, vol. 11, 277; Elizabeth Annin to Jackson, January 23, 1878, SJC, reel 2, vol. 7, 249–250.

27. Mrs. Gorman, "Samuel Gorman," 308–331; Stapleton, "History of Baptist Missions"; HBS to "My dear sister," August 1, 1860, HBS letters, Woodward Collection, SRCA.

28. John Menaul to John Lowrie, May 20, 1873, American Indian Correspondence, box M, vol. 1, letter 139.

29. Mary Ealy to Jackson, August 16, 1878, SJC, reel 2, vol. 8, 199; Mrs. Ladd, "History of the University of New Mexico," UNM- SC, 20–22.

30. John Menaul to John Lowrie, May 20, 1873, American Indian Correspondence, box M, vol. 1, letter 139; W. F. Hall to John Lowrie, April 29, 1873, American Indian Correspondence, box M, vol. 1, letter 126.

31. Harriet S. Kellogg, *Life of Mrs. Emily J. Harwood* (Albuquerque, N. Mex.: El Abogado Press, 1903), 53; Barber and Agnew, *Sowers Went Forth,* 14; Danielson and Danielson, "New Mexico's First Protestant Preacher."

32. Bender, *Missionaries, Outlaws, and Indians,* 94; José Ynez Perea to Jackson, December 8, 1879, SJC, reel 2, vol. 9, 305–306; Shields family genealogy, Jemez Springs, N. Mex., file, Menaul Historical Library; Ben M. Thomas, *Annual Report of the Commissioner of Indian Affairs, 1882* (Washington, D.C.: Government Printing Office, 1882), 130; Mercereau, "Life of Some Home Missionaries," 6; HBS to "My dear dear sister," June 29, 1852, HBS letters, Woodward Collection, SRCA.

33. Other women who combined maternity with missionary work in the territory include Ann Eliza Nicholson, Mary Ealy, Emily Shields, Isabelle Shields, Susan Perea, Mrs. Tolhurst, Amanda McFarland, Harriett Ladd, Elizabeth Annin, Mrs. J. D. Perkins, Mrs. A. H. Donaldson, and Mrs. Henry Palmer. And although she did not have children of her own, Charity Ann Gaston, who married the widower John Menaul, filled the maternal role as stepmother to Menaul's daughters.

34. U.S. Bureau of the Census, Population Schedules of the Seventh Census of the United States, 1850. New Mexico: Santa Ana and Santa Fe counties. National Archives (NA) M–432, reel 468; HBS to "My dear friends," July 23 and August 13, 1852, HBS letters, Woodward Collection, SRCA; Mercereau, "Life of Some Home Missionaries," 2–3.

35. HBS to "My dear mother," October 10, 1852, and HBS to "Dear Mother, brothers, & sisters," March 22, 1858, HBS letters, Woodward Collection, SRCA. Bender, *Missionaries, Outlaws, and Indians,* 127.

36. Bender, *Missionaries, Outlaws, and Indians,* 166; Shields genealogy; Mercereau, "Life of Some Home Missionaries," addendum; HBS to "My dear mother and sister," January 12, 1854, HBS letters, Woodward Collection, SRCA. For a discussion of contraception and abortion on the frontier, see Myres, *Westering Women,* 154–156.

37. Mrs. Gorman, "Samuel Gorman," 321; HBS to "My dear sister," August 1, 1860, HBS letters, Woodward Collection, SRCA.

38. Taylor Ealy to Jackson, February 27, 1879, quoted in Bender, *Missionaries, Outlaws, and Indians,* 104; and James M. Roberts to John Lowrie, September 13, 1870, American Indian Correspondence, box B, vol. 2, letter 147.

39. HBS to "My dear sister," August 11, 1854, and HBS to [her mother], August 12, 1854, HBS letters, Woodward Collection, SRCA.

40. For a discussion of medicine in the West, see Richard Dunlop, *Doctors of the American Frontier* (Garden City, N.Y.: Doubleday and Company, 1965); see also Myres, *Westering Women,* 156–158.

41. Mercereau, "Lives of Some Home Missionaries," 7; HBS to "Dear Mother," July 2, 1861, HBS letters, Woodward Collection, SRCA; Mary Ealy to Jackson, November 18, 1878, quoted in Bender, *Missionaries, Outlaws, and Indians,* 90; HBS to "Dear Mother," January 25, 1860, HBS letters, Woodward Collection,

SRCA; Mercereau, "Lives of Some Home Missionaries," 6–7; HBS to "My Dear Mother and Sister," August 11, 1854, HBS letters, Woodward Collection, SRCA.

42. See Frances Sage Bradley and Margaretta A. Williamson, "Rural Children in Selected Counties of North Carolina," in *Child Care in Rural America* (New York: Arno Press, 1972), 33, ♥9. This volume contains reprints of five Children's Bureau Publications (1917–1921), published by the U.S. Department of Labor. HBS to "My dear Mother and Sister," August 11 and November 12, 1854, HBS letters, Woodward Collection, SRCA.

43. Hiram W. Read, "Extracts from Rev. H. W. Read's Journal," *Home Mission Record* (April 1853); Mercereau, "Lives of Some Home Missionaries," 6–7; HBS to "Dear friends," January 2, 1861, HBS letters, Woodward Collection, SRCA.

44. Mrs. J. D. Perkins to Jackson, September 12, 1880, SJC, reel 3, vol. 10, 90; Mrs. Gorman, "Samuel Gorman," 320; J. M. Shields to Jackson, March 16, 1883, SJC, reel 3, vol. 13, 70; HBS to "Dear Mother and Sister," November 7, 1860, HBS letters, Woodward Collection, SRCA.

45. HBS to "my dear friends," July 10, 1853, HBS letters, Woodward Collection, SRCA; Danielson and Danielson, "New Mexico's First Protestant Preacher"; Barber and Agnew, *Sowers Went Forth,* 12; Bender, *Missionaries, Outlaws, and Indians,* 138; Shields genealogy.

46. Barber and Agnew, *Sowers Went Forth,* 14; Mercereau, "Lives of Some Home Missionaries," 8; Mrs. A. H. Donaldson to Jackson, May 21, 1880, SJC, reel 3, vol. 10, 160–161.

47. Unfortunately, no records exist to indicate whether Mrs. Nicholson died in Santa Fe; HBS to "My dear mother," January 26, 1852, HBS letters, Woodward Collection, SRCA.

48. HBS to "My Dear Mother and Sister," January 12, 1854, HBS letters, Woodward Collection, SRCA; Mrs. Gorman, "Samuel Gorman," 322; letter of John Milton Shaw, July 8, 1862, *Home Mission Record* (September 1862); J. M. Shields to Jackson, November 8, 1878, SJC, reel 2, vol. 8, 296.

49. J. M. Shields to Jackson, November 8, 1978, SJC, reel 2, vol. 8, 296.

50. J. M. Shields to Jackson, November 8, 1878, SJC, reel 2, vol. 8, 296; J. M. Shields to Jackson, November [n.d.], 1878, SJC, reel 2, vol. 8, 288; B. M. Thomas to Jackson, January 3, 1879, SJC, reel 2, vol. 9, 66–67.

51. J. M. Shields to Jackson, January 6, 1879, SJC, reel 2, vol. 9, 67–68.

52. H. Kendall to Jackson, February 26, 1879, SJC, reel 2, vol. 9, 120–122.

53. J. M. Shields to Sheldon Jackson, July 28, 1879, SJC, reel 2, vol. 9, 253–254.

Chapter Two

1. For example, see Patricia Stallard, *Glittering Misery: Dependents of the Indian Fighting Army* (San Rafael, Calif.: Presidio Press, and Fort Collins, Colo.: Old Army Press, 1978); Sandra L. Myres, "Romance and Reality on the American Frontier: Views of Army Wives," *Western Historical Quarterly* 13 (October 1982): 410–427; Sherry L. Smith, "'Civilization's Guardians': Army Officers' Reflections on Indians and the Indian Wars in the Trans-Mississippi West, 1848–1890," (Ph.D. diss., University of Washington, 1984), includes a chapter entitled "Army Wives, Indians and the Indian Wars," 321–360. Joan Ingalles deals primarily with the decade 1850 to 1860 in "Family Life on the Southwest Frontier," *Military History of Texas and the Southwest* 14 (1978): 203–213. Information about women who married enlisted men is included in Darlis Miller, "Cross-Cultural Marriages in the Southwest: The New Mexico Experience, 1846–1900," *New Mexico Historical Review* 57 (October 1982): 335–359.

An examination of women other than officers' wives and their interaction with the army is Darlis Miller, "Foragers, Army Women, and Prostitutes," in *New Mexico Women: Intercultural Perspectives,* ed. Joan M. Jensen and Darlis A. Miller (Albuquerque: University of New Mexico Press, 1986). Chapters Three and Four in the present work address the experiences and writings of Ellen Williams, a laundress and nurse in New Mexico during the Civil War, and Josephine Clifford, who eventually fled from her abusive and insane husband, an officer in the Third Cavalry.

2.	Myres, ed., *Cavalry Wife: The Diary of Eveline M. Alexander, 1866–1867* (College Station: Texas A & M University Press, 1977); Robert C. and Eleanor R. Carriker, *An Army Wife on the Frontier: the Memoirs of Alice Blackwood Baldwin, 1867–1877* (Salt Lake City: Tanner Trust Fund, University of Utah Library, 1975); Mrs. Orsemus B. [Frances] Boyd, *Cavalry Life in Tent and Field,* intro. Darlis Miller (1894; reprint, Lincoln: University of Nebraska Press, 1982); Maria Brace Kimball, *My Eighty Years* (Boston: privately printed, 1934); Lydia Spencer Lane, *I Married a Soldier, or Old Days in the Old Army* (1893; reprint, Albuquerque, N. Mex.: Horn and Wallace, 1964); Genevieve La Tourrette, "Fort Union Memories," *New Mexico Historical Review* 26 (October 1951): 276–286; Marian Russell, *Land of Enchantment* (1954; reprint, Albuquerque: University of New Mexico Press, 1981); Martha Summerhayes, *Vanished Arizona: Recollections of the Army Life of a New England Woman* (1911; reprint, Lincoln: University of Nebraska Press, 1979); unpublished accounts include Ione Bradley, "Recollections of Army Life," Luther Bradley Papers, box 6, U.S. Army Military History Institute, Carlisle Barracks, Pa.; and Ellen Dixon Wilson, "My Aunt's Reminiscences," (unpublished manuscript of the reminiscences of Mrs. W. P. Wilson, Fort Union National Monument, N. Mex.).

3.	Russell, *Land of Enchantment,* 124.

4.	Catherine (Katie) Bowen letters from Fort Union, N. Mex., 1851–1853, typescripts in the Arrott Collection, Donnelly Library, New Mexico Highlands University, Las Vegas, N. Mex. (hereafter cited as Bowen letters, AC, NMHU); Anna Maria Morris diary, Morris Collection, University of Virginia Library, Charlottesville, Va., microfilm (hereafter cited as Morris diary, UV). A portion of Anna Maria Morris's diary was published in Kenneth Holmes, ed., *Covered Wagon Women: Diaries and Letters from the Western Trails, 1840–1890,* vol. 2 (Glendale, Calif.: Arthur H. Clark Co., 1983), 15–43.

5.	Holmes, *Covered Wagon Women,* 2: 16; Gwladys Bowen to author, February 7, 1985.

6.	Some historians have argued that women were reluctant pioneers; see, for example, Lillian Schlissel, *Women's Diaries of the Westward Journey* (New York: Schocken Books, 1982); and John Mack Faragher, *Women and Men on the Overland Trail* (New Haven, Conn.: Yale University Press, 1979). Others have demonstrated more convincingly that many women accepted the challenge of westering gracefully and enthusiastically; see Sandra Myres, *Westering Women and the Frontier Experience, 1800–1915* (Albuquerque: University of New Mexico Press, 1982); and Glenda Riley, *Frontierswomen: The Iowa Experience* (Ames: Iowa State University Press, 1982).

7.	Unfortunately, Anna Maria Morris's letters have not yet come to light, although entries in her journal indicate that she wrote numerous letters to her father and sisters. The letters of Katie Bowen in the Arrott Collection are those she wrote to her parents; additional letters to other family members remain in the possession of her granddaughter. Chris Emmett quoted extensively from these letters in *Ft. Union and the Winning of the Southwest* (Norman: University of Oklahoma Press, 1965) but misquoted on numerous occasions. Thus, I chose to consult the letters themselves rather than rely on his quotes. Many of Morris's journal entries are terse, and she evidently kept the diary for her own use, expressing herself at length in the letters she wrote home. During the first part of her journey, she made two copies of the journal, sending home portions of it as mail service permitted. For example, see diary entries of June 10 and June 12, 1850, Morris diary, UV. Apparently, she discontinued that practice when she arrived in New Mexico and instead wrote letters.

8.   Morris diary, June 28, 1850, UV; Bowen letters, September 28, 1851, AC, NMHU.

9.   Morris diary, July 6, 1850, UV; Bowen letters, July 1, 1853, and August 24, 1851, AC, NMHU; and Morris diary, July 12, 1850, UV.

10. Morris diary, August 31, 1850, UV; Bowen letters, September [n.d.] 1851, and November 2, 1851, AC, NMHU.

11. For example, Lydia Spencer Lane moved many times during her years as a military wife; see Lane, *I Married a Soldier.* Morris diary, July 27 and August 13, 1851, UV. Robert W. Frazer, *Forts and Supplies: The Role of the Army in the Economy of the Southwest, 1846–1861* (Albuquerque: University of New Mexico Press, 1983), 64–66, corroborates Mrs. Morris's entries regarding her husband's assignments.

12. Bowen letters, February 29 and May 28, 1852, AC, NMHU. Frances Boyd and her family, including three children, were forced to live in one room at Fort Clark, Texas; see Boyd, *Cavalry Life,* 273. Lydia Spencer Lane also had occasion to lament the roof of her quarters. During her tenure at Fort Union, ceilings received a coat of plaster, a solution that was not particularly satisfactory. After preparing a meal for seventeen, she placed the dishes on the table and called her guests. Before they sat down, however, "down fell half the ceiling . . . filling every dish with plaster to the top." Lane, *I Married a Soldier,* 146.

13. Morris diary, July 31 and September 15, 1851, UV.

14. Bowen letters, May 28, 1852, AC, NMHU; Morris diary, November 22, 1851, UV.

15. Frances Boyd, for example, was dismayed to discover her dishes broken into fragments when goods arrived at Camp Halleck, Nevada. Boyd, *Cavalry Wife,* 52–53.

16. Morris diary, June 18, 1851, UV; Bowen letters, August 24, 1851, AC, NMHU.

17. Kate H. Parker, "'I Brought with Me Many Eastern Ways': Euro-American Income-Earning Women in New Mexico, 1850–1880" (Ph.D. diss., University of New Mexico, 1984), 51, 58.

18. La Tourrette, "Fort Union Memories," p. 283; Bowen letters, November 2, 1851, and February 2, 1852, AC, NMHU; Morris diary, July 13, 1851. No male black servant was listed with the Morris family on the census of 1850. Albino Lopez, a sixteen-year-old Hispanic male, did appear as the family's servant on this enumeration in December 1850, and it is possible that he fathered Louisa's child (born July 13, 1851), whose name was Hispanic. U.S. Bureau of the Census, Population Schedules of the Seventh Census of the United States 1850: New Mexico: Santa Fe county, National Archives (NA) M–432, reel 468.

19. Frances Boyd, for instance, complained that during the two years her husband served at Camp Halleck, their rations consisted only of bacon, flour, beans, coffee, rice, tea, and sugar. Boyd, *Cavalry Life,* 55.

20. For some references to food preserving, see Bowen letters, September 14, 1851, and January 1, 1852, AC, NMHU; Morris diary, September 4, September 13, September 24, September 20, and September 23, 1850, UV. Frances Boyd and Lydia Spencer Lane expressed pride in their ability to make butter; see Boyd, *Cavalry Life*, 231, and Lane, *I Married a Soldier*, 141. Bowen letters, September 14, 1851, AC, NMHU.

21. Bowen letters, September 2, 1851, AC, NMHU; Morris diary, October 4, 1851.

22. Bowen letters, April 28, 1853, AC, NMHU; Morris diary, November 5, 1850, and February 8, 1851; Bowen letters, September 3, 1853, AC, NMHU.

23. Bowen letters, September 28, 1851, AC, NMHU.

24. Bowen letters, April 28 and September 3, 1853, AC, NMHU. Mrs. W. P. Wilson related a similar experience when she arrived at Fort Union and met a woman who had lived for several years at Fort Defiance. "She had been nearly six years away from dressmakers and fashion papers, and Oh, how odd her clothes looked that day she first called on me and how utterly unconscious she was of her dress or mine." Wilson, "My Aunt's Reminiscences."

25. Bowen letters, November 30, 1851; January 1, 1852; and March 31, 1852, AC, NMHU.

26. How valuable the services of army doctors proved to expectant mothers varied; Marian Russell, for example, recalled that the imminent birth of her daughter reduced the "young army surgeon" at Fort Bascom to "a hopeless wreck," and a nearby rancher's wife acted as midwife instead. Russell, *Land of Enchantment*, 110. Bowen letters, February 2 and March 31, 1852, AC, NMHU; Morris diary, July 23, 1850, UV.

27. Marian Russell's first daughter, for example, died in infancy of an unnamed complaint, and Frances Boyd nearly lost her infant son to whooping cough. Lydia Spencer Lane's son "was ill unto death for days" before he finally recovered from an unspecified illness. Russell, *Land of Enchantment*, 113; Boyd, *Cavalry Life*, 271; Lane, *I Married a Soldier*, 140. Anna Maria Morris also referred to illness resulting in the death of a child in a friend's family. Morris diary, January 25, 1852, UV.

28. Gwladys Bowen to author, February 28, 1985; the Bowens' daughter Agnes was born in Albuquerque in 1854; Gwladys Bowen to author, May 2, 1985; Bowen letters, February 29, 1852, and no date (probably March 1852), AC, NMHU.

29. Lydia Spencer Lane also took care to secure vaccination against smallpox in the Southwest; see Lane, *I Married a Soldier*, 71. Bowen letters, May 28, 1852; January 3 and March 29, 1853, AC, NMHU. Frances Boyd echoed Katie's endorsement of the New Mexican climate, maintaining that "in the Southwestern climate ordinary diseases do not prevail, and if any of the epidemics which mothers usually dread break out, the absolute pureness of the air renders them innocuous," Boyd, *Cavalry Life*, 224.

30. Bowen letters, July 1, 1853; November 2 and 30, 1851; and October 3 and November 1, 1852, AC, NMHU. Gwladys Bowen to author, May 2, 1985. Marian Russell's husband also received injuries when he fell from his horse. Russell, *Land of Enchantment*, 109.

31. Bowen letters, September 1, 1852, AC, NMHU. Frances Boyd also reported her pride in her daughter. Boyd, *Cavalry Life*, 171.

32. Morris diary, July 14, 1852, and April 13, 1853, UV.

33. Bowen letters, March 29, 1853; August 1, 1852; August 15, 1853; November 1, 1852; and July 1, 1853, AC, NMHU. See Robert L. Griswold, *Family and Divorce in California, 1850–1890: Victorian Illusions and Everyday Realities*

(Albany: State University of New York Press, 1982), 10–17. Katie Bowen's correspondence is enlightening regarding relationships between spouses and parents' responses to their children. Although Frances Boyd and Lydia Spencer Lane portray their husbands favorably, both men seem somewhat distant from their families; see Boyd, *Cavalry Life*, and Lane, *I Married a Soldier*. In the narrative of Martha Summerhayes, her husband, Jack, appears as a rigid and domineering figure; indeed, Mrs. Summerhayes provides several hints that her marriage was not particularly rewarding. Summerhayes, *Vanished Arizona*. Marian Russell and her husband Richard apparently shared a close and affectionate relationship similar to that of Katie and Isaac Bowen. Russell, *Land of Enchantment*. Anna Maria Morris also seems to have been happily married; her journal entries are usually terse, but on several occasions she broke with that pattern. For example, she once wrote "I am exceedingly anxious about the Maj. He is in the midst of hostile foes. I pray God to protect and watch over him" (Morris diary, February 1, 1852, UV).

34. Morris diary, May 18, May 28, March 7, and February 27, 1852, UV. Bowen letters, November 30, 1851, AC, NMHU.

35. Bowen letters, November 2, 1851, and January 1, 1853, AC, NMHU. Most of the Bowen letters and many of the entries in Mrs. Morris's journal allude to social functions, which provided a sense of community for army families.

36. Bowen letters, February 2, 1852, AC, NMHU; and Morris diary, August 30, January 1, and January 3, 1852, UV. Stallard, *Glittering Misery*, 61–68, discusses the caste system that kept officers' ladies and enlisted men's wives apart and mentions other instances where women of different social levels assisted each other.

37. Sarah Bowman, who also used the surnames of Bourgett, Borginnis, and Burgett, was a famous prostitute of the El Paso area. She acquired her nickname during the Mexican War. Nancy Hamilton, "The Great Western," in *The Women Who Made the West*, Western Writers of America (New York: Doubleday, 1980), 186–197; H. Gordon Frost, *The Gentlemen's Club: The Story of Prostitution in El Paso* (El Paso, Tex.: Mangan Books, 1983), 15–16. A native of Tennessee, Sarah (using the name Bourgett) lived at Socorro in December 1850. She gave her age as thirty-three and admitted that she could neither read nor write. At the time of this census, her family included five children (aged two to sixteen) named Skinner. U.S. Bureau of the Census, Population Schedules of the Seventh Census of the United States, 1850: New Mexico: Valencia county, NA M–432, reel 468. Apparently this family is the same family that Mrs. Morris mentioned in her journal entry of May 4, 1851, which reads "in the evening Mr. Casey called to bring the little girl for Mrs. Graham [another officer's wife and friend of Mrs. Morris]. I am to keep her till Mrs. G. comes down. She is the daughter of a Calafornia emigrant who died at El Paso. The mother also died leaving five little daughters. Mr. St. Vrain has taken one. The one I have is about 8 years old called Diantha Skinner." Her references to "the Great Western" occur in Morris diary, September 18 and October 3, 1852, UV.

38. Bowen letters, n.d. [March 1852?], AC, NMHU; Emmett, *Ft. Union*, 141–144, and Stallard, *Glittering Misery*, 71–72, mention these events.

39. Morris diary, July 11, 1851, UV; Bowen letters, February 29, 1852, AC, NMHU; Morris diary, July 21 and September 2, 1850, UV; Bowen letters, July 1, 1853, AC, NMHU; Morris diary, September 6, 1850, UV. Lydia Spencer Lane also found an infant's funeral distressing and admitted that she could not drink

from a dirty cup she found at a hostelry; Lane, *I Married a Soldier*, 71–72, 148–149.

40. Morris diary, July 7, 1850, and February 5, 1851, UV; Bowen letters, September 28, 1851, and February 29, 1852, AC, NMHU; Morris diary, March 30, 1851, UV.

41. Bowen letters, May 28 and March 31, 1852, AC, NMHU; Morris diary, August 11, August 15, and August 16, 1851, UV.

42. Eveline Alexander, for example, became very interested in the Navajo, Pima, and Papago; see Alexander, *Cavalry Wife*. Several authors have recently examined women's responses to native Americans. See, for example, Myres, *Westering Women*, 37–64; Glenda Riley, *Women and Indians on the Frontier, 1825–1915* (Albuquerque: University of New Mexico Press, 1984); and Smith, "'Civilization's Guardians,'" 321–360. These writers agree that fear usually preceded actual contact and suggest that this emotion later gave way to others, including sympathy and curiosity.

43. Morris diary, July 2, 1850; Mrs. White's story was widely circulated at the time it happened, and different versions about the outcome have evolved. All agree, however, that the Apaches murdered Mrs. White immediately before the search party reached them; the fate of the child and servant is unclear. See W.W.H. Davis, *El Gringo, or New Mexico and Her People* (1857; reprint, Lincoln: University of Nebraska Press, 1982), 44–46; Hubert Howe Bancroft, *History of Arizona and New Mexico, 1530–1888* (1889; reprint, Albuquerque, N. Mex.: Horn and Wallace, 1962), 463–464, and Clinton E. Brooks and Frank D. Reeve, eds., *Forts and Forays, James A. Bennett: A Dragoon in New Mexico, 1850–1856* (Albuquerque: University of New Mexico Press, 1948), 23–26.

44. Bowen letters, January 1, 1852, and January 30, 1853, AC, NMHU.

45. Morris diary, August 3, 1851; January 29 and July 7, 1852, UV.

46. Morris diary, 1853–1858, UV; Holmes, *Covered Wagon Women*, 2: 19.

47. Bowen letters, November 3, 1853, AC, NMHU. Gwladys Bowen to author, February 7 and May 2, 1985. Isaac Bowen's brother raised the three remaining children.

48. Summerhayes, *Vanished Arizona*, 24.

Chapter Three

1. Patricia Stallard, *Glittering Misery: Dependents of the Indian Fighting Army* (San Rafael, Calif.: Presidio Press, and Fort Collins, Colo.: Old Army Press, 1978), provides the most complete picture of the lives of women married to enlisted men and other women who served the army as laundresses. Miller J. Stewart, "Army Laundresses: Ladies of the 'Soap Suds Row'," *Nebraska History* 61 (Winter 1980): 421–36, is based almost exclusively on Stallard's earlier work, and, not surprisingly, offers similar conclusions. A recent study that illuminates the experiences of some women affiliated with the army in New Mexico is Darlis Miller, "Foragers, Army Women, and Prostitutes," *New Mexico Women: Intercultural Perspectives*, ed. Joan M. Jensen and Darlis A. Miller (Albuquerque: University of New Mexico Press, 1986). Maria Bracc Kimball, *My Eighty Years* (Boston: privately printed, 1934), devotes several chapters of her memoirs to descriptions of enlisted personnel and domestic servants. Prostitution in the frontier army is also treated in Anne M. Butler, *Daughters of Joy, Sisters of Misery: Prostitutes in the American West, 1865–90* (Urbana: University of Illinois Press, 1985). Women's roles as nurses and hospital matrons at frontier posts merit scholarly study.

2.   I am indebted to Marc Simmons, who first called my attention to Mrs. Williams's work. Ellen Williams, *Three Years and a Half in the Army, or History of the Second Colorados* (New York: Fowler and Wells Company, 1885). In a bibliography of army women in the West, Sandra Myres notes that "accounts by enlisted men's wives and families are . . . difficult to find" and lists only two, Mrs. Williams's work and Alice Mathews Shields, "Army Life on the Wyoming Frontier," *Annals of Wyoming* 13 (October 1941): 331–343, which describes army life after 1865; see Sandra Myres, comp., "Army Wives in the Trans-Mississippi West, A Bibliography," in Teresa Vielé, *Following the Drum*, ed. Sandra Myres (Lincoln: University of Nebraska Press, 1984), 257–273. Don Rickey, Jr., provides references to several items enlisted men authored in *Forty Miles a Day on Beans and Hay: The Enlisted Soldier Fighting the Indian Wars* (Norman: University of Oklahoma Press, 1963), but (aside from the Shields article) none are accounts that women wrote. The lives of working-class women in the West have not received as much attention as those of other groups, largely because they left so few written records. The writings of Anne Ellis, detailing her experiences in Colorado mining camps of the late nineteenth century, are noteworthy exceptions. See, for example, her *Life of an Ordinary Woman* (Lincoln: University of Nebraska Press, 1980), *Plain Anne Ellis: More About the Life of an Ordinary Woman* (Lincoln: University of Nebraska Press, 1984), and *Sunshine Preferred* (Lincoln: University of Nebraska Press, 1984).

3.   Kate H. Parker, "'I Brought with Me Many Eastern Ways': Euro-American Income-Earning Women in New Mexico, 1850–1880" (Ph.D. diss., University of New Mexico, 1984), 44. Charles Williams, Pension Application Files, Civil War Series, Records of the Veterans Administration, Record Group (RG) 15, National Archives (NA), Washington, D.C. Mrs. Williams's pension applications are filed with her husband's; Williams, *Three Years and a Half*, 2–3; Regimental Descriptive Book, Second Colorado Infantry and Cavalry, 52, Office of the Adjutant General, Volunteer Organizations, Civil War, Colorado, RG 94, NA, does not contain the names of any women who served the company as laundresses or nurses. A description of Charles Williams indicates that at the time of his enlistment in October 1861, he was forty years old, five feet eight inches tall, with brown eyes and hair and a dark complexion.

4.   "The captain of each company had the right to appoint the washerwomen." Stallard, *Glittering Misery*, 59. During this period, a company could employ one laundress for each twenty men, and thus Mrs. Williams likely was not the only laundress for the company. Her book clearly indicates that other women married to enlisted men accompanied the company, as did the wives of some of the officers. Pension Application Files, RG 15, NA; Marc Simmons, *New Mexico: A Bicentennial History* (New York: W. W. Norton, 1977), 141–149, discusses the Civil War in New Mexico. See also Hubert Howe Bancroft, *History of Arizona and New Mexico, 1530–1888* (1889; reprint, Albuquerque, N. Mex.: Horn and Wallace, 1962), 688–700. Company B's experiences in New Mexico are chronicled in Alonzo Ferdinand Ickis, *Bloody Trails Along the Rio Grande: A Day-by-Day Diary of Alonzo Ferdinand Ickis (1836–1917), A Soldier and His Activities with Company B . . .* (Denver: Old West Publishing Co., 1958). The First Regiment of Colorado Volunteers also participated in Civil War battles in New Mexico; part of this regiment was later incorporated (along with independent Companies A and B and other groups) into the Second Colorado Cavalry. See Ovando Hollister, *History of the First Regiment of Colorado Volunteers*, ed. Richard Harwell (Chicago: R. R. Donnelley & Sons, 1962).

5. Williams, *Three Years and a Half,* 9–11; Charles Williams, Pension Application Files, RG 15, NA.
6. Williams, *Three Years and a Half,* 14.
7. Ibid., 19, 15.
8. Ibid., 32, 14–17.
9. Ibid., 19.
10. Ibid., 19–20; Charles Williams, Pension Application Files, RG 15, NA; *Santa Fe Gazette,* April 26, 1862.
11. Williams, *Three Years and a Half,* 20, 25; *Santa Fe Gazette,* April 26, 1862; Harvey Halcomb, "Confederate Reminiscences," ed. Lansing Bloom, *New Mexico Historical Review* 5 (July 1930): 320; Max L. Heyman, Jr., *Prudent Soldier: A Biography of Major General E.R.S. Canby, 1817–1873* (Glendale, Calif.: Arthur H. Clark Co., 1959), 183.
12. Charles Williams, Pension Application Files, RG 15, NA; Williams, "When Shall We Hear the Joyous Cry!" *Santa Fe Gazette,* June 28, 1862.
13. Charles Williams, Pension Application Files, RG 15, NA; *Santa Fe Gazette,* July 5, 1862; Williams, *Three Years and a Half,* 30–31.
14. Williams, *Three Years and a Half,* 33–34.
15. Ibid., 35, 38–44.
16. Charles Williams, Pension Application Files, RG 15, NA; Williams, *Three Years and a Half,* 138.
17. Williams, *Three Years and a Half,* 139; U.S. Bureau of the Census, Population Schedules of the Ninth Census of the United States, 1870: Iowa. Wayne and Webster counties, NA M–593, reel 425. Charles Williams's mother raised Mary Jane to adulthood, when she joined her father and stepmother. Charles Williams, Pension Application Files, RG 15, NA.
18. Charles Williams, Pension Application Files, RG 15, NA; Williams, *Three Years and a Half,* v.
19. Williams, *Three Years and a Half,* 140–143; pp. 2–3 of Mrs. Williams's narrative replicate exactly a "compendium of history" that appeared in the [Fort Riley, Kansas] *Soldier's Letter,* vol. 1, no. 1 (no date). No author's name appears on the column, and an introduction refers to "he"; however, a possibility remains that Mrs. Williams and her husband collaborated on this project.
20. See, for example, Martha Summerhayes, *Vanished Arizona: Recollections of the Army Life of a New England Woman* (1911, reprint, Lincoln: University of Nebraska Press, 1979), 8; Charles Williams, Pension Application Files, RG 15, NA.
21. Charles Williams, Pension Application Files, RG 15, NA.
22. Ibid. The application of June 5, 1893, alludes to an earlier application that was denied, but this document is no longer in the file.
23. Ibid.
24. Ibid. Widows of veterans were, in fact, luckier than most widows in an era when few public assistance programs existed. A recent study of widows in the Southwest is Arlene Scadron, ed., *On Their Own: Widows and Widowhood in the American Southwest, 1848–1939* (Urbana: University of Illinois Press, 1988). In an essay in that volume, Joyce Goodfriend notes that "in an era when the federal government scrupulously avoided involvement in any form of public welfare program, one favored category of citizens — veterans and widows of veterans — was singled out for special treatment." Joyce D. Goodfriend, "The Struggle for Survival: Widows in Denver, 1880–1912," in Scadron, *On Their Own,* 172.

Chapter Four

1. Josephine Clifford McCrackin, "Toby," in *"Another Juanita" and Other Stories* (Buffalo, N.Y.: Charles Wells Moulton, 1893), 105. I have used her spelling throughout this chapter. Josephine Clifford wrote under that name until her marriage in 1882 to Jackson McCrackin. Thereafter, she wrote as Josephine Clifford McCrackin. I have cited the works according to the name the author used at the time of publication.

2. Collections of Clifford's (McCrackin's) autobiographical sketches and short stories include *Overland Tales* (Philadelphia: Claxton, Remsen & Haffelfinger, 1877), *"Another Juanita,"* and *"The Woman Who Lost Him" and Tales of the Army Frontier* (Pasadena, Calif.: George Wharton James, 1913). Women's accounts of frontier military life in New Mexico following the Civil War include Mrs. Orsemus B. [Frances] Boyd, *Cavalry Life in Tent and Field,* intro. Darlis Miller (1894; reprint, Lincoln: University of Nebraska Press, 1982); Lydia Spencer Lane, *I Married a Soldier, or Old Days in the Old Army* (1893; reprint, Albuquerque, N. Mex.: Horn and Wallace, 1964); Marian Russell, *Land of Enchantment* (1954; reprint, Albuquerque: University of New Mexico Press, 1981); Sandra Myres, ed., *Cavalry Wife: The Diary of Eveline M. Alexander, 1866–1867* (College Station: Texas A & M University Press, 1977); and Robert C. and Eleanor R. Carriker, *An Army Wife on the Frontier: The Memoirs of Alice Blackwood Baldwin, 1867–1877* (Salt Lake City: Tanner Trust Fund, University of Utah Library, 1975).

3. Ann Douglas Wood, "The Literature of Impoverishment: The Women Local Colorists in America, 1865–1914," *Women's Studies* 1 (1972): 4; Josephine Clifford McCrackin, "Reminiscences of Bret Harte and Pioneer Days in the West," *Overland Monthly* n.s. 67 (January 1916): 7–15; and Josephine Clifford McCrackin, "Ina Coolbrith Invested with Poet's Crown," *Overland Monthly* n.s. 66 (November 1915): 448–450.

4. To date, Clifford's experiences as an army wife have been overlooked by historians. An undergraduate student at the University of California at Berkeley, however, recognized the autobiographical nature of Josephine's writings about her abusive marriage; see Jacquelyn Marie, "Josephine Clifford McCrackin: Battered Wife and Writer," American Literary Miscellany #71, 12/1912, Bancroft Library, University of California at Berkeley, Berkeley, California. This author and I independently reached similar conclusions about Josephine's experiences, and even chose the same quotation to introduce our subject.

5. Teresa Vielé, *Following the Drum: A Glimpse of Frontier Life,* ed. by Sandra Myres (1858; reprint, Lincoln: University of Nebraska Press, 1984); Mrs. D. B. Dyer, *"Fort Reno"; or, Picturesque "Cheyenne and Arrapahoe Army Life,"* Before the Opening of Oklahoma (New York: G. W. Dillingham, 1896); Martha Summerhayes, *Vanished Arizona: Recollections of the Army Life of a New England Woman* (1911; reprint, Lincoln: University of Nebraska Press, 1979).

6. For a discussion of family discord, see Patricia Stallard, *Glittering Misery: Dependents of the Indian Fighting Army* (San Rafael, Calif.: Presidio Press, and Fort Collins, Colo.: Old Army Press, 1978), 103–129. Melody Graulich examines family violence through western American literature in "Violence Against Women in Literature of the Western Family," *Frontiers* 7 (1984): 14–20.

7. McCrackin, "Reminiscences of Bret Harte," 9–11.

8. Francis B. Heitman, *Historical Register and Dictionary of the United States Army from Its Organization, September 29, 1789, to March 2, 1903,* 2 vols.

(Washington, D.C.: Government Printing Office, 1903), 1: 310. The date and place of Clifford's marriage to Josephine is difficult to determine precisely. Josephine's autobiographical sketches mention that she met Clifford in St. Louis and that they married; she neglected to give the date and place, however. During an investigation of a pension claim in the 1890s, Josephine first maintained she could not remember the date or place; later, she vaguely stated that she married Clifford in Brooklyn, New York, sometime during the 1860s. An investigator for the Pension Office, however, examined her divorce petition, made in 1868, and discovered that at that time Josephine gave the date and place of marriage as November 26, 1864, in Baltimore. Her mother, who appeared as a witness in the divorce proceedings, gave the same place and date and added that she witnessed the ceremony. The materials relating to the divorce, granted in the fifteenth Judicial District in San Francisco, California, perished in the great fire and earthquake of 1906. See James A. Clifford, Pension Application Files, Record Group (RG) 15, National Archives (NA), Washington, D.C. Other evidence, however, suggests that the marriage probably took place earlier. Josephine's article "Something About My Pets" in *Overland Monthly* 6 (January 1871): 58–67 (later included in *Overland Tales*) indicates that the couple was married for at least several months before they left St. Louis. Moreover, Josephine gave the date and place of her first marriage as November 1863 in Missouri on a card she filled out for the California State Library. See Josephine Clifford McCrackin, Bio-Card-File, California State Library, California Section, Sacramento, California; Court Martial File of James A. Clifford, RG 153, 00 2180, box 1398, NA; Josephine Clifford, "Down Among the Dead Letters," *Overland Monthly* 3 (December 1869): 517–522, reprinted in *Overland Tales;* and Pension Application Files, RG 15, NA.

9. Lane, *I Married a Soldier,* 131–132; Lane did not specifically mention Mrs. Clifford in her memoirs, but Josephine mentions Lane in her writings; see, for example, Clifford, "Marching with a Command," in *Overland Tales,* 327, 334.

10. Clifford, "Marching with a Command"; "Something About My Pets"; "Toby," 103–104.

11. See, for example, *Cavalry Wife,* 53, 64–65; Frances Roe, *Army Letters from an Officer's Wife* (1909; reprint, Lincoln: University of Nebraska Press, 1981), 45–50; Pension Application Files, RG 15, NA.

12. Josephine Clifford to General W. S. Hancock, March 2, 1867, Letters Received by Headquarters, District of New Mexico, September 1865 to August 1890, NA M–1088, reel 6.

13. McCrackin, "Crossing the Rio Grande," in *"Another Juanita,"* 68.

14. Clifford, "Marching with a Command," 345.

15. Clifford, "Marching with a Command," 349–351.

16. Clifford, "An Officer's Wife in New Mexico," *Overland Monthly* 4 (February 1870): 152–154, also included in *Overland Tales.*

17. McCrackin, "Crossing the Rio Grande," 66, and "Toby," 103–107.

18. McCrackin, "Toby," 106.

19. McCrackin, "Toby," 105. A sociologist who has studied abused wives maintains that "the fewer resources a wife has and the less power she has, the more likely she is to stay with her violent husband." He also notes that "external constraint" (that is, social pressures and role expectations) "influences the actions of abused wives." See Richard J. Gelles, "Abused Wives: Why Do They Stay," *Journal of Marriage and the Family* 38 (November 1976): 659–668. Another scholar emphasizes the important role that fear plays in causing wives to

remain with abusive husbands, calling it "the most understandable explanation, and paradoxically the one most commonly disregarded." For the victims, she adds, "fear immobilizes them, ruling their actions, their decisions, their very lives." Del Martin, *Battered Wives* (San Francisco: Glide Publications, 1976), 75–76. Also see Leonore E. Walker, *The Battered Woman* (New York: Harper & Row, 1979).

20. Lieutenant James Clifford to Lieutenant Colonel Alexander Duncan, January 9, 1867, NA M–1088, reel 5. McCrackin, "Toby," 111.

21. For discussions of the behavior of wife-beaters, see Martin, *Battered Wives,* and Walker, *The Battered Woman.* Not infrequently alcohol plays a major role in abuse situations. Moreover, alcohol addiction and paranoia (symptoms of which Clifford frequently exhibited) are not mutually exclusive; thus, a person may be insane, alcoholic, and abusive. While it would be difficult to formulate an exact diagnosis of Clifford's mental illness, his history and symptoms suggest that he may have suffered from a personality disorder rather than a psychosis; as a psychopath, he could have suffered from periods of paranoia, particularly when under stress. My thanks to William E. Foote, clinical psychologist, for his insights and assistance in sorting out and understanding Clifford's behavior. McCrackin, "Toby," 111.

22. McCrackin, "Toby," 129–130; also see General James H. Carleton to Lieutenant Colonel Alexander Duncan, February 9, 1867, NA M–1088, reel 5.

23. McCrackin, "Flight: A Sequel to 'Toby,'" in *"Another Juanita",* 136–138.

24. General James H. Carleton to Brevet Major Joseph G. Tilford, February 17, 1867, NA M–1088, reel 4. Summarizing other research, Gelles states that "an official acceptance of violence between 'consenting' adults and the belief that violence is a private affair" is an attitude that "police, the courts and the citizenry" espouse. Gelles, "Abused Wives," 666. Moreover, as Martin notes, by the time authorities intervene, "the wife may be so terror-stricken — so threatened and intimidated by her husband — that she may . . . even turn the officers away." The authorities are glad to avoid involvement in such cases. Martin, *Battered Wives,* 76.

25. McCrackin, "Flight: A Sequel to 'Toby'," 138–140.

26. McCrackin, "Flight: A Sequel to 'Toby'," 143–146.

27. J. Tilford to commanding officer of Fort Selden, April 19, 1867, NA M–1088, reel 5.

28. McCrackin, "Flight: A Sequel to 'Toby'," 164–166; William I. Cain to Brevet Major DeForrest, April 16, 1867, NA M–1088, reel 5; unfortunately, Eveline Alexander's diary ends in January 1867, and any additional letters she may have written during this period have not yet come to light; see *Cavalry Wife,* and Sandra Myres to author, February 14, 1985. Also see Pension Application Files RG 15, NA.

29. Court-martial File of Clifford, RG 153, 00 2180, box 1398, NA, and Pension Application Files, RG 15, NA.

30. James Carleton to Nelson Davis, February 17, 1867, NA M–1088, reel 4.

31. Pension Application Files, RG 15, NA.

32. Ibid.; see also Heitman, *Historical Register,* vol. 1, 310. Family tradition and records indicate that Margaret had nine children to Clifford; interview with Jeanne McIntosh (James and Margaret Clifford's great-grandaughter), August 1986.

33. Pension Application Files, RG 15, NA. A copy of Clifford's letter of February 1866 to Margaret is included in the pension file.

34. Court-martial File, RG 153, 00 2180, box 1398, NA; army doctors who examined Clifford apparently determined his mental status by their observations and experiences with him. That he was able to manipulate their impressions to his own advantage (as records suggest) strengthens the suspicion that Clifford was indeed a psychopathic personality. Under stress, he also exhibited symptoms of paranoia. While Clifford probably suffered from a personality disorder rather than a psychosis, his associates in the frontier army of the nineteenth century could not have made such a distinction at that time; such aberrant behavior fell under a more general category of "insane." Interview with William E. Foote, clinical psychologist.

35. Court Martial File, RG 153, 00 2180, box 1398, NA; Pension Application Files, RG 15, NA.

36. Pension Application Files, RG 15, NA; Donald S. Dreesen, "Founders of Albuquerque: Families Living in Bernalillo County and the Rio Abajo During the 17th and 18th Centuries," (manuscript, University of New Mexico Library, Special Collections Department).

37. Pension Application Files, RG 15, NA. *Who's Who in America, 1910–1911,* vol. 6 (Chicago: A. N. Marquis & Co., 1910), 1215. Also see George Wharton James, "The Romantic History of a Remarkable Woman — Josephine C. McCrackin," *National Magazine* 35 (March 1912): 795–800 (later republished in James's magazine, *Out West,* in 1913, and as a preface to a collection of McCrackin's works he published in 1913 as *"The Woman Who Lost Him" and Tales of the Army Frontier*).

38. McCrackin, "Reminiscences of Bret Harte," 12; see also Ella Sterling Cummins Mighels, *The Story of the Files: A Review of Californian Writers and Literature* (San Francisco: Cooperative Printing Co., 1893).

39. Josephine DeWitt Rhodehamel and Raymund Francis Wood, *Ina Coolbrith: Librarian and Laureate of California* (Provo, Utah: Brigham Young University Press, 1973), 97–98, 331–332; McCrackin, "Ina Coolbrith Invested with Poet's Crown," 448–450. See also Robert L. Griswold, *Family and Divorce in California, 1850–1890: Victorian Illusions and Everyday Realities* (Albany: State University of New York Press, 1982), 1, 79.

40. Josephine stated in her deposition, made in 1896, for Margaret's pension claim, that she had learned about Clifford's death from Anton Roman some fifteen or sixteen years previously. Mrs. McCrackin gave her religion as Roman Catholic in her entry in *Who's Who.* In several of her short stories, women who are divorced nonetheless wait to remarry until they are assured of their former husbands' death; see, for example, "Her Red Hair," in *"The Woman Who Lost Him,"* 47–121, and "La Graciosa," in *Overland Tales,* 13–50. See also James, "Romantic History," 795–800.

41. That Josephine wrote these stories about the time she learned of Clifford's death seems likely because she commented "the iron horse now goes snorting and shrieking by a strip of fair country which in those days lay . . . entirely outside the reach of civilization" ("Toby," 103). The Santa Fe and Southern Pacific met at Deming, New Mexico, in 1881, and reached Silver City in 1882. David F. Myrick, *New Mexico's Railroads: An Historical Survey* (Golden, Colo.: Colorado Railroad Museum, 1970), 148. Moreover, she probably hesitated to publish these stories about her life with Clifford while he was still alive because she feared that he might locate her. She apparently knew of Clifford's death by the time the stories appeared in *Californian* in 1881. See note 40, above, and her handwritten list of her publications in Josephine Clifford

McCrackin papers, California State Library, California Section. James, "Romantic History," 779; "In the Realm of Bookland," *Overland Monthly* n.s. 63 (February 1914): 207; Bertha Snow Adams, "A Seventy-six-year-old Woman Reporter," *American Magazine* 79 (June 1915): 51.

42. "La Graciosa," "The Gentleman from Siskiyou," "Manuela," "Her Name was Sylvia," "Juanita," and "A Lady in Camp" appear in *Overland Tales;* "Another Juanita" and "That Ranch of His" are included in *"Another Juanita"*; "Her Red Hair," "Penitencia," and "Desdemona" are in *"The Woman Who Lost Him"*; "An Episode of Fort Desolation" appears in *"Another Juanita"* under that title and also in *Overland Tales* as "A Woman's Treachery."

43. James, "Romantic History," 800–801.

44. James, "Romantic History," 802; Josephine C. McCrackin to Ina Coolbrith, August 11, 1917, Henry E. Huntington Library, San Marino, Calif., quoted in Rhodehamel and Wood, *Ina Coolbrith*, 332–333; *Santa Cruz Sentinel*, December 22, 1920.

45. Merrit Cross, "Josephine Woempner Clifford McCrackin," in *Notable American Women, 1607–1950: A Biographical Dictionary*, ed. Edward T. James, 4 vols. (Cambridge: Belknap Press of Harvard University Press, 1971), 2: 455; Beverly Seaton, "Josephine Woempner Clifford McCrackin," in *American Women Writers: A Critical Reference Guide from Colonial Times to the Present*, ed. Lina Mainiero, 4 vols. (New York: Frederick Ungar, 1981), 3: 76.

46. McCrackin to James D. Phelan, July 19, 1914, James Duval Phelan Correspondence, C-B-800, Bancroft Library; Carmony quoted in Mighels, *The Story of the Files*, 145; Mighels, *The Story of the Files*, 159; Hubert Howe Bancroft, *The Works of Hubert Howe Bancroft*, vol. 38, *The Essays and Miscellany* (San Francisco: History Co., 1890), 632.

47. James, "Romantic History."

Chapter Five

1. An earlier version of this chapter appeared as Cheryl J. Foote, "Alice Blake of Trementina: Mission Teacher of the Southwest," *Journal of Presbyterian History* 60 (Fall 1982): 228–242. For a discussion of "home" mission activity (so-called to distinguish it from foreign missions) in the West, see Colin B. Goodykoontz, *Home Missions on the American Frontier* (1939; reprint, New York: Octagon Books, 1971); T. Scott Miyakawa, *Protestants and Pioneers: Individualism and Conformity on the American Frontier* (Chicago: University of Chicago Press, 1964); Robert F. Berkhofer, Jr., *Salvation and the Savage: An Analysis of Protestant Missions and American Indian Response, 1787–1862* (1965; reprint, New York: Atheneum, 1972); and Gary Topping, "Religion in the West," *Journal of American Culture* 3 (Summer 1980): 330–350. The present study focuses upon Presbyterian work in New Mexico, in part because many Presbyterian records are available at Menaul School in Albuquerque and partially because Presbyterian efforts in the Southwest have been the subject of more studies than other denominations. See, for example, R. Douglas Brackenridge and Francisco O. Garcia-Treto, *Iglesia Presbiteriana: A History of Presbyterians and Mexican-Americans in the Southwest* (San Antonio, Tex.: Trinity University Press, 1974), and Ruth K. Barber and Edith J. Agnew, *Sowers Went Forth: The Story of Presbyterian Missions in New Mexico and Southern Colorado* (Albuquerque, N. Mex.: Menaul Historical Library of the Southwest, 1981).

2. Barber and Agnew, *Sowers Went Forth*, 12. Sandra Myres, ed., *Cavalry Wife: The Diary of Eveline M. Alexander, 1866–1867* (College Station: Texas A & M University Press, 1977), includes a brief biography of Mrs. Alexander. The teacher this association funded was Charity Ann Gaston, who later married John Menaul; her career as missionary wife is discussed in Chapter One.

3. A thorough discussion of the formation of the Woman's Board of Home Missions — and opposition to it from Presbyterian women who feared such an organization would harm women's support of foreign missions — appears in Lois A. Boyd and R. Douglas Brackenridge, *Presbyterian Women in America: Two Centuries of a Quest for Status* (Westport, Conn.: Greenwood Press, 1983), 15–34. Elizabeth Howell Verdesi, *In But Still Out: Women in the Church* (Philadelphia: Westminster Press, 1975), 51–58.

4. Ann Douglas, *The Feminization of American Culture* (1977; reprint, New York: Avon, 1978); Boyd and Brackenridge, *Presbyterian Women*, 159–173; Barbara Welter, "'She Hath Done What She Could': Protestant Women's Missionary Careers in Nineteenth-Century America," in *Women in American Religion*, ed. Janet Wilson James (Philadelphia: University of Pennsylvania Press, 1980), 110–125; Rosemary Skinner Keller, "Lay Women in the Protestant Tradition," in *Women and Religion in America, vol. 1: The Nineteenth Century*, ed. Rosemary Radford Ruether and Rosemary Skinner Keller (San Francisco: Harper & Row, 1981), 242–253. As Boyd and Brackenridge note, some unmarried women had entered the mission field as early as 1840; for example, one woman came to New Mexico as an assistant to Samuel and Catherine Gorman, Baptist missionaries to New Mexico in the 1850s. Boyd and Brackenridge, *Presbyterian Women*, 164.

5. Boyd and Brackenridge, *Presbyterian Women*, 168.

6. Welter, "'She Hath Done What She Could,'" argues that women's involvement in missionary work expanded as the significance of the endeavor itself was declining. Thus, she suggests, the expansion in women's roles did not indicate a rise in women's status. Boyd and Brackenridge, *Presbyterian Women*, and Keller, "Lay Women in the Protestant Tradition," maintain, however, that as women participated in new ways and greater numbers in church work, they also began to seek power within the church hierarchy. All agree that individual women found personal satisfaction and self-fulfillment from their involvement in expanded female roles.

7. Barber and Agnew, *Sowers Went Forth*, 159–160; Edith Agnew and Ruth Barber, "The Unique Presbyterian School System of New Mexico," *Journal of Presbyterian History* 49 (Fall 1971): 197–221.

8. Berkhofer, *Salvation and the Savage*, 9.

9. Alice A. Blake, "A History of Presbyterian Missions in Northern New Mexico," typescript in Menaul Historical Library of the Southwest, Albuquerque, N. Mex., 216.

10. Blake, "Presbyterian Missions," 102.

11. Mrs. Roy Blake (wife of Alice Blake's nephew) to author, March 13, 1981; Executive Record Books, 1882–1898, Territorial Archives of New Mexico (TANM), State Records Center and Archives (SRCA), Santa Fe, New Mexico.

12. Blake, "Presbyterian Missions," 216.

13. Ibid., 220–221.

14. Ibid., 216.

15. See Michael C. Coleman, "Not Race, but Grace: Presbyterian Missionaries and American Indians, 1837–1893," *Journal of American History* 67 (June 1980):

41–60; Alice Blake, "Quarterly Report," *Home Mission Monthly* 4 (December 1889): 38.

16. Blake, "Presbyterian Missions," 216.
17. *El Abogado Cristiano,* October 1, 1895.
18. *Revista Católica,* March 14, 1897, and December 13, 1891.
19. Missionary reports with pictures of Penitente rites appear in many issues of *Home Mission Monthly.* See also Marta Weigle, *Brothers of Light, Brothers of Blood: The Penitentes of the Southwest* (Albuquerque: University of New Mexico Press, 1976).
20. U.S. Bureau of the Census, Population Schedules of the Twelfth Census, 1900: New Mexico: San Miguel county, National Archives (NA) T–623, reel 40; Blake, "Quarterly Report," (December 1889), 38; Blake, "Presbyterian Missions," 221; Alice Blake, "Quarterly Report," *Home Mission Monthly* 7 (November 1892): 161.
21. Blake, "Presbyterian Missions," 222–23; interview with Edith Agnew, March 14, 1981; Alice Blake, "Quarterly Report," *Home Mission Monthly* 9 (November 1894): 12; Boyd and Brackenridge, *Presbyterian Women,* 167–168, discuss problems missionary women faced when forced to reside with other women; *Annual Report of the Superintendent for Public Instruction, 1897,* 48, TANM, reel 72.
22. Blake, "Presbyterian Missions," 225–226; "Annual Reports of the Woman's Home Missionary Society of the First Presbyterian Church of Morristown, New Jersey, 1898–1899, 1899–1900, 1900–1901," furnished by Mrs. Max R. Spencer, Morristown, New Jersey; Alice Blake, "Quarterly Report," *Home Mission Monthly* 14 (May 1900): 146.
23. Alice Blake, "A Needed Lever — Christian Education," *Home Mission Monthly* 15 (November 1900): 11–12.
24. Blake, "Presbyterian Missions," 226; Robert W. Larson, "Statehood for New Mexico, 1888–1912," *New Mexico Historical Review* 37 (July 1962): 164.
25. Blake, "Presbyterian Missions," 227.
26. Interview with Edith Agnew; S. Omar Barker, "Trementina: Memories of a Mission Village," *Albuquerque Journal* (September 23, 1980).
27. Interview with Edith Agnew.
28. Ibid.; for descriptions of flooding of the Trementina Arroyo, see Alice Blake, "A Flooded Arroya," *Home Mission Monthly* 17 (November 1902): 5; and Blake, "Devastating Floods," *Home Mission Monthly* 19 (December 1904): 42. Mary Stright diary, December 3, 1882, Menaul Historical Library; Anna McKee letters, October 19, 1884, Colorado Historical Society, Denver, Colorado.
29. Alice Blake, "Two Communities in Contrast," *Home Mission Monthly* 23 (November 1903): 11; Herbert J. Hagerman, Letters Received January 1906–April 1906, Records of the Territorial Governors, 1846–1912, TANM, roll 156.
30. Barker, "Trementina," *La Aurora,* August 27, 1903.
31. Alice Blake, "A Remote Center of Civilization," *Home Mission Monthly* 25 (November 1910): 8; and Blake, "Advantages of Isolated Districts," *Home Mission Monthly* 24 (November 1909): 12.
32. Blake, "Advantages of Isolated Districts," 13; and Alice Blake, "Quarterly Report," *Home Mission Monthly* 6 (November 1891): 12.
33. Alice Blake, "Trementina's Scourge," *Home Mission Monthly* 18 (February 1904): 105–106; editorial, *Home Mission Monthly* 18 (September 1904): 259; "News Items," *La Aurora,* January 15, 1904.

34. *La Aurora,* September 15, 1904; April 15, 1905; August 15, 1913; "From North, East, South and West Our Workers Gather," *Home Mission Monthly* 38 (July 1914): 210–212.
35. Alice Blake, "Encouragements and Outlook among Mexicans in the United States," *Home Mission Monthly* 22 (November 1907): 3–5.
36. Interview with Edith Agnew; Alice Blake, "Trementina, New Mexico," *Home Mission Monthly* 26 (November 1911): 17.
37. U.S., Department of Labor, Children's Bureau Publication no. 38, *April and May Weighing and Measuring Test, Part I* (Washington, D.C.: Government Printing Office, 1918); Alice Blake, "After Eighteen Years," *Home Mission Monthly* 33 (May 1919): 165.
38. Blake, "After Eighteen Years," 165.
39. Alice Blake, "New Outlook on an Old Field," *Home Mission Monthly* 34 (May 1920): 165; interview with Edith Agnew.
40. Ruth Streeter, "A High Way," *Home Mission Monthly* 36 (May 1922): 159.
41. L. T. Brooks, "Touching the Problem at Several Points," *Home Mission Monthly* 35 (May 1921): 160.
42. Interview with Edith Agnew; Mrs. Roy Blake to author, March 13, 1981.
43. Interview with the Reverend Alfonso Esquibel, March 14, 1981; Mrs. Roy Blake to author, March 13, 1981.
44. Barker, "Trementina."
45. "Wearers of the Service Pin of the Woman's Board of Home Missions," *Home Mission Monthly* 35 (November 1921): 14.

Chapter Six
1. Neil M. Judd, *The Bureau of American Ethnology: A Partial History* (Norman: University of Oklahoma Press, 1967), 3–12; Curtis M. Hinsley, Jr., *Savages and Scientists: The Smithsonian Institution and the Development of American Anthropology, 1846–1910* (Washington, D.C.: Smithsonian Institution Press, 1981), 145–162, 192.
2. *First Annual Report of the Bureau of Ethnology to the Secretary of the Smithsonian Institution, 1879–'80* (Washington, D.C.: Government Printing Office, 1881), xxx. The word American was added to the Bureau's title in 1894. Hinsley, *Savages and Scientists,* 182, n.8.
3. Matilda Coxe Stevenson, "The Zuni Indians: Their Mythology, Esoteric Fraternities, and Ceremonies," in *Twenty-Third Annual Report of the Bureau of American Ethnology to the Secretary of the Smithsonian Institution, 1901–1902* (Washington, D.C.: Government Printing Office, 1904), 18.
4. For an excellent discussion of this subject, see Hinsley, *Savages and Scientists,* 145-89.
5. "James Stevenson," in *The Dictionary of American Biography,* ed. Dumas Malone, vol. 17 (New York: Charles Scribner's Sons, 1935), 631–632; Nancy O. Lurie, "Matilda Coxe Evans Stevenson," in *Notable American Women, 1607–1950: A Biographical Dictionary,* ed. Edward T. James. 4 vols. (Cambridge: Belknap Press of Harvard University Press, 1971), 3: 373–374; Joy McPherson, "Matilda Coxe-Stevenson Papers," (manuscript, National Anthropological Archives of the Smithsonian Institution [NAA], Washington, D.C.), 1.
6. Stevenson, "Zuni," *Twenty-Third Annual Report,* 17–18; *Third Annual Report of the Bureau of Ethnology to the Secretary of the Smithsonian Institution, 1881–'82* (Washington, D.C.: Government Printing Office, 1884), xx; *Fourth Annual Report of the Bureau of Ethnology to the Secretary of the Smithsonian*

Institution, 1882–'83 (Washington, D.C.: Government Printing Office, 1886), xxxiv; *Fifth Annual Report of the Bureau of Ethnology to the Secretary of the Smithsonian Institution, 1883–'84* (Washington, D.C.: Government Printing Office, 1887), xxiii. Josephine was Bandelier's first wife; of her, his biographers state "her true personality and the role she played always remain rather obscure. It is certain that she never shared the professional aspects of Bandelier's life as did Fanny, the second wife." Charles H. Lange and Carroll L. Riley, eds., *The Southwestern Journals of Adolph F. Bandelier, 1880–1882* (Albuquerque: University of New Mexico Press, and Santa Fe, N. Mex.: School of American Research, 1966), 65–66. Fanny, whom Bandelier married in 1893 after he left New Mexico, assisted him greatly in his work until his death in 1914. William E. Curtis, *Children of the Sun* (1883; reprint, New York: AMS Press, 1976), notes of Emily Cushing "she does not and cannot share his [her husband's] fascination for the work in which he is engaged," 41.

7.   Nancy O. Lurie, "Women in Early American Anthropology," in *Pioneers of American Anthropology: The Uses of Biography,* ed. June Helm [MacNeish] (Seattle: University of Washington Press, 1966), 58; *Fifth Annual Report,* xxiii, 533–555.

8.   *Fifth Annual Report,* l–li; Stevenson, "The Religious Life of the Zuni Child," in *Fifth Annual Report,* 542; "Stevenson," *Notable American Women,* 373.

9.   Joan Mark, *Four Anthropologists: An American Science in Its Early Years* (New York: Science History Publications, 1980), 67. *Organization and Historical Sketch of the Women's Anthropological Society of America* (Washington, D.C.: Women's Anthropological Society, 1889), 14, 16, 19, 20–21.

10.   *Seventh Annual Report of the Bureau of Ethnology to the Secretary of the Smithsonian, 1885–'86* (Washington, D.C.: Government Printing Office, 1891), xxi, xxiv, xxv. James Stevenson, "Ceremonial of Hasjelti Dailjis and Mythical Sand Painting of the Navajo," *Eighth Annual Report of the Bureau of Ethnology to the Secretary of the Smithsonian Institution, 1886–'87* (Washington, D.C.: Government Printing Office, 1891), 229.

11.   *Tenth Annual Report of the Bureau of Ethnology to the Secretary of the Smithsonian Institution, 1888–'89* (Washington, D.C.: Government Printing Office, 1893), xxv.

12.   *Eleventh Annual Report of the Bureau of Ethnology to the Secretary of the Smithsonian Institution, 1889–'90* (Washington, D.C.: Government Printing Office, 1894), xxx.

13.   Stevenson, "Zuni," *Twenty-Third Annual Report,* 406; Lurie, "Women in Early American Anthropology," 43–54; Hinsley, *Savages and Scientists,* 154.

14.   Hinsley, *Savages and Scientists,* 197; Lurie, "Women in Early American Anthropology," 55–64; Triloki Nath Pandey, "Anthropologists at Zuni," *Proceedings of the American Philosophical Society* 116 (August 15, 1972): 321–337; Jesse Green, ed., *Zuni: Selected Writings of Frank Hamilton Cushing* (Lincoln: University of Nebraska Press, 1979), 24–25, n. 4; Edmund Wilson, *Red, Black, Blond and Olive. Studies in Four Civilizations: Zuni, Haiti, Soviet Russia, Israel* (New York: Oxford University Press, 1956), 21. Mark, *Four Anthropologists,* 121; J. Walter Fewkes, "Oraibi in 1890," in "Contributions to Hopi History," *American Anthropologist* n.s. 24 (July–September 1922): 273; Lurie, "Women in Early American Anthropology," 233, n. 41; Peggy Golde, "Odyssey of Encounter," in *Women in the Field: Anthropological Experiences,* ed. Peggy Golde (Chicago: Aldine Publishing Company, 1970), 75; Leslie A. White, *The*

Pueblo of Sia, New Mexico, Bulletin of American Ethnology no. 184 (Washington, D.C.: Government Printing Office, 1962), 7.

15. Judd, *Bureau of American Ethnology,* 67; Pandey, "Anthropologists at Zuni," 326; Green, *Zuni,* 25, n. 4. *Historical Sketch of the Women's Anthropological Society,* 18; Stevenson, "Zuni," *Twenty-Third Annual Report,* 406.

16. Matilda wrote these comments on the back of a photograph of Cushing now in box no. 1, Hodge-Cushing Collection, Southwest Museum, Los Angeles, California, quoted in Green, *Zuni,* 24, n. 4. Most scholars who have studied Cushing concur that he was a genius; their evaluations of his contributions to ethnology, however, vary considerably. See, for example, Green, *Zuni,* 1–24; Mark, *Four Anthropologists,* 96–130; Wilson, *Red, Black, Blond and Olive,* 15–19; Pandey, "Anthropologists at Zuni," 322–326; Raymond Stewart Brandes, "Frank Hamilton Cushing: Pioneer Americanist" (Ph.D. diss., University of Arizona, 1965); and Hinsley, *Savages and Scientists,* 190–230. Stevenson to William Holmes, June 29, 1906, Bureau of American Ethnology, Letters Received from Matilda Coxe Stevenson (hereafter cited as BAE, LR MCS) 1906, folder 2, NAA. Stevenson, "Zuni," *Twenty-Third Annual Report,* 204; Norman Bender, *Missionaries, Outlaws, and Indians: Taylor F. Ealy at Lincoln and Zuni, 1878–1881* (Albuquerque: University of New Mexico Press, 1984), 123; Report of Zuni Inspection by Inspector Howard, July 1882, Reports of Inspections of the Field Jurisdiction of the Office of Indian Affairs, 1873–1900, National Archives (NA) M–1070, reel 41; Curtis, *Children of the Sun,* 17–18, 41–42.

17. John Gregory Bourke, "Diary" (manuscript copy, University of New Mexico Library, Special Collections) vol. 54, 2601; Hinsley, *Savages and Scientists,* 229, n. 111.

18. Bourke, "Diary," 54: 2600; Golde, *Women in the Field,* 9.

19. *Historical Sketch of the Women's Anthropological Society,* 16–17; "Washington's Women of Science," William H. Holmes collection, NAA, 3.

20. Stevenson, "Zuni," *Twenty-Third Annual Report,* 380; Helen Codere, "Field Work in Rwanda, 1959–1960," in *Women in the Field,* 152, and Ernestine Friedl, "Field Work in a Greek Village," *Women in the Field,* 208; Lurie, "Women in Early American Anthropology," 60–61; John Wesley Powell to T.E. [Matilda] Stevenson, March 15, 1890, BAE LR MCS, 1890, NAA.

21. Stevenson and White use the spelling "Sia" in their studies of this pueblo. Except in referring specifically to their works, I have chosen the spelling commonly used today, Zia. Stevenson, "The Sia," in *Eleventh Annual Report,* 15.

22. Stevenson to Powell, June 13, 1890, BAE LR MCS, NAA.

23. Stevenson, "Zuni," *Twenty-Third Annual Report,* 379–380; Curtis, *Children of the Sun,* 41; Reports of Inspections of the Field Jurisdiction of the Office of Indian Affairs, 1873–1900, Pueblo and Jicarilla Agency, "Report of Zuni Inspection by Inspector Howard, July 1882," and "Synopsis of Report of Inspector Pearsons, November 1885," NA, M–1070, reel 41.

24. Stevenson, "Zuni," *Twenty-Third Annual Report,* 310–313, 380, photograph, 373. Lurie, "Women in Early American Anthropology," 55, asserts that Matilda's choice of "a transvestite as her first pupil" demonstrates her "ability to rise objectively and matter of factly above her sheltered rearing," but Matilda clearly stated that when she selected We'wha she had no idea that We'wha was "a man wearing woman's dress." As she explained, "so carefully was his sex concealed that for years the writer [Stevenson] believed him to be a woman." Stevenson, "Zuni," *Twenty-Third Annual Report,* 310. In addition,

though Mrs. Stevenson relied heavily on We'wha as an informant, evidence suggests that Wilson ignored Mrs. Stevenson's other associations at Zuni when he stated that her "friendship with We'wha" represented "her single really close link" with the pueblo. Wilson, *Red, Black, Blond and Olive*, 21.

25. W. H. Holmes, "In Memoriam: Matilda Coxe Stevenson," *American Anthropologist* n.s. 18 (October–December 1916): 559; *Fifteenth Annual Report of the Bureau of Ethnology to the Secretary of the Smithsonian Institution, 1893–'94* (Washington, D.C.: Government Printing Office, 1897), xxvii, xxx, xxxiv, liii, lvi, lvii, lxi, lxiv; *Sixteenth Annual Report of the Bureau of American Ethnology to the Secretary of the Smithsonian Institution, 1894–'95* (Washington, D.C.: Government Printing Office, 1897), xx, xxiv, xxvii, xxxii, xxxvii, xxxix, xli, xliv, xlix, lii, lvi; *Seventeenth Annual Report of the Bureau of American Ethnology to the Secretary of the Smithsonian Institution, 1895–'96* (Washington, D.C.: Government Printing Office, 1898), liv; *Eighteenth Annual Report of the Bureau of American Ethnology to the Secretary of the Smithsonian Institution, 1896–'97* (Washington, D.C.: Government Printing Office, 1899), xxvii; Stevenson, "Zuni," *Twenty-Third Annual Report*, 381, 312.

26. Stevenson, "Zuni," *Twenty-Third Annual Report*, 392, 312; Ealy's report is quoted in Marc Simmons, *Witchcraft in the Southwest: Spanish and Indian Supernaturalism on the Rio Grande* (Flagstaff, Ariz.: Northland Press, 1974), 125.

27. Simmons, *Witchcraft*, 112–114.

28. Stevenson, "Zuni," *Twenty-Third Annual Report*, 396–397; in writing about her field experiences, Stevenson never used the first person pronoun "I," but always "she."

29. Stevenson, "Zuni," *Twenty-Third Annual Report*, 398–406; Simmons, *Witchcraft*, 119.

30. Stevenson to L. Bradford Prince, December 28, 1892, Records of the Territorial Governors, 1846–1912, L. Bradford Prince, 1889–1893, Letters Received, Territorial Archives of New Mexico (TANM), reel 112, frames 1376–1381; and Stevenson to Prince, January 10, 1893, reel 113, frames 126–131.

31. Simmons, *Witchcraft*, 120–121; Stevenson, "Zuni," *Twenty-Third Annual Report*, 406; George Wharton James, *New Mexico: The Land of the Delight Makers* (Boston: The Page Co., 1920), 91–92; C. Gregory Crampton, *The Zunis of Cibola* (Salt Lake City: University of Utah Press, 1977), 150; Francis E. Leupp, *Notes of a Summer Tour Among the Indians of the Southwest* (Philadelphia: Office of the Indian Rights Association, 1897), 14. The possibility exists, however, that the Zunis merely exercised greater care to carry out trials and executions in secrecy.

32. Lurie, "Women in Early American Anthropology," attributes one of Powell's strokes to a confrontation with Matilda (234, n. 53). Hinsley, *Savages and Scientists*, 247–249. Powell to Stevenson, June 20, 1901, cited in Powell to Henry Teller, January 21, 1902, BAE LR MCS, 1902, NAA.

33. W. J. McGee to Stevenson, June 5, 1901; Stevenson to Powell, July 31, 1901; R. Rathbun to Powell, July 24, 1901; Stevenson to Powell, January 9, 1902; Stevenson to Powell, January 13, 1902; Powell to Teller, January 21, 1902; Powell to Stevenson, January 25, 1902; S. R. Langley to Powell, March 6, 1902; McGee to Langley, March 13, 1902; Stevenson to Powell, May 13, 1902, BAE LR MCS, 1902, NAA.

34. Stevenson, "Zuni," *Twenty-Third Annual Report*, 18; *Twenty-Fourth Annual Report of the Bureau of American Ethnology to the Secretary of the Smithsonian*

Institution, 1902–1903 (Washington, D.C.: Government Printing Office, 1907), xiv; Stevenson to Powell, August 30, 1902, BAE LR MCS, 1902, NAA; in the same collection, see also Stevenson's letters dated July 29–August 5, October 9, October 10, and November 7, 1902.

35. *Twenty-Fourth Annual Report,* xxvii; *Twenty-Fifth Annual Report of the Bureau of American Ethnology to the Secretary of the Smithsonian Institution, 1903–1904* (Washington, D.C.: Government Printing Office, 1907), xv–xxiv; *Twenty-Sixth Annual Report of the Bureau of American Ethnology to the Secretary of the Smithsonian Institution, 1904–1905* (Washington, D.C.: Government Printing Office, 1908), xvii–xviii; the Zuni exhibit was to include a party from Zuni, which Stevenson organized, but the appearance was canceled because, in Matilda's words, "at the last moment I received a request to reduce my estimate for the expense in bringing the Indians, which I refused to do. And so the Zuni with their weird rites were omitted from the department of anthropology at the Exposition." Stevenson to Charles Fuergerson, November 18, 1905, MCS Collection, NAA.

36. "Will Live with Indian Friends," *Santa Fe New Mexican,* February 8, 1906 (reference courtesy of Hana Samek); Stevenson to Holmes, March 15, March 18, and March 21, 1906, BAE LR MCS, 1906, folder 1, NAA; Stevenson to Holmes, April 7, April 18, May 7, May 21, May 29, June 12, and June 15, 1906, BAE LR MCS, 1906, folder 2, NAA.

37. Stevenson to Mr. Clayton, August 15, 1906, BAE LR MCS, 1906, folder 2, NAA.

38. Stevenson to Holmes, October 6, 1906, BAE LR MCS, 1906, folder 2, NAA.

39. Report of H. S. Traylor to Cato Sells, April 29, 1916, Bureau of Indian Affairs (BIA), Record Group (RG) 75, Central Classified Files 1907–1939, Pueblo Day Schools, 125049-15-154, NA, Washington, D.C.; B.C. Terry to Clara True, July 10, 1913, in Report of Supervisor A. K. Kneale and Recommendations of E. B. Linnen re. Coggeshall-Wilson-Tucker Affair, February 24, 1914, BIA RG 75 Central Classified Files 1907–1939, Santa Fe SF 671-14-154, NA; C. J. Crandall to the Commissioner of Indian Affairs, November 9, 1907, Archives of the Indian Pueblo Cultural Center, Albuquerque (reference courtesy of Hana Samek).

40. Folder 11, MCS Collection, NAA, contains Mrs. Stevenson's correspondence with her attorney, A. B. Renehan, about the lawsuit; deeds, title searches, and related materials can be located in the Renehan-Gilbert papers, State Records Center and Archives, Santa Fe, N. Mex.; Stevenson to Charles Walcott, June 10, 1910, MCS, folder 3, Walcott-Stevenson Correspondence, 1907–1909 [sic], NAA. Also numerous items are in BAE LR MCS, 1908, NAA, including letters from Stevenson to Holmes and copies of letters written by Clara and Frances True and sent to Stevenson and her attorney, Renehan.

41. Stevenson, "Ethnobotany of the Zuni Indians," *Thirtieth Annual Report of the Bureau of American Ethnology to the Secretary of the Smithsonian Institution, 1908–1909* (Washington, D.C.: Government Printing Office, 1915). Stevenson to Walcott, November 17, 1908, BAE LR MCS, 1908, NAA; a copy of this letter also appears in MCS Collection, folder 3, Walcott-Stevenson Correspondence, NAA. Lurie mentions Matilda's alcoholism in "Women in Early American Anthropology," based on personal reminiscences. Matilda, however, vehemently denied charges that she drank; see Stevenson to George Wharton James, October 14, 1914, PE 211, Bancroft Library, University of California, Berkeley.

42. Hodge to Stevenson, June 2, 1911, BAE LR MCS, 1911, NAA; Stevenson, "Strange Rites of the Tewa Indians," *Smithsonian Miscellaneous Collections* 63 (1913): 73–80; Stevenson, "The Sun and the Ice People Among the Tewa Indians of New Mexico," *Smithsonian Miscellaneous Collections* 65 (1914): 73–78.

43. Stevenson, "Strange Rites," 80; Cleofas Jaramillo, *Shadows of the Past* (1941; reprint, Santa Fe, N. Mex.: Ancient City Press, 1980), 19; Simmons, *Witchcraft*, 127–134; Bourke diary, 55: 2654–2655.

44. Stevenson to Hodge, February 3, 1914, Hodge-Stevenson Correspondence, MCS Collection, NAA; Stevenson to Hodge, January 1, 1915, Stevenson to Hodge, January 12, 1915, Hodge to Stevenson, January 27, 1915, Hodge to Stevenson, April 19, 1915, Stevenson to Hodge, April 22, 1915, Hodge to Stevenson, April 24, 1915, BAE LR MCS, 1914, 1915, NAA.

45. See civil case #8067 and civil case #8003, First Judicial District, Santa Fe County District Court Records, Judicial Complex, Santa Fe, N. Mex.; Stevenson to James, October 14, 1914, PE 211, Bancroft Library, University of California, Berkeley. Stevenson to Hodge, June 21, 1913, Hodge-Stevenson correspondence, MCS, NAA, Hodge to Renehan, June 3, 1914, BAE LR MCS, 1914, NAA.

46. Hodge to Renehan, June 3, 1914, BAE LR MCS, 1914, NAA; Renehan to Hodge, April 15, 1915, LR BAE MCS, 1915, NAA.

47. Stevenson to Hodge, April 2, 1915, LR BAE MCS, 1915, NAA; Herman Gasch to Walcott, June 24, 1915, LR BAE MCS, 1915, NAA. Other anthropologists have been reluctant to address Stevenson's controversial assertions; Ruth Bunzel, for example, commented that Stevenson "published some rather startling but inconclusive papers" about the ceremonies of the eastern pueblos. Margaret Mead and Ruth L. Bunzel, eds., *The Golden Age of American Anthropology* (New York: George Braziller, 1960), 206.

48. Pandey, "Anthropologists at Zuni," 326, and Lurie, "Women in Early American Anthropology,". 55, suggest that animosity toward anthropologists originated with Matilda; interestingly, however, a number of anthropologists have continued to study at Zuni, which suggests that they are still able to secure information and that they are willing, as was Matilda, to persist in their endeavors despite opposition. All make the judgment, it would seem, that their need to study native peoples is more important than the native peoples' need to avoid such scrutiny. Hinsley, *Savages and Scientists*, 193; White, "Sia," 4.

49. Stevenson's works remain standard references; see, for example, William Sturtevant, ed. *Handbook of North American Indians, vol. 9, Southwest*, ed. Alfonso Ortiz (Washington, D.C.: Smithsonian Institution, 1979), 669. Hodge to Stevenson, June 2, 1911, BAE LR MCS, 1911, NAA; Lurie, "Women in Early American Anthropology," 73; Pandey, "Anthropologists at Zuni," 329.

Conclusion

1. Susan Magoffin, *Down the Santa Fe Trail and into Mexico,* ed. Stella M. Drumm (1926; reprint, New Haven and London: Yale University Press, 1962), 28.

2. Marian Russell, *Land of Enchantment* (1954; reprint, Albuquerque: University of New Mexico Press, 1981), 1.

Reference List

Manuscript and Archival Materials

Archives of the Indian Pueblo Cultural Center, Albuquerque

C. J. Crandall to the Commissioner of Indian Affairs, November 9, 1907.

Bancroft Library, University of California at Berkeley

Jacquelyn Marie. "Josephine Clifford McCrackin: Battered Wife and Writer." American Literary Miscellany #71, 12/1912.

James Duval Phelan Correspondence, C-B-800.

Matilda Coxe Stevenson Correspondence, PE 211.

California State Library, California Section, Sacramento

Bio-Card-File, Josephine Clifford McCrackin.

Josephine Clifford McCrackin papers.

Colorado Historical Society, Denver

Anna McKee letters.

Fort Union National Monument, New Mexico

Ellen Dixon Wilson. "My Aunt's Reminiscences."

Menaul Historical Library of the Southwest, Albuquerque

Alice A. Blake. "A History of Presbyterian Missions in Northern New Mexico."

Mary Maude Roberts Mercereau. "Story of the Life of Some Home Missionaries in the Early Days." James M. Roberts file.

Shields family genealogy. Jemez Springs, New Mexico file.

Mary Stright diary.

National Anthropological Archives of the Smithsonian Institution, Washington, D.C.

Bureau of American Ethnology. Letters Received from Matilda Coxe Stevenson.

"Washington's Women of Science." William H. Holmes Collection.

Joy McPherson. "Matilda Coxe-Stevenson Papers."

Matilda Coxe Stevenson Papers.

National Archives, Washington, D.C.

U.S. Bureau of the Census. Population Schedules of the Seventh Census of the United States, 1850. New Mexico: Santa Ana, Santa Fe, and Valencia counties, M–432, reel 468.

U.S. Bureau of the Census. Population Schedules of the Eighth Census of the United States, 1860. New Mexico: Santa Fe and Socorro counties, M–653, reel 714.

U.S. Bureau of the Census. Population Schedules of the Ninth Census of the United States, 1870. Iowa: Wayne and Webster counties, M–593, reel 425.

U.S. Bureau of the Census. Population Schedules of the Twelfth Census, 1900. New Mexico: San Miguel county, T–623, reel 40.

Regimental Descriptive Book. Second Colorado Infantry and Cavalry, 52. Office of the Adjutant General. Volunteer Organizations, Civil War, Colorado. Record Group 94.

Records of the Office of the Judge Advocate General (Army). Court Martial File of James A. Clifford. Record Group 153.

Letters Received by Headquarters, District of New Mexico, September 1865 to August 1890. M–1088, reel 6, Record Group 393.

Reports of Inspections of the Field Jurisdictions of the Office of Indian Affairs, 1873–1900. M–1070, reel 41, Record Groups 48 and 75.

Bureau of Indian Affairs Central Classified Files, 1907–1939. Pueblo Day Schools. Record Group 75.

Bureau of Indian Affairs Central Classified Files, 1907–1939. Santa Fe. Record Group 75.

New Mexico First Judicial District, Judicial Complex, Santa Fe

Santa Fe County District Court Records. Civil Cases #8003 and #8067.

New Mexico Highlands University Library, Las Vegas

Catherine Bowen letters, Arrott Collection.

New Mexico State Records Center and Archives, Santa Fe

Renehan-Gilbert Collection.

Harriett Shaw letters, Dorothy Woodward Collection.

Territorial Archives of New Mexico. Microfilm.

Presbyterian Historical Society, Philadelphia

American Indian Correspondence: The Presbyterian Historical Society Collection of Missionaries' Letters, 1833–1893. Microfilm.

Sheldon Jackson Correspondence. Microfilm.

United States Army Military History Institute, Carlisle Barracks, Pennsylvania

Ione Bradley. "Recollections of Army Life." Luther Bradley Papers.

University of New Mexico Library, Special Collections, Albuquerque

John Gregory Bourke Diary. Photostatic copy of original at West Point, N.Y.

Donald S. Dreesen. "Founders of Albuquerque: Families Living in Bernalillo County and the Rio Abajo During the 17th and 18th Centuries."

Mrs. Horatio Oliver Ladd. "History of the University of New Mexico for Our Children." Ladd Collection.

University of Virginia Library, Charlottesville

Anna Maria Morris diary. Morris Collection. Microfilm.

In possession of the author

"Annual Reports of the Woman's Home Missionary Society of the First Presbyterian Church of Morristown, New Jersey, 1898–1899, 1899–1900, 1900–1901." Furnished by Mrs. Max R. Spencer, Morristown, N.J.

Government Publications

Bureau of Ethnology (Bureau of American Ethnology)

First Annual Report of the Bureau of Ethnology to the Secretary of the Smithsonian Institution 1879–'80. Washington, D.C.: Government Printing Office, 1881.

Third Annual Report of the Bureau of Ethnology to the Secretary of the Smithsonian Institution 1881–'82. Washington, D.C.: Government Printing Office, 1884.

Fourth Annual Report of the Bureau of Ethnology to the Secretary of the Smithsonian Institution 1882–'83. Washington, D.C.: Government Printing Office, 1886.

Fifth Annual Report of the Bureau of Ethnology to the Secretary of the Smithsonian Institution 1883–'84. Washington, D.C.: Government Printing Office, 1887.

Seventh Annual Report of the Bureau of Ethnology to the Secretary of the Smithsonian Institution 1885–'86. Washington, D.C.: Government Printing Office, 1891.

Eighth Annual Report of the Bureau of Ethnology to the Secretary of the Smithsonian Institution 1886–'87 Washington D.C.: Government Printing Office, 1891.

Tenth Annual Report of the Bureau of Ethnology to the Secretary of the Smithsonian Institution 1888–'89. Washington, D.C.: Government Printing Office, 1893.

Eleventh Annual Report of the Bureau of Ethnology to the Secretary of the Smithsonian Institution 1889–'90. Washington, D.C.: Government Printing Office, 1894.

Fifteenth Annual Report of the Bureau of Ethnology to the Secretary of the Smithsonian Institution 1893–'94. Washington, D.C.: Government Printing Office, 1897.

Sixteenth Annual Report of the Bureau of American Ethnology to the Secretary of the Smithsonian Institution 1894–'95. Washington, D.C.: Government Printing Office, 1897.

Seventeenth Annual Report of the Bureau of American Ethnology to the Secretary of the Smithsonian Institution 1895–96. Washington, D.C.: Government Printing Office, 1898.

Eighteenth Annual Report of the Bureau of American Ethnology to the Secretary of the Smithsonian Institution 1896–97. Washington, D.C.: Government Printing Office, 1899.

Twenty-Third Annual Report of the Bureau of American Ethnology to the Secretary of the Smithsonian Institution 1901–1902. Washington, D.C.: Government Printing Office, 1904.

Twenty-Fourth Annual Report of the Bureau of American Ethnology to the Secretary of the Smithsonian Institution 1902–1903. Washington, D.C.: Government Printing Office, 1907.

Twenty-Fifth Annual Report of the Bureau of American Ethnology to the Secretary of the Smithsonian Institution 1903–1904. Washington, D.C.: Government Printing Office, 1907.

Twenty-Sixth Annual Report of the Bureau of American Ethnology to the Secretary of the Smithsonian Institution 1904–1905. Washington, D.C.: Government Printing Office, 1908.

Thirtieth Annual Report of the Bureau of American Ethnology to the Secretary of the Smithsonian Institution 1908–1909. Washington, D.C.: Government Printing Office, 1908.

Books

Bancroft, Hubert Howe. *Essays and Miscellany.* San Francisco: History Co., 1890.

———. *History of Arizona and New Mexico, 1530–1888.* 1889. Reprint. Albuquerque, N. Mex.: Horn and Wallace, 1962.

Barber, Ruth K., and Edith J. Agnew. *Sowers Went Forth: The Story of Presbyterian Missions in New Mexico and Southern Colorado.* Albuquerque, N. Mex.: Menaul Historical Library of the Southwest, 1981.

Bender, Norman. *Missionaries, Outlaws, and Indians: Taylor F. Ealy at Lincoln and Zuni, 1878–1881.* Albuquerque: University of New Mexico Press, 1984.

Berkhofer, Robert F., Jr. *Salvation and the Savage: An Analysis of Protestant Missions and American Indian Response, 1787–1862.* 1965. Reprint. New York: Atheneum, 1972.

Billington, Ray A. *The Protestant Crusade, 1800–1860: A Study of the Origins of American Nativism.* 1938. Reprint. Chicago: Quadrangle Books, 1964.

Boyd, Lois A., and R. Douglas Brackenridge. *Presbyterian Women in America: Two Centuries of a Quest for Status.* Westport, Conn.: Greenwood Press, 1983.

Boyd, Mrs. Orsemus B. [Frances]. *Cavalry Life in Tent and Field.* 1894. Reprint with an introduction by Darlis Miller. Lincoln: University of Nebraska Press, 1982.

Brackenridge, R. Douglas, and Francisco O. Garcia-Treto. *Iglesia Presbiteriana: A History of Presbyterians and Mexican-Americans in the Southwest.* San Antonio, Tex.: Trinity University Press, 1974.

Brooks, Clinton E., and Frank D. Reeve, eds. *Forts and Forays, James A. Bennett: A Dragoon in New Mexico, 1850–1856.* Albuquerque: University of New Mexico Press, 1948.

Butler, Anne M. *Daughters of Joy, Sisters of Misery: Prostitutes in the American West, 1865–90*. Urbana: University of Illinois Press, 1985.

Carriker, Robert C., and Eleanor R. Carriker. *An Army Wife on the Frontier: The Memoirs of Alice Blackwood Baldwin, 1867–1877*. Salt Lake City: Tanner Trust Fund, University of Utah Library, 1975.

Clifford [McCrackin], Josephine. *"Another Juanita" and Other Stories*. Buffalo, N.Y.: Charles Wells Moulton, 1893.

Cott, Nancy F. *The Bonds of Womanhood: "Woman's Sphere" in New England, 1780–1835*. New Haven, Conn.: Yale University Press, 1977.

Crampton, C. Gregory. *The Zunis of Cibola*. Salt Lake City: University of Utah Press, 1977.

Curtis, William E. *Children of the Sun*. 1883. Reprint. New York: AMS Press, 1976.

Davis, W.W.H. *El Gringo, or New Mexico and Her People*. 1857. Reprint. Lincoln: University of Nebraska Press, 1982.

Douglas, Ann. *The Feminization of American Culture*. 1977. Reprint. New York: Avon, 1978.

Dozier, Edward. *The Pueblo Indians of North America*. New York: Holt, Rinehart, and Winston, 1970.

Dunlop, Richard. *Doctors of the American Frontier*. Garden City, N.Y.: Doubleday and Company, 1965.

Dyer, Mrs. D. B. *"Fort Reno"; or, Picturesque "Cheyenne and Arrapahoe Army Life," Before the Opening of Oklahoma*. New York: G. W. Dillingham, 1896.

Ellis, Anne. *The Life of an Ordinary Woman*. Lincoln: University of Nebraska Press, 1980.

———. *Plain Anne Ellis: More About the Life of an Ordinary Woman*. Lincoln: University of Nebraska Press, 1984.

———. *Sunshine Preferred*. Lincoln: University of Nebraska Press, 1984.

Emmett, Chris. *Fort Union and the Winning of the Southwest*. Norman: University of Oklahoma Press, 1965.

Faragher, John Mack. *Women and Men on the Overland Trail*. New Haven, Conn.: Yale University Press, 1979.

Frazer, Robert W. *Forts and Supplies: The Role of the Army in the Economy of the Southwest, 1846–1861*. Albuquerque: University of New Mexico Press, 1983.

Frost, H. Gordon. *The Gentlemen's Club: The Story of Prostitution in El Paso*. El Paso, Tex.: Mangan Books, 1983.

Goodykoontz, Colin B. *Home Missions on the American Frontier*. 1939. Reprint. New York: Octagon Books, 1971.

Green, Jesse, ed. *Zuni: Selected Writings of Frank Hamilton Cushing*. Lincoln: University of Nebraska Press, 1979.

Gregg, Josiah. *Commerce of the Prairies*. Edited by Max L. Moorhead. Norman: University of Oklahoma Press, 1954.

Griswold, Robert L. *Family and Divorce in California, 1850–1890: Victorian Illusions and Everyday Realities*. Albany: State University of New York Press, 1982.

Harwood, Thomas. *History of New Mexico Spanish and English Missions of the Methodist Episcopal Church from 1850 to 1910 in Decades*. 2 vols. Albuquerque, N. Mex.: El Abogado Press, 1908–1910.

Heitman, Francis B. *Historical Register and Dictionary of the United States Army from Its Organization, September 29, 1789, to March 2, 1903*. 2 vols. Washington, D.C.: Government Printing Office, 1903.

Heyman, Max L., Jr. *Prudent Soldier: A Biography of Major General E.R.S. Canby, 1817–1873*. Glendale, Calif.: Arthur H. Clark Co., 1959.

Hinsley, Curtis M., Jr. *Savages and Scientists: The Smithsonian Institution and the Development of American Anthropology, 1846–1910*. Washington, D.C.: Smithsonian Institution Press, 1981.

Hollister, Ovando. *History of the First Regiment of Colorado Volunteers*. Edited by Richard Harwell. Chicago: R. R. Donnelley & Sons, 1962.

Holmes, Kenneth, ed. *Covered Wagon Women: Diaries and Letters from the Western Trails, 1840–1890*. Vols. 1 and 2. Glendale, Calif.: Arthur H. Clark Co., 1983.

Ickis, Alonzo Ferdinand. *Bloody Trails Along the Rio Grande: A Day-by-Day Diary of Alonzo Ferdinand Ickis (1836–1917), A Soldier and His Activities with Company B. . . .* Denver: Old West Publishing Co., 1958.

James, George Wharton. *New Mexico: The Land of the Delight Makers*. Boston: Page Co., 1920.

Jaramillo, Cleofas. *Shadows of the Past*. 1941. Reprint. Santa Fe, N. Mex.: Ancient City Press, 1980.

Jeffrey, Julie Roy. *Frontier Women: The Trans-Mississippi West, 1840–1880*. New York: Hill and Wang, 1979.

Jensen, Joan M., and Darlis A. Miller. *New Mexico Women: Intercultural Perspectives.* Albuquerque: University of New Mexico Press, 1986.

Judd, Neil M. *The Bureau of American Ethnology: A Partial History.* Norman: University of Oklahoma Press, 1967.

Kellogg, Harriet S. *Life of Mrs. Emily J. Harwood.* Albuquerque, N. Mex.: El Abogado Press, 1903.

Kimball, Maria Brace. *My Eighty Years.* Boston: privately printed, 1934.

Lamar, Howard Roberts. *The Far Southwest, 1846–1912: A Territorial History.* New York: W. W. Norton, 1970.

Lane, Lydia Spencer. *I Married a Soldier, or Old Days in the Old Army.* 1893. Reprint. Albuquerque, N. Mex.: Horn and Wallace, 1964.

Lange, Charles H., and Carroll L. Riley, eds. *The Southwestern Journals of Adolph F. Bandelier, 1880–1882.* Albuquerque: University of New Mexico Press and Santa Fe, N. Mex.: School of American Research, 1966.

Leupp, Francis E. *Notes of a Summer Tour Among the Indians of the Southwest.* Philadelphia: Office of the Indian Rights Association, 1897.

Magoffin, Susan Shelby. *Down the Santa Fe Trail and into Mexico: The Diary of Susan Shelby Magoffin 1846–1847.* Edited by Stella M. Drumm, 1926. Reprint. New Haven, Conn.: Yale University Press, 1962.

Mark, Joan. *Four Anthropologists: An American Science in Its Early Years.* New York: Science History Publications, 1980.

Martin, Del. *Battered Wives.* San Francisco: Glide Publications, 1976.

McCrackin, Josephine Clifford. *Overland Tales.* Philadelphia: Claxton, Remsen & Haffelfinger, 1877.

———. *"The Woman Who Lost Him" and Tales of the Army Frontier.* Pasadena, Calif.: George Wharton James, 1913.

Mead, Margaret, and Ruth L. Bunzel, eds. *The Golden Age of American Anthropology.* New York: George Braziller, 1960.

Mighels, Ella Sterling Cummins. *The Story of the Files: A Review of Californian Writers and Literature.* San Francisco: Cooperative Printing Co., 1893.

Miyakawa, T. Scott. *Protestants and Pioneers: Individualism and Conformity on the American Frontier.* Chicago: University of Chicago Press, 1964.

Myers, Lewis A. *A History of New Mexico Baptists.* N.p., Baptist Convention of New Mexico, 1965.

Myres, Sandra. *Westering Women and the Frontier Experience, 1800–1915*. Albuquerque: University of New Mexico Press, 1982.

————, ed. *Cavalry Wife: The Diary of Eveline M. Alexander, 1866–1867*. College Station: Texas A & M University Press, 1977.

Myrick, David F. *New Mexico's Railroads: An Historical Survey*. Golden, Colo.: Colorado Railroad Museum, 1970.

Organization and Historical Sketch of the Women's Anthropological Society of America. Washington, D.C.: Women's Anthropological Society, 1889.

Report of the Commissioner of Indian Affairs to the Secretary of the Interior for the Year 1871. Washington, D.C.: Government Printing Office, 1872.

Rhodehamel, Josephine DeWitt, and Raymund Francis Wood. *Ina Coolbrith: Librarian and Laureate of California*. Provo, Utah: Brigham Young University Press, 1973.

Rickey, Don, Jr. *Forty Miles a Day on Beans and Hay; the Enlisted Soldier Fighting the Indian Wars*. Norman: University of Oklahoma Press, 1963.

Riley, Glenda. *Frontierswomen: The Iowa Experience*. Ames: Iowa State University Press, 1982.

————. *Women and Indians on the Frontier, 1825–1915*. Albuquerque: University of New Mexico Press, 1984.

Roe, Frances. *Army Letters from an Officer's Wife*. 1909. Reprint. Lincoln: University of Nebraska Press, 1981.

Russell, Marian. *Land of Enchantment*. 1954. Reprint. Albuquerque: University of New Mexico Press, 1981.

Scadron, Arlene, ed. *On Their Own: Widows and Widowhood in the American Southwest, 1848–1939*. Urbana: University of Illinois Press, 1988.

Schlissel, Lillian. *Women's Diaries of the Westward Journey*. New York: Schocken Books, 1982.

Simmons, Marc. *New Mexico: A Bicentennial History*. New York: W. W. Norton, 1977.

————. *Witchcraft in the Southwest: Spanish and Indian Supernaturalism on the Rio Grande*. Flagstaff, Ariz.: Northland Press, 1974.

Smith, Mrs. Lewis. *Sermons of Rev. Lewis Smith with a Biographical Sketch of the Author*. Auburn, N.Y.: Wm. J. Moses, 1867.

Spicer, Edward. *Cycles of Conquest: The Impact of Spain, Mexico, and the United States on the Indians of the Southwest, 1533–1960*. Tucson: University of Arizona Press, 1962.

Stallard, Patricia. *Glittering Misery: Dependents of the Indian Fighting Army.* San Rafael, Calif.: Presidio Press, and Fort Collins, Colo.: Old Army Press, 1978.

Stratton, David. *The First Century of Baptists in New Mexico, 1849–1950.* Albuquerque: Woman's Missionary Union of New Mexico, 1954.

Sturtevant, William, ed. *Handbook of North American Indians, Vol. 9, Southwest.* Edited by Alfonso Ortiz. Washington, D.C.: Smithsonian Institution, 1979.

Summerhayes, Martha. *Vanished Arizona: Recollections of the Army Life of a New England Woman.* 1911. Reprint. Lincoln: University of Nebraska Press, 1979.

U.S., Department of Labor, Children's Bureau Publication no. 38, *April and May Weighing and Measuring Test, Part I.* Washington, D.C.: Government Printing Office, 1918.

Verdesi, Elizabeth Howell. *In But Still Out: Women in the Church.* Philadelphia: Westminster Press, 1975.

Vielé, Teresa. *Following the Drum: A Glimpse of Frontier Life.* 1858. Reprint, edited by Sandra Myres. Lincoln: University of Nebraska Press, 1984.

Walker, Leonore E. *The Battered Woman.* New York: Harper & Row, 1979.

Wallace, Susan. *Land of the Pueblos.* Troy, N.Y.: Nims & Knight, 1889.

Weigle, Marta. *Brothers of Light, Brothers of Blood: The Penitentes of the Southwest.* Albuquerque: University of New Mexico Press, 1976.

White, Leslie A. *The Pueblo of Sia, New Mexico.* Bulletin of American Ethnology no. 184. Washington, D.C.: Government Printing Office, 1962.

Williams, Ellen. *Three Years and a Half in the Army, or History of the Second Colorados.* New York: Fowler and Wells Company, 1885.

Wilson, Edmund. *Red, Black, Blond and Olive. Studies in Four Civilizations: Zuni, Haiti, Soviet Russia, Israel.* New York: Oxford University Press, 1956.

Articles

Adams, Bertha Snow. "A Seventy-six-year-old Woman Reporter." *American Magazine* 79 (June 1915): 51.

Agnew, Edith, and Ruth Barber. "The Unique Presbyterian School System of New Mexico." *Journal of Presbyterian History* 49 (Fall 1971): 197–221.

Armitage, Susan. "Women and Men in Western History: A Stereoptical Vision." *Western Historical Quarterly* 16 (October 1985): 381–395.

Bieber, Ralph P., ed. "Letters of William Carr Lane, 1852–1854." *New Mexico Historical Review* 3 (April 1928): 194–196.

Bloom, John P. "New Mexico Viewed by Americans, 1846–1849." *New Mexico Historical Review* 34 (July 1959): 165–198.

Bradley, Frances Sage, and Margaretta A. Williamson. "Rural Children in Selected Counties of North Carolina." In *Child Care in Rural America*. New York: Arno Press, 1972.

Codere, Helen. "Field Work in Rwanda, 1959–1960." In *Women in the Field: Anthropological Experiences,* edited by Peggy Golde, 143–164. Chicago: Aldine Publishing Company, 1970.

Coleman, Michael C. "Not Race, but Grace: Presbyterian Missionaries and American Indians, 1837–1893." *Journal of American History* 67 (June 1980): 41–60.

Cross, Merrit. "Josephine Woempner Clifford McCrackin." In *Notable American Women, 1607–1950: A Biographical Dictionary,* edited by Edward T. James, vol. 2: 455–456. Cambridge: Belknap Press of Harvard University Press, 1971.

Danielson, Betty, and Dale Danielson. "New Mexico's First Protestant Preacher." *Albuquerque Journal Impact Magazine* (June 30, 1981).

Fewkes, J. Walter. "Oraibi in 1890." In "Contributions to Hopi History," *American Anthropologist* n.s. 24 (July–September 1922): 268–283.

Foote, Cheryl J. "Alice Blake of Trementina: Mission Teacher of the Southwest." *Journal of Presbyterian History* 60 (Fall 1982): 228–242.

———. "The History of Women in New Mexico: A Selective Guide to Published Sources." *New Mexico Historical Review* 57 (October 1982): 387–394.

Friedl, Ernestine. "Field Work in a Greek Village." In *Women in the Field: Anthropological Experiences,* edited by Peggy Golde, 195–217. Chicago: Aldine Publishing Company, 1970.

Gelles, Richard J. "Abused Wives: Why Do They Stay." *Journal of Marriage and the Family* 38 (November 1976): 659–668.

Golde, Peggy. "Odyssey of Encounter." In *Women in the Field: Anthropological Experiences,* edited by Peggy Golde, 67–93. Chicago: Aldine Publishing Company, 1970.

Goodfriend, Joyce D. "The Struggle for Survival: Widows in Denver, 1880–1912." In *On Their Own: Widows and Widowhood in the American Southwest, 1848–1939,* edited by Arlene Scadron, 166–194. Urbana: University of Illinois Press, 1988.

Gorman, Mrs. Samuel. "Reverend Samuel Gorman—Memorial." *Old Santa Fe* 1 (January 1914): 308–331.

Graulich, Melody. "Violence Against Women in Literature of the Western Family." *Frontiers* 7 (1984): 14–20.

Grimshaw, Patricia. "'Christian Woman, Pious Wife, Faithful Mother, Devoted Missionary': Conflicts in Roles of American Missionary Women in Nineteenth-Century Hawaii." *Feminist Studies* 9 (Fall 1983): 488–521.

Halcomb, Harvey. "Confederate Reminiscences," edited by Lansing Bloom. *New Mexico Historical Review* 5 (July 1930): 320.

Hamilton, Nancy. "The Great Western." In Western Writers of America, *The Women Who Made the West,* 186–197. New York: Doubleday and Company, 1980.

Holmes, W. H. "In Memoriam: Matilda Coxe Stevenson." *American Anthropologist* n.s. 18 (October–December 1916): 552–559.

Horner, Patricia V. "Mary Richardson Walker: The Shattered Dreams of a Missionary Woman." *Montana, the Magazine of Western History* 32 (Summer 1982): 20–31.

"In the Realm of Bookland." *Overland Monthly* n.s. 63 (February 1914): 207.

Ingalles, Joan. "Family Life on the Southwest Frontier." *Military History of Texas and the Southwest* 14 (1978): 203–213.

James, George Wharton. "The Romantic History of a Remarkable Woman—Josephine C. McCrackin." *National Magazine* 35 (March 1912): 795–800.

Jensen, Joan M., and Darlis A. Miller. "The Gentle Tamers Revisited: New Approaches to the History of Women in the American West." *Pacific Historical Review* 49 (May 1980): 173–214.

"Josephine Clifford McCrackin." In *Who's Who in America, 1910–1911.* Vol. 6. Chicago: A. N. Marquis & Co., 1910.

Keller, Rosemary Skinner. "Lay Women in the Protestant Tradition." In *Women and Religion in America, vol. 1, The Nineteenth Century,* edited by Rosemary Radford Ruether and Rosemary Skinner Keller, 242–253. San Francisco: Harper & Row, 1981.

La Tourrette, Genevieve. "Fort Union Memories." *New Mexico Historical Review* 26 (October 1951): 276–286.

Lacy, James M. "New Mexican Women in Early American Writings." *New Mexico Historical Review* 34 (January 1959): 41–51.

Larson, Robert W. "Statehood for New Mexico, 1888–1912." *New Mexico Historical Review* 37 (July 1962): 164.

Lurie, Nancy O. "Matilda Coxe Evans Stevenson." In *Notable American Women, 1607–1950: A Biographical Dictionary,* edited by Edward T. James, vol. 3: 373–374. Cambridge: Belknap Press of Harvard University Press, 1971.

———. "Women in Early American Anthropology." In *Pioneers of American Anthropology: The Uses of Biography,* edited by June Helm [MacNeish], 31–81. Seattle: University of Washington Press, 1966.

McCrackin, Josephine Clifford. "Ina Coolbrith Invested with Poet's Crown." *Overland Monthly* n.s. 66 (November 1915): 448–450.

———."Reminiscences of Bret Harte and Pioneer Days in the West." *Overland Monthly* n.s. 67 (January 1916): 7–15.

Meyer, Marian. "Mary Donoho: New First Lady on the Santa Fe Trail." *Wagon Tracks* 1 (August 1987): 1.

Miller, Darlis. "Cross-Cultural Marriages in the Southwest: The New Mexico Experience, 1846–1900." *New Mexico Historical Review* 57 (October 1982): 335–359.

———."Foragers, Army Women, and Prostitutes." In *New Mexico Women: Intercultural Perspectives,* edited by Joan M. Jensen and Darlis A. Miller, 141–168. Albuquerque: University of New Mexico Press, 1986.

Malone, Dumas, ed. "James Stevenson." In *The Dictionary of American Biography,* vol. 17: 631–632. New York: Charles Scribner's Sons, 1935.

Myres, Sandra L. "Romance and Reality on the American Frontier: Views of Army Wives." *Western Historical Quarterly* 13 (October 1982): 410–427.

———. "Women in the West." In *Historians and the American West,* edited by Michael P. Malone, 369–386. Lincoln: University of Nebraska Press, 1983.

———, comp. "Army Wives in the Trans-Mississippi West, A Bibliography." In Teresa Vielé, *Following the Drum: A Glimpse of Frontier Life.* 1858. Reprint, edited by Sandra Myres. Lincoln: University of Nebraska Press, 1984.

Pandey, Triloki Nath. "Anthropologists at Zuni." *Proceedings of the American Philosophical Society* 116 (August 15, 1972): 321–337.

Paredes, Raymund A. "The Mexican Image in American Travel Literature, 1831–1869." *New Mexico Historical Review* 52 (January 1977): 5–25.

Reeve, Frank D. "The Old University of New Mexico at Santa Fe." *New Mexico Historical Review* 8 (July 1933): 202–210.

Seaton, Beverly. "Josephine Woempner Clifford McCrackin." In *American Women Writers: A Critical Reference Guide from Colonial Times to the Present,* edited by Lina Mainiero, vol. 3: 75–77. New York: Frederick Ungar, 1981.

Shields, Alice Mathews. "Army Life on the Wyoming Frontier." *Annals of Wyoming* 13 (October 1941): 331–343.

Stevenson, James. "Ceremonial of Hasjelti Dailjis and Mythical Sand Painting of the Navajo." In *Eighth Annual Report of the Bureau of Ethnology to the Secretary of the Smithsonian Institution, 1886–'87.* Washington, D.C.: Government Printing Office, 1891.

Stevenson, Matilda Coxe. "Ethnobotany of the Zuni Indians." In *Thirtieth Annual Report of the Bureau of American Ethnology to the Secretary of the Smithsonian Institution, 1908–1909,* 31–102. Washington, D.C.: Government Printing Office, 1915.

———. "The Religious Life of the Zuni Child." In *Fifth Annual Report of the Bureau of Ethnology to the Secretary of the Smithsonian Institution, 1883–'84,* 533–555. Washington, D.C.: Government Printing Office, 1886.

———. "The Sia." In *Eleventh Annual Report of the Bureau of Ethnology to the Secretary of the Smithsonian Institution, 1889–'90,* 9–165. Washington, D.C.: Government Printing Office, 1894.

———. "Strange Rites of the Tewa Indians." *Smithsonian Miscellaneous Collections* 63 (1913): 73-80.

———. "The Sun and the Ice People Among the Tewa Indians of New Mexico." *Smithsonian Miscellaneous Collections* 65 (1914): 73-78.

———. "The Zuni Indians. Their Mythology, Esoteric Fraternities, and Ceremonies." In *Twenty-Third Annual Report of the Bureau of American Ethnology to the Secretary of the Smithsonian Institution, 1901–1902,* 3–634. Washington, D.C.: Government Printing Office, 1904.

Stewart, Miller J. "Army Laundresses: Ladies of the 'Soap Suds Row'." *Nebraska History* 61 (Winter 1980): 421–436.

Topping, Gary. "Religion in the West." *Journal of American Culture* 3 (Summer 1980): 330–350.

Trulio, Beverly. "Anglo-American Attitudes Toward New Mexican Women." *Journal of the West* 12 (April 1973): 229–239.

Welter, Barbara. "The Cult of True Womanhood: 1820–1860." *American Quarterly* 18 (1966): 151–175.

———. "'She Hath Done What She Could': Protestant Women's Missionary Careers in Nineteenth-Century America." In *Women in American Religion,* edited by Janet Wilson James, 110–125. Philadelphia: University of Pennsylvania Press, 1980.

Wood, Ann Douglas. "The Literature of Impoverishment: The Women Local Colorists in America, 1865–1914." *Women's Studies* 1 (1972): 4.

Theses and Dissertations

Banker, Mark T. "They Made Haste Slowly: Presbyterian Mission Schools and Southwestern Pluralism." Ph.D. diss., University of New Mexico, 1987.

Brandes, Raymond Stewart. "Frank Hamilton Cushing: Pioneer Americanist." Ph.D. diss., University of Arizona, 1965.

Kenneson, Susan R. "Through the Looking-Glass: A History of Anglo-American Attitudes Towards the Spanish-Americans and Indians of New Mexico." Ph.D. diss., Yale University, 1978.

Parker, Kate H. "'I Brought with Me Many Eastern Ways': Euro-American Income-Earning Women in New Mexico, 1850–1880." Ph.D. diss., University of New Mexico, 1984.

Smith, Sherry L. "'Civilization's Guardians': Army Officers' Reflections on Indians and the Indian Wars in the Trans-Mississippi West, 1848–1890." Ph.D. diss., University of Washington, 1984.

Stapleton, Ernest. "The History of Baptist Missions in New Mexico, 1849–1866." Master's thesis, University of New Mexico, 1954.

Warner, Michael J. "Protestant Missionary Work with the Navajo Indians from 1846 to 1912." Ph.D. diss., University of New Mexico, 1977.

Newspapers and Religious Periodicals

El Abogado Cristiano (Methodist). 1895.

Albuquerque Journal. 1980–1981.

La Aurora (Presbyterian). 1903–1905.

Home Mission Monthly (Presbyterian). 1889–1921.

Home Mission Record (Baptist). 1850–1853.

La Revista Católica. 1891–1897.

Santa Cruz [Calif.] *Sentinel.* 1920.

Santa Fe Gazette. 1862.

Santa Fe New Mexican. 1906.

The Soldier's Letter [Fort Riley, Kans.]. 1864.

Interviews and Personal Correspondence

Edith Agnew. Interview with author, March 14, 1981.

Mrs. Roy A. Blake. Correspondence with author, 1981.

Miss Gwladys Bowen. Correspondence with author, 1985.

Alfonso Esquibel. Interview with author, March 14, 1981.

William E. Foote. Interviews with author, August 1985.

Jeanne McIntosh. Interview with author, August 1986.

Sandra L. Myres. Correspondence with author, 1985.

Index

More Than an Ally

More Than an Ally

*A Caring Solidarity Framework
for White Teachers of
African American Students*

Michael L. Boucher Jr.

ROWMAN & LITTLEFIELD
Lanham • Boulder • New York • London

Published by Rowman & Littlefield
An imprint of The Rowman & Littlefield Publishing Group, Inc.
4501 Forbes Boulevard, Suite 200, Lanham, Maryland 20706
www.rowman.com

6 Tinworth Street, London SE11 5AL, United Kingdom

British Library Cataloguing in Publication Information Available

Library of Congress Cataloging-in-Publication Data

Names: Boucher, Michael Lee, Jr., author.
Title: More than an ally : a caring solidarity framework for white teachers of African American
    students / Michael L. Boucher Jr..
Description: Lanham : Rowman & Littlefield, [2020] | Includes bibliographical references and index.
    | Summary: "White teachers in multiracial schools are looking for ways to understand how to
    make a difference with their students of color in their classrooms. This book will help teachers
    make that difference"— Provided by publisher.
Identifiers: LCCN 2020004843 (print) | LCCN 2020004844 (ebook) | ISBN 9781475826531 (cloth) |
    ISBN 9781475826548 (paperback) | ISBN 9781475826555 (epub)
Subjects: LCSH: African American youth—Education. | Teachers, White—United States. | Race
    awareness—United States. | Teacher-student relationships—United States. | Academic achieve-
    ment—United States.
Classification: LCC LC2717 .B584 2020 (print) | LCC LC2717 (ebook) | DDC 370.11/5—dc23
LC record available at https://lccn.loc.gov/2020004843
LC ebook record available at https://lccn.loc.gov/2020004844

♾ ™ The paper used in this publication meets the minimum requirements of American
National Standard for Information Sciences Permanence of Paper for Printed Library
Materials, ANSI/NISO Z39.48-1992.

For Karen, who made everything possible.

Contents

Acknowledgments

There are so many people who guided me over the years and have made it possible for me to produce this book. First, I want to thank my brilliant, amazing wife, Karen Burgard, for her unwavering support and willingness to read and edit every word that went into, and came out of, this book. It would not have been possible without you, Dollface. Second, I want to thank my hero and mentor, Robert Helfenbein. Rob, you are my model for how professors in the academy should approach research with communities and someone who truly understands the impact of centering those communities in that research. I will be forever grateful for your counsel and encouragement, especially when I needed it the most.

I want to thank Lynne Boyle-Baise, who offered me the opportunity to study at Indiana University, and Jesse Goodman, Mary McMullen, and Crystal Morton, for their support throughout my dissertation. The questions you raised and the support you provided were invaluable. My excellent teachers at IU and IUPUI provided me with a different approach to discussing the complex issues raised in this work, and I appreciate the perspectives they provided. I want to thank the teachers who participated in the study on which this book is based. Their commitment to working in the community allowed me to see that solidarity comes in stages and in different packages but is crucial to successful teaching across the color line.

There are so many people in Minneapolis who have made this work become a reality. My life there in classrooms shaped me as an urban educator. Minneapolis will always be at the foundation of my understandings and worldview, and the lived experiences of my students will always be with me. I want to thank my students from Folwell and Sheridan, who taught me so much as a young teacher, and I now have the privilege of seeing them grown up with kids of their own and accomplishing so much. I am proud to call them friends. To our cadre of once-young teachers—Jeff Sommers, Amy Strickland Johnson, and Laura Yost-Manthey—we set out to change the world, and we succeeded.

My students from South High School in Minneapolis continue to inspire and teach me as doctors, activists, artists, writers, parents, and academics. They taught me the meaning of solidarity and created it with me. Each student I taught at South still holds an important and special place in my heart, but I would like to take a moment to identify a few: Isiah Edwards, who helped me see solidarity when I wasn't looking, and Sha'Dasha Whitner, who taught me so much about myself as a White teacher and that solidarity is needed at all times. I also want to acknowledge my student and friend Vince Moniz for his poetry, friendship, jokes, and encouragement. Vince, your words bring me home in so many ways.

I also want to express my deep appreciation for my colleagues at South High School. They laughed with me, encouraged me, and challenged me over the years, especially Doug Berglund, Diane Manley-Bagley, Tiffany Moore, Phyllis Hayes, Melinda Bennett, and Brian Fitzgerald. Thank you all for your belief in me and your abiding commitment to students. I still tell the stories about you in my classes and hold you all as examples of what great teaching can be.

I am so grateful to my students and colleagues at Texas A&M University–San Antonio, especially Dean Carl Shaperis and the provost, Mike O'Brien, for their support and advice as I finished this project. Their commitment to encouraging and supporting junior scholars and their passionate commitment to the community of San Antonio's South Side is very exciting. I am so proud to be part of this work. With their continued support, I intend to extend my research and advocacy to the communities in this city.

I want to thank the editors with whom I have worked at Rowman & Littlefield. Suzanne Canavan, Tim Koerner, and Carlie Wall have encouraged me along the way and did not give up on me, even as the world seemed to do everything in its power to keep me from finishing. *Mil gracias* to Sara Eiranova for her great design work on the diagram for caring solidarity, to South alum Greta McClain for her work in Minneapolis and for allowing me to use images of her murals on the cover, and to Courtney Perry for allowing the use of her amazing photographs of Greta's work.

I want to thank my family, Vicki and Mike Boucher, and my sister, Beth Edgar, and her family. Thank you all for always taking an interest in this work and supporting me throughout its completion. Your questions about the process and the book's progress these past two years have touched my heart. Finally, I want to acknowledge and thank my son, Joshua Boucher. Joshua, you know that our long talks about supporting communities and being an activist for equality and justice have meant everything to me. They helped shape and mold this work, and you will hear our conversations throughout the pages. You make me so proud every day as you work in solidarity with your community as a journalist. You get it, Buddy. You always have.

Introduction

Great Teachers Need a Framework to Talk about Race

Race has moved from a taboo topic to the center of political and social discourse as people of color have continued the long tradition of advocating for themselves and their children. There was a move into public consciousness that was accelerated after the acquittal of George Zimmerman for the killing of Trayvon Martin in 2013 (Love, 2014), with the use of social media and the Twitter hashtag #BlackLivesMatter by Alicia Garza, Patrisse Cullors, and Opal Tometi. This new generation of activists was stirred after the killing of Michael Brown in Ferguson, Missouri. Corresponding events and movements such as the Movement for Black Lives have pushed White Americans who want to work toward a more equitable society to examine history, structures, and the essential nature of the country.

This examination means that people are talking about race on a regular basis, yet the conversations are not yet producing the kind of increased awareness and empathy that lead to substantial change. Why is that? When race is discussed, the solution is seldom dismantling the structures that keep powerful people in power and others on the margins. In schools, talking about race, when it's done at all, is done *to* people and not *with* them—making solutions elusive not because they are truly impossible but because their cost in money, place, and privilege is perceived as too high. Thus, the talk continues without results, often devolving into blaming the victims of racism.

After a successful career of teaching in urban schools, I began this research in 2009 when it seemed like Americans were ready to talk with clarity about race. The United States had just elected its first Black president, who campaigned on hope and unity. More people of color were coming into leadership positions in both the public and private sectors. From social media to popular culture, it seemed that Americans were on the verge of finally having an honest dialogue about race. What many of us did not fully understand, however, was that there was a storm of resentment brewing against that progress.

The election of 2016 blew in and exploded the fragile structure of White racial understanding (see "Capitalizing White" in the introduction). Instead of moving forward, many White people have become confused about the difference between lie and fact, concerned with their own position, and defensive of their personal status (DiAngelo, 2011; Coates, 2017). The last decade has been dizzying and has left many well-intentioned White people convinced that something must change but without a clear framework as to what that change should look like.

White teachers who seek relationships with students based on solidarity see #BlackLivesMatter and want to create classrooms that reflect that their students matter and that their experiences matter. However, other teachers have sometimes participated in the varied backlashes to the movement, such as denying that race exists, deliberately misunderstanding (#AllLivesMatter), and silencing student protests.

The election of Donald Trump was a gut punch to White people who assumed that the country was moving ahead in race relations (Sondel, Baggett, & Dunn, 2018). The current news climate has only increased the tempo and frequency of race conversations, but again they are frequently unproductive. As race, racism, and White supremacy are being debated hour by hour, the absurdity of our current discourse can be overwhelming to White teachers looking to create a more just and inclusive America. These teachers are trying to understand how they can become more than just casual observers of racism and more than nonracists. They are seeking to move to a deeper level of solidarity with people of color (Applebaum, 2011; Gaztambide-Fernández, 2012).

Given the tenor of the conversation around race, picking up this book and considering its contents is either an act of defiance or one of devotion. Whether it is defiance in the face of increasing polarization across the political and social landscape in all its forms, or if the motivation comes from a devotion to the art, craft, and calling of being an impactful educator, this book should be helpful in either endeavor. It is an attempt to empower White teachers and teacher candidates[1] to do the hard work of interrogating their own racial privilege and joining in caring solidarity with their students.

---

1. The term *teacher candidate* is used throughout to refer to university students enrolled in a teacher education program or during student teaching. Other names used in the literature are *teachers in training* or *preservice teachers*. This wording is an attempt to avoid confusion when referring to "students" in a pre-K–12 context.

My research over the last decade has shown that White teachers seeking success in their work that serves predominantly African American students should look within and interrogate their own whiteness. They should look for ways to dismantle structures of racial oppression and privilege in their schools and communities. However, the road to that self-awareness is fraught with pitfalls.

NO ONE CAN JUST CLOSE THE DOOR AND TEACH

Sullivan (2014) argued that the tendency of *racially aware* White people to enter spaces where they feel they can have an impact, such as a racially segregated neighborhood, does more harm than good. She argued that when these White people move into these new spaces, they express their own privilege and assume a missionary or savior standpoint (Warren & Talley, 2017). She exhorted, "Rather than setting aside one's whiteness in an attempt to learn about other races, white people can begin to do effective racial justice work by cleaning up their own house" (p. 20).

Even in teacher education programs, because of segregated patterns of living in America, most teacher candidates have never had a meaningful exchange about race with a person racially different from themselves. It can be scary, treacherous, and unsafe to talk about race, and given the opportunity, most people avoid talking about it outside of their own racial or social groups. However, as educators devoted to students and to equity and justice in education, these uncomfortable conversations are necessary and should lead to action.

While Sullivan makes a compelling argument for self-knowledge before doing the work of dismantling privilege, White teachers working in schools with African American students have already crossed color lines and are living in the racial dynamic, meaning that inaction or delayed action is not a viable choice. White teachers in multicultural and multiracial schools do not have the luxury of deciding where and when to make a difference by waiting and assessing the situation from the sidelines. These teachers currently work across the color barrier, and thus it is not a question of whether they will influence their students and communities because, for better or worse, they do so every day.

The work of dismantling structures of oppression is currently being done in many fields and from many angles, including law, politics, policy, faith, and education. While all White people should participate in these multisided efforts, teachers have a special responsibility to care for, and about, our students and communities of color. This means that teachers must take control of the one place over which we have control, our schools.

In frustration, teachers will often say that they just close their door and do their work, effectively shutting out the cacophony outside. However, schools in a healthy republic are the gardens of democratic thinking, reasoning, and skills, not marketplaces engaged in a crass exchange of services. If anything is exchanged, it should be the narrow, flattened ideas of childhood for the complex, rich ideas of adulthood. Instead, too many view education as a value-laden transaction where those who shout the loudest are privileged in the marketplace of ideas while other voices are further marginalized.

Classrooms are the place to build a more equitable and sustainable society and should not be some neutral, or neutered, conduit for received knowledge. It is a foolish fantasy to believe that any neutrality is even possible, but to actively argue that schools should be mere conveyors of received knowledge is to reject our democratic ideals. In order to create a space where the pluralistic ethic can flourish, the mask of neutrality of culture in schools must be lifted. Thus, teachers in multicultural and multiracial schools are in the best position to do the work of dismantling structures of oppression and White supremacy and create a new, more equitable society. However, it will take more than reading the "I Have a Dream" speech every January and a bulletin board of heroes every February.

This book explains a new concept in teaching, caring solidarity. Building on the work of Gloria Ladson-Billings's *The Dreamkeepers* (1994) and that of other scholars, the hope is to change the conversation about how White teachers approach teaching African American students. Solidarity with students and communities is built by replacing fear with understanding, discomfort with empathy, and avoidance with courage. Through education, care, and solidarity, educators committed to dismantling these structures move first themselves and then others to a deeper understanding and connection to empower and inspire students.

Even in teacher education programs, because of segregated patterns of living in America, most teacher candidates have never had a meaningful exchange about race with a person racially different from themselves. It can be scary, treacherous, and unsafe to talk about race, and given the opportunity, most people avoid talking about it outside of their own racial or social groups. However, as educators devoted to students and to equity and justice in education, these uncomfortable conversations are necessary and should lead to action.

WHO AM I?

In order to discuss the positionality of teachers and gain the historical and personal context for how they can work in solidarity with students, it is important to have at least an outline of my personal history and positionality so that my identity and worldview can also be placed in context. Personal and family histories matter in that they have shaped and continue to have influence over us. Thus, one of the first steps to interrogating my own standpoint is to understand how I came to that position. In short, I am a mostly White male who grew up in the suburbs of Minnesota and taught in an inner-city high school in Minneapolis.

As for my family history, on my mother's side, my ancestors came from Poland and England along with many other immigrants in the 1800s. On my father's side, beginning in 1830, some of my ancestors were removed by the United States during the Trail of Tears from their homes and farms in what is now Mississippi and Alabama. They were placed in southern Oklahoma "Indian Territory." By blood quantum, my grandmother was a quarter Choctaw and Irish, and my grandfather was mostly English from a poor family of farm laborers. I am a registered and voting member of the Choctaw Nation of Oklahoma.

When I was very young, my father obtained a position in Minnesota, and that is where I grew up and spent most of the first forty-five years of my life. Growing up in Minnesota, all my friends' parents were White, middle class, and college educated. It was the stable, uncomplicated life that my parents wanted for me. Yet I felt there was a piece of me that belonged somewhere else. I was discontent identifying with the cultural norms of the Minnesota mix of Norwegians, Germans, and Swedes of my suburban upbringing. Even though we only went to Oklahoma a few times in my youth, I was always proud to be "something else" that others did not share.

I have had little contact with Choctaws in Oklahoma other than extended family, but I feel that the Choctaw Nation is an important part of who I am. In college, I began carrying my Choctaw identification card in my wallet. That ID card is a good metaphor for my connection to the tribe. It is something that I keep with me, but it is not outwardly visible.

It is my own indicator of difference from the society around me and, growing up, I felt that it gave me permission to be an outsider whenever I felt like it. However, as an adult, I came to realize that for all my imaginings of being an outsider, I was deeply rooted in the privilege afforded me by whiteness and my middle-class economic status.

Upon graduating from college with a degree in social studies education, I gained a position in the Minneapolis public schools where I began the process of becoming an urban educator. There I found the diversity I had been wanting. I was able to experience cultures, ideas, and people that taught me how to be a more complete teacher and person. I taught middle and high school social studies for eighteen years until I left to pursue my doctorate in education and became a teacher educator. For the purposes of this discussion, I position myself as a mostly White male former high school teacher, now teacher educator.

STRATEGIC ESSENTIALISM AND DIVERSITY

The focus of this work is the teaching of African American students by White teachers. These categories are imposed in order to begin a dialogue, but there is no assumption that these categories are static or isolated from the history of colonization, slavery, segregation, and White supremacy. However, unless artificial categories are overlaid to some extent, the discussion becomes so watered down as to become meaningless. This specific type of essentialism allows for a conversation about race.

According to Azoulay (1997), strategic essentialism is a "prerequisite for dialogue" about race (p. 102). Strategic essentialism opens up the intellectual space by grouping people together, even in ways that do not always reflect people's lived reality. To understand that race is a socially constructed concept should not get in the way of understanding that it is also a historical reality. To deny this leads people to the kind of color-blind ideology that only reifies the current social and political structure of White privilege and "color-blind racism" (Bonilla-Silva, 2010, p. 40).

Strategic essentialism should not be confused with essentialized frameworks like White supremacy, which assumes that White people are fundamentally better and more equipped to run things than people of color. White supremacy essentializes others who are not assumed to be White and places them in the category of diverse or non-White, while White people are considered normal and outside of race (Irving, 2014). All over the world, White people have created spaces for themselves and pushed others to the margins. However, in each context blackness and the response to it are different. The binary of Black and White does not work in all global contexts and does not even scratch the surface of the range of human diversity.

A caveat is important here. Strategic essentialism is a device meant to be used temporarily to give space for discussion of real historical issues. Thus, when talking about Black and White people, the tool of essentialized racial categories allows for the discussion of race in the United States and in the study of diverse classrooms. If strategic essentialism is never abandoned, the danger is that it will become real essentialism and move away from its original intent.

With that danger in mind, it is important for teachers and researchers to acknowledge that while some group identifications are real, and while historical inequity and racism are real, the racialized concepts that ground these notions are socially constructed and are not based on any biologically determinable differences (Helfenbein, 2003).

CAPITALIZING WHITE

Throughout this text, I have capitalized the word *white* when referring to White people. This has been my practice as a way to state that whiteness, in this context, is not a mere description like hair or eye color. White, instead, is a socially constructed grouping of people based on their racialization in the U.S. context, not a scientific or empirically observable characteristic. White, Black, and Brown are all racialized descriptors of group membership, not neutral descriptions of actual skin colors.

I have also used the terms *racialization* or *racialized* when referring to how people are perceived. It is a shift in thinking for many White people from the assumption that race is old and descriptive to seeing it for what it is, a relatively new way to categorize people. People are not naturally dropped into races. They have race imposed upon them as they are categorized by others. Thus, people are racialized in order to place them in the racial categories used to decide who is in power and who is excluded.

As part of this book's strategic essentialism, I have not specifically discussed the experiences of people who identify as mixed race. As a matter of history, all people in the United States are mixed from different parts of the world. Sometimes this causes identity conflicts as people do not know where they fit in a racialized America. This volume will not deal with the specific issue of the very important work of how mixed-race people relate to the concept of race.

Therefore, as a matter of definition, "White people" refers to the people of European descent who hold both social and economic power that comes with being perceived as a member of the White race. Whiteness and blackness have historically been fluid and contextual. Quotations from scholars and their capitalizations, or not, have been preserved, so the reader will need to be ready for different cases within paragraphs, but my explanations will use the capital *W*.

Some scholars and activists use the lowercase *w* in referring to White people or use *whyte* rather than *white* in order to decenter whiteness in academic literature, and I applaud their work and some are cited in this book. In this case and after much deliberation, with an eye toward my intended audience and the future, I have chosen to capitalize *White* in an effort to help teachers and newer scholars to see whiteness, sometimes for the first time.

So much of whiteness is taken for granted as normal or even as the only way to do things, and ways of decentering whiteness further its disintegration (Michael, Coleman-King, Lee, Ramirez, & Bentley-Edwards, 2017). For a definition, *whiteness* is the intersection of privilege based on the perception of being a member of the White race and the assumption of normality that being White has in the United States.

My project here is to uncover whiteness and separate it from normativity so that teachers will then be equipped to enter into relationships of caring solidarity with their Black students. That is only possible if White people see their own whiteness and develop what Helms (1990) referred to as a positive White racial identity. I have also capitalized *Black* and *Brown* when referring to racialized groups in the same way.

THE TASK AT HAND

From August to June, teachers meet young people in schools to teach them the ideas, skills, and knowledge needed to become successful in the wealthiest, most powerful society ever created by humankind. The responsibility is awesome. With the mechanisms that teachers provide, these students will vote, earn a living, raise a family, and leave their own legacies to society. The work teachers do in the classroom every day shapes the future. There are many jobs that pay more and carry more prestige, but it would be difficult if not impossible to find a job with as much influence over as many people as being the teacher.

If an adult conversation is to be had about teachers working across the color barrier, whiteness both as a concept and a fact must be addressed. The waters ahead are not easily navigated, but unless the gaps between teachers and students in terms of race, culture, income, political power, and privilege are embedded in the structure of reforms, they will not address the issues facing today's schools.

The project of this book is focused on the teaching of African American students by White teachers, but that is not the only project that needs a full examination. Being strategically essential allows for a focus on this one area, but the intersectionality of sexual orientation, colorism, sexism, anti-indigenousness, and a multiplicity of other oppressions also impacts students and their teachers.

However, as with all research, the question used to collect the data for this volume narrowed the focus to examining the phenomenon of White teachers in classrooms of mostly African American students. That is the focus here, but there are many other foci that need to be explored. The goal is that the theory herein will be applicable to many contexts.

A NEW PARADIGM

There are several elements to becoming a teacher in solidarity that have emerged from my research and, more importantly, the research of the myriad scholars of color who have so generously taught me over the years and are cited throughout this book. While working toward caring solidarity with students, it is important to consider that there will always be an ebb and flow in this journey, and each individual is different in their growth and their situation.

This framework is for teachers who are looking for a way to move toward solidarity with students and for researchers looking for a way to describe teachers who work in solidarity with students. It was created to be both descriptive and aspirational. It can be used to describe teachers in the field who are currently working in caring solidarity with their students, and it can be used to train or develop teachers with intentions toward caring solidarity.

Caring solidarity builds upon current frameworks such as Culturally Sustaining Pedagogy (Paris & Alim, 2017) and abolitionist pedagogy (Love, 2019c) and is a way to map a journey for White teachers toward those pedagogies. Everyone starts from somewhere. The path is winding and long, but the goal, to create an equitable and humane classroom, is worth the trip. The purpose of this framework is to point the way.

Chapter One

Caring Solidarity, Race, Teachers, and Schools

The framework of caring solidarity addresses both the mind-sets that allow a person to move toward caring solidarity and also the skills of empathy, alliance, and being an accomplice. As Katsarou, Picower, and Stovall (2010) stated, "to truly teach in solidarity with schools and communities requires of teachers both specific mindsets and skill sets" (p. 152). This framework addresses critical perspectives on solidarity that include White allies (Patel, 2011), false empathy (Delgado, 1996; Warren & Hotchkins, 2014), and White savior syndrome (Straubhaar, 2014). Caring solidarity asks teachers to delve deeply into their own position and explore the mechanisms, conditions, and mental commitments necessary to do that work.

As communities of color come under increasing attack from above and below, teachers must be the vanguard of equity and diversity in our schools and our society. Caring solidarity is situated in second-wave White teacher–identity studies (Jupp, Berry, & Lensmire, 2016) and is applied to students and teachers. However, the majority of the theoretical basis for the framework comes from scholarship done by African American scholars in elementary school settings. Their insights are crucial to the construction of the theories behind the framework, and they are quoted and cited widely in this book.

This new framework is rooted in critical theory, critical whiteness studies, and multicultural understandings, but seeks to move to a deeper commitment that will allow White teachers to meet the deep challenges of the present age and usher in a new one that fulfills the promise of an equitable, empowering, and democratic education for all of our students. The theoretical work relies on culturally relevant and sustaining pedagogies and seeks to be an extension or precursor needed for White teachers to build solidarity with Black stu-

1

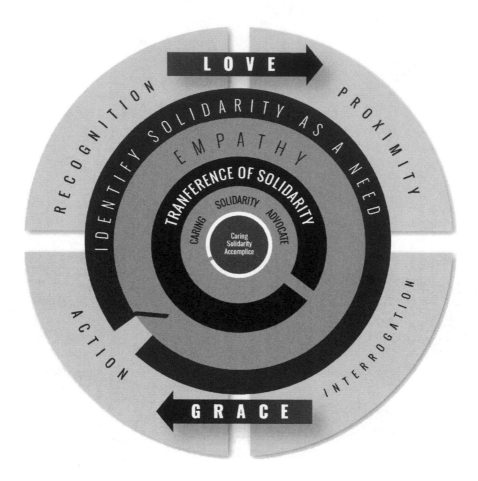

Caring solidarity framework.

dents. It is also meant to be a mechanism to more fully integrate these frameworks into daily teaching.

The caring solidarity framework is meant to be both descriptive of teachers who seek solidarity across the color line and aspirational for teachers seeking to create classrooms where Black students know they are valued and learn to thrive. It asks White teachers to deeply examine their roles, positions, ideas, and methods used when they teach African American students. Caring and solidarity are concepts that have been explored separately and tangentially in education for decades but have not been placed together as a specific way to describe the effort of teachers who work across the color line.

These first few chapters summarize some of that research to give a portrait of how schools disempower and disenfranchise Black students. It begins with discussion of the current White teaching force and race. The second chapter explains the imperative of the moment with an outline of the deepest moral failure of our schools, the school to prison pipeline. The third chapter reviews the concept of multicultural education and its ineffectiveness to meet the current challenges. The conversation then turns to ways to meet the challenges and begins the move from allyship and other asset pedagogies to a new framework of caring solidarity.

No other profession has the potential to reshape and redirect this age where science, reason, and equality have been all but abandoned. Teachers can effect societal change through their work in and out of classrooms. They can expose their students to truths that are unavailable to them anywhere else. Teachers are world changers, and teaching effectively is essential to creating needed change in the country, the world, and our communities.

THE WHITE TEACHING FORCE

Before explaining the framework that will allow White teachers to succeed across the color line, it is important to examine the current state of teaching and learning in the United States. In order to understand the moral imperative of dismantling the school to prison pipeline and to solve the current crisis in the education of African American children, we must look at who is teaching, why they are teaching, and how they are teaching.

The American teaching force, according to the National Center for Education Statistics (NCES), is 80 percent White, middle-aged, and middle-class (Feistritzer, Griffin, & Linnajarvi, 2011; Loewus, 2018; Taie & Goldring, 2017). That is slightly down from 82 percent in the last survey in 2012. About 77 percent of teachers are women. In pre-K through sixth-grade schools, nearly 90 percent are women; in high schools, women make up around 66 percent. Thus, it is safe to say that most teachers are White women. Nine percent of teachers identify as Hispanic, slightly up from 2012, and the 7 percent of teachers who identify as Black has not changed in the last seven years.

In 1972, the first year the U.S. Department of Education collected demographic data for the newly desegregated schools, students of color accounted for 22 percent of total enrollments, and teachers of color constituted 12 percent of the teaching force, a ten-percentage-point gap between the two groups. A decade later, the disparity had grown to seventeen percentage points, with students of color making up 27 percent of total enrollments and teachers of color accounting for only 10 percent of the teaching workforce (p. 283). In 2017, students of color made up 40.6 percent of the total U.S. public school population, and in the largest cities, a much higher percentage (Ingersoll & May, 2011; Musu-Gillette, de Brey, McFarland, Hussar, & Sonnenberg, 2017). Given the overwhelming percentage of teachers who are White, it is not uncommon that students of color will spend their entire day taught by White teachers. This fact makes the ideology, behavior, and position of White teachers a priority if we are to structure schools to meet the needs of all students.

THE QUICK FIX?

Systems and their leaders look for quick fixes to intractable problems. One answer put forth to make schools more diverse and to increase the buy-in of students of color is to bring more teachers of color into the classroom. Education leaders work to bring new teachers from racially and ethnically diverse backgrounds into the profession, but their efforts have not been enough. Once teachers of color are in schools, they face challenges from students and adults, and schools of education are often not ready to aid teacher candidates of color in dealing with the micro- and macroaggressions that teachers of color experience.

Research has indicated that Black students who have even one Black teacher in their[1] schooling experience in low-income schools have 29 percent greater interest in school and are 39 percent less likely to drop out before completing high school (Gershenson, Hart, Lindsay, & Papageorge, 2017). But as Milner (2006) explained, having a Black teacher in the classroom is not necessarily the panacea it is often hoped to be unless they are also culturally competent and refuse to engage in deficit models. Also, the assumption that Black students are merely in need of *role models* is also insufficient and again assumes no responsibility on the part of White teachers (Brown, 2012; Milner, 2006; Williamson, 2011).

It is imperative to approach the problem of student disenfranchisement from as many angles as possible. As the number of students of color continues to outpace the pool of teachers of color, increasing the number of teachers of color in our schools is an important aspirational goal (Stotko, Ingram, & Beaty-O'Ferrall, 2007; Villegas, Strom, & Lucas, 2012). However, White teachers are the predominant demographic of professionals working in schools, and there will not be enough teachers of color to change that experience for many years (Milner, 2006). So, it is crucial that these White teachers be the ones who work to break the structures that impede students of color (Sleeter, 2001b). Schools need more counselors. They need more and better multicultural curricula, more teachers of color, and more administrators of

---

1.   I have chosen to use *they*, *them*, and *their* in replacement of *he/she* or other gender binary phrasing, especially when referring generally to people or students and gender is not part of the discussion. Also, this use has been recently added to the seventh edition of the APA manual.

color, but if White teachers are not part of the changes, they will not be implemented in time to catch this generation.

IS THE NEW GENERATION OF TEACHERS THE SAME AS THE OLD GENERATION?

Scholars have noted that White teacher candidates wrap deeply held racism in the language of care, believing that students of color do not value education and need to be motivated to learn with external reward systems like prizes, candy, or money. Often these preconceived deficit notions range from a clinical model of pathology, to wholesale condemnation of students' culture, to an appeal that students should learn whiteness as a way to success (Osei-Kofi, 2005; Payne, 2013; Valencia, 2010). When candidates then go into the field, these stereotypes are often reinforced through teacher talk, an incomplete understanding of what they are seeing in classrooms, and a lack of awareness of their own biases (Sleeter, 2001b).

The cycle is perpetuated from candidacy to teaching to mentoring, and even as teachers join the professorate in schools of education, many still cling to their deficit models and seek to help candidates get "good placements," meaning in wealthy White schools in the suburbs, and do not ask the larger questions about oppressive structures (see Mervosh, 2019).

As Valencia (2010) clarified, "deficit thinking typically offers a description of behavior in pathological or dysfunctional ways—referring to deficits, deficiencies, limitations, or shortcomings in individuals, families, and cultures" (p. 14). These models are not only the default for many teachers and teacher candidates, but they also blame students for a lack of success in the classroom (Boucher & Helfenbein, 2015; Gorski, 2006; Osei-Kofi, 2005).

According to Eslinger (2013), teachers fall victim to a savior mentality and a White supremacist belief structure that must be quelled in order to create a culturally responsive classroom. While teachers come to the profession as caring individuals, their models of care are often missing the aspects needed by Black students, that of solidarity with them, and deep knowledge of who students are—culturally, racially, and individually.

Teachers live in the intersection of theory, practice, societal forces, and economic realities. The data are clear that many White teachers see students as a bundle of deficits or as a threat to the learning environment. Britzman (2003) explained that teachers come to the profession with "chronologies" negotiated through their own classroom lives both as students and as teachers. When combined with their frames around "power, knowledge, dependency, and negotiation," teachers negotiate their own socializations depending on their many interactions with culture and identity. If White teachers have not interrogated their own position as White people, they carry frames of White normality and supremacy into the classroom.

Britzman rejected the notion that there is one monolithic culture of teachers, stating, "Within any given culture, there exists a multiplicity of realities—both given and possible—that form competing ideologies, discourses, and the discursive practices that are made available to them" (p. 70). The ability to transcend racial divisions is not embedded in the potential teacher as an innate talent. Instead, teachers develop the required skills in a process that can take years depending on their understandings and experiences.

Because of the need for White teachers to stand in solidarity with students of color, it is crucial that while discussing teachers, they are portrayed as able to move into antiracism and caring solidarity no matter where they start. Casey (2017) extends this caveat: "We often make the mistake of treating white people who have little experience thinking through issues of race and racism as resistant racists, rather than as learners. We would never fault someone who had not taken geometry for not being proficient in their first efforts in a geometry course; why do we insist on faulting white people for not being proficient in their first efforts to understand what it means to be white in a white supremacist society and what this means for them as social actors?" (p. 96).

Having an awareness of the world is a crucial aspect of being educated and, even more so, of being an educator. Through writing, activism, and political action, people of color and White allies are purposefully making it increasingly difficult to argue that someone can justifiably be ignorant of racism, privilege, and White supremacy. Therefore, it is incumbent on White teachers to educate themselves and heed the perspectives of people with funds of knowledge in the communities where their students are living.

This is especially true for those White teachers who teach across the color line. Conversely, to avoid all discussion of race and whiteness while interacting with Black students means that teachers are not listening to their students and are finding ways to avoid the onslaught of information about activism and social change. Thus, rather than adopting a default position of approaching teachers as racists who need to be cleansed, teacher educators and researchers should approach teachers as learners who are more or less resistant to the understandings that must be achieved to be successful in their chosen field (Jupp, Berry, & Lensmire, 2016).

TALKING ABOUT RACE OUT LOUD

Before going further, it is important to back up a bit and explain what race is and what it is not in order to move beyond the surface level of understanding the structures keeping students from succeeding. First and foremost, race is a socially constructed experience in American life that has no biological basis (Kolbert & Hammond, 2018; Painter, 2010). In reality, all color designations are based on perceptions of color, and yet they matter because Americans imbue skin color with power, fear, intelligence, and ability.

More or less skin melanin does not make a person more or less safe, dangerous, smart, or talented, but it does change the way a person is perceived in the world. Race is not a neutral designation but a tool of anti-blackness. Despite this brute fact, or because of it, the deep historical roots of race in America have shaped who we are as Americans and the structures of our society. Our relationships with each other and the structures of our society, employment, justice system, real estate, health care, schooling, and all other aspects of our communal life are influenced or defined to a greater or lesser degree by race. Whether we want it to or not, race defines how we interact with each other.

As Allen & Liou (2018) explained, "Whites are what people of color are not, or so the logic of Whiteness goes. If Whites depict people as culturally backwards and deprived, then that means Whites are by default depicting themselves as culturally progressive and enlightened. If the controlling image depicts people of color as lazy and unintelligent, then Whites are by default constructing themselves as smart and hardworking" (p. 686).

According to Solorzano (1997), racism is defined using three touchstones, "(1) one group believes itself to be superior; (2) the group which believes itself to be superior has the power to carry out the racist behavior; and (3) racism effects multiple racial/ethnic groups" (p. 8). The use of this definition allows the comprehension that racism is the exercise of power in structures and institutions that exclude people of color, not just individual hatred or acts of violence, which can also be racist. The feeling or belief that White people, culture, or ways of being are superior and the ability to enact policies that reflect this belief is racism.

Most people imagine that racism is under the strict purview of backward, unsophisticated degenerates who burn crosses, sympathize with Nazi Germany, and march with tiki torches. While that is all true, the small acts of segregating oneself from racially different people, racial jokes, financial barriers to school and college admission, the whiteness of the curriculum, and teachers' deficit thinking about students are also racism. All institutions are structured by individuals, and individual decisions support and maintain them. There is no way to point to any one subgroup or socioeconomic level and say that they alone are racist and the rest of society is not.

Despite its status as a myth, race, in fact and in practice, is real. It is real because people make it real through ideology and actions. It is often hard for White people to fathom how many of their own mental models are based on race. Race has been central to the American story from the exploration by Europeans, to the creation of the republic, to the Civil War, to today.

In popular discourse, some use the fact that race is not biologically based to demand a moratorium on talking about it. The thinking goes that talking about race is the reason for racism. These people hope that by keeping quiet, racism will evaporate. Avoidance seems like a simple answer to a vexing problem, but the hidden meaning of this sentiment is that everyone should stop demanding equality with the people in power, since much of that power is based on race.

That power is economic, political, and personal. Most White Americans do not consider themselves racists, yet there is large support for policies that hoard power and privilege in the White populace. In America, the people in power are, by and large, White. So, the thinking goes, if people of color would just be satisfied with White people holding the majority of wealth, power, and privilege in society, then we can all get along. Thus, when African Americans march, kneel, walk, or demand to be heard at all as Americans, they are accused of *causing division* because they are seeking to divide White people from their privilege.

Race denial is a violent stance in that it refuses to see the facts and the brutality that is happening in plain view. To take the perspective that race is unreal because it does not affect the speaker disregards both evidence and reason. The same goes for those who accept that race exists but refuse to accept that it matters. Both are constructed from a standpoint of privilege, in that they are asking people who experience racism to *get over it* or to *stop playing the victim* (Coates, 2008). Race has been used to justify slavery and segregation, but the lines of definition between the different races are always changing. Even with those changes, one constant remains: the mistaken notion that whiteness is normal and the most desirable (Painter, 2010).

Race has been used to justify slavery and segregation, but the lines of definition between the different races are always changing. Even with those changes, one constant remains: the mistaken notion that whiteness is *normal* and the most desirable (Painter, 2010). Candidates and teachers also conflate race and culture. In contrast to race, culture refers to institutions, norms, and all aspects of life that humans do together. "The word *culture* derives from the Latin *colere* and refers to terms we use today like inhabit, settle, defend and cultivate. Culture comprises many pieces like language, rituals, institutions, foods, art and technologies. It encompasses all the things we do and say that make us human and part of the group" (Kohl, 1992, p. 135). While culture is positive and expansive, race is selective and narrowing. Whereas culture enriches life and helps define who we are as part of a larger family, race is a way to define who is in and who is out. Unfortunately, people who want to avoid race will often substitute culture as a way to construct a caricature of people who they view as different. This conflation allows racism and the denigration of cultures to go on without condemnation, but ultimately it is just as damaging to both the speaker and the receiver. Whiteness, then, as a function of White normality and white supremacy, is passed to the next generation because of the unwillingness of adults to deconstruct the concepts.

REQUIRING WHITENESS AS NORMALITY

To understand the interplay of race, power, and pedagogy in classrooms headed by White teachers, it is important to understand the power of whiteness as a concept and as a force in the classroom. According to Frankenberg (1993), there are three dimensions to whiteness. First is the "structural advantage" of the White power structure and its accompanying privileges. Second is the "standpoint" or positionality of being White and seeing the world through that lens. Third, whiteness "carries with it a set of ways of being in the world, a set of cultural practices, often not named as 'white' by white [people] but looked on instead as 'American' or 'normal'" (p. 54).

The powerful concept of normality allows White people to assume that all others are abnormal or diverse and that their diversity from the norm is pathology. Oftentimes a cure is sought through the education system. As Levine-Rasky, (2000) explained,

> traditional solutions to inequitable educational outcomes for racialized groups of students have been directed to the putative problems of these racialized others ("them") and to the challenges in implementing culturally sensitive pedagogy (the space between "us" and "them") rather than to the workings of the dominant culture itself. (p. 272)

This division between us (White, middle class, legacy educated, dominantly cultured) and them (anything not in that list). Levine-Rasky (2000) continued,

> There is a willingness, for example, to increase the skills of marginalized groups through programmes catering to "their needs," such as special education, remedial reading, and segregated behavioural classes. There is a concomitant failure, however, to penetrate the source of marginalization for these identified groups, and thus little commitment to provide these students with the same possibilities as those available to dominant groups. Indeed, the need for special programmes and the student failure observed in them continues to be explained by problems residing with the students and their families. (p. 272)

One example is the enforcement of standard English in classrooms. Whiteness allows teachers who enforce rules about what is acceptable speech in the classroom to think they are caring and equipping the next generation to cope in a world where the values and language of whiteness are the norm. These teachers are able to view themselves as empowering their students by acculturating them more deeply in the culture of whiteness. Frustratingly, many acts of White supremacy are so wrapped up in how White teachers show caring that it is often difficult for White people to even see themselves as having this mental framework (Gaztambide-Fernández, 2012; Gray, 2019).

The debate over African American Vernacular English (AAVE) rages among teachers and scholars of different backgrounds (Gay, 2010; Seltzer, 2019). Godley et al. (2006) found that teacher attitudes about and against AAVE result in deficit thinking and stigmatization, which lead to lower expectations of students who use AAVE. However, AAVE is not a deficit. It is a fund of knowledge and a community asset. It allows communication within the group, and White teachers of African American students would be well served by being versed in it.

Teachers in solidarity with students around the issues of communication and language understand that strategizing with students, enabling them to code-switch between AAVE and the dominant register in class is necessary for long-term success (Delpit, 1988/2006). To insist on a White culturally specific register as the only way to speak in a classroom alienates teachers from students, inhibiting the creation of solidarity (Souto-Manning, 2013).

NAMING THE UNMENTIONABLE: WHITE SUPREMACY

As hooks (2013) explained, while people usually associate racism with overt "acts of aggression by whites against blacks." White supremacy, as a way to understand social structures, "addresses the ideological and philosophical foundations of racism" (p. 177). White supremacism is the most divisive, cancerous, and self-defeating mental and social construct of our time, and yet it has largely gone unnoticed in the telling of U.S. history. The term *White supremacy* conjures up racist hate groups and Klan rallies burning crosses, and most educated people disavow that version of White supremacy.

No one wants to be labelled as a bad person and few phrases make people feel uncomfortable as being associated with racism or White supremacy. These words like these make White people profoundly uncomfortable. The power any phrase possesses to hurt others does not come from its sound or even its surface meaning. The meanings of words are important, but so is their social context (DiAngelo, 2017). Nice White people always want to avoid being called *racist* and want others to understand that they are looking for common ground (Renkle, 2018). Constructive conversations about racism are the often subverted by the feelings of White people insert themselves into the foreground in race conversations, and because of that, little has changed that truly removes White supremacist ideology from society.

When people tiptoe around the feelings of White people, they will always be in solidarity with whiteness. *White supremacy* is one of those terms that has a simple meaning, the assumption that White people are better than others, but is often unheard because it has been used in social context to describe the most violent and detestable sections of society.

Sociologist Robin DiAngelo (2017) has written extensively about the term: "White supremacy captures the all-encompassing centrality and assumed superiority of people defined and perceived as white, and the practices based upon that assumption. White supremacy is not simply the idea that whites are superior to people of color (although it certainly is that), but a deeper premise that supports this idea—the definition of whites as the norm or standard for human, and people of color as an inherent deviation from that norm."

As DiAngelo (2018) explained, "White people raised in Western society are conditioned into a white supremacist worldview because it is the bedrock of our society and its institutions. Regardless of whether a parent told you that everyone was equal, or the poster in the hall of your white suburban school proclaimed the value of diversity, or you have traveled abroad, or you have people of color in your workplace or family, the ubiquitous socializing power of white supremacy cannot be avoided. The messages circulate 24-7 and have little or nothing to do with intentions, awareness, or agreement" (p. 129).

Allen and Liou (2018) explained, "In describing White supremacy as a social system, we are referring to a larger society that, despite times of what may seem like racial progress (e.g., the Civil Rights Era or Reconstruction), is fundamentally arranged to ensure that Whites remain in control of society, as they work to unjustly and immorally construct a higher social status over people of color" (p. 687).

DiAngelo (2017) challenged all White people to name the real issue in our politics and to begin the work of dismantling White supremacist ideologies in ourselves and the culture:

> Naming white supremacy changes the conversation because it shifts the problem to white people, where it belongs. It also points us in the direction of the life-long work that is uniquely ours; challenging our complicity with and investment in racism. Yes, this work includes all white people, even white progressives. None of us have missed being shaped by the white supremacy embedded in our culture. (p. 33)

The ideology of White supremacy is found in every corner of American history and life, from the first Conquistadors and Pilgrims to the founding of a nation that espoused liberty but still protected slavery. It includes Jim Crow, crime bills that caused mass incarceration, and crowds calling for a wall on the southern border. White supremacist ideology allows White people to justify their lack of faithfulness to the democratic ideals of the founders and their own moral principles. Its purpose remains to define White people as superior. White supremacy, once it is named, can be seen everywhere in society and though it is often more hidden, in the school structure. As hooks and other scholars pointed out, it is the root of how school is structured from preschool to graduation.

CENTERING RACE, NOT TALKING ABOUT RACE, OFFENSE, AND AVOIDANCE

McIntosh (2001) observed that there are unearned privileges given to Whites based on the fact that they are White people in a country where whiteness is normalized. James Baldwin clarified that whiteness is an illusion (Coates, 2015). Allen and Liou (2018) have explained whiteness as being "rooted in the active pursuit of White racial interests through the creation of institutional norms framed by the White supremacist social structure and its related normalized systems of practices" (p. 679).

Bonilla-Silva (2010) explained that there is a pervasive practice in schools referred to as "color-blind racism" (p. 2). This tendency allows White teachers to blame Black students for their failure, and Black parents can be ignored for not attending to their child's schooling. Ideological color blindness is a major force in the larger society (DiAngelo, 2018). As Hayes and Juarez (2012) explained, "holding on to a color-blind framework allows people to address only the egregious forms of racism" (p. 7).

The practice of color-blindness allows White people to ignore "the very knowledge of culturally responsive teaching and social justice that is needed to transform the whiteness of education" (Hayes & Juarez, 2012, p. 7). In multicultural classrooms, centering race and culture is an exercise in freedom for both teacher and students. If race and culture are not out in the open but are left unsaid, secret, taboo, and untouchable, the messages conveyed to students reinforce oppression and privilege and devalue students of color (DiAngelo, 2018).

It seems counterintuitive to some White people that talking about race is the best way to combat racism. The avoidance of race talk largely derives from a misunderstanding of race combined with an unwillingness to begin dismantling White supremacy in individuals and structures. *Not* talking about cancer did not lead to a cure for cancer. *Not* talking about sexual assault has not led to an end to sexual violence. *Not* talking about a subject has never solved it.

For example, Arizona has a troubled past and present when it comes to race and culture in the classroom, even taking the unusual step of banning "ethnic studies" courses in 2010. The climate of fear that surrounds schools in many states when talking about race and culture means that when teachers do engage in discussions, they risk infuriating White parents and legislators (Palos & McGinnis, 2012). Yet, when they do not have these conversations, students will act out in ways that reflect their lack of understanding.

In January 2016, the senior class of Desert Vista High School in Ahwatukee, Arizona, near Phoenix made black T-shirts with one gold letter per shirt spelling out "BEST*YOU'VE*EVER*SEEN*CLASS*OF*2016" in large gold letters. After the picture, six White female students stood together laughing and photographed themselves with their shirts spelling out "NI**ER" using the letters and asterisks from the previous photo formation.

The photo went viral on social media and created a storm that enveloped the students and the school. The students were immediately punished with five-day suspensions, and one student gave a public, tearful apology for "offense" while insisting that she was "not racist" (White & Ruelas, 2016).

When these students apologized for their offense, they did not understand that while their actions were indeed offensive, they were offensive because the students were both disrespectful and dismissive of the history of that word and its use as a tool of oppression. They tried to explain that to them it was just a "bad word," and they were just breaking the rules of decorum, not trying to subjugate their classmates or neighbors. They considered the word to be a vulgarity on the same level as swear or curse words that they could not use in school. They refused to see that this action was different. It was an act of oppression, and the administration reinforced that impression through inaction.

The language around offense places the blame on those who receive the disrespect, not on those who wield words as weapons. In schools and our social discourse, we have dealt with the language and not the reasons for the language. These students argued that their actions were not racist because their White privilege allowed them to avoid seeing that they were not only being offensive but oppressive. These personal actions were not understood by them as racism because to them only bad people are racist, and they did not perceive themselves as bad people. Instead, it was a professed act of rebellion, using a "bad word" they knew was taboo.

In the investigation that followed, the tearful apologies were accepted, and the students returned to school. However, the most important question was not asked by the administration: Against whom was this a rebellion? The rebellion was against the idea that, as White people, there is something that is forbidden for them to say or do.

In the effort to paint racists as bad without dealing with the roots of White supremacy, schools have made oppressive language forbidden fruit that can only be experienced among trusted associates. By avoiding race and the history of colonial oppression from Arizona's founding, the Arizona school's approach fed racism and pushed White students toward White supremacy rather than extinguishing it.

White America's unease and denial about race, the history of race, and White supremacist structures create the ability to be "bad" in safe contexts. These words, when used in these contexts, are supposed to be fun, festive, or risqué. These spaces allow White people to vent their anger at perceived transgressions against White supremacy.Ultimately, by not teaching explicitly about racism, oppression, and race, schools are perpetuating the worst of these things.

ENDING COLOR BLINDNESS

So then, is the answer to just ignore difference and treat all kids the same? Kids are kids, right? That is the refrain stated in conversations with teachers and sometimes even in the halls of teacher preparation programs. However, research shows that kids are not all the same. Kids are individuals, but they are also members of identity groups, families, and communities. This race-evasive phrase is a way to avoid looking at students as different from their White teachers, but students are almost always different from their teachers racially, ethnically, and culturally on many levels.

Even if a teacher racially identifies as being in the same group, there will be differences based on economic status, age, and social groups, and social media has accelerated these divides and how teachers interact with students. This makes a statement like "kids are kids" one that is meant to let adults off the hook. If there is no difference in kids, then there is no need to meet the different needs of students. Bartolomé (1994) explained that this "kids are kids" approach to children's learning has been skewed by the mentality that frames adults as whole and fully human and some kids as broken. It also seeks to erase racial and cultural differences between White kids and kids of color. It tries to rise above difference but instead enforces whiteness on everyone as though that were the cure to some kind of pernicious ailment. Because they are not broken, there is not, nor should there be, a magic method that would fix students of color. Kids are not broken, and kids of color are not broken White kids.

To sum up, as Black students will see and experience the overwhelming whiteness of teachers for most, if not all, of their schooling experience in America, to be successful, White teachers must understand their own positions as White people and of how that impacts their teaching. As Love (2019b) explained, learning about race leads to uncomfortable but crucial understandings of American history and society:

> Teachers who disregard the impact of racism on Black children's schooling experiences, resources, communities, and parent interactions will do harm to

children of color. This ignorance is not just a painful sign of a blatant lack of information—a function of racism is to erase the history and contributions of people of color—it is a dangerous situation as these teachers go on to take jobs in schools filled with Black and Brown children. This turns schools into places that mirror society instead of improving it. The hard truth is that racism functions as a "superpredator" of Black and Brown children within our schools.

Until race is centered in conversations about White teachers, there can be no real progress toward a more inclusive curriculum or pedagogical framework (Sleeter, 2005). Until educators at all levels begin the project of dismantling White supremacist structures in schools and then the larger society, there will be no progress toward the multicultural goals they espouse. The current discourse of inclusion has proved insufficient to meet the challenges of today's versions of White supremacy. More is needed and more is required from White teachers to solve the largest problems in American education.

MEET THE PARTICIPANTS

It is important to ground the approach presented in this book in empirical research. The method is available in other works (Boucher, 2013, 2016, 2018; Boucher & Helfenbein, 2015). To study the relationships of solidarity built by White teachers of African American students, teachers were interviewed and observed using a technique called photo-elicitation (Boucher, 2018). This technique allows for the observation of interactions between the teacher and an African American student. The photos taken during the observation are then shown to the participant, who is able to theorize about pedagogy and practice. These photos were then intentionally destroyed as their purpose was only to elicit responses from the teacher participants.

Each session began with the simple question, "What is happening in this photo?" From there, teachers would tell their stories and their truths about their teaching and how they built solidarity relationships with students. Included in this book are vignettes from three of the participants in the study.

Table 1.1. The Participants

Pseudonym	Gender	School	Grade	Degree	Years of teaching	Persona
Frieda Kohn	F	Central	9–10	MA	22	The Warm Demander
Bianca Romano	F	Central	7 & 11	MA	2	The Care Bear
Mark Johnson	M	Westview	11	BA	9	The Fighter

These participants demonstrated some form of solidarity with their students, but in very different ways. Two are female, and one is male. All are White teachers of different ages. All of them taught high school in segregated schools with largely African American populations in a medium-sized city in the Midwest. The grounding of the framework in both research and theory can aid White teachers in their quest to build a more equitable classroom where African American kids, and their teachers, succeed, thrive, and find joy in learning.

Chapter Two

Gaps and the School-to-Prison Pipeline

After lifting the veil on the White supremacist structures in schools and society, those structures become impossible to ignore. The largest of them, and arguably the most destructive, is the school-to-prison pipeline (Hirschfield, 2008). This pipeline is created and maintained through laws and policies at every federal and state level, and it is implemented through the individual actions of teachers and principals (Bryan, 2017). Solidarity with students begins with the teacher's understanding of these structures and then refusal to become part of the system. This radical act of saying NO is the first step in building relationships that lead to caring solidarity.

ORIGINS OF THE "GAP"

Scholarship has long revealed that there is a persistent difference in achievement between White students and African American students (Ladson-Billings, 2006, 2007, 2008). In all ways that it is measured, whether by test scores, graduation rates, or college admissions, African American students succeed in the current education system at a lower rate than their White counterparts. This gap starts in preschool and extends through college (Haskins & Rouse, 2005).

Despite decades of concentration in research and practice on this gap, it still permeates American schools (Howard, 2010). It exists in public and private education and in every area of the country. It is not exclusively an urban problem, as many assume, but extends wherever students of color are schooled in the United States (Bradbury, Corak, Waldfogel, & Washbrook, 2015; Ladson-Billings, 2006, 2007, 2008). However, the questions that are asked and who decides the definition of success defines who is, and who is not, in that gap.

Beginning with the 1966 Coleman report, formally titled "Equality of Educational Opportunity" (1966), education scholars, theorists, and teachers worked to explain and then eliminate a gap in standardized test performance between African Americans and White students. The report itself deservedly blamed this *achievement* gap on segregation but wrongly concluded that simply putting Black students in majority White schools would solve the problem. However, scholars and the federal government have concluded that segregation is worse than ever, and yet the gap persists irrespective of the level of segregation or desegregation of a school (Coleman, 1966; EdBuild, 2016; Kucsera, 2014; Orfield, Frankenberg, Ee, & Kuscera, 2014).

The desegregation efforts of the 1970s had successes but were then reversed in the 1990s as Whites began to find new ways to segregate schools, including a shift toward community schools and deliberately dividing existing districts to separate students by race (Nazaryan, 2017). Unfortunately, as U.S. government reports have shown, schools are as segregated now as they were at the time of the Coleman report (EdBuild, 2016; Kucsera, 2014; Orfield, Frankenberg, Ee, & Kuscera, 2014).

Under slavery and segregation, beyond economic, religious, and other personal factors, it was the power that Whites coveted for themselves that created the systems we now live in. The purpose of American segregation was not only separation but also subjugation. Today, few would argue for the kind of separation that was normal in the United States through the 1990s, but the underlying power structure of whiteness has only recently come into question.

The scholarship is unambiguous in finding that the cause of this disparity is an assemblage of structural inequalities of the schooling system combined with the decisions made by individual schoolteachers and administrators. Black kids in schools that are majority White are less likely to graduate, are less likely to go to college, and tend to have lower test scores than their White counterparts. The same is true if Black kids go to a segregated, majority Black school. Given this information, people must choose: Do they believe that (a) Black kids are naturally inferior to White students, or (b) is the entire education system is stacked against Black students? Given the evidence, it is either one or the other. Simply put, the answer is b. From the first day that Black students walk through the doors of their school, they face a labyrinth of roadblocks, challenges, insults large and small, and closed doors.

As Love (2019c) explained, successful teaching across the color line requires an approach that does not assume students are damaged by their blackness, nor by their communities, but by the White power structures that oppress them. To navigate this system, African American children walk the thinnest line of behavior. To survive, they must be better by far than their White peers and outstanding in personal courage.

Many meet this challenge, and it is a proud testament to the resilience of extraordinary human beings. Yet faith endures, and there is always the hope that this year, this school, this teacher will be different. This year *can* be different if there is a change in how students and schools are treated and conceptualized.

THE OPPORTUNITY GAP AND EDUCATION DEBT

The achievement gap, as a concept, assumes shortcomings of students, families, and communities of color. However, there are other ways to look at the gap. Adults in the education system know that a good education leads to opportunities and success in life. Generally, people who go into the field of education were good at many parts of schooling. People who go into teaching are often those who found success and fulfillment in school and have a desire to bring those experiences to their students (Britzman, 2003; Danielewicz, 2001). This experience, combined with the assumption that schooling is the path to success, means that teachers, especially White teachers, assume that the ways students are currently educated is both normal and desirable (Solomona, Portelli, Daniel, & Campbell, 2005).

Because the entire system assumes White normality, it ignores that fact the students are not succeeding and cannot fathom that standardized tests, graduation rates, and college admissions are neutral elements that are not racially or culturally defined. This creates a formula that ignores the real situation of Black kids in schools. Ladson-Billings (1995) explained that the language around the achievement gap uses words that assume students are deficient and that the gap in question is based on a neutral set of factors (2006, 2007, 2008).

Researchers have shifted this discourse on achievement and sought to change the narrative from a gap in *achievement* to a gap in the *opportunities* afforded students of color (Darling-Hammond, Friedlaender, & Snyder, 2014; Ladson-Billings, 2006, 2007, 2008; Love, 2019c). Scholarship shows that teachers of all varieties look at students of color, or even lower-income White students, with models that focus on their deficits rather than their strengths and resilience. Looking at the achievement gap from the other side, these questions can help to elucidate the structures that are often unnamed and unchallenged.

- What if the gap exists not because students are failing in schools but because schools are failing the students?
- What if this failure stems from the suppositions of White people and their belief in their own goodness and normality?

• How would it change teacher behavior if schools and systems were understood to be failing the students rather than the students failing in the systems?
• What if we assumed that teachers of low performing students have a gap in their ability to meet the needs of their students rather than students having a gap in their achievement?

These questions begin the process of becoming conscious of White supremacist structures that many White teachers have never considered questioning. Scholars have reframed the gap to focus on opportunities, resources, and support that is lacking rather than seeing students as deficient in their ability to achieve standards normed from White communities.

Income, race, and geographic location are still the main predictors of school success, and the methods used by school systems to close the achievement gap have largely focused on Black students. However, educators have often refused to see themselves as anything but blameless, benevolent actors in the daily drama of schools and kids. Ullucci (2012) explained, "The challenge arises in helping teachers come to terms with the ways whiteness and privilege function within these systems, and how they can either be complicit with or rupture these mechanisms" (p. 90). White educators often do not look at the gaps as opportunities to change and reorient curriculum and the space of schooling but instead have used them as bludgeons against students, parents, and communities, explaining away the failure of Black children under their tutelage (Crocco & Costigan, 2007).

Ladson-Billings correctly pointed out that the Coleman report's exhortation to integrate schools was erroneously taken by many to mean that Black students were culturally inferior and that exposure to White schools was an answer to that cultural deficiency. Instead of a gap, Ladson-Billings defines a debt owed to students of color. She explained that there were both market and nonmarket effects of the assumption of inferiority. For example, historically, spending on Black segregated schools has been much less than on White schools and still is today.

Ladson-Billings pointed out that if schools that educate mostly Black and Brown students were funded at the same levels as schools in wealthy, White suburbs, students would have been performing better all along. Add to that additional spending to address social ills like low wages, the inability to negotiate for higher wages because of the destruction of unions, and food deserts, and there would be a narrowing of the education debt and thus of the gap in achievement in most areas of schooling.

Ladson-Billings explained that while the labor of Black people was being exploited, the wealth from that labor built the country and the wealthy classes within it. Even today, Black labor is being used to power the economy through a prison system where prisoners' labor is exploited and subsidized by taxpayers (Browne, 2007). The debt is owed because African American people have been blocked from access to the economy, to education, and to civil rights since the founding of the republic. Yet researchers have the audacity after this history to talk of a "gap."

GRIT

Another frame that reinforces White supremacy is the concept of grit, as explained by Duckworth et al. (2007), It has gained traction as a way to describe and then build resiliency in students. According to Duckworth, grit is a concept that describes students who work "strenuously toward challenges" and are able to sustain that effort over years despite "failure, adversity, and plateaus in progress" (p. 1088). According to this theory, high achievement does not come to those who are the smartest or even the most talented but to those who persevere, especially against great odds. Grit is evidenced by that success. Duckworth also surmised that grit is connected to self-discipline and the ability to deny immediate gratification for long-term success.

At first glance, grit sounds like the kind of resilience that schools should be instilling in all students. It is portrayed as the ability to stand in the face of adversity and trudge on when the going is difficult. However, this concept is used not only to commend those who make it through but to blame those who do not. The thinking often goes that those without grit are somehow unworthy of success and that the educator's job is to create grit in their students (Stokas, 2015).

In her book *We Want to Do More than Survive*, Love (2019c) explained that the for-profit company the Character Lab produces materials and friendly research studies on grit, relating it to everything, including the young adult novel *The Hunger Games*. But Love asked why students are expected to navigate a racist system and when they rebel are seen as somehow deficient in grit.

The Character Lab insists that it is interested in building skills to help students achieve their long-term goals. But Love (2019a) asked a pertinent question that seems to allude grit ideologists:

> But what if your long-term goal is fighting racism? Is four hundred years long enough? We have rebelled, fought, conformed, pleaded with the courts, marched, protested, boycotted, created timeless art that reflects our lives, and become president of the country that disposes of us with little to no relief of our oppression. Is that not grit? (pp. 72–73)

Love explained that good teaching is "to abandon teaching gimmicks like 'grit' that present the experiences of dark youth as ahistorical and further pathologize them and evoke collective freedom dreaming" (p. 12). It is a testament to the deep faith in America and the potential of their children that parents send their students to schools that over and over again, generation after generation, disrespect and devalue their children and describe their hardships in an oppressive system as character building "grit" experiences (Duckworth & Quinn, 2009). Grit ideology mocks that resilience and assumes that oppression is good for kids who do not deserve any other life..

Some schools may work at equipping students for life in a White supremacist society, but seldom are they equipping students to dismantle it. As Love (2019c) explained, "pedagogies that promote social justice must have teeth. They must move beyond feel-good language and gimmicks to help educators understand and recognize America and its schools as spaces of whiteness, White rage, and White supremacy, all of which function to terrorize students of color" (p. 13). Students build resilience out of the struggles that people with privilege do not have to endure. Schools act as though these struggles are the normal course of the life of students of color without asking why and never assume that White students should have to face analogous challenges or depravations (Ris, 2015).

THE DISCIPLINE GAP

Continuing to work on seeing the structures of White supremacy, our attention should also turn to the unequal disciplinary actions taken against Black students. In the attempt to improve test scores without changing how students are taught, reforms have created a pipeline for Black students directly from schools to the correctional system (Fuentes, 2012; Hirschfield, 2008; Wald & Losen, 2003).

The ideology of the achievement gap pervades schools where African American students attend and is a tool to reinforce the concepts of White supremacy and normality. Methods to close the gap have largely focused on Black children themselves and have not treated it as an opportunity to change perceptions of race and the measures used to qualify success. Rather, the solution is often to treat the gap as a pathology afflicting Black students. School bureaucracies use deficit models and interventions that constrain the curriculum, eliminate the arts, enforce strict disciplinary codes, and focus on holding teachers and students accountable for raising test scores (Crocco & Costigan, 2007). These models have led to reforms such as zero-tolerance policies that have created a pipeline directly from schools to the correctional system for Black students (Fuentes, 2012; Hirschfield, 2008; Kim & Geronimo, 2009; Morris & Perry, 2016; Wald & Losen, 2003).

The research is clear that the pipeline begins early in the educational careers of Black students. According to a 2016 report by the U.S. Department of Education, the gap in discipline and punishment of African American students begins before students are five years old. The report states that Black public preschool students (two to four years old) were 3.6 times more likely to be suspended from school than White preschool children, and while Black students make up 19 percent of enrollments, they make up 47 percent of out-of-school suspensions. According to the report, "Black boys represent 19% of male preschool enrollment, but 45% of male preschool children receiv[ing] one or more out-of-school suspensions. Black girls represent 20% of female preschool enrollment, but 54% of female preschool children receiv[ing] one or more out-of-school suspensions" (CRDC, 2016).

As Love (2019c) explained, "for too many, suspension is a birthright of being young and Black" (p. 5). This exclusion from school has real consequences for Black students' achievement over their educational lives. The problem of preschool and elementary school suspension has caught the attention of some administrators. In Minneapolis, the superintendent banned suspensions for all students in preschool, kindergarten, and first grade for the 2014 school year (Matos, 2015). However, the ban only lasted one year after teachers and administrators complained that it left them without options for student behaviors that they found unacceptable.

Morris and Perry (2016) found that African American students in a large Kentucky school system were suspended out of school, thus excluding them from the learning process, at a rate nearly six times that of their White peers. They further explained that segregation of Black students within the district could account for about 12 percent of out-of-school suspensions. Not surprisingly, the schools with the highest rates of African American students had the highest rates of suspension, but even in schools that were more integrated, "each additional percentage of the student body that is black is estimated to increase the annual number of school suspensions by about ten, controlling for school size and socioeconomic composition" (p. 76).

Morris and Perry's (2016) analysis of exclusion from school and the achievement test performance of excluded students highlights the effects of segregation and disciplinary bias:

> The suspension disparity operates at both the school and individual levels such that black students are more likely than white students to attend schools that employ higher levels of exclusionary discipline, and black students are also more likely to be suspended than their white peers within the same schools. In turn, racial and ethnic minorities underperform on reading and math achievement tests relative to white students in this school system. (Morris & Perry, 2016, p. 81)

They concluded that "the effects of suspension are long lasting, setting into motion a trajectory of poor performance that continues in subsequent years, even if a student is not suspended again. Indeed, our results show that academic growth drops precipitously after one early suspension" (p. 82).

Gregory and Weinstein (2008) argued that there is a "discipline gap" in schools when it comes to White teachers and African American students (p. 456). The disproportionate number of suspensions of African American students, specifically males, leads to lower achievement and therefore a more negative attitude toward school, which can display itself in self-destructive or defiant behaviors, thus leading to more suspensions. This cycle can quickly lead to students being referred to the justice system and eventual incarceration (Gregory & Weinstein, 2008).

These are only a small sample of the large number of studies that show the detrimental effects of educational exclusion, which snowball as students grow into adolescence, so it would seem that the practice would be abandoned, and yet it keeps going. Preschool students excluded from the learning environment fall behind and become elementary students suspended who fall further behind. Students who are slightly behind in elementary school, without purposeful intervention, become students who are behind in middle and high school.

This cycle of suspensions to low scores to more suspensions leads to behaviors that further disrupt the classroom that is focused on raising test scores. When a student then comes in contact with police resource officers in middle or high school, the consequences of boredom, low achievement, low self-confidence, and the constant drip of failure in school can wash students into the justice system.

HOW THE PIPELINE IS BUILT AND MAINTAINED

It would be simple to dismiss the evidence of the school-to-prison pipeline by acknowledging that White teachers are good people doing the best that they can. That is a true statement. The vast majority of White teachers go to school every day to change the world and make it a better place, yet they carry with them biases, frames, and ideologies that cause them to do permanent damage to African American students, families, and communities. There is overwhelming evidence that White teachers perceive Black students as a threat to the learning environment in their classrooms and that administrators are complicit in this, thus making this perception the basis for individual actions. This perception of threat by White teachers is the entryway to the school-to-prison pipeline. Teachers who lack the ability or desire to prevent students from entering the pipeline by inspiring them with thought-provoking curriculum and instruction in behavior self-regulation within the classroom create a self-fulfilling prophecy that students of color are unmanageable. This is the agonizing reality, and it must be dealt with.

According to Wald and Losen (2003), a lack of effective behavioral interventions, harsh school removal policies, and a get-tough discipline system in schools and juvenile facilities have coalesced to create a pipeline from the schoolyard to the prison yard (p. 10). This school-to-prison pipeline criminalizes childish behaviors and, according to Hirschfield (2008), has created a system of school governance where teachers and administrators have ceded authority to "criminal justice professionals" (p. 93). Hirschfield explained that fear of people who are not White and middle class, combined with pressure to have all students perform well on standardized tests, has driven this move to criminalization.

As demonstrated by the school-to-prison pipeline and the uneven success of students based on race, schools are not neutral but instead are heavily biased in favor of White teachers and White children. The whiteness of school spaces is part of the curriculum as much as the ABCs. Students of color are continually disinvited from participating as equal entities. They are welcome to be in school as long as they are willing to follow the rules. These rules do not take into them account, do not value their input nor their presence. The rules are made to sift the acceptable from the unacceptable.

The rules are also there for teachers. Teachers feel a great deal of pressure to keep in line and not make trouble. These rules make it so teachers cannot afford to have students disrupt classroom procedures because of their need to adhere to strict timelines dictated by administrators. This causes any behavior that diverts the teacher from the daily plan to be labeled as disruptive and results in action. The proliferation of school resource officers arresting students has progressed from being the discipline of last resort to a primary disciplinary strategy in schools. These resource officers have come under increased scrutiny as student videos of officers in South Carolina, Texas, and Florida have shown officers "slamming" students as young as twelve years old to the ground and even dragging them across desks. Children as young as three years old are being handcuffed. Young children are being jailed with adults. Historically, Black students have a reasonable assumption of unfair treatment by police, causing a complete breakdown of any social contract between the administration, teachers, and students. Instead of learning to be citizens in a democracy who trust and value the system, kids learn that their futures are filled with harassment, arrest, and violence from authority figures.

As Goff et al. (2014) found, an "atmosphere of dehumanization" has pervaded school discipline (p. 10). Part of what they found was that police officers overestimated Black children's ages and perceived them to be 4.53 years older than they were. They concluded that Black children, in contexts of dehumanization, are prematurely treated as adults, leading to an increased use of violence to control behavior and an assumption of guilt.

Rather than school officials and educators working to keep students in schools, they have handed discipline over to police officers who become the conduit introducing Black students to the school-to-prison pipeline for both major and minor incidents. Hirschfield (2008) explained, "Teachers and administrators often perceive little choice but to summon repressive means to swiftly remove disruptive students from the classroom and the school" (p. 93).

This attitude, when added to the many cases each year of police abusing students in schools, shows that any good that comes from having an armed police officer in schools is outweighed by the negative impact their presence has on teaching, administration, and student well-being. White teachers without the capacity to culturally connect with their students are more likely to depend on police officers, suspension, and exclusion as a form of punishment.

Testing regimes, teacher accountability, and a narrowing of the curriculum to meet testing requirements have made schools less safe for Black students as teachers struggle to meet the demands placed upon them from outside the classroom. More reliance on testing as a way to measure teacher performance, educators are less likely to invest in students whose test scores are lower. Because of punitive reforms, teachers are increasingly accountable for student achievement on standardized tests, yet teachers' incapacity to meet the demands placed on them has created the perception that harsh methods are needed to control student behavior. Added to this mix, schools with higher minority populations use a narrower curriculum that focuses almost exclusively on math and reading in order to try to meet those testing targets. Teachers are increasingly unable to use exploratory projects and trips that build interest in learning.

This drill curriculum lowers interest in class work and creates boredom for students, causing them to act out. To deal with these behaviors that disrupt the drill-test learning environment, teachers increasingly turn over authority to administrators and law enforcement in a futile attempt to force students to meet imposed academic standards (Fallis & Opotow, 2003). While this state of affairs has become the norm throughout the United States, it is hardest felt in large cities, where high percentages of Black males are increasingly introduced to the correctional system at an early age by being pushed out of the school system (Bowditch, 1993; Fuentes, 2012; Hirschfield, 2008; Wacquant, 2001).

Bowditch (1993) found that students with lower grades and attendance were systematically encouraged to drop out of high school through the disciplinary process. "The activities of the discipline office, which routinely identified 'troublemakers' and 'got rid of' them through suspensions and involuntary drops, may be one important but largely unacknowledged mechanism through which schools perpetuate the racial and class stratification of the larger society" (p. 506). Gregory and Weinstein (2008) argued that there is a "discipline gap" between Black and White students and that this gap results in suspensions by administrators (p. 456).

Hirschfield (2008) explained, "Teachers and administrators often perceive little choice but to summon repressive means to swiftly remove disruptive students from the classroom and the school" (p. 93). Cuellar and Markowitz (2015) found a significant jump in the probability that students who are suspended out of school will become involved in the judicial system when they are not in school: "being suspended out of school on a school day is associated with a more than doubling of the probability of offense" (p. 105). Further, they explained that "school suspension policies designed to handle problem behavior in school may contribute to overall crime rates out of school, highlighting a significant potential disadvantage of using out-of-school suspension as part of a school disciplinary policy" (p. 105). These and other studies show that there is a bias toward harsher discipline in schools for students of color and that when students are excluded from the school environment, they are more likely to end up incarcerated either during their school years or shortly thereafter.

In summary, schools are admittedly facing unprecedented challenges, the adults in the schools are tempted to try and meet them by changing student populations rather than changing their pedagogy. The resulting handover of authority, combined with the economic incentive to post improved test scores, has resulted in a consistent trend toward using the juvenile justice system to divert students from school systems unable to meet student needs (Fuentes, 2012).

The process that moves students from classroom to cellblock begins with behaviors that in the past would have resulted in little more than a suspension or a parent meeting now result in criminal charges and confinement, thus introducing students to the justice system and increasing the chance of adult incarceration (Cuellar & Markowitz, 2015). These interventions or altercations may involve police officers trained in school discipline, but oftentimes they are not. Either way, the unstated goal of officers in schools is to maintain student compliance, not to keep students in the learning environment (p. 93).

Harsh school removal policies have resulted from the inability to create behavioral interventions that would deescalate situations. Instead of more humane structures that take time and resources, schools created zero-tolerance and get-tough policies that led to more suspensions and juvenile detentions. The effects of these policies, procedures, and biases in the system have been devastating for African American students across the country.

For these students and the rest of society, the loss of academic achievement, the expense of a system of monitoring students, the increased police presence and the retraining of police, mass incarceration, and the shattering effects on individuals and families are not justified by the outcomes. We are not more educated and secure as a nation because lives are lost and futures are ruined. We do not gain by more police, more incarceration, more rules, and more exclusion of students.

COPS BUT NO COUNSELORS

According to the ACLU, 90 percent of schools in the United States do not have enough counselors and social workers to meet the needs of students as schools are increasing their police presence. The ACLU report titled *Cops and No Counselors: How the Lack of School Mental Health Staff Is Harming Students* (2017) found in a nationwide survey that

- 1.7 million students are in schools with police but no counselors;
- 3 million students are in schools with police but no nurses;
- 6 million students are in schools with police but no school psychologists;
- 10 million students are in schools with police but no social workers; and
- 14 million students are in schools with police but no counselor, nurse, psychologist, or social worker. (Whitaker et al., 2017, p. 3)

Skiba et al. (2011) monitored the disciplinary practices of 364 middle and elementary schools and found that African American students received harsher and more frequent discipline than their White peers. These exclusions are disproportionately placed on Black students despite the fact that their behaviors are perceptibly similar to White students who did not receive the same types of punishment (Monroe, 2005). Skiba et al. (2002) found

> no evidence that racial disparities in school punishment could be explained by higher rates of African American misbehavior. . . . White students were significantly more likely to be referred to the office for smoking, leaving without permission, obscene language, and vandalism. In contrast, black students were more likely to be referred to the office for *disrespect, excessive noise, threat, and loitering* [emphasis added]. (p. 334)

Evidence overwhelmingly points to the fact that implicit bias, fear, and suspicion of Black children; a lack of knowledge about cultural differences and the structures in place that impede students of color from wealth and mobility; and pressure for all students to perform well on standardized tests has pressed schools to exclude rather than teach Black kids (Morris & Perry, 2016; Okonofua & Eberhardt, 2015; Skiba, Peterson, & Williams, 1997).

Love (2019b) described her perceptions of White teachers: "Let me be clear: I do not think White teachers enter the profession wanting to harm children of color, but they will hurt a child whose culture is viewed as an afterthought." The lack of cultural awareness and competency has caused control to be the foremost goal of schooling and made law enforcement officials the first rather than the last resort for controlling student behavior. With uniforms, deadly weapons at the ready, and an attitude of confrontation, police are embedded into the disciplinary structure, often without training in education.

Pane and Rocco (2014) explained that "exclusionary school discipline is commonly practiced when teachers perceive heightened misbehavior and classroom discipline combined with the fear of losing control in the classroom. Exclusionary school discipline practices include the referral of disruptive students out of the classroom and their subsequent suspension and expulsion from school" (p. 29). They explained that the pipeline begins with referrals for disruption from individual teachers, then suspension from administrators, school failure, dropping out or expulsion, juvenile incarceration, and then adult prison (Losen & Skiba, 2010). The ACLU found in 2017 that:

- Students with disabilities were arrested at a rate 2.9 times that of students without disabilities. In some states, they were 10 times more likely to be arrested than their counterparts.
- Black students were arrested at a rate 3 times that of white students. In some states, they were 8 times more likely to be arrested.
- Pacific Island/Native Hawaiian and Native American students were arrested at a rate 2 times that of White students.
- Latinx students were arrested at a rate 1.3 times that of White students.
- Black girls made up 16 percent of the female student population but were 39 percent of girls arrested in school. Black girls were arrested at a rate 4 times that of White girls. In North Carolina, Iowa, and Michigan, Black girls were over 8 times more likely to be arrested than White girls.
- Black and Latino boys with disabilities made up 3 percent of students but 12 percent of school arrests. (Whitaker et al., 2017, p. 5)

The evidence is overwhelming that American schools, especially secondary schools, are not places that embrace and nurture African American students. Instead, the evidence shows that schools are gauntlets that only the most resilient, the most exceptional are able to navigate (Love, 2019a, 2019b, 2019c). Love refers to this slow, deliberate, daily process of dehumanization, disenfranchisement, and criminalization of African American youth as "spirit murdering" (Love, 2014).

Duncan (2018) described the work that Black teachers in multicultural schools do to gird their students against the racism of their White teacher colleagues. Duncan chronicled the emancipatory practices of these teachers, which included interrupting racist and deficit-oriented speech by colleagues, transparently holding students to higher standards, and interceding with White colleagues on behalf of students.

While Duncan's work shows the lengths to which teachers of color will go to sustain their Black students, schools should not depend solely on Black teachers to do all of the work to dismantle the White supremacy that pervades schools and school structures. That work must be done, in collaboration with their colleagues of color, by the White teachers who make up the majority of the workforce.

White teachers who seek to take a stance of caring solidarity with their students of color must become dismantlers of White supremacist structures in schools and school systems. It is immoral and unsustainable to assume that any curriculum or pedagogy that does not save students from going to prison is anything more than window dressing on a system that is intended to oppress and subjugate people of color. White teachers must stand in the way of the school-to-prison pipeline, not just with words but with action.

PARTICIPANT 1: FRIEDA KOHN, THE "WARM DEMANDER"

Frieda Kohn's room at Central High School is covered with even more of the posters anyone would expect to see in a social studies classroom. Posters of heroes such as Martin Luther King Jr. and Shirley Chisholm overlay world and state maps and float above the U.S. Constitution, Declaration of Independence, and Pledge of Allegiance. Maps of ancient Rome and a diagram of the Renaissance all combine to create a wall-sized collage of history and geography.

Over these posters are layered pennants from the local colleges and, finally, on top of the colorful backdrop, exemplary work done by students in her class. The rules of the classroom are simple and written out using an eclectic collection of markers and handwriting styles on one corner of the collage:

1. Be on time.
2. You may only use three passes per grading period.
3. Once in the room, do not exit without permission or a pass.
4. Respect the lesson. Be attentive and participate.
5. Respect the classroom. Leave it better than you found it.
6. Electronics, other than your laptops, will be confiscated if visible.

These rules were created in collaboration with her students at the beginning of the school year as one of their first exercises in the kind of engaging citizenship education Frieda practices. During my observations, students were often dispersed around tables with laptop Macintosh computers, working on a semester-long project that culminated in their making movies about the judicial process.

In each of Frieda's classes of between fourteen and twenty-five students, approximately 70 percent were African American, 20 percent were Latino, and 10 percent were White. The groups were not assigned, and there was no division in the room according to ethnicity. Most groups, however, were likely to have a majority of one gender.

For the unit observed, each group was given a scenario of a crime committed in order to understand the judiciary system and the rights of citizens under arrest. Students assigned their own roles, wrote scripts, and shot their own videos to explain the process from arrest and arraignment to acquittal or incarceration. They were proud of their work and eager to show Ms. Kohn their work on days dedicated to assessing their progress.

A self-described "short, fat, White woman," Frieda chose the typical path of a four-year degree in social studies education from a major midwestern public university. She then entered into the profession of teaching immediately after graduating and had a master's degree at the time of the interviews. She taught in two different states, one in the East and one in the Midwest, and described "falling in love" with urban education while teaching in the eastern United States.

Frieda described herself as a "warm demander."[1] "Our former principal used the term 'warm demander' a lot, and there's a lot of research out there on what warm demanders are in public education. I do think I fit into that role." She was calm and reassuring to students but in a way that made sure to get the point across if there was a need to correct a behavior. She used an example to illustrate her pedagogy:

> One young man I've had now since he was a freshman. He's [currently] a junior. I had him in one class freshman year and two classes last year and I had him again this year for two classes, and he'll say, "Ms. Kohn never cusses you out, but sometimes by the time she's done talking, you feel like you have been."

Frieda felt that she fit the identity of a warm demander and that through high expectations for behavior and academics, she helped students attain their potential.

She explained that she expected a great deal out of her students, but she was only able to do that because of the relationships she had built with them. However, sometimes having the expectation was not enough:

---

1. First coined in Kleinfeld (1975), warm demanders are first concerned with the climate of the classroom and with building rapport with students, but they are also deeply committed to student achievement. To accomplish both, warm demanders use a combination of adopted or appropriated cultural norms along with school structural and cultural values to build relationships and move students toward academic achievement.

I don't do a lot of write-ups; I tend to do the "let's talk about it" and come to a mediated mutual understanding. I call them F.O.G., "fear of God," meetings. And there are times when [a student] will come up and say, "I know I've messed up here and I need to talk," and I'm the one that they are going to talk to. It's just that relationship building. I'm willing to do that with any of the kids. At times I've done that with a lot of them. They just need an adult who cares for them.

According to Kleinfeld (1975), one of the traits of a warm demander is that the teacher respects the student's culture and is willing to adopt certain traits or values of the student's home culture as a connection point.

However, the other part of the warm demander is that the teacher is willing to demand a high degree of academic achievement from students. This balance is the hallmark of the warm demander identity, and Frieda worked to do both, as she described in her work with a student who had been homeless.

Frieda: He has been homeless, living from hotel to hotel to hotel. He has really matured this year, and we're seeing that. Last year he had attendance issues. He still has some organization issues. He still doesn't get things turned in on time necessarily, but he is so much improved.

Michael: So, he has a warmth with you, even more so than the rest. Where do you think that comes from?

Frieda: I think it comes from, pulling them out and taking the time to sometimes say, "I'm going to kick you in the butt today and this is why." It's the old story of, kids need structure, and they want that because structure is how you know you're safe and cared for. And there are times when he has screwed up in class where I could have written them up and drop the hammer on him.

Frieda's discussion showed that, in her language, her approach, and her mannerisms, she was willing to meet students where they were and yet demand that they meet her expectations for academics and work. She was willing to bend the expectations in specific circumstances, but the bar is always high, and it got higher as the relationship bond with the students cemented.

Frieda's Solidarity with Students

As a teacher who embraced warm demander pedagogy, Frieda worked to build relationships of solidarity with students in and out of the classroom. She met with parents and participated in the community. She knew the parents and grandparents of students and invested in their lives.

Besides being a warm demander, Frieda saw herself in solidarity with her students against the larger world. That solidarity came out in the depth of her relationships with her students, her willingness to confront students on harmful behaviors, and her work to inspire students to go to college.

But this kind of solidarity did not happen without cultivation. Sometimes students needed to be corrected, and Frieda was not reluctant to do that. During the observation, many students sought out Frieda's counsel on a variety of issues having to do with schoolwork, home life, college aspirations, grades, and sports. Each one of these students received a similar kind of individual attention. Frieda showed that she was listening carefully to their concerns by nodding and asking clarifying questions. After each student had explained the problem, Frieda would question the student until he or she came up with an answer they could both agree on. She would often have her hand on the student's shoulder or their arm as she was listening.

As Frieda looked at the pictures I took as part of the study, she had a story about each of the students in one particular working group.

> [This one walks to school], and if he is going to be late, he will sometimes stay home. He has had issues with truancy, even truancy court. So he is one that you pull out in the hall and give a swift kick in the rear end. "You still need to be here. You can't miss the whole day just because you're going to be tardy. Get here and get here on time."

Frieda created a system for this student to have a friend call him in order to make sure that he was at school, where, Frieda said, he stayed late:

> Just because he needs a quiet place to study. He lives with his grandmother, and she is very supportive. I've called her a few times in the past and said, "Hey, he is slipping a little on grades." She says, "Okay, he's yours." So he stays after. She just wants to make sure she knows where he is.

This type of communication goes beyond the typical professional model of teaching and is especially important when working across the color line. In her deep caring for students, her continual emphasis of solidaristic relationships made her a successful teacher in this underresourced, urban school.

Chapter Three

Multicultural Education as Implemented and Caring Solidarity

Since the 1970s, multicultural education (MCE) has been the framework on which all efforts at education across difference are draped. Multicultural education as envisioned by venerable scholar and educator James Banks (1995) is an outgrowth of the civil rights movement and seeks to integrate those ideals into the teaching practices of all teachers for all students. Banks's work with schools, textbooks for teacher education, and scholarly mentorships are directed toward the goals of creating a school system where everyone is included, valued, and part of the learning community.

Banks described the beginnings of the multicultural movement as extending back to the early years of the last century with W. E. B. Du Bois and Carter G. Woodson. Both Du Bois and Woodson argued for the end of segregation from a political and humanitarian standpoint. Du Bois asked why the basic standards of humanity were not applied to Black people:

> What do we want? What is the thing we are after? . . . We want to be Americans, full-fledged Americans, with all the rights of other American citizens. But is that all? Do we want simply to be Americans? Once in a while through all of us there flashes some clairvoyance, some clear idea, of what America really is. We who are dark can see America in a way that white Americans cannot. And seeing our country thus, are we satisfied with its present goals and ideals? (Du Bois, 1903/1994, p. 290)

Writing in 1933, Carter G. Woodson (1933) blamed the education of African Americans as a contributing factor to the mind-set of segregation, stating that Black inferiority and White superiority were drilled into all people in almost every class and "in almost every book" (p. 2). He explained that the school curriculum was not used as a tool for enlightening and questioning the current state of affairs but for engraining White supremacy into the minds of African American children, thereby ensuring continued suppression.

Woodson declared that "to handicap a student by teaching him that his black face is a curse and that his struggle to change his condition is hopeless is the worst sort of lynching. . . . This crusade (for a curriculum that lifts up Black people) is much more important than the anti-lynching movement, because there would be no lynching if it did not start in the schoolroom. Why not exploit, enslave, or exterminate a class that everybody is taught to regard as inferior?" (p. 3).

James Banks explained that during the 1960s, as a response to the civil rights movement and the women's movement, many educators began to ask if there were other voices that could be added to the curriculum. "Sometimes in strident voices, African Americans, frustrated with deferred and shattered dreams, demanded community control of their schools, African-American teachers and administrators, and the infusion of Black history into the curriculum" (Banks, 1995, p. 18).

Throughout the 1970s and 1980s, with leadership from scholars like James Banks and Geneva Gay, amid limited success and frequent lapses, schools have worked to instill in all American students an appreciation of all cultures and races. Banks (1997) included six goals, here paraphrased, for a multicultural curriculum:

1. Help students view curriculum from diverse cultural and ethnic perspectives.
2. Contribute to a healthy nationalism and national identity.
3. Develop students' abilities to make reflective decisions about ethnicity and culture, take personal and social responsibility, and become active in creating a more just world.
4. Help students understand their own cultures and reduce self-segregation.
5. Help students understand that all people have cultures and that one is not superior to another.
6. Help students develop important school skills while also learning about culture and being human. (Banks, 1997, pp. 25–28; Payne & Welsh, 2000)

Gay (2010) explained that culture matters in educating students of color. She rejected the proposition that cultural blindness creates equality in the classroom and proposed that cultural neutrality is a fallacy and that educational reform should be grounded in "positive beliefs about the cultural heritages and academic potentialities of these students [of color]" (p. 23). To create a validating curriculum, Gay explained that teachers should see culturally different students as assets to the classroom and listed many other characteristics of an inclusive learning environment. She also called for instruction that incorporates multicultural materials into the classroom. In Gay's discussion of the comprehensive approach to culturally responsive teaching, a teacher who practices this approach will use culture as a way to mediate curriculum and educate the "whole child" (p. 32).

Gay argued that academic success can best be attained through the teacher's cultural awareness and a use of collective effort rather than competition. In her description of the multicultural curriculum as multidimensional, she advocated for a comprehensive approach to teaching. Curriculum, climate, instruction, and assessment can all be brought together under the umbrella of one common set of goals. She explained, however, that "to do this kind of teaching well requires tapping into a wide range of cultural knowledge, experiences, contributions, and perspectives" (p. 34).

However, Banks's and Gay's laudable and democratic goals are perceived as a threat to White conservatives. Critiques of multicultural education, especially in popular books by authors on the right, all have a common theme. In their imaginings, multicultural curricula weaken our national unity that was forged in Europe (Sleeter, 2001a). As discussed in earlier chapters, U.S. schools are becoming increasingly diverse and concerned about culture but are also doing all they can to address that diversity while at the same time avoiding discussion of race (Fry, 2009; Kobayashi & Peake, 2000). The need for a multicultural framework for U.S. schools did not spring from a lack of awareness that other people exist; it came from people of color working to gain and hold power over the education of their children.

MULTICULTURAL EDUCATION DOES NOT GO FAR ENOUGH

In 2001, noted multicultural writer and teacher educator Christine Sleeter explained that "conservatives hope to destroy public support for multicultural education and mobilize public opinion to endorse a conservative definition of how young Americans will be taught to view the United States in its diversity, and the positions of the United States and European Nations within a hierarchical, capitalistic, global order made up of diverse people" (2001a, p. 89).

These definitions include the conservative belief that schools are not the place for cultural expression and should be intellectual spaces where culture is an unnecessary add-on. They advocate that education should be a tool for assimilation, making attendance to culture a diversion from the American project. Sleeter also argued that the goals of multicultural education are hampered because most teachers do not know enough about non-European cultures to help students broaden their worldview, they are likely doing more harm than good through their ignorance.

Schools have worked to foster a sense of multiculturalism without asking White people to change their own framework toward race. They have sought to accomplish this monumental task of infusing tolerance or appreciation of other races and cultures without disrupting White supremacy (May, 1999).

There is little question that all of these conservative notions are prevalent in education and are constantly being shoved into the discussion of how best to teach children. If these conceptions are to be rejected as ineffectual and harmful, they need a replacement that will inspire teachers and students to adopt a more democratic mind-set. However, a more relevant critique of multiculturalism is that it has not gone far enough and that it still reinforces whiteness in order to avoid as much conflict with conservatives as possible.

Paris (2012) explained that before multiculturalism, teachers saw all aspects of culture that were not part of whiteness as a deficit to be overcome through education: "Deficit approaches to teaching and learning, firmly in place prior to and during the 1960s and 1970s, viewed the languages, literacies, and cultural ways of being of many students and communities of color as deficiencies to be overcome in learning the demanded and legitimized dominant language, literacy, and cultural ways of schooling" (p. 93).

MCE practices have undoubtedly improved the educational experience of students, but they have not gone far enough to change how White teachers, as well as the majority culture, see people who look different from them. On a day-to-day basis, schools, teachers, and communities still tell students of color that their cultural and racial selves are not normal and that their expressions of cultural identity are not welcome. Schools police students' hair, clothes, and language in racially and culturally biased ways that enforce White normality and cultural values on students. In order to be truly multicultural, teachers must move beyond deficit thinking and a condensed, essentialist view of the cultures in their classrooms.

THE FOODS AND FESTIVALS APPROACH

In common usage, the multicultural practices should have led to an examination of the power of whiteness. Instead, they have led to a parade-of-cultures approach to multiculturalism that is criticized as a shallow dip into the cultures of people who are not considered White. In this approach, clothing, foods, language, and other characteristics are "celebrated" without the assumption that there will be any deep understanding or solidarity with the cultures on parade.

Teachers often use what Ladson-Billings and Tate (1995) called the "foods and festivals approach" to celebrating diversity (p. 61). For example, the culture of Mexico is paraded with food and clothing from southern and central Mexico, but there is no assumption of an understanding of the political struggles of indigenous peoples against the Mexican government or the U.S. involvement in the destruction of Honduras that has led to migration through Mexico to the United States.

The additive foods-and-festivals approach allows White teachers to feel like they are inclusive in the curriculum and that they are doing their part to educate students about people within or beyond their communities, but these essentialized images do little to educate any students about their diverse world, they do not address the power of whiteness, and they do not empower students of color to see themselves as anything but the Other in the classroom. Hoffman (1996) referred to this as "hallway multiculturalism" when she described the trip down the hallway of her teaching college covered with multicultural posters made by education students (p. 547). The approach in classrooms uses buzzwords, tropes, and essentialized images in an unsuccessful attempt to teach about the complex world. It is a world that does not fit into these neat, colorful categories. Hoffman explained:

> As an anthropologist of education, I knew I ought to applaud such efforts at fostering multicultural awareness. Yet, every time I walked down the hall, my instinctive reaction was far from positive. I was not sure exactly what bothered me, but it seemed somehow that the overall effect was one of ideological conformity—as if the students had all been programmed to think in exactly the same way, with the same images and same words. The very fact that the "lessons" of multiculturalism were so codified seemed to undermine the essential multicultural theme—an inherent openness and flexibility. . . . It seemed to me all too pre-packaged, a parroting of the "right" themes—a lesson, in a sense, too well learned. (p. 547)

In most MCE curriculum and practice, there is little attempt to interrogate the power dynamic of the classroom. Instead, teachers and their students are taught that whiteness is normal and that all who are not perceived that way are diverse. Thus, being normal, the white teacher presumes that he or she has perfect knowledge. This perfect knowledge assumes that the set of understandings and communication pathways of White teachers are above question. Helfenbein (2003) was concerned about this attitude: "This model . . . assumes that the cultural identities of both parties [teachers and students] are closed systems and that no mediation of the message occurs in the process of communication" (p. 11). Thus, rather than building relationships based on interconnectedness, MCE, if poorly implemented, can push students toward a more essentialized view that divides the world between us and them.

Beyond that, teachers doing MCE curriculum often avoid talking about race and racism and enforce colorblindness, often to avoid controversy that will attract unwanted attention from parents or administrators. As May

(1999) explained, "in effect, essentialist racialized discourses are 'disguised' by describing group differences principally in cultural and/or historical terms—ethnic terms, in effect—without specifically mentioning 'race' or overtly racial criteria" (p. 13). The ahistorical foods-and-festivals approach ignores White supremacy, colonialism, and genocide for a version of culture that avoids any indictment of Americans or Europeans and has the effect of otherizing people of color both in the classroom and around the world.

The foods and festivals approach to MCE stands in the way of the democratic project of MCE. A truly multicultural education would interrogate whiteness, seek to de-power it, and create a classroom where everyone is part of the diversity. It would create a deep understanding that the nature of culture is fluid, dynamic, and rich. According to Helfenbein (2003), this knowledge would lead to "new possibilities and better truths" (p. 11).

SCHOOLS REINFORCE WHITE SUPREMACIST STRUCTURES

What would schools look like if Black students' lives really, truly mattered?[1] How would our schools be different? What would our school days be like? What would the curriculum look like? The buildings? The halls? How would our teaching be different? According to the Pew Research Center (2015), students of color outnumber White students in schools, but that is not the experience of most children. This is because, while aggregate numbers show an increase in the percentage of students of color, White students are the majority in most districts where they reside because of segregation and other demographic patterns (Krogstad & Fry, 2014).

Even given this segregation, the language and concepts of inclusion and multiculturalism have successfully permeated curriculum and school culture. There is no doubt that in innumerable ways, MCE has changed teaching for the better. Teachers now look beyond Dick and Jane to teach reading and beyond the White presidents for heroes to depict on their walls. Inclusion of other people's stories and depictions of Brown and Black children has become an imperative in the classroom. However, while representation is vital, the fundamental structures have changed little as the names and faces changed in the curriculum.

While MCE works to include all people in the curriculum, it has not succeeded in decentering the White majority's hold on the structures of schooling or the curriculum. Culturally relevant pedagogy and multicultural education have been part of staff development and have been studied by educators in university programs for decades. Bulletin boards in hallways celebrate difference, and days are set aside for ethnic celebrations. But look-

---

1. Thanks to Denise Taliaferro Baszile, PhD, and Boni Wozolek, PhD, for giving me the time and space to explore this question for the American Educational Research Association.

ing at White students, have these efforts made them any smarter about race? As evidenced by current conversations about race, lessons on tolerance, acceptance, and inclusion have not changed White Americans' thinking about race.

There is a gap between the multicultural commitments of schools and the follow-through on those understandings when students graduate. School systems have worked to implement culturally responsive pedagogy into practice and have conducted hours of professional development. But the main indicators of success have not moved. Critics contend that while multicultural education has not been a failure, it has not been a success either. If multicultural education had been a success, the United States should be further along in terms of racial equity and access to capital, law, and education (Kanpol & McLaren, 1995). A successful multicultural curriculum would result in a country that values all people and is committed to equity. However, what we have seen instead, is racial segregation, colorblindness, and political and economic disparity.

MOVING BEYOND MULTICULTURALISM: CRITICAL MULTICULTURALISM

When solutions are sought, the adults and their behaviors, attitudes, or mental models are not considered as causes or even as variables. When blame is passed out, it goes to the students, communities, and parents. Whether that blame is in the form of a "culture of poverty" as in Ruby Payne (2013) or in false caring based in White supremacy, teachers who are not in solidarity with students blame students' parents and communities for their perceived inadequacies (Smiley & Helfenbein, 2011). There are two problems with the implementation of MCE that are often seen in classrooms. First, the term *culture* in MCE is often a stand-in for *race* in common discussions; thus, Crayola crayons that are various skin colors are marketed as multicultural. People conflate race and culture and improperly use physical characteristics as if they were indicators of culture. That conflation also leads to a furthering of racism because it imparts traits to people based on skin color. This is the process that critical multiculturalism seeks to avoid and is the focus of much of the critique.

Schools have been tasked with the democratic responsibility of building a multicultural society but have failed to help White Americans gain a democratic identity that would ward off the assault of racism and White supremacists. While certainly a toxic stew of bigotry, cable news and right-wing outlets cannot bear all the blame for dismantling Americans' commitment to democracy and multiculturalism. The way MCE has been implemented does not demand any identity work from White students, and they easily throw it off with their graduation caps. It is inevitable that, when they leave the warm embrace of schools, White people become vulnerable to antidemocratic ideologues, fearmongers, and racists. These former schoolchildren were not equipped to combat falsities or dismantle false equivalencies, nor were they schooled in democratic sensibilities, so they follow conspiracy theorists and authoritarians rather than use the tools that should have been provided to them when they were students.

The children in classes since the 1970s have learned the lessons of multicultural education, but as adults they continually disparage multicultural education as nothing more than political correctness. The reasons for this have been explained by hooks: "Structural racial integration with no fundamental change in white supremacist thinking and values has simply meant that black people, though 'integrated' into various areas of mainstream life over time, were and still are seen as inferior" (hooks, 2013, p. 178). Even for schools where students share the same space, the social construction of White supremacy is a primary hidden curriculum for students of color.

This halfway integration and multicultural education has not been enough to eliminate White supremacist ideology among the White U.S. population. According to a *Wall Street Journal* poll in 2015, "only 34% of Americans believe race relations in the U.S. are fairly good or very good, down from a high of 77% in January 2009, after the election of Barack Obama as America's first black president" (Nasaw, 2016). Before Obama's inauguration, conservatives and liberals hailed the election of an African American president as proof that America had moved past racial divisions and dropped old prejudices to create a new, cosmopolitan future, a new postracial society.

However, things have only become more divided. In a 2017 poll by the Pew Research Center, 70 percent of Republicans (86 percent of whom were White) stated that White people face some or a lot of discrimination. As these poll numbers illustrate, White people are feeling that they do not have a stake in a multicultural society. Racist language has now reached fever pitch, such that the use of veiled racist language and outright slurs against racial minorities has become commonplace even in the highest echelons of power (Sondel, Baggett, & Dunn, 2018).

For decades there have been calls for a more critical approach to the MCE curricular reform movement (Goldberg, 1995; Kanpol & McLaren, 1995; May, 1999). According to May (1999), the critical multicultural approach works to avoid some of the problems with multicultural education while addressing the criticism that there is not really a plan given by its critics to address the White supremacist structures in schooling.

Helfenbein (2003) explained that educators should avoid essentializing students in a static version of a cultural identity: "Culture plays a role in the construction of human reality, but only a role. Any static notion of cultural relations fails to recognize the complexity of social interactions and reifies misconceptions, stereotypes, and prejudice as truth" (p. 11).

Helfenbein opened up a new way to look at multicultural education. He called for a larger discussion of the "untidy elements of culture" and asked if identity can be better explored through "creolization, meztizaje, and hybridity" (p. 13). This take on critical multiculturalism asks students to deeply explore not only others but themselves and their cultural influences. To accomplish this, uncomfortable conversations and direct teaching about colonialism, slavery, and race must take place, even with young children.

Paris (2012) called for a more robust multicultural approach to curriculum and pedagogy. He explained that the terms used to discuss the teacher's role around culture in the classroom do not do enough to help teachers see themselves as more than just instructors who "tolerate" the differences of language and culture in their classroom but who actually advocate for the needs of their students. "I question the usefulness of 'responsive' and 'relevant'—like the term 'tolerance' in multicultural education and training, neither term goes far enough" (p. 95).

As Love (2019b) explained, "White teachers need to want to address how they contribute to structural racism. They need to join the fight for education justice, racial justice, housing justice, immigration justice, food justice, queer and trans justice, labor justice, and, above all, the fight for humanity."

Schools have spent years continually trying *this* technique and *that* strategy; teachers and administrators, exhausted and ill equipped, place blame on anyone but themselves. Despite years of scholarship, the teaching done in colleges of education, and the in-service training of the teaching force, there has been little change in White people's attitudes about race in America.

Multicultural education theorist Sonya Nieto (1999) explained that multicultural education must be antiracist education: "teaching does not become more honest and critical simply by becoming more inclusive" (p. 4). The curriculums are set so that they do not challenge racism, so that they do not ask students to see themselves as members of a society built upon racism, and they avoid making students feel like they have a stake in tearing down the structures that have been put in place specifically to benefit White people.

Bettina Love (2019b) challenged White teachers to go beyond the MCE curriculum:

> So, the question is not: Do you love all children? The question is: Will you fight for justice for Black and Brown children? And how will you fight? I argue that you must fight with the creativity, imagination, urgency, boldness, ingenuity, and rebellious spirit of abolitionists to advocate for an education system where all Black and Brown children are thriving. I call this abolitionist teaching. To love all children, we must struggle together to create the schools we are taught to believe are impossible: Schools built on justice, love, joy, and anti-racism.

In summation, multiculturalism, with its worthy and reachable goals of curricular inclusion, has not done the work that many had hoped of dismantling the structures of racism in our schools. To have a multicultural curriculum that does not grapple with colonialization and slavery flattens the narrative and essentializes the people under study. The goal of multicultural curriculum and pedagogy should be to complicate the narratives and to build students' identities to include culture, race, ethnicity, gender, and sexual preference and to let all of our students explore their own identities and become open to the identities of others.

A NEW PARADIGM IS NEEDED

Pedagogically, educators often go only as far as to try and clip the edges off the sting of racism, but to be truly effective in the call to create a more just and equitable world for students, teachers must attack the root of the problem: White supremacy in curriculum, structures, pedagogy, and practice.

Teachers who are ill equipped to work with Black students try to overcome, overpower, and overtalk their students. For these teachers, the purpose of the classroom is to train students in proper behavior, not the content. In other words, these teachers try to bend their students to their whiteness and acculturate them into that system. This often plays out in how new teachers think and talk about "respect" and the "real world." They see the real world as the world run and maintained by White people for the benefit of White people. To them, that is not a troubling notion but a comfort. These teachers perceive it as a goal for their students to be successful in that White world without disrupting it.

Milner (2010) described the positioning of a teacher/participant and listed four elements that allowed a White male teacher to succeed with students who are racially different from him: (1) learn from the students and adjust practices accordingly, (2) develop a "deeper understanding of the impact of race," (3) develop relationships with students that "transcend cultural boundaries," and (4) understand how to take advantage of opportunities to learn from students (p. 46). However, helping teachers make connections between their whiteness and their classroom practice is a difficult task.

Thus, even though multicultural education has been the norm since the 1970s, a new paradigm is needed to meet the needs of students in diverse communities. Multitudes of phenomena, including mass incarceration, the rise of White supremacist groups and terrorism, and the election of populists and xenophobes across the globe, show two things: (1) the multicultural curriculum enacted since the 1970s has not produced the desired effect of eliminating White supremacy as an ideology for a significant percentage of the population, and (2) the level of threat to students of color has ramped up, so the response must be much more robust than before.

Let's return to the question, what would school look like if Black students' lives really, truly mattered? Teachers would stand in solidarity with their students by interrogating their own whiteness and dismantling the oppressive, White supremacist structures in their schools, classrooms, and communities. And they would stand up for their Black students, demanding that they be treated as full citizens and human beings in all areas of society.

Teachers in multiracial schools will say that they have chosen a life with children because they want to have a positive and transformative impact on students' lives (Duncan-Andrade, 2007). To do so, they need the tools. Great teaching changes lives. Great teachers shape the future. Great teachers carry with them into the classroom a healthy mixture of defiance and devotion.

To demolish the structures that create whiteness, White teachers must make a daily commitment to interrogate and dismantle the power of whiteness. If teachers are going to cross the color line and teach students of color effectively, they must do more than just *tolerate* the diversity of their students in the classroom (Paris, 2012). To be successful, teachers who commit to this work must make a clear decision to do so with understanding, empathy, and caring solidarity with students. While dismantling structures of whiteness is a challenge and not a threat, some cannot tell the difference. The work will be hard. It will cost. It will have failures. But for those who persevere, the rewards will be beyond measure.

If the conversation is framed away from the perceived deficits of students of color to areas where teachers need to deeply reorient their own self-perceptions and actions in the communities of color they serve, then White teachers can begin to build the needed mind-set to move beyond the multicultural to solidarity.

PARTICIPANT 2: BIANCA ROMANO, THE "CARE BEAR"

Bianca Romano's Central High classroom at the end of the hall was a colorful sensory experience. On the way out the door, the room narrowed in a V shape so that the students were funneled as they left the classroom, an architectural feature that she used to full advantage. At the end of class periods, each student was given a high five and a verbal affirmation as they walked out the door. These affirmations were often academic in nature, "Good work today," but were more often personal: "I love those shoes" or "Your hair is awesome today!" When asked about these interactions, Bianca expounded,

> It's a way to guarantee you checked in with every single kid every single class by saying you have to high-five my hand, as dumb as that is, so I can say,

"Bye, Jeremy," "Bye, Shonda," "Bye, Derrick." And it literally gives you a moment with every single kid even if I didn't talk to them during the class.

However, it takes a great deal of foundational work to create the kind of classroom climate where this is possible. When asked if there is resistance by any of the students to this ritual, Bianca responded,

Yes, there can be resistance, but the high-five, that is a rule. That is the bare minimum. [Even if there is] resistance, [the high five] turns into some kind of relationship. And so, Alex is a junior and he tries really hard. He'll sneak and stand behind me, but even that is a form of interacting. So, by you trying really hard not to give me a high five, we are now having this interaction, and I'm trying to catch you. You know, it's funny, even if they're walking down the hallway and I say, "Get back here," they'll stomp back and high-five my hand. Even the fact that you're willing to stomp back, you're still . . . it's just part of the way things work, and I think most students have accepted that.

Bianca was a twenty-four-year-old second-year teacher who came to teaching with a background in psychology and business from a private four-year institution in the Midwest. She saw this ritual of the high five as a way that she was absolutely certain she was connecting with each of her students in some way during the day.

This level of familiar contact was a hallmark of Bianca's pedagogy. She sought to make those connections every day and said that it is the little things that showed she was on their side. Bianca's style of continual positive interaction was similar to the style of the warm demanders in that she had high standards and a continual dialogue around work and personal responsibility. Yet she did not do a lot of *other mothering* as described by Ware (2006). She showed caring solidarity in ways that involved verbal affirmations, meeting basic needs, and physical affection.

The room itself was particularly large and could easily have accommodated two classrooms. Across from the windows were two columns of orange chart paper framing an area for student work emblazoned with "wild and wondrous work!" On another part of the long wall were handmade student project posters of various U.S. history heroes and events, leftovers from previous reports. Dotted around the room were uplifting statements, some on printed posters and some handmade: "Life is full of choices: choose carefully," "we the people," and "Courage is what it takes to stand up and speak."

Bianca divided the room into two spaces, one with couches and cabinets for books, and the other a traditional instructional space, with student tables in rows facing a whiteboard. In these seats, Bianca's twenty-five students were scattered at the desks. In the class I repeatedly observed, all but two were African American or Latino. Between these two spaces, against a wall of windows, was her small desk, surrounded by a tumble of chairs, arm desks, and stools. Most days, although there were many chairs and options for seating in the spacious classroom, six students vied for the chance to cram themselves into these seats and use a small corner of her desk as a writing space. The big prize was to sit in her worn and creaky office chair and be the "director" who pushed the arrow key for PowerPoint presentations.

On the forty-foot wall of windows, painted in bright colors, created using a bingo dabber, was one word in each window two feet across: in the first window, "Courage"; in the second, "Scholarship"; then "Excellence" and "Respect." Then on the next four windows were "We the People of Room 352. WE WILL be . . . Scholars, Leaders, Teammates, and Achieve 80% Mastery." Most of these signs were a reflection of Bianca's values, and some were emblems of the pressure she was under to obtain high student scores on district and state tests. She worked to create an atmosphere where students are expected to do well, and she was pleased at their progress. "We have an 80% mastery expectation in this class that we reach a lot of the time." Bianca's definition of high expectations for her students included their ability to meet these expectations on all assignments and exams. Her strategy paid off in that she reported that her students had the highest growth on the district social studies test.

In Bianca's class, every moment possible was full of positive talk. "Good work," "Nice job," and "High five" were all part of the moment-by-moment talk in her classroom, and students worked for these encouragements. Students brought things to her attention in order to gain high fives and red stamps on papers.For Bianca, the relationships she built with her students were the most important part of her identity as a teacher.

Over the weeks of observations, I noted the skills of a teacher in solidarity, with high expectations and the mixture of academic and behavioral achievement with constant positive affirmation of students. During one observation, I counted twelve positive comments directed toward students over four minutes. Bianca worked hard at maintaining relationships with students and saw it as a tool that allowed her access to assess student learning.

> That takes having a foundation built, so it's not like, "Why are you talking to me?" Just having enough of a relationship to always have a foot in the door. The longer I teach, the more I realize that [a standoffish student attitude] is usually a cover for, "I don't understand what I'm supposed to be doing" or "I don't understand the assignment."

Bianca's Solidarity with Students

At the end of her first year, Bianca reported that her students had received the highest gains in the district over the previous year's students on their state standardized test. The next year Bianca reported that her students received top scores on the district benchmark tests.

Bianca built deep relationships with her students and struggled with curriculum planning, but as a young teacher, what she lacked in steady confidence she made up for in sheer energy. Bianca struggled with truly understanding what she was supposed to teach, although there is no question why she wanted to teach.

> I want everything for them. I do want the naive hope. Education is the ultimate equalizer, and the reality is that until education is equal, it won't be the ultimate equalizer. I want everything for them, but I also realize I can't give them everything, so I just give them everything within my realm of my control.

Bianca was adamant that she had chosen the types of students she taught, and she believed she was making a difference, one of the main contributors to job satisfaction. Bianca explained that even though she was still learning how to be a good teacher, she was committed to growing into the identity:

> I don't see myself ever working with a different demographic. I laugh harder with my kids because that is a really genuine quality of mine and it works for me. I can differentiate personally because I know what will work for [individual students].

Bianca's identity as a teacher in solidarity extended to her identity as a White teacher of students of color as well. When asked what it takes to be an effective urban teacher, she responded,

> Have ridiculously high expectations for your students and don't have excuses but have understanding. [Don't] make [teaching] an "us-them" thing. You are in it together. That's the thing about teaching.

This concept of being "in it together" in a relationship of solidarity was a crucial part of Bianca's pedagogy. Whether it was the high fives, the hugs, the inspirational posters, the painting on the windows, or the conversations with students about their work, Bianca was always working to create bonds of solidarity that were meant to move students toward achievement. Bianca said, however, that this culture of learning was not a constant at Central High School. "We've really developed a culture [within my classroom] of 'I want to learn.' And at Central that culture isn't there. There really isn't a cohesive anything." Yet when asked to define her relationship with students, she explained that she was primarily a "role model" and an agent who introduced them to the world.

Bianca attempted to model a solidaristic relationship with students, mentoring them to meet their potential. While Bianca was still unsure about *what* to teach, she was absolutely clear on *why* she wanted to teach and why this population. In Bianca's narrative, I saw a choice to challenge herself to meet her students across the racial divide. She was demonstrably comfortable with her students, which showed in every interaction I observed. Bianca's solidarity was a caring solidarity, deeply rooted in her personal understandings of race, the importance of education, and her desire to make a difference in students' lives.

Chapter Four

The Asset Pedagogies

Caring, Allyship, and Solidarity

After laying out the issues and the imperative of action to move beyond multicultural education to a more robust response to the current crisis for students of color, it is important to look at the pedagogies that are making positive changes in schools and in the lives of children. These are often called the *asset pedagogies* in that they view children of color with respect to their assets rather than assuming that language, racial, and cultural differences are deficits.

Charged with helping districts follow the law after *Lau v. Nichols* (1974), the federal government established a mandate to teach English to students who were not proficient. Cazden and Leggett (1976) called for schooling that was "more responsive to cultural differences among children" (p. 3). They explained, "School systems are asked to consider cognitive and affective aspects of how different children learn so that appropriate teaching styles and learning environments can be provided that will maximize their educational achievement" (p. 3).

Since then, as Paris and Alim (2014) pointed out, "collaborations between researchers and teachers proved deficit approaches untenable and unjust" (p. 87). Paris and Alim (2014) used the term *asset pedagogies* to explain the approaches that lift students up as resilient, inquisitive, and knowledgeable about themselves and their communities and not as others have typically cast them, as deficient intellectually or culturally (Payne, 2013; Valencia, 2010).

In her 1994 book *The Dreamkeepers*, Gloria Ladson-Billings challenged teachers and researchers to reject deficit models and recognize the inherent strengths of African American children. She explained that culture should be at the center of pedagogy in multiracial and multicultural classrooms and discussed "principles at work" that combine high expectations and awareness of African American culture to create a classroom where "culturally relevant pedagogy" (CRP) could take place (p. 17). She outlined an approach resting on three criteria: (1) students must experience academic success, (2) students must develop and maintain cultural competence, and (3) students must develop a critical consciousness through which they challenge the status quo of the current social order (p. 160). Her subsequent work, especially her 1995 article, "Toward a Theory of Culturally Relevant Pedagogy," has created hallmarks of asset pedagogical research and practice.

Elements of CRP include identification with and commitment to the African American community, viewing students as extended family members, stress on mastery of math and literacy, and judicious use of authority in the classroom. In order to move past strictly linguistic differences or passive cultural asynchronization as explanations for Black students' lack of achievement in classrooms, Ladson-Billings (1994) explained culturally relevant teaching this way:

> [It] uses student culture in order to maintain it and to transcend the negative effects of the dominant culture. The negative effects are brought about, for example, by not seeing one's history, culture, or background represented in the textbook or curriculum or by seeing that history, culture, or background distorted. (p. 17)

In her other writings, Ladson-Billings's (1995a and 1995b) explanation of culturally relevant pedagogy echoed that of other theorists who have called for a more humane and democratic approach to teaching by tapping into students' cultural strengths (Brown-Jeffy & Cooper, 2011; Hermes, 2005; Phillippo, 2012; Shevalier & McKenzie, 2012). Called "culturally responsive teaching" by Gay (2010), the current body of literature uses the two terms nearly interchangeably. Both Ladson-Billings and Gay have argued that through culturally appropriate interactions and relationship building, teachers learn to raise expectations as students rise to meet them.

Geneva Gay, in her book *Culturally Responsive Teaching: Theory, Research, and Practice*, reasoned that teachers' understanding of their students' cultures can improve their ability to tailor curriculum and pedagogy to students' needs:

> For example, teachers need to know (a) which ethnic groups give priority to communal living and cooperative problem solving and how these preferences affect educational motivation, aspiration, and task performance; (b) how different ethnic groups' protocols of appropriate ways for children to interact with adults are exhibited in instructional settings; and (c) the implications of gender role socialization in different ethnic groups for implementing equity initiatives in classroom instruction. This information constitutes the first es-

sential component of the knowledge base of culturally responsive teaching. (Gay, 2010, p. 107)

Paris (2012) called for students to be treated in a way that used culture as an asset in learning, but he asked that teachers go even further to embrace and sustain culture and language plurality in classrooms. Teachers are not explicit enough in their support for students to "support the linguistic and cultural dexterity and plurality necessary for success and access in our demographically changing U.S. and global schools and communities" (p. 95). Paris challenged teachers to go beyond the learning of cultures and the facile essentializing of culture to truly embrace all cultures in the classroom and to help students preserve their own cultural identities.

In a later work, Paris and Alim (2014) sought to reposition the discourse on the research, pedagogy, and curriculum applied to and provided to students of color. This demographic and linguistic approach confirmed that the United States will become increasingly diverse and that centers of power will flow out of White cultural norms and Dominant American English (DAE) as people of color increase and other forms of English, along with other languages, increase. Paris (2012) explained that culturally sustaining pedagogy "seeks to perpetuate and foster—to sustain linguistic, literate, and cultural pluralism as part of the democratic project of schooling" (p. 95).

McCarty and Lee (2014) posited that indigenous students need even more than the culture-sustaining pedagogy promoted by Paris. In their framework, called culturally sustaining/revitalizing pedagogy (CSRP), they argued that students on and off of tribal lands are "in a fight for cultural and linguistic survival" and that sovereignty, self-determination, and self-identification are a struggle that Native youth experience against a backdrop of colonization and ethnocide. They identified three components of this framework: first, attention to power relations with the "goal of transforming legacies of the colonizer" (p. 103); second, an emphasis on native language acquisition; and third, a focus on community, "respect, reciprocity, responsibility, and the importance of caring relationships" (p. 103). This framework, grounded in indigenous pedagogy, is instructive for all work with colonized and oppressed communities.

Beyond the questions of demographic or moral appeals to multiculturalism, and despite the popularity of Gay's, Ladson-Billings's, and Paris's work among educators and teacher educators, the prevalence of deficit models and White supremacy in schools and society as dominant ideologies has not abated. The hard evidence shows that schools are still places of trauma for students of color, from the suspension of preschoolers and early elementary students (Malik, 2017) and of African American middle and high school students (Monroe, 2005; Skiba et al. 2011) to the recent round of bullying that has taken place since the 2016 election (Southern Poverty Law Center,

2017) and the continued existence of the school-to-prison pipeline that washes students from schools into the justice system (Wald & Losen, 2003). So while ll these ways of teaching are a vast improvement over past pedagogies, the urgency of the need has only increased since their development.

CARING FOR AFRICAN AMERICAN STUDENTS AND WARM DEMANDER PEDAGOGY

Gay (2010) described caring as an important part of teaching in multicultural classrooms. "Caring is one of those things that most educators agree is important in working effectively with students, but they are hard-pressed to characterize it in actual practice" (p. 48).

According to Gay (2010), for teachers to care for students, they need to celebrate them and enjoy their differences but still expect a great deal from them. "Teachers who really care for students honor their humanity, hold them in high esteem, expect high performance from them, and use strategies to fulfill their expectations" (p. 48). Gay argued that this is a type of "authentic caring" where teachers and students develop "sustained, trusting, respectful, and reciprocal relationships" (p. 49). Trust is a difficult thing to build across the color line. Many students have trusted, and that trust has not been reciprocated by White teachers, or worse, students have been betrayed by teachers who say one thing but do another. A teacher who cares must build trust and help students unlearn reasonable distrusting behaviors through consistency and care.

Ware (2006) explored ways that White teachers form bonds and create success with African American students. She identified a type of teacher who uses what she calls "warm demander" pedagogy (see also Gay, 2010, p. 75; Kleinfeld, 1975). This refers to a set of highly organized, discipline-oriented, caring behaviors that use culture as a tool for connecting to students. The White teachers that Ware described have taken on what she perceives as an African American cultural identity in order to more clearly communicate with their students (p. 45).

First coined in Kleinfeld (1975), warm demanders are first concerned with the climate of the classroom and building rapport with students, but they are also deeply committed to student achievement. To accomplish both, warm demanders use a combination of adopted or appropriated cultural norms along with school structural and cultural values to build relationships and move students toward academic achievement. Love (2019c) described her third-grade teacher, who fit the warm demander profile—"Mrs. Johnson did not just love her students, she fundamentally believed that we mattered. She made us believe that our lives were entangled with hers and that caring for us meant caring for herself"—and the classroom where Love learned and felt valued: "It was a collective spirit of accountability, love, and purpose. She genuinely listened to us, took up our concerns in her teaching, and made sure each voice in the classroom was heard" (pp. 47–48).

Cooper (2003) observed teachers who used culturally relevant pedagogy in the classroom and examined the conceptual beliefs of successful White teachers of Black elementary school children. The teachers had high expectations for their students and a well-developed work ethic of their own, they were able to reflect on their performance, and they viewed themselves as effective teachers. Cooper also found that the teachers had a developing racial consciousness, defined as being "involved [in] specific articulation of race matters, including racism in the teacher's personal and professional lives" (p. 423). Further, Cooper included respect and commitment to the Black community, empathy for Black children, and a willingness to learn from the Black community.

Ladson-Billings (1994) and Cooper (2003) similarly found that successful teachers of Black elementary school children use techniques described as "authority" in the classroom and that they are a "second mother" to their students (p. 414). The authors described this function as beyond what many would view as the role of a teacher. Teachers in these classrooms monitor every aspect of a student's well-being, care, and feeding during the time they are in the classroom. These teachers are quick to correct students and praise them as the situation requires. They use sharp voices to point out infractions but use terms of endearment like "sweetie" or "baby" when praising (Cooper, 2003, p. 423).

The ethic of caring as defined by Noddings (1986) also sheds light on the discussion. It is related to but distinct from the description given by Ladson-Billings (1994), Gay (2010), and Cooper (2003). According to Noddings, the masculine orientation of the current system has failed to create the kind of ethical citizenry that democratically minded individuals are looking for, but instead people who compete rather than care. Noddings believed that schools could teach students to care about each other, themselves, the world, and right action, as well as their academic subjects.

To Noddings, "the primary aim of every educational institution and of every educational effort must be the maintenance and enhancement of caring" (p. 172). Noddings theorized that caring involves engrossment, where the attention of one person is entirely taken up by another person, and motivational displacement, where one person's goals and success are the main reason for the relationship with the other. Noddings's belief that schools should be places where people take care of one another emotionally has its roots in the feminine ethic of caring. She explained that caring is a central part of teaching and parenting and explained six ways that schools can become more caring:

1. Be clear that the goal of schooling is to produce competent, caring, loving people.
2. Take care of needs for affiliation with peers and adults.
3. Worry less about control of students.
4. Eliminate the hierarchies of programs and curriculum.
5. Give part of the day to "themes of care," where spiritual and emotional needs are met.
6. Teach the students that caring means they are competent. (p. 368)

Noddings's (1986) ethic of caring is a different way of being when placed in the educational environment. It reflects a difference in the cultural competencies expected of teachers. According to the other theorists mentioned, marginalized students require caring that is expressed differently than that described by Noddings. These differences extend to the way teachers approach caring for students—a gentle approach, whereas Gay's (2010) was empathetic, and Howard (2002), Cooper (2003), and Ladson-Billings (1994) described caring teachers who have a sharper tone. However, part of the difference is that Howard, Cooper, and Ladson-Billings assessed a deeper need for teacher intervention in the lives of students.

Coleman (2007) and Bidwell (2010) found similar trends in their studies of Black teachers of Black middle school students. Coleman found that students value teachers they described as "nice." Coleman described Black students' perceptions of their academic success as attributable to what their teachers personally thought of them. They valued teachers who demonstrated that they cared, communicated with students on a personal and academic level, gave affirmative feedback, and simplified and explained content matter (Coleman, 2007). Bidwell found that three strategies were essential to teachers' success with African American students: forming meaningful relationships with the students, engaging students in racial conversations, and reflecting both individually and with colleagues.

Howard (2002) interviewed African American students to record their understanding of what makes a successful teacher. From student interviews and observations, Howard identified terms students used to categorize an "effective" teacher (p. 429). First, teachers whom students perceived as effective were able to structure their classrooms in ways that made students feel like the classroom was a "home" and like the members of the class were a "family" (p. 431). Howard explained that this home feeling was built not only on the relationships formed within the classroom but also on the rituals and traditions developed there. To give one example, as part of the school curriculum, students took part in a "morning circle," during which they were able to speak to friends and develop interpersonal relationships (p. 432).

Howard (2002) also identified "culturally connected caring" as a way to frame student responses (p. 434). Howard explained,

Culturally connected caring refers to a display of caring that occurs within a cultural context with which students are familiar. Behavioral expectations, nurturing patterns, and forms of affection take place in a manner that does not require students to abandon their cultural integrity. (p. 434)

Thus, Howard advocated for a type of caring that is deeply rooted in students' cultural understandings and communication styles.

Second, Howard found that a teacher's "passion" was an integral trait leading to success. Howard found that the communication style and types of affirmation that students reported showed teachers' caring for students included "hollering or yelling" (p. 437). Students reported that teachers expressed their caring by asking about students' lives outside of school and demonstrating real investment in student success. "Students seemed to believe that teachers who were not as emotionally and passionately concerned with their learning were teachers who 'don't even care about us'" (p. 437).

As a way to attempt to bridge the gap between CRP and caring, Parsons (2005) and Eslinger (2013) have both worked to integrate the two concepts in order to demonstrate a way of being in the classroom that most effectively meets the needs of racialized students. Eslinger focused on White teachers and their caring relationships with students and posited that the answer might come in the form of culturally responsive caring. "A substantial part of White teachers' inability to adequately convey their care, I contend, is their resistance to addressing issues of race and racism" (p. 5). Eslinger explained that successful teachers interrogate their own whiteness and privilege and their a priori knowledge and attitudes about race and racial minorities. "White teachers need: 1) to develop a rich, and culturally diverse knowledge base; 2) to interrogate their identities and the privileges associated with them; and 3) to critically examine curriculum and pedagogy" (p. 5).

ALLYHOOD AND ALLYSHIP

The discussion around the schooling of African American students seldom focuses on the adults who work in the buildings or the structures where the schooling takes place. Instead it often focuses on the students themselves and their families, but addressing the inequalities of schooling must begin not with the students but with the adults and the structures that monitor, act upon, and cause that inequality (Harvey & Reed, 1996).

Adopting strength-based techniques and CRP are helpful, but until White teachers who teach across the color line join in caring and solidarity with their students to dismantle White supremacist structures in the classroom, school, and larger society, the "achievement gap" will continue, and teachers will blame the victims of racism for its effects (Ladson-Billings, 2006, 2007).

In an attempt to move teachers into a more direct act of solidarity, some activists and researchers have embraced the concept of allyship as a way to describe their work as advocates and allies of their students of color (Patel, 2011). During the time of desegregation in the 1970s, a great deal was written on White teachers employed in still-segregated or newly desegregated systems (Paley, 2000). Today there has been a rise in literature that uses the concepts of "critical White allies," "allyship," and "allyhood" (Case, 2018; Patel, 2011; Reason, Millar, & Scales, 2005; Waters, 2010).

The concept of allyship is rooted in a framework of social justice work and asks White people to "deconstruct cycles of privilege and oppression" through cognitive understanding of the nature of privilege and interpersonal experiences with people of color (Waters, 2010, p. 6). But, as Utt (2013) pointed out, White privilege allows allies to pick which parts of the alliance they are comfortable with: "part of the privilege of your identity is that you have a choice about whether or not to resist oppression."

Allyhood is increasingly being discussed as a move toward solidarity, not as an end in itself, because it is still a step away from creating relationships of solidarity (Love, 2019c; Patel, 2011). As Masoom (2017) explained, allyhood as often expressed in White social justice culture is "perfectly contradictory to everything you'd expect the ideal 'ally' to be. Just as both the privileges and oppressions we face don't take breaks, neither can true solidarity. Discussions regarding being an 'ally' inherently imply choice—the choice to step back, and not engage." Utt (2013) also explained that, "as a White person, I have a responsibility to stand up to racism and work to bring White people into the anti-racist conversation in a way that they can hear and access." Under this definition, the White ally is more than someone who shows sympathy but is active in their empathy, yet still retains privilege enough to remove themselves at any time.

Allyship as a form of alliance came about as a result of the increasing need for action to defend against conservative attacks on people of color demanding justice. It is part of an increasing awareness that White people need to be part of the solution, but allyship is seldom ready to define White people and structures as the reason for and the definition of the problem. Allyship still allows White people to be comfortable in their lives and their privilege and to continue using and enjoying White supremacist structures in society. While allyship is not bad, it is inadequate to face the pressing challenges faced by schools and teachers. While allyship is a step towards solidarity, White teachers cannot call themselves allies or say that they are in solidarity while continuing to do some justice and some injustice as part of an overall strategy.

SOLIDARITY

The focus of this book is the definition and creation of relationships of solidarity. Solidarity has been discussed in relation to teaching but has not been brought forward as a major factor in the ability of White teachers to successfully teach their African American students (Duncan-Andrade & Morrell, 2008; Gay, 2010; Milner, 2010; Paris, 2012; Sleeter & Soriano, 2012). But given its use and lack of a clear definition in education, it is important to look at all available definitions.

Gaztambide-Fernández (2012) explained that "solidarity is often mobilized as an expedient way of expressing certain political ideals without any concern for articulating what precisely is meant by solidarity, often confounding multiple meanings" (p. 46). According to Wilde (2007), the concept of solidarity has been "confined to the realm of rhetoric while serious theoretical work has concentrated on other aspects of political association such as democracy, nationalism, community, multiculturalism and human rights" (p. 171).

Wilde defined solidarity as "the feeling of reciprocal sympathy and responsibility among members of a group which promotes mutual support" (p. 171). But because of its connection with feelings of love and friendship, solidarity has largely been neglected as a central concept in much of the education literature. It has been relegated to being an undefined phrase, part of a definition of cultural responsiveness and as an element of social justice. However, those who have discussed it have described a more political standpoint in teaching and pedagogy.

Bayertz (2013) explained that the term *solidarity* has its roots in the shared responsibility of common debts within a family in Roman law but over the centuries has become "a mutual attachment between individuals," yet despite its frequency in the literature of political movements like unionization, solidarity as a concept has seldom been dissected and analyzed and has largely an assumed meaning (p. 3). He explained, "Although in everyday politics the term solidarity is freely used, as when required, in order to mobilize a readiness to act and/or make sacrifices, it has seldom been the object of elaborated theory" (p. 3).

Bayertz worked to define *solidarity* and divided it into two levels, the factual level, which defines common ground between individuals, and the normative level, which defines the mutual aid that humans receive when necessary. He explained that solidarity is often combined with terms that generally mean things like community spirit or charity. Bayertz attempted to differentiate between four concepts of solidarity and explain their uses.

The first use of the term *solidarity* is essentially the same as fraternity or kinship. In this understanding, there is a universality that is possible under the idea that we are all "God's children" and have a common human root;

thus solidarity is possible if humans let go of difference and embrace the commonality of humans.

Second, solidarity is used as a device to explain the whole of a society. People divide labor, get in lines, and generally weave through others as they work and play. This highly surface aspect of solidarity is one where we generally follow norms and laws in order to have a life uninterrupted by violence or crime. This interpretation is driven by self-interest and largely depends on the assumption that all are included in the society and none are specifically excluded from its benefits. If this assumption is not met, there is no solidarity, and self-interest will devolve into selfishness (see also Scholz, 2012).

The third version of Bayertz's solidarity involves groups standing up against the greater powers for common interests. On the positive side, it can be people who come together to right a wrong and protest against injustice. But it can also be negative, as in criminal conspiracies, police who refuse to give up their own even when wrongdoing is pervasive, and mob violence against the innocent. This form of solidarity can be based on class, race, ethnicity, and any other affiliation. It is, however, motivated toward a group goal.

Lastly, under the welfare state, solidarity is the justification for redistributing the resources of individuals and society for the greater good. Thus taxation and the limiting of income inequality are the central tenets of this form of solidarity. The concept here is that the fruits of all our labor should be enjoyed by all of us (Bayertz, 2013).

When it comes to teaching and learning, critical pedagogy as expressed by Freire (2014) articulated a form of solidarity with students and what that looks like. To Freire, the concept of solidarity begins with the "dialectical unity" of knowledge production, solidarity, and action. These three concepts form the basis for "praxis" that moves the educator to a higher ability to connect with students and a higher purpose of empowering the oppressed (p. 38). He explained that the oppressed are forced into a duality and often internalize their own oppression to survive. Solidarity, then, is a means to ending that oppression, but it is a fearful step.

> The conflict lies in the choice between being wholly themselves or being divided; between ejecting the oppressor within or not ejecting them; between human solidarity or alienation; between following prescriptions or having choices; between being spectators or actors; between acting or having the illusion of acting through the action of the oppressors; between speaking out or being silent, castrated in their power to create and re-create, in their power to transform the world. This is the tragic dilemma of the oppressed which their education must consider. (p. 48)

This internalization of oppression allows for survival in an oppressive system but robs all people of their humanity. Through relationships of solidarity, the oppressed can open up their humanity and throw off oppression, first within themselves and then in the world outside (Gaztambide-Fernández, 2012; Harvey, 2007).

Freire (2014) also addressed the oppressor. He explained that, even if a member of the oppressor class begins to understand the oppression they have been inflicting, that does not necessarily mean that they will join in solidarity with those in the oppressed classes:

> Discovering himself to be an oppressor may cause considerable anguish, but it does not necessarily lead to solidarity with the oppressed. Rationalizing his guilt through paternalistic treatment of the oppressed, all the while holding them fast in a position of dependence, will not do. Solidarity requires that one enter into the situation of those with whom one is solidary; it is a radical posture. (p. 49)

Thus, when discussing teachers and students of color, teachers of any position or identity may see the oppression of their students and still work to keep their students in the system. Rules about pants, hair, language, and other weapons of oppression are internalized not only by young people but also by adults so that sometimes even teachers of color will engage in assimilationist narratives with students rather than liberatory ones.

Once a person has acknowledged the humanity of the oppressed, the next step is to act and work to alleviate that oppression:

> True solidarity with the oppressed means fighting at their side to transform the objective reality which has made them these "beings for another." The oppressor is solidary with the oppressed only when he stops regarding the oppressed as an abstract category and sees them as persons who have been unjustly dealt with, deprived of their voice, cheated in the sale of their labor—when he stops making pious, sentimental, and individualistic gestures and risks an act of love. (Freire, 2014, p. 50)

He understood that these actions engender risk. This risk can mean loss of status, income, and respect by others in the same field or school. It could also mean the loss of a job. Standing in true solidarity is more than mouthing the words; it is doing the actions that are required to pull down the structures of oppression that the privileged have enjoyed. Freire continued, "True solidarity is found only in the plenitude of this act of love, in its existentiality, in its praxis. To affirm that men and women are persons and as persons should be free, and yet to do nothing tangible to make this affirmation a reality, is a farce" (p. 50). Love in action, action in concert with the oppressed, not toward them, is the essence of Freire's solidarity. Action pedagogy is created when teachers go beyond instilling facts and testing standards to truly know-ing, caring, loving, and acting on behalf of their students.

As Freire pointed out, "one cannot impose oneself, nor even merely co-exist with one's students. Solidarity requires true communication" (p. 76). Solidarity is a requirement in the pursuit of true humanity but is only possible in "fellowship" and cannot "unfold in the antagonistic relations between oppressor and oppressed." To build trust, the person who seeks the relation-ship of solidarity must be the one who works to be trustworthy and then makes the overture. To be trusted, the trustee must prove to be trustworthy.

The term *solidarity* is seldom used to describe the behaviors of successful teachers in education. Teachers who advocate for students against systems of oppression are too often ignored in favor of more technocratic descriptions of the act of teaching. Solidarity in education can often be described as an emotional connection with students, but the political aspect is equally impor-tant for teachers who cross the color line. Sleeter and Soriano (2012) ex-plained that education theorists see solidarity as a step toward teaching for social justice wherein "teachers empathize with and care deeply about their students and therefore work with students' communities within the broader political project of identifying and eliminating oppression" (p. 4).

De Lissovoy and Brown (2013) delineated two models of solidarity in education: (1) a model that is based on a struggle, where people come togeth-er for a common cause or a movement to accomplish a task, and (2) a model referred to as "solidarity as alliance":

> Seeks to negotiate rather than overcome differences between participating in-dividuals or groups in order to achieve a strategic goal. This approach views differences not merely as obstacles, but potentially as positive political re-sources. Pioneered in the civil rights movement, and more subtly worked through in more recent antiracist and gender equity advocacy, this paradigm is familiar to anti-oppression movements that recognize a basic division (among those involved in the struggle) between "target" and "ally" groups. (p. 7)

Gaztambide-Fernández (2012) summed up the concept:

> First, solidarity always implies a relationship among individuals or groups, whether as a way to understand what binds people together or what brings them together for civic or political action. Second, solidarity always implies an obligation, or a sense of duty regarding what is just or equitable, whether it is construed in relationship to some notion of human rights or a social contract, or to commitments to struggles against particular forms of oppression. Third, solidarity always implies a set of actions or duties between those in the soli-dary relationship. (p. 50)

Drawing on the scholarship of feminist authors, Gaztambide-Fernández pro-posed a "pedagogy of solidarity" that seeks to break the colonial relationships between teachers and students and also between students and the curriculum. His theory involves three modes of solidarity that can lead to an anti-oppressive, antiracist, and decolonizing pedagogy.

Relational. This form of solidarity is expressed in a deliberate commitment to building a relationship based on mutual respect. "To think of the pedagogy of solidarity as relational is, first, to acknowledge being as co-presence, by deliberately taking as a point of departure that individual subjects do not enter into relationships, but rather subjects are made in and through relationships" (p. 52). This conception of solidarity expresses itself in the ability to know, as much as possible, the one with whom the relationship is sought and leaves room for the creation of self and the other, together and separately.

Transitive. This is about the act of creating solidarity; as Gaztambide-Fernández stated, a person can solidarize with another person or group. This act of solidarity arises from Freire's concept praxis: "the pedagogy of solidarity is about an action that also affects or modifies the one who acts—to solidarize oneself with" (p. 54). It also stands in contrast to a type of solidarity as performance that seeks to aggrandize oneself rather than pull together in the interest of the marginalized and disenfranchised. This type of solidarity is in contrast to the allyship described earlier. While an allyship approach addresses some of the behaviors of successful White teachers, it is not adequate to explain teachers who build deeper, political relationships of solidarity with students in conditions that allow them to make a difference in their students' lives (Alonso, Anderson, Su, & Theoharis, 2009; Duncan-Andrade, 2007; Wilde, 2007). Allyhood still allows for a White supremacist framework and often results in teachers who have false empathy (Delgado, 1996; Patel, 2011; Warren & Hotchkins, 2014) or a White savior syndrome (Straubhaar, 2014).

Creative. Creative solidarity seeks to upend the relations that currently govern human interactions and asks those who seek solidarity to redefine identity, culture, and the relationships these involve. Creative solidarity "involves 'creatively' engaging with others in unexpected and perhaps even inopportune ways that might rearrange the symbolic content of human exchanges by mobilizing that which always exceeds the very terms of the encounter" (p. 56).

Gaztambide-Fernández's concepts of solidarity nestle into caring solidarity as a way of describing the project of White teachers who seek a deeper, more impactful teaching experience across the color line. As defined, solidarity is a crucial element of successful teaching in multiracial classrooms, but building that solidarity in classrooms across the color line takes commitment and patience and must be renewed each fall when a new set of students comes through the classroom door.

Only teachers in relationships of caring solidarity with their students are able to fully implement culturally relevant pedagogy in which teachers foster student success, maintain their own and student cultural competence, and develop critical perspectives that challenge White supremacist and inequitable social structures (Ladson-Billings, 1995a and 1995b). To expect to implement culturally relevant or culturally responsive pedagogy without first creating relationships based on caring solidarity will result in teachers feeling like they are failing and are unable to reach African American students. Trying to build a culturally relevant or sustaining pedagogy without first building relationships of caring solidarity is like building a house on a foundation of sand.

PARTICIPANT 3: MARK JOHNSON, THE "FIGHTER"

Mark Johnson taught social studies at Westview High on the second floor in a neat classroom with all of the bases covered. On the blackboard behind his desk were the objectives and standards that would be met in the ninety-minute lesson. The desks were in rows in an L shape, so most students faced the smartboard, and ten faced the open classroom. In front of the smartboard, a stand included all the accouterments of a teacher who knows his craft, including markers, pencils, books, and Post-It Notes. His students were mostly African American, some were Latinx, and four were White. In the opposite corner, on a table next to Mark's desk, next to a miniature Zen garden, was a small fountain that had stopped working a few days before. "Sometimes when a kid is stressed or just needs a moment, they will come over and just rake the sand."

On my first observation day, it appeared there had been a lot of raking lately as sand was strewn both on and under the table. As his sophomores filed in, they were given a writing activity to get them mentally prepared for the upcoming lesson in his world history class on the Holocaust.

Mark was a native of the state and entered urban education after taking courses at the local state college. He mentioned that he chose to teach in the city rather than a small town like the one he grew up in because he found that the students were different than he expected before he entered the program, and he felt like city students needed him more.

> The teachers that are in the suburban schools, not that the kids don't need them, they just need someone in that position. It could be just about anyone, even an ineffective teacher is more effective there than an ineffective teacher here in the urban setting because kids come a little more prepackaged. I call it Wonder-Breadland. Everything is presliced and ready to go. Here, these kids need a dedicated individual who truly cares about being here and cares about these students.

Mark had been at Westview for his entire nine-year career and had seen a lot of turnover and budget cuts, which had made him concerned. He lamented that he was one of the more seasoned veterans at Westview.

> I have been here for nine years now. I can count on two hands the number of people who are here and have been here since I started here, and this is a big building. That's sad. I should not be considered one of the most veteran teachers in the building at nine years. That shouldn't happen. That's hard.

Mark was seeing part of the larger trend in urban education of rapid turnover. Urban schools have always had a higher degree of turnover and teachers leaving the profession, but this trend has accelerated in recent years and has had a devastating effect on many urban programs that rely on consistency of staff to keep the vision and to build relationships with students and the community.

High teacher turnover often means that students who are the most vulnerable in our society have the least experienced teachers or the most transient. Loeb, Darling-Hammond, and Luczak (2005) enumerated the reasons for teacher turnover, including working conditions, such as large class sizes, little influence in decision making, and low salaries. Mark added that there are many outside and political pressures on teachers, and he believes that the governor, the legislature, and the media do not respect teachers as professionals.

However, Mark was a fighter. He was determined that the students in his class would succeed and that no one would get in the way of that. He saw teaching as a calling, part of which is to defend his students against the rhetoric thrown at his school and district by politicians. Mark's version of peaceful combat against the larger forces that threatened his students demonstrated his ability to build relationships of solidarity with them.

Mark's Solidarity with His Students

Mark's radio-quality baritone voice carried well in his classroom, and he cut through the chatter of a room full of teenagers without raising the volume. His classroom demeanor was comfortable both in front of the class explaining a concept or telling a story, as well as talking one-on-one with students. He laughed often during class and had inside jokes with his students. He stood outside the door between classes to observe students' hallway behaviors and to give him information he then used for relationship building inside the classroom.

When asked what kinds of pedagogy and practices work in his classroom, Mark's answer was quick: "individualized attention." He explained that teachers should find out the interests of their students: "Figure out what they like, what they don't like, what style of learning they enjoy the most. I've found that the more choice [based on that knowledge] I can add into a lesson the better the lesson goes over."

He also explained that the classroom is not just a place to disseminate information. Students need to process their thinking and their feelings about the curriculum and many other things:

> They want to be able to talk about what they're thinking and what they're doing. They want to be able to ask questions both of each other and of me, and they want to be able to feel like their opinions somehow matter and influence those around them.

To meet those needs, Mark has created a classroom climate open to questioning, where students feel able to discuss class content in a safe atmosphere in which the teacher supports their efforts.

> I try to give time to as many voices as I can. I let them say what they want to say and acknowledge that they have said it. Then, even if 90 percent of what they said was wrong, I acknowledge the thing that was right, and I help guide them to where I want them to be. I try to find positive in whatever they've said, no matter what it was.

Mark also worked to create lesson plans that build in time to create relationships with students. He explained that he wants to talk with as many students as possible one-on-one on any given day.

> I build lessons that are diverse in learning style so I can see what they do well on and what they don't do well on. I build time into the way I teach that lets me sit right next to the kid, talk to him for two, three minutes, move on to the next kid, and tell them a joke or two. Don't just stay on topic when you sit with them. Get them off topic for two minutes and put them right back.

These personal lessons were a hallmark of Mark's pedagogy. He saw these moments as the most important part of what he did in the day. Teachers who build solidarity with their students spend these small moments with them building their self-esteem, correcting their behavior, and helping them plan for the future. Grand gestures may mean less than the small moments in these classrooms where burgeoning adults are guided by caring mentors who see them not for who they are but for who they can be.

Beyond the classroom, Mark also had an identity within the school, where he felt as though he was part of the institution and the community. Because of the way classes were scheduled, Mark saw nearly every sophomore in the school, and beyond that he made it a point to be involved in the school beyond the school day. He saw students where they worked after school, in shops and at the local grocery store, and he went to school sporting events where he talked with parents, siblings, and current and former students. He felt that he had been in the school long enough that students knew what to expect when they came to his class, and having Mark as a teacher was seen as part of the Westview experience.

> They know my style. I've been in this building now for nine years. Their brothers and sisters have seen me. They know who I am, and I think that's a big part of success in urban education is that I'm not this new guy coming into their territory. I'm part of their territory. Yeah, I'm part of this place, and they accept me as such. So they feel like I'm on their side. That's . . . like, I go to their games, I go . . . I talk to their parents. I come to the restaurants where they eat. I don't just leave here at 2:45 and never see this place again. I'm here after school. They see me, and they know me. So they feel comfortable with me.

Mark has worked diligently to create an atmosphere of solidarity with his students and explains that being "on their side" is an important part of urban teaching. He offered this example:

> A basketball player was right on the verge of being eligible to play [because of his grade point average]. He just had a bad day when he took my final exam. I knew it was a bad day. I could see it when he came in. He was not doing . . . it was a district test, and I couldn't excuse him from it, so he had to take it. He didn't do too well, and he ended up not being eligible for basketball. He came back to me on January 7 when we came in and said, "What can I do?" I said, "Well, you bombed that final exam." He goes, "I know, but I know it, I know it." I said, "Then let's take it again." So I gave him a chance to take it again, and he passed the test with an 85 percent. I changed the test around a little bit, so it's not like he memorized the answers from a friend or anything like that. So I know he knew what he was doing. He just had a bad day. I understand that.

Mark's actions were directed not by the needs of the system but by his students' needs. He understood that he was working with young people, and sometimes that means they are not able to perform a certain task on a certain day. Mark showed his empathy and caring by putting the needs of his student ahead of the needs of the school by making an accommodation while still retaining high standards.

> The kid is seventeen years old. You have bad days, and because I allowed him that chance, he didn't shut down on me, he didn't give up, he's still plugging away. He's doing great, he's playing basketball now. He's on the team. The entire basketball team is now very happy that he's with them. Not that they [basketball players] were causing a problem in my classroom, but they're now even more engaged because they saw that I cared enough about one of their teammates to give him a second chance.

Beyond making accommodations for young people and understanding that they sometimes need some extra chances, Mark believed that what he is doing in the classroom and community was making a tangible difference in the lives of young people.

> I know these kids. I know that if in the past I had not been here, there were several kids who probably wouldn't have made it . . . personally. I know that in my heart, and I know that for a fact. These kids said these words. I knew that going into urban education, that these kids needed someone who truly cared.

Mark explained that he has made a choice of careers and lifestyle. He saw teaching as more than a career choice; it was a calling, and he felt it was a good choice for him. He was confident in his ability to reach his students, and his students' test scores reflected that. Westview's state test scores and graduation rates were improving. From 2007 to 2011, Westview's state test in English and math scores rose from 30 percent to a 42 percent passing rate, and the graduation rate rose from 43 percent to 77 percent.

> Could I get a job in [a suburb]? Absolutely. Could I have gotten a job as a lawyer or as an engineer or any of the other things that I thought about when I got into college? Yeah, and I probably would have been happy with it too. But the idea of making a difference in kids' lives is a very big one for me. The idea of being that one piece of consistency that they may experience in their lives is a critical one for me, and that's why I stay in urban education. That's why I stay here at this school, and I have fought very hard to stay at this school. With the kind of numbers that I produce, other schools have asked for me, and I have turned them down. I like being here. I want to be here, and I want to stay with these kids.

Mark was keenly aware of the power he wielded as a mentor and as an adult in the building, but he was able to avoid power struggles with students by cultivating camaraderie and relationships of solidarity.

> I make a conscious effort. When a power struggle emerges, I know that teenagers, if they are backed into a corner, are going to lash out. That's the fight-or-flight idea, so give a kid an easy out. I could throw a giant fit about a seventeen-year-old boy that can't come to class with a pencil, or I could have a drawer full of extra pencils that I find on the ground. I buy a set of pencils at the beginning of the year, and I never buy any more. I just find them on the ground, and I put them in my drawer. They know that if they come in and they need a pencil, they need paper, they need whatever they need for the day, it's in there, no penalty. Just grab it. Just go. I only make a big deal out of it if you sit there for thirty minutes and then don't say . . . if I have to find you that you haven't done anything. Help yourself before I have to come and tell you to help yourself.

During one ninety-minute period, I observed Mark handing out four pencils to students. He responded,

> So, I don't make a big deal out of it because, why? What am I actually here to do? I'm here to teach them the content that I have, to teach them how to function in society. Yes, I know they need to be prepared, and they know that too, but sometimes it's not their fault. And understanding that, where the fight should be and where the fight shouldn't be, is kind of where I go.

I asked Mark to clarify where the fight should be, if not over pencils and materials. Many teachers would see the box of pencils as indulgent, and they would advocate teaching students to be responsible through points for materials and shutting kids out of class who come unprepared. Mark was clear that he would engage a student who is refusing to learn, but with compassion for the situation.

> The fight should be, "I don't want to learn this today." "That's fine, but you need to do it. You either need to give me a reason that I need to send a social worker for to get some help, or you need to suck it up and do it." Did you notice me over there talking to the gentleman second period? He was having a bad day. I got him to do a little bit. I could not break through to him the entire time, but I kept at him. I kept going, kept going, kept going. That is my equivalent of a fight. That's as aggressive as I get when it's something like that because I don't see a reason to make that an issue.

Mark's solidarity with his students came from deep within his being. He found a sense of purpose in his teaching, and he defended his students. He saw teaching as a calling, and that mind-set gave him the energy to fight the battles against those who would interrupt his task of educating and mentoring his students.

Mark's pedagogy is deeply rooted in his ability to build solidarity using caring, empathetic practices. He builds solidarity with students, parents, community members, and other adults in the school as a web of care that helps students succeed and attain their goals.

Chapter Five

A New Framework

Even if schools make a concerted effort to diversify school curriculum, personnel, and pedagogy but keep the structures of White supremacy, they have not met their obligations as educators committed to justice. A multicultural school that still imposes White supremacy is only slightly more liberatory than a school committed to segregation.

Bettina Love (2019a) shared from her own experience:

> For Black and Brown children in the United States, a major part of their schooling experience is associated with White female teachers who have no understanding of their culture. That was certainly my experience. My K-12 schooling was filled with White teachers who, at their core, were good people but unknowingly were murdering my spirit with their lack of knowledge, care, and love of my culture.

To stop the type of violence that Love describes will take a personal and structural overhaul of the school system and the people teaching in it. To accomplish this overhaul, changes must be made to how teachers see themselves in the classroom as well as to how schools are structured.

Specifically, there is a need for a school environment and teacher commitment framework that addresses the needs of Black students taught by White teachers in order for the curricular framework of multicultural education and the pedagogical frameworks of culturally relevant and other asset pedagogies to flourish. The literature on the relationships, power dynamics, and pedagogy across the divide of racial difference is vast and has a long history, and scholars now address these power relationships using the counternarratives of people of color challenging the paradigm of White supremacy (see De Lissovoy, 2010; Love, 2019a, 2019b; Solorzano & Yosso, 2002).

The caring solidarity framework attempts to fill a gap in teacher education and professional development by proposing a theoretical and paradigmatic change in the ways of describing successful White teachers of African American students. The purpose of this framework is to build the capacity of teachers using multicultural curriculum to create culturally relevant or sustaining classrooms and to describe teacher behaviors and commitments for creating solidarity with students.

THE CARING SOLIDARITY FRAMEWORK

Caring solidarity is an attempt to create a model that is both (1) descriptive of teachers who are working in solidarity with their students of color and (2) aspirational in helping teachers to move from solidarity with whiteness and the deficit models that accompany that mind-set to caring and solidarity with their students and communities. The framework of caring solidarity (see the figure in chapter 1) begins with four commitments: recognition, proximity, interrogation, and action. People seeking to work in caring solidarity move from one commitment to another using the conduits of love and grace, as described in this chapter. Chapter 6 explains how these commitments allow people to identify solidarity and empathy as needs. Between empathy and caring solidarity, however, is a barrier called transference of solidarity, which is described in chapter 7. Within the level of caring solidarity, there are two sublevels where the degree of teacher commitment and action distinguish between advocates and accomplices (also described in chapter 7).

Teachers grow into these commitments as they have more contact with students and the day-to-day realities of teaching. However, changes in circumstances, whether positive, like students winning an award or an infusion of funding, or negative, like a school closing or a traumatic event inside the school, can impede a teacher's growth disproportionately in one or more areas, even after attaining a level of solidarity in another situation. As White teachers are met with students of color, they learn and grow into their roles as educators crossing the color line.

Depending on their life experiences, the environment of the school, their own curiosity and commitments, and the mentorship and leadership they experience in their preparation and in their workplace, they may have more or less ability to move to new levels. For example, a teacher could be successful in her teaching at a racially and culturally diverse school with a majority White population, but through demographic changes she may find herself with a majority-minority population.

That shift will require growth into the new situation and maybe a renewal of old commitments and the attainment of new ones. The new situation will require a deeper level of commitment and a new sense of how relationships of caring solidarity are formed. No matter the situation, however, this model of caring solidarity, when applied to White teachers who cross the color line, can help them to succeed and thrive in their new environment.

There are two mind-set conduits that move teachers from one commitment to the other. The first is love, which moves people from recognition to proximity. The other is grace, which moves people from interrogation to action. To move to relationships of caring solidarity with students, the commitments are met at different levels: level 1, empathy; level 2, caring solidarity as an advocate; and level 3, caring solidarity as an accomplice (Indigenous Action Media, 2014; Powell & Kelly, 2017).

It is important to note that this is not a straightforward progression, and it is not automatic. Accomplices are not grown like trees. It is not a natural process. It is a decision, and it has consequences. Sometimes White people will make the choice to move, and then, upon seeing the opposition, will retreat until they are stronger. Sometimes they never make that choice. However, the choice to move toward caring solidarity comes with its own rewards, not the least of which is a more successful classroom, school, and community.

COMMITMENT TO RECOGNITION

Moving from the outside of the diagram (in chapter 1) in the upper lefthand quadrant, the first of the four commitments is to recognition. This recognition allows teachers to see their students as they really are, not as they are in the imagination of the teacher. As most White teachers do not have vast experience living with people of color before becoming teachers, the world of imagination is all that new teachers know about working in multiracial schools. Sometimes this is informed by solid teacher preparation, but often movies and the news inform new teachers about the students they will meet.

As explained earlier, the normality of whiteness in media, schools, and the social world all reinforce a detailed curriculum of White normality, White supremacy, and anti-blackness. So, being taught their whole lives that they are the standard by which all cultures, beauty, and behaviors should be measured, White teachers walk into classrooms of Black students and must unlearn the very paradigm of their existence. New White teachers who come to schools without exposure to other races and cultures oftentimes come to these schools with an idea that they will become the White savior (Straubhaar, 2014). They have seen movies like *Dangerous Minds* (1995) and *Freedom Writers* (2007), where teachers make inspiring speeches that turn young ruffians into scholars (Cammarota, 2011; Hughey, 2010). A part of whiteness is often that White people believe there is no place they cannot go and their presence is ostensibly good. The stance of the missionary, or the fixer, allows them to perceive students as in need of their values, not just guidance (Warren & Talley, 2017).

When these new teachers meet their students, White teachers bring into the classroom little that allows them to frame the experiences they will have from day one if they are seeking solidarity. Eventually, the White teacher will begin to see the students for who they are and will experience what can be referred to as the *shock of recognition*. In Herman Melville's 1850 essay "Hawthorne and His Mosses," he summed up how people who have no history with each other can acknowledge one another:

> Take that joy to yourself, in your own generation; and so, shall he feel those grateful impulses in him, that may possibly prompt him to the full flower of some still greater achievement in your eyes. And by confessing him, you thereby confess others, you brace the whole brotherhood. For genius, all over the world, stands hand in hand, and one shock of recognition runs the whole circle round. (Melville, 1850)

Recognition and Critical Theory

The caring solidarity model of recognition is rooted in the work of contemporary critical philosopher Axel Honneth (1995). Honneth's recognition gives a solid foundation in critical theory to caring solidarity as a framework for teachers who encounter diversity, often for the first time in their lives. Honneth's recognition is more than a glance around the room; it is a commitment to a relationship built upon understanding the other person as a person, not for what can be done for one party or the other.

Recognition is not an exchange but the creation of a bond that can only happen when both parties are able to see beyond the external and acknowledge the humanity of the other person. To Honneth, solidarity is built upon the recognition of the status of others. The level of that recognition comes from the intersubjective "esteem" that is built between them (Blunden, 2003). In his signature volume, *The Struggle for Recognition: The Moral Grammar of Social Conflicts* (1995), Honneth explained that the system of ethical life is based in struggle. Combatants are struggling for recognition in the eyes of the other, and there is no assumption of status without struggle.

Honneth's volume reconceptualizes the state of nature as described by Hegel, Hobbes, and other social contract theorists of the Enlightenment. Using Hobbes's concept of a mythical natural state before civilization, Honneth poses a question that has vexed philosophers: what made people decide to abandon the rule of the strong, give up their rights as individuals, and bind together to create civilizations and society? For Hegel, it was the conflict that arises between individuals for recognition, or status or esteem, as Honneth explained. The esteem that arises through conflict allows the parties to recognize each other legally, socially, and morally.

Recognition, then, does not happen without conflict, and esteem does not come without cost. Recognition is an earned state, not a natural one. Conflict creates the conditions for recognition, and the esteem or respect that grows out of the encounter establishes the humanity of both individuals in the other's eyes. Extending Honneth's framework to classrooms, recognition is only possible when two entities with differences recognize each other's humanity and are able to meet in a place where teachers can teach and students can learn.

The shock of recognition is the experience White teachers have when they realize that their students are, indeed, not what they have been taught they are but are fully human themselves. In the teacher-student relationship, there is a demand for respect from teachers and an equally strong demand for recognition from students. New White teachers in classes with Black students assume that they will have authority based on economic, structural, and racial status; however, students often do not immediately hand over that status without the teacher proving their worthiness. As children grow into adolescence, the demand for recognition grows.

The longer recognition is withheld from students who are not truly seen, the more strongly they will withhold respect/recognition until it is earned by the teacher. This struggle for recognition—on the students' part to be seen in all their humanity, and on the teacher's part to be appreciated as an authority—is the root of the conflict between the White teacher and the Black student. Neither can do their jobs to their fullest potential until that conflict is resolved. Recognition involves a different way of looking at the interactions between White teachers and their students. The shock of recognition, if correctly negotiated, can launch a teacher down the road to success across the color line. This shock of recognition is the beginning of the process toward solidarity.

While the shock of recognition is a momentary experience, the unlearning and learning needed after that shock is a long and revealing process. To do it, a White teacher must be willing to spend the time, the effort, and the emotional labor to recognize the humanity of students who are racialized in society and in the mind of the teacher. Recognition is the act of seeing Black people/children for who they are, not through the lens of whiteness.

Shibboleths as Signs of Recognition

After the initial stages of recognition, the White teacher seeking caring solidarity will begin to move toward the next stage. To do that, communication must become possible. However, many teachers do not come with the tools to speak with people who are racially and culturally different from themselves. As recognition progresses, words that will help teachers move into the group of students can be used.

Language, gestures, and customary greetings are powerful ways that humans communicate recognition of another person. The way that people are spoken to says much about the value that one person places on another. The overall term for these words and actions is a *shibboleth* (Du Bois, 1903/1994). A shibboleth is a way of saying something that shows group membership. The use of the word comes from the ancient biblical story of two Hebrew peoples, the Ephramites and the Gideonites, who were at war but could not tell each other apart visually.

These two groups were so similar in culture and custom that it was difficult to decipher whose side people were on. So to make sure only the right people got through the lines, the guards made everyone say the word *shibboleth*, Hebrew for *grain*. There was no "sh" sound in Ephramite vernacular, so Ephramites could not say the word to the Gideonites' satisfaction, and 42,000 Ephramites were killed.

Bloodshed aside, the shibboleths referred to here are words, phrases, and pronunciations that identify one as part of a group. Using the vocabulary that students use when discussing a topic with teens is a shibboleth. It can also be an accent. In my area of Texas, mixing Mexican Spanish pronunciation of names and places, even if the conversation is not in Spanish, establishes that a person is from southern Texas. Shibboleths, then, can be used by members of the "in group" to exclude outsiders or as code to characterize insiders. However, they can also be used as a way to show that an outsider wants to be accepted by insiders.

The use of shibboleths by outsiders, if done respectfully and within an attempt at solidarity, can be accepted by the in-group. However, for White teachers, the use of shibboleths should be done as part of an overall expression of solidarity. If not, the teacher may be perceived as phony or even mocking. As Milstein (2015) reminded, "identity does not automatically mean solidarity" (p. 65). Such phoniness sometimes exhibits itself when, rather than respectfully using shibboleths to make connections, outsiders misappropriate aspects of students' cultures into their own identity.

Misappropriation occurs when an outsider like a new teacher assumes that they are in the in-group and uses shibboleths without permission or inappropriately. Teachers sometimes intentionally use words as a way to mock students or to try and overpower them. That is a misuse of shibboleths and does not build solidarity. It will rightfully be rejected, further separating students from the teacher. This of course should be avoided and rebuked if it is done to anyone.

Teachers should always keep in mind the colonial aspects of such acts of misappropriation and seek to ameliorate them by owning their difference and being hyperaware that they are using other people's culture to make connections and not to commandeer behaviors and words as their own. For White teachers to be successful in multiracial and multicultural classrooms, they need a deeper level of understanding of cross-cultural communication.

There is an argument made that White students may feel alienated if the teacher speaks a language other than Standard English in the classroom. But consider the alienation that happens moment-to-moment for students of color when every interaction seeks to erase their culture, identity, and difference. Wouldn't all students benefit from a broadened appreciation of language and culture?

In these types of pushback, the narrative is that when other cultures are moved to the front, there is an assumption of displacement of White people. To some people, that is intolerable. White supremacy does not allow for the possibility that White students and teachers have a deficit in monolingualism or monoculturalism. Whiteness and White supremacy do not allow for differences to usurp whiteness. Differences can be tolerated as long as they do not take on more importance than whiteness. Thus, the complaint of unfairness when others are put forth is rooted in White supremacy. White teachers in multicultural classrooms where solidarity is sought will come upon this argument and must be ready to educate White parents or other educators that whiteness should not be front and center in the curriculum.

Successful White teachers who cross the color line immerse themselves in the culture of the school, the neighborhoods, and their students' cultural setting. They learn the language of the community, and they exchange shibboleths. These shibboleths allow for the exchange of ideas and allow teachers and students to trust one another. If done correctly, shibboleths are an outward sign of the commitment to recognition. They are a mechanism for showing students they are being seen for who they are and not for their approximation to, or distance from, whiteness.

The respectful, humble use of shibboleths to show respect is often welcomed, even if initially mistrusted, and is a way to show respect. If done with consideration and as a way to recognize and own the cultural differences between White teachers and students of color, the use of shibboleths can be a part of building relationships of solidarity between teachers and students.

Love as a Mind-Set Conduit to Proximity

As shown in the upper portion of the chapter 1 figure, the conduit from recognition to proximity is love. Love moves people from recognition to proximity. When people declare their love, they move in together, they marry, and they make deep commitments. They establish lives together. Family members share homes, and friends share bonds and often express love, sometimes as brothers or sisters. Love heals. Love permeates. Love envelopes. As hooks (2000) stated, "only love can heal the wounds of the past. However, the intensity of our woundedness often leads to a closing of the heart, making it impossible for us to give or receive the love that is given to us" (p. xxvii).

Ask any teacher on most days, and they will tell you that they love their students. Sometimes secondary school teachers are less likely to say so as there currently are taboos over the language of love, but even they will declare their love of their job, their school, or their team.

The love of one's students is an outgrowth of recognition. Without recognition, there can be no love, nor solidarity, as there is no relationship. There are many ways to discuss love as a concept, but for this discussion, it is important to frame love as action that moves a person toward solidarity with another. That kind of love, the political act of commitment to another outside themselves and outside their kin, is a commitment that many say they have when entering the teaching profession but of which in practice they often fall short (Matias, 2016a).

To frame the love that leads to solidarity, Frankfurt School critical theorist Erich Fromm's work *The Art of Loving* (1956) elucidates the active loving relationship of solidarity:

> Love is an activity; if I love, I am in a constant state of active concern with the loved person, but not only with him or her. For I shall become incapable of relating myself actively to the loved person if I am lazy, if I am not in a constant state of awareness, alertness, activity. (p. 118)

To be active in loving as a teacher means to care for students. It means that a teacher will put the needs of their students first, that they will do what is necessary for students to succeed and not hold students in contempt. It means the teacher does not belittle the students. As hooks (2000) explains, love is an action:

> To begin by always thinking of love as an action rather than a feeling is one way in which anyone using the word in this manner automatically assumes accountability and responsibility. We are often taught we have no control over our "feelings." Yet most of us accept that we choose our actions, that intention and will inform what we do. (pp. 12–13)

In this context, the kind of love that moves a person to action is a choice that all people make. It is not merely a feeling or a preference for one over the other, as in the love of ice cream. The love that leads to caring solidarity transcends the day-to-day feelings a person may or may not have. It is a commitment to love and to be with the other person or people. That is why it leads to proximity. Loving a community or an individual is possible only when a commitment to solidarity is made as well (Matias & Allen, 2013).

For Fromm (1956), the act of loving required one to forego the selfish narcissism that is a hallmark of the young and grow into a person with the capacity to embrace faith in the one who is loved:

> The ability to love depends on one's capacity to emerge from narcissism, and from the incestuous fixation to mother and clan; it depends on our capacity to grow, to develop a productive orientation in our relationship toward the world and ourselves. This process of emergence, of birth, of waking up, requires one quality as a necessary condition: faith. The practice of the art of loving requires the practice of faith. (p. 112)

This act of growing up, of leaving the childish imaginary behind, is an important step. As Fromm explained:

> Thought and judgment are not the only realm of experience in which rational faith is manifested. In the sphere of human relations, faith is an indispensable quality of any significant friendship or love. "Having faith" in another person means to be certain of the reliability and unchangeability of his fundamental attitudes, of the core of his personality, of his love. (p. 114)

New White teachers, as discussed earlier, often arrive with a set of imaginary students in their heads, but if they are dedicated to their craft, they will experience the shock of recognition. That shock is a startling, waking experience that should move them away from the imaginary to the real people in front of them. It is only through that recognition that love is possible, and love, if correctly cultivated, moves them toward solidarity.

The love Fromm describes is only possible if it is not an exchange, for example, love in exchange for love back. The love that leads to solidarity is based in caring for someone outside of oneself. It does not depend on reciprocation and is unconditional:

> Unconditional love corresponds to one of the deepest longings, not only of the child, but of every human being; on the other hand, to be loved because of one's merit, because one deserves it, always leaves doubt; maybe I did not please the person whom I want to love me, maybe this, or that—there is always a fear that love could disappear. (p. 39)

Beyond the lack of conditions, Fromm frames his concept of love that leads to solidarity as respect. This is not an authoritarian form of respect but a loving respect that rests on recognition of the other person's humanity and on one's ability to love unconditionally. It is a gift freely given as a free person, not with a payment demanded:

> Respect means the concern that the other person should grow and unfold as he is. Respect, thus, implies the absence of exploitation. I want the loved person

to grow and unfold for his own sake, and in his own ways, and not for the
purpose of serving me. (p. 26)

The love that leads to solidarity, built on a foundation of recognition, is only
possible between free people who love, not out of need, but as an outgrowth
of freedom and the recognition of the dignity of the person loved. It is an act
of loving that moves people toward a relationship of solidarity.

For Fromm, there were three elements of this kind of love that needed to
be in place for this respect to flourish. These three elements resonate with
teachers and are certainly part of a teacher's identity and daily practice:
discipline, concentration, and patience "throughout every phase" of life (p.
102).

Discipline

As with anything one has to work at to become proficient, love takes discipline. Fromm equated the art of loving with learning to play an instrument or
Zen archery. The discipline of love as an educator means that teachers will
get up early to make copies, prepare activities, go to morning practices, or
grocery shop before school to make sure students have food.

Secondary schools often start before dawn, and teachers are there as early
as possible to get started on the day's activities. Sometimes with coffee in
hand, grabbing food as they walk, or eating while driving through the snow
to get to school and meet their students, teachers who display this type of
discipline are love in action.

After students arrive, sometimes sleepy and oftentimes with empty stom-
achs, teachers are there to care for them: "It is essential, however, that discipline should not be practiced like a rule imposed on oneself from the outside,
but that it becomes an expression of one's own will; that it is felt as pleasant,
and that one slowly accustoms oneself to a kind of behavior which one would
eventually miss, if one stopped practicing it" (Fromm, 1956, p. 103).

Throughout the day, teachers distribute love in the form of questions,
answers, feedback, compliments, sarcasm, bad puns, and silly sayings. These
things, to be effective, do not come from mandates or canned lesson plans
but from inside teachers' hearts and souls.

Great teachers recognize that their discipline of themselves is necessary
for teaching students effectively. The teacher who is undisciplined will not
plan for student learning effectively, will not create an environment condu-
cive to learning, and will not build those relationships of caring solidarity
because they are not secure on their own. Discipline brings the conditions
necessary for love and success into the classroom.

Concentration

Fromm's concept of concentration was the ability to be alone with oneself. It is the ability to spend time without even thinking that allows for real rest. The ability to be alone allows a person to be independent of others and therefore able to love. "If I am attached to another person because I cannot stand on my own feet, he or she may be a lifesaver, but the relationship is not one of love" (Fromm, 1956, p. 103). For teachers, to be in relationships of caring solidarity with their students means that they must understand themselves and be confident in their pedagogy, practice, and who they are in the school and the world.

This is not something that can happen on the first day or often even in the first few years of a teaching career. Navigating and negotiating relationships across race and culture barriers is hard work and takes a never-ending commitment to self-understanding as well as maturity in the position of teacher. They must have a sense of who they are as White people in a school across the color line and have presence that comes with time and concentration:

> To be concentrated means to live fully in the present, in the here and now, and not to think of the next thing to be done, while I am doing something right now. Needless to say, that concentration must be practiced most of all by people who love each other. (p. 106)

To be ready to make caring solidarity relationships, the teacher must have enough sense of self to be ready to absorb the inevitable mistakes and failures that will accompany the teaching journey without crumbling. To do this takes a type of courage to face, not an outside opponent, but the enemy within: the nemeses of perfection, the fear of students, the fear of being wrong, looking silly, or being misunderstood.

It takes presence of mind, courage, and faith to build relationships across difference. As Fromm stated, this kind of concentration

> requires courage, the ability to take a risk, the readiness even to accept pain and disappointment. Whoever insists on safety and security as primary conditions of life cannot have faith; whoever shuts himself off in a system of defense, where distance and possession are his means of security, makes himself a prisoner. To be loved, and to love, need courage, the courage to judge certain values as of ultimate concern—and to take the jump and stake everything on these values. (p. 116)

Successful teachers across the color line value their students and communities. They value a curriculum where students are recognized and represented. They value the cultures of their students and do not assume their own cultures are superior to the culture of their students. They are continually learning from their students and communities. These values allow for love to flow from the teacher to the students and then back.

Teachers who do not have this ability to love will not receive love in return. There is no guarantee that a teacher who does all of these things will receive love in return, but it is guaranteed that if they do not do these things, love will not flow back.

Patience

As with any art, Fromm's active loving is an art that must be patiently mastered over time. The act of teaching is not something that can be mastered in a course or a program. It takes time with students, with books, and with oneself in quiet reflection. Fromm explained, "Eventually, a condition of learning any art is a *supreme concern* with the mastery of the art. If the art is not something of supreme importance, the apprentice will never learn it. He will remain, at best, a good dilettante, but will never become a master. This condition is as necessary for the art of loving as for any other art" (Fromm, 1956, pp. 101–102).

The art of teaching across the color line also requires the practice of patience, a commitment to students, and especially a commitment to learning from students. The discipline needed to be a successful teacher across the color line is multifold, but among the most important is the ability to reflect on one's own standpoint. Great teachers are constantly revisiting their practice and their mental frameworks. They are willing to be challenged, even uncomfortably, and use that challenge as an opportunity to learn and grow. They are disciplined in their study of pedagogy, practice, and content. They are students of their students. In other words, they study their students and learn from them. They learn how to meet their students in caring solidarity through disciplined observation, interaction, and study.

Successful teachers are willing to be patient with students and with themselves. They learn and grow with their students. They lead students to new understandings while also learning from them. White teachers who meet their Black students with patience, secure in their own knowledge of pedagogy and content and open to new understandings about race, power, and culture, are able to create a powerful, loving environment for students, where students feel valued, cared for, and cared about. In return, the students enliven the classroom and enrich the life of the teacher.

COMMITMENT TO PROXIMITY

In the caring solidarity framework, the movement is from recognition, using the conduit of love, to the commitment of proximity. When a White teacher is first hired at a multiracial school, the first active commitment they make is the act of crossing the color line. That physical movement is often the first time White teachers have interacted with people of color on a regular and meaningful basis. It is often the first time that these White people have been asked to care for a child who does not look like them, and most are not adequately equipped to make that journey.

Once teachers are able to recognize their students, they are able to move closer to them and live, be, and exist inside the cultural parameters of the students' community. This will be part of the process of creating teachers' identity. The identity will be shaped by the experiences of living, working, and moving in spaces that are not defined primarily by whiteness.

Proximity begins with White teachers teaching in the school, but it cannot end there if teachers are to achieve relationships of solidarity (Harvey, 2007). Many teachers declare they are in solidarity with students but stop short of moving into communities where people of color live, shop, school their children, and participate politically. However, until a teacher is willing to be a member of the community, they will always have a distance between themselves and the students they teach.

That is not to say they cannot be a good teacher, or even an effective ally for their students, but to teach all day in communities of color and then go home to White enclaves avoids the steps necessary to move into solidarity. Unless a person is willing to be in proximity to the ones that they declare they love, that love is hollow and perhaps not love at all. Teachers who take positions in diverse schools who have not made any commitment to teaching across the color line are often disastrous.

That is not to say they cannot be good teachers or even effective allies for their students and live away from them, but to teach all day in communities of color and then go home to White enclaves avoids the steps necessary to move into solidarity. Unless people are willing to be in proximity to the ones that they declare they love, that love is hollow and perhaps not love at all. The journey begins in teacher candidacy. Teacher candidates are often unaccustomed to students of color and bring with them their own attitudes about how students should speak, act, and learn. Those ways are based in their own experiences and their own preferred learning method, but students who are racially or culturally different have different ways of being that will be perceived as incorrect or disrespectful if the context is not understood. If this set of attitudes is not informed through the process of teacher certification, newly hired teachers will have even more hardened ideas about schools and students when they begin teaching. And so teachers who take positions in diverse schools but have not made any commitment to teaching across the color line are often disastrous.

When a White teacher takes a teaching position in a diverse school, they should do so with the expressed intention of crossing race and class lines, effectively a choice in defining their teacher identity. To be successful, they perform a conscious act. This proximity is a choice. There are plenty of communities across the nation that have few students of color attending, and teachers often make more money in these districts. So no White teacher should work in diverse schools without a commitment to bonding their identity to their students through recognition and then proximity. To do otherwise sets everyone up for failure.

The Caveat: Neoliberalism, Reform, and Gentrification

The concept of proximity faces reasonable criticisms. Gentrification, or the immoral displacement of people of color in neighborhoods that newly appeal to middle- and upper-class White people, has been a topic of scholarly and political discussion since the 1990s (Lipman, 2013; Wyly & Hammel, 2004). The displacement of already marginalized communities by White people is a consideration that must be taken into account by White teachers who want to teach successfully in those neighborhoods. Adding to such displacement will not engender solidarity. However, without proximity, there will always be a distance that impedes the relationship. This causes a quandary that is important to explore.

White people tend to believe that their presence is unquestionably good, and this tendency allows them to move into spaces that have been refit to meet White standards. Sullivan (2014) explained that White people are ontologically expansive; in other words, they tend not only to see themselves as the norm but also to assume that all spaces are theirs for the taking. She explained that White people have a "habit, often unconscious, of assuming and acting as if any and all spaces—geographical, psychological, cultural, linguistic, or whatever—are rightfully available to and open for white people to enter whenever they like" (p. 20).

When White teachers teach in places where Black kids are brought *to* them, as in suburban magnet schools, charter schools, or private schools that are not rooted in communities of color, that is not the same kind of proximity that brings about caring solidarity. It may bring about allyship or even advocacy because the teacher may care a great deal about her students, but caring solidarity involves moving oneself to the people with whom caring solidarity relationships are sought (Milstein, 2015).

The issue is this: teachers have already moved into these spaces. As pointed out in chapter 1, White teachers are already teaching Black students in their communities. The case is settled that White teachers will interact with communities of color. The question is how and to what degree. If teachers are to be successful in advocacy and allyship with students, they must know the communities where students live. To move to caring solidarity, White teachers move from recognition of people who do not look like them, through love, to proximity.

As degreed professionals, teachers are aware that they have choices in life. White teachers should make choices out of conviction. That conviction may or may not lead them to work with students who do not share their White identity. Those choices range from where they want to live to whom they want to teach. As McIntosh (2001) famously stated, "White privilege is like an invisible weightless knapsack of special provisions, maps, passports, codebooks, visas, clothes, tools, and blank checks" (p. 188). One of the privileges of whiteness is the ability to go places and do things without restrictions based on race.

While privilege itself does not preclude caring about others, privileged status allows the choice of altruism as one of many alternatives and the reasons for choosing to teach (Danielewicz, 2001). However, altruism linked to privilege will impede caring solidarity because it will invariably ask for gratitude in return.

The politics and implications of gentrification and place are real and difficult to navigate, so it may take time for new White teachers to move into proximity with students, while others are able to dive in from the first school bell. This privilege also extends to the choices White people are able to make about where to live and what type of lifestyle they wish to have (Lipman, 2013).

The successful teacher who seeks to engage in caring solidarity must be committed to proximity. Allyship can mean proximity at school alone, but to move to greater levels of solidarity with students, teachers in caring solidarity will have to live, raise families, and become deeply involved, socially, politically, and culturally, in the neighborhoods where their students are living.

COMMITMENT TO INTERROGATION

Whiteness and Its Power

Moving along the outside of the caring solidarity framework diagram, the next commitment is the interrogation of whiteness. Whiteness, to give a simple definition, is the intersection of White normality and White privilege. The construction of American society was specifically created to increase the privilege of White people. To understand the influence of whiteness, we must define it. According to Frankenberg (1993), there are three dimensions to whiteness. First is the "structural advantage" of the White power structure and its accompanying privileges. Second is the "standpoint" or positionality of being White and seeing the world through that lens. "Thirdly, it carries with it a set of ways of being in the world, a set of cultural practices, often not named as 'white' by white folks but looked on instead as 'American' or 'normal'" (p. 54).

McIntosh (2001) observed that there are unearned privileges given to Whites based on the fact that they are White people in a country where whiteness is normalized. While this concept causes discomfort for many White people, especially new teachers (see, e.g., Michie, 2007), it is not surprising to people of color, for whom whiteness has always been a part of daily life. As hooks (2013) explained,

> It is living in a culture of white supremacy that is often an unconsciously debilitating force diminishing the spirit. This is not new news for most black folks. From slavery to the present day, black folks have known that dealing with traumatic exploitation and oppression based on race creates life-threatening stress and concomitant illness that come in its wake. (p. 185)

This powerful concept of normality allows White people to assume that the ways they live their lives are normal and expected while all others are abnormal or diverse, as explained in this book's introduction. Bonilla-Silva (2010) explained that there is a pervasive practice referred to as "color-blind racism" that allows White people to claim that they are not racist by denying that race matters (p. 2). "I don't see a person's race" is a common phrase that teacher candidates will state at the beginning of their programs. Oftentimes this comes from their own constructs of justice and integrity because they equate racism with overt acts of discrimination and hate, something they vow they will never do.

As Hayes and Juarez (2012) explained, "holding on to a color-blind framework allows people to address only the egregious forms of racism" (p. 7). It allows White people to be blind to "the very knowledge of culturally responsive teaching and social justice that is needed to transform the whiteness of education" (p. 7).

Eslinger (2013) explained that successful teachers of students of color interrogate their own whiteness and their a priori knowledge and attitudes about race, racial minorities, and privilege. "White teachers need: 1) to develop a rich and culturally diverse knowledge base; 2) to interrogate their identities and the privileges associated with them; and 3) to critically examine curriculum and pedagogy" (p. 5). According to Eslinger, teachers also fall victim to a savior mentality and a "White supremacist" belief structure that must be quelled in order to create a culturally responsive classroom (p. 8).

For White teachers to be successful in the hypercultural classrooms of today's urban schools, they need a deeper level of understanding than simple cross-cultural communication. Thus, in terms of whiteness, it is less about pigment in the skin than about power, privilege, and the ability to act without care or regard to the feelings, positions, and standpoints of others who are not seen as White.

To deeply understand what whiteness is and why it matters takes an examination of self, identity, and ideology. Individuals doing their own internal investigation are practicing what Cochran-Smith (2003) described as interrogation. To interrogate one's whiteness means that a person shines a proverbial light into their own attitudes, feelings, and mental frameworks to investigate where these stem from (Keating, 1995). To interrogate, teachers look at their own ideas about themselves, their students, the families of their students, and the communities where they teach. For anyone taking this journey, to interrogate their own whiteness is an act of courage.

Working to break down one's own privilege can be difficult and frightening, and many abandon the project before it even begins. It is much easier to retreat from the day-to-day grind of holding oneself accountable and default to blaming students for their lack of middle-class sensibilities (Payne, 2013). Nearly every day, teacher educators hear someone say that the "kind of kids we get" or "those kids" are the problem, not the teachers' responses to differences or the structures of inequality that students endure. Done correctly, this interrogation can lead to a sensibility that allows one to take risks in and out of the classroom (Love, 2014).

Cochran-Smith (2003) explained that there are several steps that can help a person to interrogate their whiteness. The first is to listen to or read stories of people of color and work to hear and believe that those experiences, although different, are as valid and real as their own. Second is for the person to begin to tell their own racialized story where they will verbalize the differences and similarities between the story they can tell of their lives and the lives of people of color. Singleton and Linton (2006) ask participants in conversations about race to "remain in the moment" and focus on the present when someone tells a story that challenges whiteness. These techniques can help White teachers begin the journey to interrogating their own whiteness, but a key component is recognition of the unearned privileges that whiteness brings in American society.

Positive White Racial Identity

The goal of interrogating one's whiteness is to come to an understanding of a positive White racial identity. In 1990, psychologist and scholar Janet Helms created a scale to identify the stages that lead a person from the default position of White supremacy to a positive White racial identity. Her stages are summarized, updated, and applied here.

Contact

The ideology of color blindness is indicative of this stage (Bonilla-Silva, 2010). The person may deny that racism still exists or declare that White supremacy is a "hoax" or a liberal talking point (Friedersdorf, 2019). This person may deny that attacks on people of color are racially based or that police shootings of unarmed Black people are the result of White supremacy or anti-blackness.

They will defend the Confederate flag and Southern pride as heritage, not hate. They may even acknowledge that racism exists but will deny that it is a problem that must be dealt with. They may even refer to people who identify race as an issue as the "real racists" against White people. They will demand that immigrants show gratitude for being allowed to stay in the United States.

White people are socialized into these ideologies from childhood and may have experienced a lack of contact with people of color. Add right-wing media to the mix, and the person is bound to have a long journey ahead of them in order to build a positive racial identity. They will be more able to move if they are confronted with the reality of the lives of people of color. This can happen if a grandchild of color is born into the family or if they are confronted for their nonracism stance by others they respect in their family, at work, at church, or in other social situations.

Disintegration

Ideally, when White people enter colleges and universities, they are confronted with stories, theories, and a new set of explanations for the world that will contradict the common sense they have been given in conservative White communities. There are, of course, ways to avoid this uncomfortable experience through strategic choices of classes or at conservative universities that shelter White students from these new understandings.

However, when White students are confronted with a deeper understanding of race, its impact on communities, and the deeper history of colonization and slavery, they can sometimes feel guilt or shame at what their ancestors or other White people have done. This guilt can then be redirected to action and antiracism. If that happens, a White person can move to the next stage, but if left without help, a person in this stage can find plenty of websites that will support them in regressing and tell them that everything they have learned is either useless or not real—or, worst of all, a conspiracy to commit "White genocide."

Reintegration

In this stage, White people blame others for the effects of White supremacist ideology. While the description of this stage seems like backsliding, it is actually an important part of the process. This is the (un)enlightened "yeah, but" person endured in social situations and college classrooms. People in this stage are willing to accept that Whites have racial privilege and that people who are not perceived as White have been oppressed, but they are still annoyed when they are told that privilege has allowed them and their families to succeed even if they are mediocre.

They are the people who bring up the repression of the Irish or their own immigrant stories to show that their journey has been just as difficult as slavery. They will also use deficit models for the achievement gap and may blame a culture of poverty for why Black students do not do as well as White students in schools.

Pseudo-Independence

This is the stage where White people will begin to have a positive and realistic White racial identity. They are ready to look to people of color to explain racism and accept that explanation. They do not question the narratives of racism encountered by people of color. They seek out the advice and counsel of people of color on matters of race. They do not assume that White people know best or that they are always the ones in charge.

However, this stage is still developmental in that people still seek to be nonracist and expect people of color to do the work of undoing racism. They do not see themselves as part of the solution or the problem, and they may still engage in "ironic" or "hipster" racism (West, 2013) or casual White supremacy when in social situations or when trying to be humorous.

Immersion/Emersion

In this stage, a White person is actively working to be an antiracist. They may call out friends who use ironic or hipster racism or join in conversations as a White ally. They may join groups seeking to stamp out racism or join in protests around race discrimination. They will speak up in classes and ally themselves with people of color. At this stage, they are still developing a positive White racial identity, but they are becoming more comfortable with the idea that they can be part of the solution to White supremacist structures and anti-blackness.

Autonomy

This last stage is characterized by a clear understanding and acceptance of a positive White racial identity. There is an understanding of the history of colonization, slavery, and segregation in America and the world. There is a desire to know more about the histories of people who are not perceived as White. There is a desire and a capacity to read literature by people of color, and this person has real friendships across the color line. From here, a person can engage in "relationships of solidarity" (Harvey, 2007).

Helms's work, rooted in psychology, has been deeply influential for scholars of color and White scholars looking to understand the creation of a positive White racial identity. While this theory helps to understand many White people's experiences, it is difficult to reconcile that, more often than not, White teachers with two years or less of training are thrust in front of children before reaching the certain degree of maturity that comes with the autonomy stage.

Therein lies the dilemma for professors of education and educational leaders. The stages take time, study, reflection, and experience—all things in short supply when they hire freshly minted teachers from undergraduate programs or, more difficult, trainees from a fast-track alternative certification program. Black students cannot wait for their teacher to come around to recognizing their humanity, so White teachers must engage in creating relationships of solidarity even before they are fully formed as autonomous antiracists (Harvey, 2007).

Things to Consider

White teachers who seek to enter into relationships across the color line based on caring solidarity must interrogate their own whiteness. As Matias stated, "it is not enough that white teachers are trained to be masters of cultural competency of the Other but are never asked to interrogate their own Whiteness" (Matias, 2016b, p. 199). To be successful, White teachers who cross the color line must immerse themselves in the long process of understanding the privilege of being White in the United States (McIntosh, 2001). The process of interrogating whiteness begins with the acknowledgment of White privilege and an examination of the history of race in America, then owning the fact that Whites are beneficiaries of the social construct of race. To that end, here are some steps, not in order, that are needed to interrogate whiteness.

Count the Cost

White people must ask themselves what they are willing to lose by understanding what other people know to be true. Truthfully, White people are deceived from birth. They are told that they are innocent. White people are told that their ancestors, neighbors, and White heroes are all innocent of theft from people who do not present as White. The first step is to decide if learning otherwise will shatter their identity and be too much to bear.

Stepping out of the shadow of these lies is freeing if a person seeks to be free, but it can be frightening and overwhelming to someone who does not have the strength to face the truth.

Study, Read, and Reflect

The work of authors of color who have explored whiteness would take a whole other book to list, but the references in this book are a good place to start. Other books by White people (like DiAngelo, 2018; Michael, 2015; and Irving, 2014) who interrogate whiteness are also great resources.

Ask Questions

Ask questions of adults, yes, but it is also important to ask questions of students. Seldom do students get asked anything of consequence, and adults in their lives are loath to admit they do not know something. Sample questions for kids are, "Why is that?" "What do you think of that?" and "How do you cope with that?" Questions that on the surface are not about race are often the beginning of wisdom about race. It will not be as effective if teachers ask about specific things they have just read or the latest new theory. Stop and listen, and things will be revealed in ways that are only possible when the hearer is ready.

Seek Learning and Professional Development

Conferences, workshops, museums, and classes can help White people to learn about race, racism, and the effects of White supremacy on all people. Seek out experts, read and reflect, and think about whiteness and how to defuse its effects on everyone, specifically students.

Engage in Dialogue but Avoid Explaining All You Know

Teachers must engage in critical dialogues about race, whiteness, and White supremacy, but they will not learn if they are in teacher or telling mode. Like people reformed from anything, reformed White people can be annoying and ridiculous to people who have lived race consciousness their entire lives.

Instead, amplify what people of color say in meetings. These meetings can be with parents or colleagues or both. Remember that, as a White person who wants to enter into relationships of solidarity, it is important to listen, learn, and be taught. However, and this is very important, do not merely repeat a phrase or idea and take it as a possession. Instead, include the speaker, as in, "I agree with what [speaker's name] said. I think it is important that we hear that." At that point, you can say the idea again and then check to make sure it was right. "Is that what you meant, [speaker's name]?" Then, afterward, talk with the person who was amplified to make sure they are OK with the amplification. If not, do not repeat it (Case, 2018).

Helms (1990) and Tatum (1992) stated that the goal of this act of discovery is the autonomy stage where White people are able to transcend their own feelings and move toward alliances with people of color. This alliance is preceded by what Tatum referred to as "antiracist" behaviors.

> The positive feelings associated with this redefinition energize the person's efforts to confront racism and oppression in his or her daily life. Alliances with people of color can be more easily forged at this stage of development than previously because the person's antiracist behaviors and attitudes will be more consistently expressed. (Tatum, 1992, p. 17)

This alliance, a deeper level in a relationship of solidarity, becomes possible because of behaviors associated with antiracism. However, to achieve antiracist behaviors, a White person must first interrogate their Whiteness through the understanding of privilege. If done with sincerity and determination, it can become liberatory from the prison of whiteness.

Freire (2014) explained that "liberation is thus a childbirth, and a painful one. The man or woman who emerges is a new person, viable only as the oppressor-oppressed contradiction is superseded by the humanization of all people. Or to put it another way, the solution of this contradiction is born in the labor which brings into the world this new being: no longer oppressor no longer oppressed, but human in the process of achieving freedom" (p. 49).

Liberation from segregation in the mind, heart, and body is only possible through deep interrogation of the person and the position of that person in society. Interrogation of whiteness allows the White teacher to move closer to creating relationships of caring solidarity with students and communities of color.

Grace as a Mind-Set Conduit to Action

One example of grace happened after a 2016 Trump rally in Fayetteville, North Carolina. Rakeem Jones, a 27-year-old pizza delivery driver who is Black attended a Trump rally to protest the racism during the campaign. After yelling a few words, he was roughly escorted out by several armed guards. As he was being hustled out, he was sucker-punched by several attendees, especially John Franklin "Quick Draw" McGraw, age 79, a social-security pensioner and part-time leather worker. Nine months later, the tape of McGraw punching Jones resulted in a charge of assault against McGraw, and the two faced each other in court, where McGraw maintained his non-racism and spoke to Jones. The *Washington Post*'s Terrence McCoy (2016) told the story:

> The judge asked McGraw whether he wanted to say something, too. "I'm extremely sorry this happened," McGraw said, and when the judge told him to explain it to Jones, not him, he turned to Jones and took a step toward him. It was the closest they'd been to each other since the rally. "This was between two men. You know what you did. And I know what I did. I'm not going to

say you were wrong or I was wrong," McGraw said. "You and I both know what occurred, and I hate it worse than anything else in the world." He stepped closer to Jones and raised a finger. "We got caught up in a political mess today," he said. His jaw began to tremble. "And you and me, we got to heal our country."

At that point, Jones forgave McGraw and the two men embraced. This scene of forgiveness went viral and people saw it as hope for our country, but in reality it is a symptom of the problem. McGraw did not apologize. He maintained that the ideology that led him to be at a Trump rally and to vote for Trump was not the problem. Instead, things just got out of hand. This kind of reconciliation has been the type that is expected from Black people across the globe. Slavery, apartheid, and segregation are in the past, and Black people are expected to forgive and move on without any recognition that great wrongs have been done to them.

McGraw believed he was justified in his actions that night, but they caused harm, and he maintained that this was not his intent; therefore, he offered an apology for the harm, not for the action. The conceptual framework of the apology is "I am sorry my White supremacy hurt you." McGraw also believed it was appropriate for Jones to apologize for his encroachment and trespass in a White space. Whiteness demands that if one is allowed to occupy space (as all space is White), then one should be humble and grateful for the opportunity to be in the presence of whiteness. So, to McGraw, Jones's sin was a lack of gratitude. When he talked about healing the country, it is not a healing that would elevate Jones to McGraw's status. Rather, it is one where Jones is grateful for being allowed to live in America.

White supremacy demands that whiteness always be the center, and so the expectation is that transgressions against whiteness are worthy of apology. At times, as part of generosity and benevolence, White supremacy can offer apologies for harm that is caused when it is exercised and causes harm, as in apologies for Japanese internment. However, there is no apology for White privilege or the ideology of White supremacy that caused the action that resulted in the harm.

Philosopher Myisha Cherry explains that this type of story, when told to victims of oppression, is used to force them into submitting to authority and offering forgiveness, even when it is not reasonable to do so. Cherry delineated between two types of "moves" that are placed on victims: the "authority move" and the "my suffering is worse than yours" move. The authority move argues that because an authority forgave, the victim should also forgive. She uses Jesus as an example: "1. Jesus forgave. 2. Whatever Jesus did, we should do. 3. Therefore, we should forgive" (p. 65).

This kind of move adds to the oppression of victims because it delegitimatizes their justifiable anger at being victimized. Cherry clarified that authority is not a moral argument; it plays on emotion and is an expression of power over the oppressed. In the "my suffering is worse than yours'" move, victims of violence is led to the conclusion that they should not feel their anger because someone else had a more difficult time than them. This move uses examples of suffering (Jesus, for example) to bludgeon its victims into relinquishing their own justifiable outrage at being abused.

These types of double victimizations are done to students all the time. Black students have been historically treated as the racial other, punished for lashing out, expected to forgive the system, and then finally expected to have complete faith that victimizations will not happen to their children (Kozol, 1995; Yasso, 2005). White teachers then complain that Black parents do not come to school for meetings and events and do not jump in and volunteer. For White teachers to reconcile and build relationships of solidarity, they must offer grace and accept grace as a daily exercise in love and faith.

As Dr. Martin Luther King Jr. (2017) reminded his audience, "Grace has a very vital place in any life. It has a very vital place in understanding the whole predicament of man and the whole predicament of the universe, for you can never understand life until you understand the meaning [of grace]" (p. 387, 388). The acceptance of grace from communities and the willingness to forgive oneself when mistakes or oversights cloud the work of building relationships of solidarity is also an important step in building it. This process will include missteps, mistakes, and downright mess-ups. The ability to keep trying when everything is crumbling is the true measure of commitment, endurance, and grace. It is the kind of grace that can lead to solidarity.

Sin, grace, and forgiveness are all wrapped up together and are sometimes difficult to untangle, but the focus on grace allows one to clearly see the path to the next commitment (action). If White people and White teachers can receive grace from their students and communities and return grace to the parties, it allows for deep recognition, love, proximity, interrogation, and action. The acceptance of grace is humbling and the opposite of supremacy.

As shown in the caring solidarity framework diagram, grace is the conduit that moves people from interrogation to action. Grace is not usually something written about in academic texts, but the concept is so crucial to the experience of solidarity that to ignore it would leave a gaping hole in the definition. Berry (2018) described grace as a "multidimensional phenomenon" (p. xvi), and the concept of grace is tied to sin and then forgiveness as a consequence of grace. As a matter of definition, grace is not earned but given. The American concept of grace is largely informed from the Protestant Church, which views grace as a central tenet of the faith.

In the late 1950s, Dr. King (2017) explained that while the gift of grace is free, the need for grace is rooted in sin. King unapologetically names sins beyond what many White people would list to include the progeny of White supremacist ideology and capitalism. The logic goes that a fallen humanity deserves death but can be redeemed through grace. The acceptance of grace is a central marker of the Protestant concept of Christianity:

> And so, it boils down that we are sinners in need of God's redemptive power. We know truth, and yet we lie. We know how to be just, and yet we are unjust. . . . We know the ways of peace, and yet we go to war. We have resources for great economic systems where there could be equitable distributions of wealth, and yet we monopolize and take it all for ourselves and forget about our brothers. And when we come to see ourselves, we discover that all of us are sinners. "All we like sheep have gone astray." (p. 384)

This need for grace because of the sin of White supremacy is deep. It has hampered the most powerful creed in human history that "all men are endowed by their creator with certain inalienable rights, among those are life, liberty, and the pursuit of happiness." It has made those words ring hollow from the moment they were penned by Thomas Jefferson, an enslaver, even as he argued to stop the slave trade through the Declaration of Independence.

Even the Great Emancipator, Abraham Lincoln, never saw past his own ideology of Black inferiority as he befriended Frederick Douglass and fought a war that eventually became one to free the slaves. There has never been a time in American history when White supremacy has not been the agreed-upon ideology of those in power.

To dismantle White supremacy, White people, especially White teachers who want to succeed across the color line, will have to become the recipients of grace from their students and communities. This will be difficult because many White people do not believe they need grace or forgiveness, as they maintain that they have not done anything that needs forgiving. They maintain that they never owned slaves, enforced segregation, or used racial slurs, so why would anyone need to forgive them?

Consider the following illustration. If a man lives in a stolen house and lives off stolen money, he may not be a thief, but he still has a responsibility to the victims of the theft. White supremacy means never having to apologize or admit wrong. But those who wish to work in solidarity with African Americans must also work to dismantle White supremacy. To do so means that they also need the grace and forgiveness of those who have been wounded by White supremacy. Dr. King (2017) offered grace even in the midst of his deep struggles against White supremacy:

> Western civilization, you've gone into the far country of imperialism and colonialism. You have trampled over more than one billion six hundred million of the people of the world. You have exploited them economically, you have dominated them politically, trampled over them, humiliated them, and segregated them. . . . And there you are in this far country of oppression, trampling over your children. But western civilization, America, you can come home and if you will come home, I will take you in. And I will bring the fatted

calf and I will cry out to all of the eternities, "Hallelujah," for my nation has come home. (p. 390)

The good news for White teachers is that children have an enormous capacity for grace. Every day they come to school full of hope and promise that the system will nurture them. If it does not nurture them today, they hope that tomorrow it will.

As Dr. King (2017) reminded his audience, "grace has a very vital place in any life. It has a very vital place in understanding the whole predicament of man and the whole predicament of the universe, for you can never understand life until you understand the meaning of [grace]" (pp. 387–388). The acceptance of grace from communities and the willingness to forgive oneself when mistakes or oversights cloud the work of building relationships of solidarity are also important steps in building them (Harvey, 2007). This process will include missteps, mistakes, and downright mess-ups. The ability to keep trying when everything is crumbling is the true measure of commitment, endurance, and grace. It is the kind of grace that can lead to solidarity.

COMMITMENT TO ACTION

Rounding out the commitments in the caring solidarity framework is a commitment to action. Once a White teacher has reconciled the shock of recognition, experienced love for students, moved into proximity with communities, interrogated their own whiteness, and accepted grace from self and community, it is time to act. The actions taken that lead to relationships of caring solidarity are threefold. They are personal, structural, and societal.

Personal

A commitment to action must include a commitment to personal growth and learning. The natural outgrowth of interrogation is personal action. The process of interrogating whiteness fundamentally changes how the world is structured for the person doing it. Before interrogation, it is as though the person is walking with blinders on that allow for only a small tunnel of the real world. But during and after interrogation, the blinders fall away and reveal a wide and complex world where easy answers are nowhere to be found. Into this new world, White teachers plunge and act regardless of understanding.

The key is that after interrogation, the teacher will be more informed to act. Freire's concept of praxis, or action/reflection, is a guide here for how we should think of action on the personal level. Freire (2014) explained, "Knowledge emerges only through invention and re-invention, through the restless, impatient, continuing, hopeful inquiry human beings pursue in the world, with the world, and with each other" (p. 72). Personal action creates the teacher who reimagines and then shapes the world.

Structural

Teachers moving to caring solidarity must take their knowledge of their communities and of themselves and act to stand against the violence that inhabits so many schools where students of color attend. The systems of suspensions, hall sweeps, bull horns, police in the hallways, and generally oppressive environments are not part of a healthy school. Teachers can and do have control over the atmosphere of their buildings. As mentioned in chapter 2, the school-to-prison pipeline begins with the actions of individual teachers and administrators. White teachers moving toward caring solidarity will be voices against the violence visited upon students. That stand includes opposition to absurdities like teachers carrying weapons in schools and zero-tolerance disciplinary policies. It includes a general demand to stop the creation of an authoritarian atmosphere in schools where Black children come to learn.

It also includes being a voice to give students a say in curriculum planning. This should include cultural studies courses so that all students can feel included and valued, and sessions and assemblies that are more than just culture day. The goal is to engage students in critical dialogues on issues that matter to them. Teachers in action will ask why students are being suspended rather than remediated or shown how to reconcile after disputes. Then they will collect data with students and share it with teachers and the community. Teachers committed to action build schools where everyone, especially the students, knows without a filament of doubt that Black lives matter and that they matter to every person in the school.

Societal

Any threat to White supremacy is a threat to the social order, the same social order that created colonialism, slavery, Jim Crow, mass incarceration, and the school-to-prison pipeline. As civil rights icon John Lewis explained in a 2016 interview, "We have been too quiet for too long. There comes a time when you have to say something, when you have to make a little noise, when you have to move your feet. This is the time. Now is the time to get in the way. The time to act is now. We will be silent no more. The time for silence is over" (Mettler, 2016). If White teachers are to move to caring solidarity, they must be ready to change society outside of the school building. This is action that comes from recognition, love, proximity, interrogation, and grace.

In July 2016, Police Officer Jeronimo Yanez shot and killed Philando Castile, a kitchen supervisor at J. J. Hill Montessori School in St. Paul,

Minnesota. Castile was in his car with his partner and child during a racially profiled traffic stop. Castile warned the officer that he had a legally purchased and licensed handgun. While sitting in his car, he was shot by Yanez with seven point-blank rounds, five of which entered his body and pierced his heart, as his girlfriend, Diamond Reynolds, broadcast the event live on Facebook. With the father of her child bleeding and dying in her car, Reynolds, distraught, was the one arrested. The police dashboard camera recorded Reynolds and Castile's four-year-old daughter attempting to comfort her and appealing to her mother, "Mom, please stop cussing and screaming 'cause I don't want you to get shooted" (Xiong & Stahl, 2017).

Later that month, at the annual meeting of the American Federation of Teachers (AFT), teachers filed out of the building and marched through the streets of the capital city and then across the bridge to Minneapolis. "Today we march to remember Philando Castile, our student, our co-worker, our union brother," Kimberly Colbert, secretary of the St. Paul Federation of Teachers, said in a statement (DeLage, 2016). Recorded by bystanders and chronicled under the hashtag #Teachers4BlackLives (2016), twenty-one teachers sat down in a circle blocking a busy street in front of U.S. Bank and Wells Fargo, Minnesota's largest banks, which finance private prisons and help cities pay off "police misconduct settlements" (Sawyer, 2016).

All twenty-one teachers[1] were arrested for blocking the Nicollet Mall in the center of the state's largest city. This demonstrates action in caring solidarity with communities. None of these teachers were the same after being arrested for their acts of solidarity with the community. They had crossed into new territory. Freire (2014) explained,

> The revolution is made neither by the leaders for the people, nor by the people for the leaders, but by both acting together in unshakable solidarity. This solidarity is born only when the leaders witness to it by their humble, loving, and courageous encounter with the people. (p. 129)

Caring solidarity requires that teachers demand more of themselves. Freire's revolution is a revolution in ourselves, in our schools, and in our communities. It will not be enough to revolutionize the classroom or even the school building if the revolution stays there. Caring solidarity is a commitment to students, communities, and then out into the world.

---

1.   Two of my former South High colleagues were arrested that day. They inspire me still.

Chapter Six

Crossing the First Boundary and Entering Solidarity

If by this point White teachers have gone from the shock of recognition through love and into proximity, interrogated whiteness, and are moving to action through grace, they will likely be good teachers across the color line. They may even be award-winning teachers, and students may respond very well to them. Parents may be happy, and the school board may be happy. White teachers can live their whole lives outside of a caring solidarity relationship with students and communities and still be forces for good in the world.

But to be a force for change, dismantling the structures that have caused the oppression of Black students and communities, will take more than the rewards that come from being good. The door that the teacher must go through is the recognition, not just of students, but of the need for solidarity. In some cases this will mean a rejection of the conservative ideologies that have hampered solidarity, whether those have come from religion, class, or the common sense of cultural and geographic locations.

American conservatism as an ideology is the process of flattening facts and narratives to fit a simple frame of White, male supremacy. Basically, because White supremacy demands that only the experiences of White people exist, conservatives assume that nothing on the other side of the color line is real. This is shown daily in conservative media and in the ways that Black children are perceived as older than they are, are more likely to be perceived as dangerous, and are more likely to be the subject of deficit models about their homes and families, as discussed in chapters 2 and 3. It also explains why conservatives continually downplay the role of racism and race in American society against all reason and historical literacy.

Conservatives assume that the only reason a White person would want to be in solidarity with Black people is that they are unable to find solidarity with anyone else, so they must be crazy, irrational, uninformed, or liars themselves. Conservative people do not believe that experiences outside of their own experiences are real. The common theme of discourse within conservatism is that when people of color demand their rights, they are ungrateful, undeserving, crazy, stupid, or larcenous.

Conservatism does not leave room for the concept that others may actually understand that justice and equality are the best way to live a life. Conservatives can only see their own power as the cornerstone of any relationship. When African American people march for #BlackLivesMatter, they are assumed by conservatives to be paid actors because White conservatives will not seriously consider that the lives of Black people are at risk, or, if they are, that they are of value. This flattening process creates half-truths, untruths, mistruths, and outright lies, but all of them serve the purpose of propping up the order that was put in place to serve White males.

White teacher candidates and teachers in multiracial schools are often ill-equipped to throw off their conservative ideology at first, but teachers who seek to move to relationships of solidarity must begin to see that perspectives other than White ones give them a larger, more comprehensive view of the world, their community, and the school. Like a house of cards, once a few of the pillars of conservative ideology fall, the whole contraption collapses and can be replaced with a more realistic and meaningful new reality.

As teachers weigh their actions, their privilege, and the consequences, they must be ready to meet conservatives' criticism. They must decide that they need and want to be in solidarity with communities of color and reject the ideologies that would keep them from acting. White people who kneel in solidarity with Black people at public events are especially vilified. They are condemned as insincere, lunatics, or attention seekers. It is outside of the White supremacist frame that anyone would willingly join with the oppressed, so there must be a sinister motive.

However, if a teacher decides to walk through that door and move toward caring solidarity, the journey will change who they are and revolutionize their teaching. As Freire (2014) stated,

> at a certain point in their existential experience, under certain historical conditions, these leaders [teachers in this case] renounce the class to which they belong and join the oppressed, in an act of true solidarity (or so one would hope). Whether or not this adherence results from a scientific analysis of reality, it represents (when authentic) an act of love and true commitment. Joining the oppressed requires going to them and communicating with them. (p. 163)

When applied to the concept of identifying the need for solidarity, Freire challenges White teachers to rationally make the choice to join in solidarity with their students.

Extending his example to schools, the emerging leaders in schools, the students, need solidarity if White teachers are to teach successfully, and the teachers need solidarity to complete the humanization that whiteness strips away. Both need each other, and both become better for the relationship.

BUILDING CARING SOLIDARITY WITH STUDENTS ACROSS THE COLOR LINE

For fourteen years I taught in a large, urban high school in the upper Midwest to a highly diverse population of ninth and tenth graders.[1] Each semester's five classes of thirty-five students comprised a rainbow of skin colors from beige to dark brown and hair colors both natural and unnatural, which gave my room a visual vibrancy that can only come from a city high school. Most of the students were Americans by birth, but several were born in countries as far away as Somalia and Ethiopia and as close as Canada and Mexico.

Deshawn (not his real name) joined the class in the autumn. He was tall for a sophomore, with dark skin and a wide smile that often distracted the girls in the class. Each day he wore a spotless, pressed, oversized white T-shirt, pressed jeans, and brilliant white shoes. From his head to his feet, Deshawn's appearance meant a great deal to him.

Attendance for some of the students, whether because of family circumstances or a lack of readiness, was a constant challenge. During the first few weeks, Deshawn began to have difficulty getting to his second-hour class at 9:30 a.m. By October, his attendance was sporadic. A discussion with him about his attendance after he missed three days in a row yielded that he was in charge of his three-year-old brother and that his mother had not been home since the weekend. The social worker was contacted and referred him to our case management team. In the case meeting, our talk was brought up. The administrator for our team was unmoved by the retelling of the story. She had already met with Deshawn and his mother, and she described Deshawn as a "thug" and "jail-bound." She then explained that he didn't "have much time left at this school."

As the semester continued, Deshawn was suspended for various infractions, from fighting to skipping classes to running in the halls. Yet three days a week he came to class. When he was there, he would listen and participate

---

1. This incident, from my teaching experience, is an expanded version of one I used in the 2016 article "More than an ally: How a successful White teacher builds solidarity with his African American students" in Urban Education, 51(1), 82–107, doi: 10.1177/0042085914542982

with his peers. He did the readings before class but did not turn in homework. He was able to discuss the ideas in the texts with any of the students in the class. He would ask questions during lectures and challenge other students' ideas during discussions. Before he left the classroom, I would tell him that his work was appreciated and ask if he would return tomorrow. He would flash that wide grin and say, "Maybe. We'll see." On days when the students were working in groups or seat assignments, I would encourage him to do homework and discuss his home situation, but he never again opened up like he did on the day he talked about his life.

A meeting that included his mother and the social worker did not help. Instead, his mother listened and then calmly gave vague warnings to her son. His head bowed, Deshawn made promises to all of us. There was no bravado that day—no winning smile—just shame and promises.

In early November, the day of the fall state exam, all the sophomores were required to enter the auditorium for testing, and it just happened to coincide with a day that Deshawn came to class. The students were delivered to the auditorium and the teachers stood to the side to help proctor the exam.

The test, the students learned as the sound system boomed and crackled, was a math exam, and everyone needed a calculator. "If you have your own calculator, you may take it out now," said the five-foot-tall math teacher who drew the short straw for overseeing this unenviable task. "If you do not have one, please come to the front and get one. These calculators are expensive, and they were bought with a special grant to the math department. You will have to give us your shoe as collateral so we get them all back."

Within a few seconds, Deshawn stood up and headed for the exit. The assistant principal who had had called him a "thug" in the case meeting intercepted him and began yelling and threatening Deshawn with suspension. Deshawn roared back that he did not care. I stepped between them and asked him what was wrong. Tears welled up in his eyes as he told me he did not have a calculator but he was not going to hand over his shoe. I understood that Deshawn had few possessions, and he was not going to toss one of them into a pile with fifty others.

I asked the assistant principal if Deshawn could go back in the auditorium if I got him a calculator. She huffed and agreed. After Deshawn was seated, I ran upstairs to my room, grabbed a cheap calculator from my desk, and quickly headed back down to the auditorium. Deshawn had calmed down by that point and received his test booklet, which he opened to begin completing the problems.

In that situation, there were multiple ways that Deshawn was set up for failure. There was little about that math test or the setting in which it took place that reflected good pedagogy. The auditorium held more than 250 students seated at small desks. The light was minimal, the preparation spare, the test extensive, and the budgeted time insufficient. This setting, along with the display of privilege in the assumption that a shoe is a utilitarian but meaningless object, is a result of school structures that value order rather than caring for individuals, especially young African American men.

Thus, when Deshawn chose noncompliance in that structure, the school had few tools other than the blunt object of suspension. Deshawn should have had a more comprehensive strategy in place to ensure his success in school. He should have had a caseworker to work with him and his family to develop strategies to keep him in school. He should have had many more support structures in place, but in that situation, in that school structure, on that day, Deshawn needed someone to be on his side.

Deshawn embodies the gaps in achievement and opportunity between White and Black students (Ladson-Billings, 2006). He was from a generationally poor, African American, single mother–led family. His grades and achievement were acceptable until eighth grade, when he began to miss school and fall behind his peers in reading and math. He valued school and knew it was the key to a better life, but his immediate needs of paying for housing and caring for his siblings fell on him at a young age, distracting him from school and causing him to find money through illegal means. When Deshawn allowed the "business" in the streets to spill over to the school, he was dragged into the school-to-prison pipeline, where too many male African American students are washed out of educational institutions into correctional settings at a young age.

There are students like Deshawn in every school, but in schools with high Black and Latino populations, the consequences for these behaviors are higher and the punishments more severe. Deshawn did what he could to navigate a school structure designed to steer students toward a diploma, but the system was ultimately ill-equipped to divert him, a young man who lacked support structures, from the justice system. Students like Deshawn are not rare, but as teachers move toward caring solidarity as an advocate and eventually an accomplice, they will be able to demonstrate their solidarity by acting to dismantle the structures that block students like him from success.

IDENTIFYING SOLIDARITY AS A NEED: IDENTITY AND THE DOOR TO CARING SOLIDARITY

Moving into the next level of the framework diagram shown in chapter 1, there is a dark ring with a door. This ring and door symbolize a wall between those who are working on the first level and those who who go deeper toward solidarity. The door is the passage to new understanding, and it is attainable only when one identifies the need to be in solidarity with students and communities. Becoming a teacher means that a person must adopt and create an identity as a teacher and view that identity as central. Danielewicz (2001) explained that identity is not a fixed condition but rather an ongoing dialectical process occurring between the individual (internal states) and other people (external conditions). This dynamic of social identification is one routine that constitutes identity. There is a role for others in making that identity: "It is not enough to assert an identity. That identity must also be validated by those with whom we have dealings" (Jenkins, as quoted in Danielewicz, 2001, p. 10).

The structure of teacher identity is fused in three important areas: (1) their ability to form bonds and personal relationships of caring solidarity with students; (2) the theory of their own practice, which includes why they chose to teach in this place with this population; and (c) their pedagogy, which is intertwined with their image of themselves as a teacher and their commitments as a person (Danielewicz, 2001).

The metaphor of the door allows for an understanding that solidarity with students and communities is fundamental to effective teaching across the color line. The decision to go through the door and live on the other side of it is an ethical one and involves the creation of an identity as an educator of Black children. Danielewicz (2001) and Britzman (2003) both argued that teaching is a process of becoming. "Education is about growth and transformation, not only of culture, but of persons too" (Danielewicz, 2001, p. 1).

To effectively teach children across the color line requires a new way of thinking about students and the teacher's role in their lives. With all of these factors considered, it is reasonable to ask what motivates a White person to become a teacher who crosses these lines of race and class. Duncan-Andrade (2007) described the commitment of teachers he worked with:

> They said that they teach because they believe their students, specifically low-income children of color, are the group most likely to change the world. They explained this belief by saying that the children most disenfranchised from society are the ones with the least to lose, and thus are the most likely to be willing to take the risks necessary to change a society. (p. 625)

To Danielewicz, teachers are constantly in the process of identity formation. While teachers adopt an identity at the beginning of their teaching career as a teacher, the definition of what *teacher* means continues to sharpen and develop over time. Good teachers are aware of this process and are open to it. They embrace the learning and growth that happens during their teaching lifetime. Danielewicz explained, "Becoming a teacher means an individual must adopt an identity as such," and the process is "so complicated and deep [because it] involves the self" (p. 9).

The identity of a White teacher in a multiracial classroom is all of this and more. According to Duncan-Andrade (2007), there are five pillars of successful teaching across the color line:

1. Critically conscious purpose, where teachers define their motives for teaching based on the needs of the community.
2. Duty, where teachers have made a commitment to living in and serving the community and their students.
3. Preparation, where teachers are hard at work making curriculum relevant and rigorous for students and constantly reflecting on their practice.
4. "Socratic sensibility," the practice of co-learning with students and never fearing to ask why. Teachers with this sensibility strike "a delicate balance between confidence in their ability as teachers and frequent self-critique" (p. 632).
5. Trust, the result of teachers sometimes standing in solidarity with students in opposition to the institutions of the school and even the community at large.

The motivation should be that the teacher sees the situation of their students in the school and society and decides that they will throw their lot in with their new communities. Moving through the door is often a way to resolve conflict within the teacher. Teachers are searching for solutions as to why their classes are not working as they want them to, why communities are not embracing them the way they feel they need to be embraced, or just a general sense that something in their identity as a teacher is not lining up with what they see at school and in the community. Honneth (1995) explained,

> Since, within the framework of an ethically established relationship of mutual recognition, subjects are always learning something more about their particular identity, and since, in each case, it is a new dimension of their selves that they see confirmed thereby, they must once again leave, by means of conflict, the stage of ethical life they have reached, in order to achieve the recognition of a more demanding form of their individuality. (p. 17)

That "more demanding form" of identity is one where solidarity is sought in and out of the classroom. Once that threshold has been crossed, the teacher will be asked to do more than many are comfortable or capable of doing. The teacher who recognizes the need for solidarity will see the world differently, and the world will see them differently as well.

EMPATHY: THE FIRST LEVEL OF SOLIDARITY

As the caring solidarity framework indicates, after passing through the barrier toward caring solidarity, there is a region of empathy. Nieto (2006) explained that empathy and solidarity are not "simply sentimental emotions." She explained that "for teachers who think deeply about their work, solidar-

ity and empathy mean having genuine respect for their students' identities—
including their language and culture—as well as high expectations and great
admiration for them (p. 466). Empathy is a form of solidarity, but it is also
the limit to what many people are able to conjure up when thinking of
solidarity or entering into it (Warren, 2013).

Empathy is an intense feeling of mutuality with a person who suffers. It
can be temporary and contextual. It can involve helping, raising money,
feeding or housing, or expressing support in a forum that matters or is meaningful to the victims and the empathizer. Empathy is situational and meaningful and is a crucial step to caring solidarity relationships.

It takes time to cross that region of empathy, and it is an individual
journey. Empathy is a deeper emotional response to conditions than sympathy is. Sympathy is when one person sees a tragedy and feels sorry for
another person. They are vibrating on the same wavelength emotionally. The
other person feels bad, and the sympathetic person feels sorry for them, but
there is never an expectation that the sympathetic person will do anything
personally to relieve that suffering. There are mechanisms for people to act in
sympathy. For example, relief organizations depend upon sympathy to help
victims of natural and human-made disasters.

People can be sympathetic to a lot of things at once. They can be sympathetic to migrants coming to the United States in search of a better life and to
the people of Paris for the loss of Notre Dame. No person can do everything
about every problem, so sympathy is a good emotion that allows people to
feel the suffering of others they will never know (Masoom, 2017). It is not
inconsistent or shallow to be sympathetic to many things at once that may be
far away from a person's experience. Empathy, on the other hand, is much
more active. Katsarou, Picower, and Stovall (2010) explain:

> Teachers need to develop empathy and see the strengths and assets of the
> students and communities in which they teach. Their classrooms must be in
> and of the community, blurring the boundaries between who teaches and who
> learns and the borders between schools and neighborhoods. It is critical that
> they are able to recognize the structural forces that impact their students' lives
> and have the sense that they are in a position to act upon them. (p. 152)

Empathy involves doing something to relieve the suffering of those in need.
It is much closer and more personal. For example, if a child is hurt in a
country thousands of miles away, an ethical, caring person would have sympathy and hope someone would be able to help that child. If a child is hurt on
the street in view of others, the ethical caring thing to do would be to get that
child necessary care and healing.

To simply look and feel sympathy in the second scenario and then walk
away would not be the act of a caring person but an unethical monster. So
empathy has as much to do with the ability to do something as it does with

the desire to do something. Empathy can also be a reason for travel, as people may go to where the pain is in order to help. Action and proximity to the issue are important distinctions between sympathy and empathy. A critical distinction between sympathy and empathy is the desire to act.

While empathy is definitely a form of solidarity, it is often confused with full solidarity. Warren (2018) described teachers who practice empathy: "Empathy is the piece of the student-teacher interaction puzzle that connects what a teacher knows or thinks about students and families to what he or she actually *does* when negotiating appropriate responses to students' needs, or when the teacher is arranging learning experiences for students" (p. 171).

It is important to avoid false empathy. False empathy occurs when one assumes that these imagined perspectives are the actual perspectives of others. In truth, we can never have a complete understanding of other people, even those with whom we are most intimate. In addition, the power structures of White privilege require constant interrogation as one travels the road toward caring solidarity. DiAngelo (2018) frames the issue of identity and of false empathy:

> I repeat: stopping our racist patterns must be more important than working to convince others that we don't have them. We do have them, and people of color already know we have them; our efforts to prove otherwise are not convincing. An honest accounting of these patterns is no small task given the power of white fragility and white solidarity, but it is necessary. (p. 129)

False empathy comes from teachers who hold deficit models of their students of color. When a teacher looks at her students as a bundle of *if onlys* (*if only* the parents . . . , *if only* the community wasn't so . . . , or *if only* they had or hadn't . . .), there is no ability to build relationships of solidarity. As Katsarou, Picower, and Stovall (2010) found with their teacher candidates,

> seeing their students only as a laundry-list of problems, these educators are unable to look past students' more challenging behavior, making meaningful and reciprocal relationships impossible. Unable to connect to their students, their efforts at classroom management and instruction fail, and they in turn blame their students for what has ultimately stemmed from their negative and stereotyped views of their students. Until this pattern is addressed, teaching for social justice is an impossible hope for such candidates. (p. 140)

There are teachers who assume that they are in solidarity with students because they are empathetic to students' needs and will even provide for them at times, but false empathy comes from a place of privilege and an unwillingness to see the world differently.

This often comes into play when teachers lower their expectations of students because of perceived differences like race or culture. Sometimes

teachers assume that because students are Black, they are from neighborhoods with violence, have a language barrier, or are not able to be challenged. These low expectations are couched in the language of caring but are
really false caring and false empathy.

Many White teachers get lost in empathy. Even if a teacher is not in false
empathy but real empathy, it can be overwhelming to constantly move from
one crisis to another, as some teachers do. It is difficult work to be empathic
and to show empathy with students who are under threat and in systems that
literally devalue their lives. The psychic energy involved in empathizing and
the emotional labor it takes can even cause teachers to leave the profession
(Herman, Hickmon-Rosa, & Reinke, 2017).

Entering into empathy should trouble one's understandings of the world
as one empathetic act uncovers the need for more empathy in places that
people do not know it is needed. Utt and Tochluk (2020) explained that when
White teacher candidates begin the journey of uncovering whiteness and
move into empathy with people of color, they can experience some proble-
matic behaviors and become culturally unmoored:

> When White teachers in urban schools cannot hold this tension of recognizing
> one's connection to Whiteness and White culture while working to regain an
> ethnic or supportive cultural grounding, they enact a number of troubling
> behaviors:
>   1. Distancing from White culture: Altering dress, manner, or behavior in
> ways that indicate a lack of self-acceptance and a wish to be something other
> than White.
>   2. Distancing from White people: Decreasing ability to effectively encour-
> age and support other White faculty to join efforts for racial justice.
>   3. Over-identifying with people of Color: Appreciating the suggestion that
> one is not really White and distancing from White identity and the responsibil-
> ity to interrogate how White privilege affects one's attitudes and behavior.
>   4. Over-identifying with European roots: Disavowing one's relationship to
> being White, leading to statements claiming that one is not part of White
> culture. There is, thus, less recognition regarding how White culture, White-
> ness, and privilege manifest in one's behavior. (p. 11)

Each of these behaviors is a result not of true empathy or solidarity but of
false empathy as described by Delgado (1996). Delgado explored this concept through a counternarrative conversation discussing the concepts of justice and empathy (Solorzano & Yosso, 2002). Delgado explained that even if
a perfect computer could be built to mete out justice, it would be unacceptable to society because it would not delineate by race. He explained that false
empathy is the belief that you would like a perfect computer, but in the end,
if it gave true justice to everyone, White people would assume that it was
unfair because it would be equal.

Delgado illustrated the predicament of false empathy. People are willing to engage in empathy as long as it does not cost them, even if that cost is measured and distributed dispassionately and equally. He contended that White people see the injustice of unequal justice as justice, and justice, handed out equally, as injustice because of false empathy.

There are always gaps, and learning will always be needed, but the act of striving to understand others' perspectives allows teachers to walk the empathetic road with students. While certainly empathy is a crucial attribute of good teaching and moral living, the expectation that one can stay in a shallow empathy for an entire career is unreasonable. It is important that White teachers move beyond these kinds of quick-fix attitudes in order to navigate toward true empathy that leads to caring solidarity. More often, empathy is able to be sustained for a while, sometimes even years. But eventually it fades, sending White teachers back through the door, away from solidarity, because of "those kids." At that point, the long undoing of all the work that led them there is seldom evident to the person it is happening to. There is exhaustion, hopelessness, and defeat.

However, if White teachers continue in their journey and move beyond empathy to the most difficult obstacle, solidarity, then there is greater purpose that leads to a more sustainable way to teach. It involves a deep self-analysis and a shedding of solidarity with whiteness. But through that barrier lies a new way to be with students. It is a new way to be in communities. Caring solidarity brings White teachers to their students and families, but it is not automatic, safe, or easy. It requires a shift in thinking, a shift in the soul.

Chapter Seven

Transference of Solidarity and Entering New Territories

Looking at the caring solidarity framework diagram in chapter 1, the thick black line near the center is labeled "Transference of Solidarity." The line is thick with a narrow opening because transferring solidarity is an obstacle that few are willing to overcome and even fewer are able. This is the most controversial of the ideas set forth in the framework. Transference of solidarity is the contention that committed White teachers who have done the work from recognition to empathy can transfer solidarity from whiteness to their Black students and communities, ending their solidarity with the privilege and White normativity that whiteness exhibits.

Because of our racialized society, White people will always be perceived as White and will always hold their privilege, no matter their place, work, or intentions. However, a positive White racial identity can produce a person who is able to use that privilege and the power structures that perpetuate White success and progress and transfer themselves toward communities and students of color. Transference of solidarity requires a positive racial identity in order to avoid false empathy or a fake identity where a person denies who they are and puts on solidarity like a cloak. True transference comes from a state of understanding and self-awareness, realistically assessing the need for solidarity to successfully live and work across the color line.

THE WHITE ALLIANCE, SOLIDARITY WITH WHITENESS, AND BECOMING A "RACE TRAITOR"

To understand how to break solidarity with whiteness and transfer it to students of color, this chapter returns to the concept of whiteness. Whiteness, as this book has discussed, is not a neutral descriptor but a designation of power and privilege at the intersection of White normality and White privilege. The question of how White people can live morally in a world that has been created for their comfort is an acute issue facing White teachers who teach across the color line. European colonialism has created a world where whiteness is a desired trait.

Frantz Fanon, author of *The Wretched of the Earth* (1961/2004), explained that the goal of colonialism is more than a conquering of the land, or even the body, but a conquering of the mind so that the colonized person is convinced that the colonizer's culture is the best, the most worthy, and the attainable perfection of human endeavor. That desire has corrupted civilizations with devastating results. Colonization not only corrupts the colonized; it deforms the humanity of the colonizer as well. The colonizer, in an effort to convince the colonized of his superiority, takes on the false persona of a person above other people. This false consciousness then extends generation after generation, sickening the culture and destroying true humanity and positive identity.

Whiteness corrupts the soul and compromises the morality of all that fall under its gaze. Most White people are casually able to live with the construct of whiteness and do all they can to avoid thinking about the fact that their success stems directly from colonization, genocide, and systemic racism. They go to work, enjoy the fruits of their labor, and do not question why their life is the way it is. This whiteness is pervasive across cultures, geography, and nations. Because of its power of normalcy, it is often hard for White people to see it.

Like the fish who does not know what water is, White people assume that their lives are the lives that they are supposed to live, and to an extent, they are correct. It is the life each person throughout the world should live. It is one where people are valued, where wealth is shared, and where police are polite. Unfortunately, that is not the world that most people of color experience. Instead, from outside of whiteness, the hoarding of riches and privilege is an affront to the promises of democracy that are broadcast from whiteness's walled fortress.

Allen (2009) explained that whiteness and its continued power derive from a unity of purpose that White people are initiated into early. He referred to it as the *White hegemonic alliance*. He argued that although class differences between White groups exist, they do not substantially affect the behaviors White people exhibit when it comes to power relations, economics, and culture.

For instance, poor White people overwhelmingly vote for wealthy White men to hold offices, with little promise that these men will do anything to improve their lives. White women vote for White men and women who repeatedly promise to limit women's rights, hurt them economically, and keep their children from health care and education. Wealthy White people have been able to convince poor White people that it is in their best interests to keep the wealthy in power.

The White hegemonic alliance makes room for many different expressions of whiteness. Whiteness allows for wealth, poverty, addiction, violence, indolence, and orientations of many kinds under the big tent of whiteness, but these extensions are not available to people of color. White boys who get into mischief are just boys, but when African American boys do the same, they are thugs or predators. The crack crisis of the 1990s yielded a war on drugs and mass incarceration of Black and Brown people, yet today's opioid crisis elicits care, compassion, and a focus on healing and a call for health-care reform and legislation to assist those addicted.

The alliance is pervasive in how schools are operated. The curriculum, the schooling structures, and the placement of programs all reflect the needs and desires of White people. White people's desires are privileged over the needs and wants of communities of color. When those communities demand better, they are accused of playing the race card and are rebuked as divisive, but when White communities seek to segregate themselves, even literally dividing towns by race, they are viewed by other Whites as bravely looking out for their children (Harris, 2019).

Allen's concept of the White hegemonic alliance allows for a type of solidarity that does not ask much from the in-group and is similar to the second version of Bayertz's (2013) solidarity as explained in chapter 4. This is the type of unquestioned solidarity that does not rely on any commitment; in fact, it relies on the opposite. It is a solidarity of the lazy. This type of solidarity comes from a lack of questioning, a lack of reflection or interrogation. It is one that refuses to look at history and refuses to acknowledge the legacy of colonialism.

Solidarity with whiteness comes with the price of loyalty without conviction, without understanding, and without consciousness. It is the default position of White people across the world and is the type of solidarity that allows people to turn away from atrocity, to deny mass murder, and to ignore science if it does not fit into the narrative of White goodness, White innocence, and White supremacy.

As an answer to this kind of unenlightened solidarity, Ignatiev and Garvey (1996) called for an end to the White race—not to the humans now considered White but to the concept of whiteness as a normative power. This is a different concept of whiteness than outlined by McIntosh (2001), who described it as a "knapsack" of passes and passports that allowed White people to walk freely in a world constructed by and for them. Ignatiev and Garvey described whiteness as a club that, while not secret, allowed members to be waved through gates that are closed to others.

However, that membership to the club only works if all members are willing to participate in the rules that keep the club exclusive and privileged. "It is based on one huge assumption: that all those who look white are, whatever their complaints or reservations, fundamentally loyal to it" (p. 36).

Ignatiev and Garvey's answer to the solidarity of whiteness was to break the rules that hold it together and become what they termed a *race traitor*, a traitor to whiteness itself:

> The way to abolish the white race is to disrupt that conformity. If enough people who look white violate the rules of whiteness, their existence cannot be ignored. If it becomes impossible for the upholders of white rules to speak in the name of all who look white, the white race will cease to exist. The abolitionists are traitors to the white race; by acting boldly they jeopardize their membership in the white club and their ability to draw upon its privileges. (p. 36)

A race traitor is a person who breaks with the solidarity imposed upon White people by society by refusing to participate in the system. Race traitors seek an end to whiteness, but what is the replacement? Whiteness and White supremacy, as this book has described, are the organizing principles of American society. The economy, politics, media, and social conventions all serve the same goal of maintaining, extending, and solidifying the illusion of White supremacy. Dropping out is certainly an option, but dropping into something else is needed.

Casey (2017) elaborated, "For me, the essential flaw in the Race Traitors theory is this: whiteness is not something individual white people are capable of manipulating" (p. 79). He went on to explain:

> Regardless of belief or intention, white people are themselves caught up in the cultural logics, discourses of power, signs and frames of domination present in the very phenotypic edifice of whiteness. And each of these things makes individual actions to "rid one's self of whiteness" more than impossible because whiteness does not exist on the individual body but on the collective bodies of white people, a shifting and complex cultural as well as racial group. (p. 80)

While certainly a race traitor–inspired disruptive strategy could work to break the hegemonic power of whiteness if a critical mass of White people participated, it is not a realistic answer to today's issues, and it does not answer the question of how to successfully teach across the color line. It assumes that a lot of White people are willing to throw off all that whiteness gives them, yet there is little evidence that this will occur.

Whiteness is a construct created by White people in order to decide who is in and who is out. Being in the in crowd has many advantages. Therefore, the idea of leaving that safe and privileged position is a hard one for White people to even imagine. Lipsitz (2006) explained that White people have an "investment" in whiteness. He described whiteness as perceived as a highly prized normal, and history has shown that White people are more invested in whiteness than they are in justice (Anderson, 2017).

WHITENESS IS PROPERTY

Critical race theorists contend that whiteness is property, a tangible means of exchange (Harris, 1993). In her groundbreaking essay "Whiteness as Property" (1993), Harris tells the story of her grandmother, who identified as Black, left Mississippi in the 1930s, and boldly took a position in Chicago at a major retailer.

There, she passed as a White woman. Harris explored the consequences of the life her grandmother led:

> Every day my grandmother rose from her bed in her house in a Black enclave on the south side of Chicago, sent her children off to a Black school, boarded a bus full of Black passengers, and rode to work. No one at her job ever asked if she was Black; the question was unthinkable. By virtue of the employment practices of the "fine establishment" in which she worked, she could not have been. Catering to the upper-middle class, understated tastes required that Blacks not be allowed. (p. 1711)

Her grandmother had to suppress herself and accept the racism that was not directed at her, because of assumed affiliation, but was part of the solidarity that comes from membership in the White alliance. While the psychological costs were high, Harris explained the benefits that came to a person who was able to move across the color line.

> Becoming white meant gaining access to a whole set of public and private privileges that materially and permanently guaranteed basic subsistence needs and, therefore, survival. Becoming white increased the possibility of controlling critical aspects of one's life rather than being the object of others' domination. (p. 1713)

These benefits of solidarity with whiteness are intentionally made invisible to White people who live in segregated suburban enclaves but are often expressly taught in places where Black and White people live in close proximity. Rothstein (2013, 2017) reminded America that in hypersegregated cities like Chicago, these lines are clear and intentional, but even in smaller cities like San Antonio, Minneapolis, Austin, and Cincinnati, *good* and *bad* neighborhoods are delineated along racial lines, making the color line a real geographic boundary.

Harris (1993) examined how that line has become normalized for White people. She observed, "Whites have come to expect and rely on these benefits, and over time these expectations have been affirmed, legitimated, and protected by the law" (p. 1713). The White hegemonic alliance has enabled White people to avoid seeing the world as it is, as White people have made it. However, for White teachers to be in caring solidarity with students and communities who do not identify, or are not identified, as White, there must be an alternative.

TRANSFERENCE OF SOLIDARITY

Because of the inability to simply throw off solidarity with whiteness without a replacement, the race traitor concept, as attractive as it is, is not a viable solution for those White teachers who already work and live across the color line. As social animals, we must be in solidarity with other people. The passive, default solidarity described by Bayertz, the emotional solidarity of empathy, and the situational solidarity of allies are all inadequate to address the current state of affairs.

Nazis are marching on college campuses, children are in cages at the border, children are being gunned down in schools, and Black children and teens are being shot by police. All of these things and many more are the consequences when colonialism and whiteness are allowed to run their natural courses. This is the world White people have created. It is time to do more than make symbolic moves. The other, less transformative versions of solidarity are also not sustainable over a career or lifetime. The solidarity that allows one to be empathetic in times of crisis but still stay in solidarity with whiteness will not be the transformative change needed to succeed as a White teacher across the color line.

However, the transference of solidarity can only happen when a White person has a positive White racial identity not based in guilt, fear, or superiority but in realism, grounded in integrity and moral empathy (Harvey, 2007). This is not a light concept or one that should be approached lightly. According to Honneth (1995), a new identity is needed to fully come to a new recognition.

This new identity comes from an understanding that the old one is insufficient for bringing about relationships of solidarity:

> A subject's personal identity presupposes, in principle, certain types of recognition from other subjects. For the superiority of interpersonal relationships over instrumental acts was apparently to consist in the fact that relationships give both interlocutors the opportunity to experience themselves, in encountering their partner to communication, to be the kind of person that they, from their perspective, recognize the other as being. (Honneth, 1995, p. 37)

It is time to throw off whiteness and adopt a new identity, one that stands against the made world and strikes out to create a new one.

White teachers who have recognized their students, interrogated their whiteness, and moved to empathy will be able to build a pathway to caring solidarity. This is not an easy or simple task for anyone. It will only be possible for the most patient, the most committed, and the most resilient. Those who do it will be perceived as radical, crazy, or ill informed. Friends and family will work to pull them back into the alliance. Such people will lose friendships and possibly alienate coworkers who choose to stay in solidarity with whiteness and impose a White supremacist frame on their teaching of Black students.

But those charges have historically been levied against people who challenge White supremacy. This is the level of solidarity that is needed. This is the level of solidarity that will change the world that students live in.

TRANSFERENCE OF SOLIDARITY VS. FALSE EMPATHY

There are those who would say that it is impossible for White people to shed their solidarity with whiteness. In his counternarrative, Delgado (1996) expressed that White people are unable to be in full solidarity with Black people because they lack "double consciousness" as W. E. B. Du Bois described in his narrative, *The Souls of Black Folk* (1903/1994).

Double consciousness, as described by Du Bois, is a sense of otherness, of not belonging in America. It is the way one feels in a foreign country, even if one speaks the language and is familiar with the landscape. It is never truly being at home. A person with double consciousness feels conscious of others looking, judging, and creating a narrative of who they are without their permission or consent.

Add to that the harsh segregation and the constant threat of deadly violence, and a sense emerges that there is no home that can be made in an America with deep roots in the subjugation of people who are not identified as White. Du Bois (1903/1994) explained,

> It is a peculiar sensation, this double-consciousness, this sense of always looking at one's self through the eyes of others, of measuring one's soul by the tape of a world that looks on in amused contempt and pity. One ever feels his twoness—an American, a Negro; two souls, two thoughts, two unreconciled strivings; two warring ideals in one dark body, whose dogged strength alone keeps it from being torn asunder. (p. 2)

Delgado's contention is that because America is home to White Americans by design, they do not have that double consciousness and therefore cannot be in solidarity with Black people who do.

Delgado (1996) continued, "He or she walks on the surface, uses the wrong metaphors and comparisons. It's a little bit like false piety, like those folks who go to church on Sunday but don't allow themselves to be seized by real religion" (p. 72). He parallels the work of White people who see themselves in solidarity with Black people and yet whose actions are the opposite, to people who go to church and yet sin with impunity at every opportunity. Even if a person with false empathy is able to do good work, it will be incomplete because they do not have the knowledge or the desire to know what is truly needed. They assume based on their own frames what is needed, and that is usually incorrect. Solorzano (1997) explained that these kinds of false empathy are used to justify the following:

> (1) having low educational and occupational expectations for Students of Color; (2) placing Students of Color in separate schools and, in some cases, separate class rooms within schools; (3) remediating the curriculum and pedagogy for Students of Color; (4) maintaining segregated communities and facilities for People of Color; and (5) expecting Students of Color to one day occupy certain types and levels of occupations. In fact, when we think of welfare, crime, drugs, immigrants, and educational problems, we racialize these issues by painting stereotypic portraits of People of Color. (p. 10)

The list above is commonplace in American schools. Some schools are demographically diverse in the aggregate but segregated within the walls. Caring solidarity stands against these practices but takes time, requiring long and specific steps before a person can be in solidarity with students and let go of solidarity with whiteness. The critique of false empathy or false solidarity is important and must be guarded against as people make this journey.

CARING SOLIDARITY AS AN ADVOCATE

The first of the two inside levels of caring solidarity is the solidarity that expresses itself in advocacy for students and communities. This level of solidarity is where the best teachers often stay. On a daily basis they meet students where they are and create lessons and experiences that empower, build, and restore. Advocacy can take many forms and is a moment-to-moment decision-making paradigm that puts the needs of students ahead of the structures of the school.

Advocates are realistic about the structures of their school as rooted in White supremacy and are annoyingly and vocally ready to call out structures and roadblocks that impede their students of color. As Harvey (2007) explained, White advocates in caring solidarity with their students of color move together toward shared goals.

First, solidarity involves at least two individuals or two groups: one is in
solidarity with another. Second, we are in solidarity with those suffering from
immorality or injustice, not from some natural disaster. Third, action may be
involved, but there seems at least to be agreement that action alone is not
enough. (p. 22)

Structures

As explained in chapter 3, few schools are places of solidarity and caring for
Black students. Instead, they are a labyrinth of potential pitfalls that will
sweep students into the school-to-prison pipeline, but teachers in solidarity
with students do all they can to advocate for students and disrupt that pipeline. Often this means standing up to other adults and even the police. Beyond that, teachers in solidarity keep their students close and resolve conflicts so that they do not get out of their jurisdiction. Once an administrator
or, worse, the police are involved, the results could be deadly. But even if the
student survives the encounter, they will never be better off for having been
removed from the learning environment.

For the teacher in solidarity, this means implementing humane and logical
classroom management techniques that make students want to be in the
classroom. Students know which teachers are in solidarity with them, even if
they do not always act as though they do. The reaction of teachers to student
who challenge their authority is the dividing line between teachers who in
solidarity and those who are not. Individual teachers and administrators make
life-and-death decisions on a daily basis, for good or bad. When the decisions
have devastating consequences, like expulsion or jail, educators rarely see
these consequences. The school-to-prison pipeline is maintained by the individual decisions of teachers and administrators, so teachers in solidarity will
do what they can to disrupt the pipeline through demands on school structures. Structurally, there are several things that can be done to make sure that
the school-to-prison pipeline is disrupted, but these two can be done immediately.

Police in Schools

Teachers in solidarity will advocate and demand that armed police officers be
removed from schools and that trained education-oriented administrative
aides and counselors be put in their place. These aides should not be armed
but should be trained in humane restraint, conflict resolution, deescalation,
and mental health crisis management. No matter how good the police officer
is in the school, they will always be the person who ultimately decides on
their own when deadly force is to be used. Since it should never be used on
children, there is literally no place for police officers as a regular part of the
school environment.

To be absolutely clear, if there is no need for deadly force, there is no need for armed police officers. If there is no need for killing a person, there is no need for a police officer because even nondeadly weapons are damaging beyond any reasonable need. Teachers in solidarity understand that the reasons for keeping police officers in schools are based on White supremacy and anti-blackness. The fact that police are in schools is a failure of leadership, pedagogy, and curriculum to empower Black students. It is a failure to understand the racial history of the United States and the function of police as forces of slavery, segregation, and anti-blackness.

Those who would equivocate on keeping police in schools are making sure that they always have the option of using deadly force against students. Taking this option away from schools will result in one of two things. Unfortunately, it could mean a decline in discipline standards as teachers who already did not understand how to relate across the color line are no longer able to use the threat of deadly force as an option to keep Black students in line. These schools, no matter how quiet the hallways, are not places of solidarity or caring, or even education for that matter, but are warehouses for youth until they leave, some with diplomas but most without.

The better option is for teachers to find a way to be in solidarity with students of color and to root themselves deeply in communities. Schools should use culturally relevant curriculum and implement humane discipline that teaches students to use their voices to call out injustice and their minds to find new ways to bend the world to themselves. These schools will do fine without police because their discipline model will be based on empowering students rather than suppressing them.

The question is a simple one. Teachers decide what kind of school they are in. "If police were removed from the school, could the school continue to run, and could teachers continue to teach?" If the answer is no, then the school is not a place of caring solidarity and is instead just one more pipeline from school to jail. If the answer is "Yes, but we have work to do," that is a place that can be in solidarity with students. It's a simple yet effective mental test that each teacher and administrator should do.

Suspensions—In and Out of School

Suspension is another structure that is a function of anti-blackness and is not a part of schools seeking to work in caring solidarity with students. Suspension is an easy out for schools that demand a consequence. The people in charge of these buildings (many are not actual schools, although they pretend to be) are under the delusion that depriving students of their proximity for the day is a punishment. For schools and teachers who are part of the school-to-prison pipeline, suspension is the opening that rinses students away from them to the jailhouse.

The other purpose of suspension is to inconvenience parents in an attempt to motivate them to get their child to comply with the orders of administrators and teachers. Sometimes it works, but it does not demonstrate or build solidarity to forcibly demand compliance.

In-school suspension is hardly better because the detention room is not a place of interactive learning. It is a place that reinforces the narrative that school is punishment and that, while the classroom may be dehumanizing and uninviting, there are options that are worse. Overall, detentions and suspensions, both in and out of school, are counterproductive if the goal is to raise students up and empower them to become engaged citizens. Simply put, engaged citizens are not compliant. Compliance is the goal of colonialism and White supremacy.

Colonialism does not wish to eliminate the colonized; it seeks to gain their compliance using punishment, shame, intimidation, and fear. These same weapons are often used in schools as a way to suppress Black students into compliance. This ultimately is not a sustainable model, and it degrades the souls of students and adults. All the people of these schools who participate in this violence, either as victims or perpetrators, are soul sick. The answer is to stop hurting and begin healing. As hooks (2013) explains, White supremacy is a sickness, and all of us have symptoms. "It is living in a culture of white supremacy that is often an unconsciously debilitating force diminishing the spirit. This is not new news for most black folks. From slavery to the present day, black folks have known that dealing with traumatic exploitation and oppression based on race creates life-threatening stress and concomitant illness that come in its wake" (p. 185).

Pedagogy

As leaders in pedagogy, advocates who have done the kind of internal work needed for caring solidarity will advocate for spaces where students can use their authentic voice in the classroom. There are many possibilities for how to do this, but here are some elements that will be evidenced in such classrooms.

Students Are Valued and Feel It

In a classroom where the teacher is a caring solidarity advocate, the students will feel valued by the teacher. There are several frameworks that will allow students to be valued and to feel valued. Asset-based pedagogies like culturally sustaining pedagogy (Paris & Alim, 2017) and hip-hop pedagogy (Stovall, 2006) are ways to teach students that let them know they matter to the teacher. Through pedagogy that reminds students daily that they are at the center of the classroom, teachers are able to build relationships of solidarity.

When it comes to management of learning, a teacher who is an advocate will not engage in classroom management in the traditional way. Instead the teacher will focus on managing learning and the environment of the classroom. Where there are students who are disinvested in learning from previous encounters, the pedagogy of the advocate will work to gain students' trust in the classroom through engagement with them. Teachers will participate with students in a contract, not a set of rules.

The contract will invite students to invest in the classroom environment and to care for and about one another. As bell hooks (1994) explained,

> To educate as the practice of freedom is a way of teaching that anyone can learn. That learning process comes easiest to those of us who teach who also believe that there is an aspect of our vocation that is sacred; who believe that our work is not merely to share information but to share in the intellectual and spiritual growth of our students. To teach in a manner that respects and cares for the souls of our students is essential if we are to provide the necessary conditions where learning can most deeply and intimately begin. (p. 13)

Students Are Being Prepared for (Actual) Adulthood

Teachers and administrators, in their language about being student-centered, sometimes forget that the goal of education is to produce adults, not kids. This is evident in the types of skills teachers focus on. Frustratingly, schools focus on behaviors that are not necessary for anyone working outside of school. Having a pencil and "being ready to learn" is an urgency for some teachers. They even keep charts and graphs of students' school skills that are literally skills only needed in school.

Pencils are seldom used outside of schools. Pens rule the workplace, and there are a lot of them. Bankers do not need to bring their own pens to the office. Lawyers do not stop lawyering for the day if they do not have a pen. Imagine a situation where school skills ruled in the business world. No work would get done until everyone stopped talking. No one would get lunch unless everyone stood perfectly still in a line. The lining up for lunch and a single-file line through the hallways is a function of anti-blackness and reinforces behaviors that are expected on a chain gang, not in the halls of power. Traveling with powerful people is an affair where gaggles of people talk and discuss all at once while engaged in meaningful work. They are not lined up and silent.

Teachers complain about testing taking too much time. Add in thirty minutes of instruction time waiting for every child to stand up straight with eyes forward and walk in lockstep. Elementary students spend much too much of their school day waiting to go from one place to another, and this practice is creeping into secondary schools as a sign of respectability politics where Black students are paraded to show off their humanity. There is one industry where these skills do matter: prisons. These practices are much too close to the ways that prisoners are paraded up and down the halls. It makes one wonder what teachers think of their students when lines and supplies are their overriding priority.

The worst part of these practices is how they are racialized. Studies show that Black children as young as four years old are systematically judged by teachers as behavior "problems" (Bryan, 2017). As explained in chapter 4, Black students are continually overcorrected and overpunished for minor infractions all the way through to the twelfth grade. This overcorrection has a devastating effect on Black students but also may have an effect on White students as well, reinforcing stereotypes given to them by adults that Black people are dangerous and need to be controlled.

As Bryan (2017) explained it, "White children not only witness the pedagogical practices of their White teachers, but they also witness the ways that teachers disproportionately target Black boys for school discipline." This overpunishment then not only perpetuates low self-esteem in Black youth, leading to a disinvestment in school, but it also teaches White supremacy to White students, dismantling the good that could come out of integrating the schools and giving students of different races the chance to interact.

Teachers in caring solidarity ready their students for adulthood by teaching skills that matter. They teach them to work together and divide tasks. They help them learn responsibility, not through punishment but by giving students age-appropriate responsibilities that build self-esteem.

Students Learn Consciousness

Teachers in caring solidarity help students explore who they are. Teachers tap into the selves of their students, and students explore unmapped areas of themselves. This extends to students of color but also includes White students. Gaining a positive White racial identity leads to resolved consciousness for White people. Uncovering White supremacy allows all students to see who they really are outside of the prison of whiteness. It is like a person waking from sleep. Consciousness is freeing.

White supremacy is an uncomfortable, unethical, and destabilizing mental condition. It makes White people miss the obvious beauty in others, destroys possibilities for friendship and love, and creates a hole in people's consciousness as they avoid uncomfortable truths about history, society, families, and themselves. Teachers in solidarity with their Black students are able to help all of their students build new frames that resolve that consciousness.

Curriculum

The curriculum, particularly the history curriculum, delivered on a daily basis to students of color is an act of violence. Students of all races learn that whiteness is goodness and innocence, that the rich have nothing but our best interests at heart, and that downtrodden peoples, when there are any, are able to peacefully appeal to White people for relief. For example, when teaching about civil rights, the lesson is that the request for relief, if constructed from the basic goodness of White people, will be granted. Sometimes it will be granted grudgingly, but the goodness and largesse of White people is never in doubt.

Students learn that only peaceful protests are productive and that unions of people are unproductive. The narrative is that a logical argument will always be well received, but anger will be met with indifference or possibly unavoidable but never excessive violence. All children are taught the basic building blocks of White supremacy beginning with their first words. Great teachers in solidarity help their students unlearn those lessons.

Fundamentally, the portrayal in American curriculum is that by default, all civilization is White, and all peoples who are not identified as White are better off for their contact with White people. Whether it is Columbus, Thanksgiving, the colonial period, or the Constitution, the story is whiteness, White innocence, and White goodness.

Even slavery is often taught as a salvation story, at least in the Northern version: people wrongly stolen from an uncivilized Africa became Americans and convinced the White people of the United States to give them their freedom. Some books even equate enslaved peoples with other immigrants (Isensee, 2015). The story continues that it took a war to convince some White people that Black people should not be enslaved, but in the end, goodness won over evil and hatred. Then some of those White people who had fought on the wrong side of the Civil War also suppressed Black people. Dr. King then made a passionate and reasonable plea on television convincing White people to save them, and now things are fine.

As ridiculous as this seems to most educated people, the average American will repeat this basic narrative if asked, and many do, even important lawmakers (Lam, 2019; Wu, 2019). As historian Walter Johnson wrote,

> at the bottom of it all, I would like for children to be taught that the modern United States was built on Indian land by African labor. No mills without plantations; no railroads without reservations. After all the quantification and qualification, those two basic historical facts remain at the foundation: extermination and enslavement. That might seem harsh, but history is harsh—though not so harsh, perhaps, that we should abandon hope of changing it. (Johnson, 2019)

This is the opposite of the hero story of U.S. history that students are usually taught, and it is one that will begin to topple the flimsy logic of White supremacy. From here, the curriculum can be revised and restored. From here, we can finally have that "new birth of freedom" that King described on that day at the Lincoln Memorial. We cannot have that rebirth until White supremacy is exposed to the disinfecting light of justice. We cannot be who we say we are until we deal with who we really are.

While social studies is the most important and most egregious of the disciplines when it comes to deciding what narrative students get from the curriculum, it is by no means alone (King, 1991). The books teachers have students read and the ones they do not, the stories they use in examples and the ones they leave out, in biology, chemistry, math, and literature classes, all teach White supremacy in overt and covert ways. Teachers who are advocates in solidarity with students will abandon the canon of White authors, but not just to add in others and "round out" the curriculum. They will seek to replace the old and see literature with new eyes.

They will work to value their Black students and challenge their White ones to see the world from perspectives that are truthfully more real than the ones we do now. For example, does *Frankenstein* teach valuable lessons? Yes. Does *Invisible Man* by Ralph Ellison teach more valuable lessons? "Absolutely," says the teacher in solidarity. Currently, there are over sixty-five movies about Frankenstein. The year 2020 is the seventy-eighth anniversary of Ellison's brilliant novel, and there are no film adaptations. Yes, *Frankenstein* is a good book with lots to teach, but Ellison's novel is much more important, especially now.

A curriculum that shows students that their school is committed to Black lives is one that empowers students to change the world. It endows students with capital that they will be able to use once they leave to make that change. Yosso (2005) listed six kinds of capital that would be instilled in a curriculum that valued Black lives and that would demonstrate caring solidarity with Black students and communities. While these types of capital overlap, she explained that they offer specific goals that a curriculum and, to a certain extent, pedagogy should impart.

Aspirational capital. The kind of resiliency that allows children to dream of a future that is brighter and bolder than their present circumstances. It is the kind of capital that adults who are not in solidarity will stamp out of students by telling them to be realistic. Realism is what got us here; aspiration will help us move forward.

Linguistic capital. Students of color are often multilingual with their friends and families. Schools often try to stamp out multilingualism rather than value students and communities for their funds of knowledge. Students who arrive speaking Spanish are taught to devalue their home language and by extension their culture by schools and teachers who feign care while crushing students' identities. Teachers in solidarity with students who demonstrate multilingualism celebrate it and guide students into code-switching skills to help them navigate the world and bend it to them, not the other way around.

Familial capital. This refers to the type of capital that comes from being connected to families and communities, "a sense of community history, memory and cultural intuition" (Yosso, 2005, p. 79). Families are an asset, yet so many deficit models see families as an impediment to a student's progress. Teachers will say, "I only have them for a few hours a day," in relation to families that they see as undoing all of the good work done by the school during the day.

Teachers who are not in solidarity with families and communities will blame them for not being engaged with the school and for not participating. Then those same teachers will not acknowledge the barriers to participation thrown up by schools, such as the times when events are offered or the inability to feed siblings before attending school events and meetings. Students' families are a source of strength, but sometimes there are challenges. Schools in solidarity with communities will help families address those challenges and join in solidarity with them to advocate for their community to meet those challenges, such as finding jobs, services, food, and housing.

Social capital. This is the capital of *who you know.* It is the capital that allows students to collect letters of recommendation for college, gain summer and after-school employment, and make connections with local elected officials and businesspeople for internships. Teachers in solidarity with their communities will connect students to people who can help them take advantage of opportunities.

Teachers can invite local politicians into the classroom. Administrators can cultivate relationships with local community leaders. All of this is done through relationships and investments in the community. It sees the people of the community as a strength and as resources to help students fulfill their potential.

Navigational capital. This refers to "skills of maneuvering through social institutions. Historically, this infers the ability to maneuver through institutions not created with communities of color in mind. For example, strategies to navigate through racially hostile university campuses draw on the concept of academic invulnerability, or students' ability to 'sustain high levels of achievement, despite the presence of stressful events and conditions that place them at risk of doing poorly at school and, ultimately, dropping out of school'" (Yosso, 2005, p. 80).

Teachers and schools should offer students classes in navigating college, filling out forms, budgeting money, and managing time that will equip them with the skills they need to navigate the world outside of school.

Resistant capital. This capital refers to the knowledge and skills necessary for building movements, resisting oppression, and creating a new world. This capital is the type of work that advocates and accomplices must do in caring solidarity. To accomplish this, teachers unveil the hidden curriculum of White supremacy, teach students the skills to organize and work together, and create meaningful data gathering and implementation of real-world prob-lem solving.

This is not a curriculum or pedagogy outside of the mainstream. It is the core curriculum for children of the elite. It is one that empowers them to make decisions, run complex organizations, and create change, yet schools constantly work to crush those same impulses in students of color. A teacher in caring solidarity will build a curriculum that does not simply pass on the White supremacist frame but empowers students to see it, analyze it, and ultimately dismantle it (Love, 2019c; Yosso, 2005).

When schools continually devalue students, marginalize them, and dem-onstrate that they are uninteresting, unimportant, and that their lives, culture, contributions, stories, and very selves are so disturbing as to be unmention-able, how can they be expected to buy into school as the pathway to success? Because of the way schools are run, it is illogical for Black students to go through thirteen years of education believing that at the end they will be successful. The ones who do succeed have undying faith, superhuman resil-iency, and brilliant minds. But children should not have to be that extraordi-nary to be educated and valued as a citizen.

Teachers in solidarity with their students challenge them with curriculum that makes them stronger, more able to fight the system, and more likely to win. Teachers in solidarity with students equip them to fight whiteness and White supremacy. They have transferred their solidarity to their students. They have joined the fight.

CARING SOLIDARITY AS AN ACCOMPLICE

As the caring solidarity framework diagram moves to the center, the circles become smaller and smaller and the openings get narrower. This symbolizes both the difficulty of moving to that space and the relative few who will occupy it. White teachers who work and live across the color line are increas-ingly needed to join the activists in a space of caring solidarity accomplices (Indigenous Action Media, 2014; Hackman, 2015; Love, 2019c; Osler, 2016; Powell & Kelly, 2017).

As this book has explained, the issue of the school-to-prison pipeline is the moral outrage of our time, and a sole focus on that would be appropriate. Yet it is certainly not the only outrage of our time, even if we narrow our focus to education. As a function of White supremacy and White normality, schools are becoming increasingly segregated. According to the nonprofit, nonpartisan organization Edbuild (2019) that is using data to expose Ameri-ca's segregation in terms of dollars,

> nationally, predominantly white school districts get $23 billion more than their nonwhite peers, despite serving a similar number of children. White school

districts average revenue receipts of almost $14,000 per student, but nonwhite districts receive only $11,682. That's a divide of over $2,200, on average, per student. (p. 4)

This funding gap is only part of the segregation story, but it is a major determining factor in students' ability to succeed in school and after graduation. Books in segregated, predominantly Black schools are old, activities are scarce, and resources for enrichment are even scarcer. In 2018 and 2019, teachers across the country went on strike. They stood up to their state governments and demanded better pay and benefits for themselves and more resources for their students.

To be clear, teachers who have to work three jobs in order to feed themselves and a cat, let alone a family, in places like Oklahoma and West Virginia are less likely to be able to spend time doing the interrogation and community building that caring solidarity requires. When a teacher is never able to focus on their students because they are too busy trying to keep their car and house in their possession, the level of education and solidarity decreases precipitously.

In 2018, teachers in Colorado, Oklahoma, West Virginia, Arizona, and Kentucky stood up and walked out of their classrooms and straight to the capital. They were fighting for their lives, their schools, their students, and their communities against Republican governors who were more interested in tax cuts for the wealthy than in providing an excellent education for students and investing in their state's economic and social wealth.

In West Virginia, for example, teachers broke the law by striking against every single county in the state. The unity was staggering, especially in a state with so much poverty. Teachers defied critics, legislators, police, and the media, singing a full-throated rendition of "We're Not Going to Take It" at the capital (Park, Levenson, & Jorgensen, 2018).

Each state's situation is different, and each one won and lost some within their own list of demands, but overall teachers put their leaders on notice that the time when teachers are easily pushed down and down while legislators demean and threaten them are over. Despite Republican losses at the polls in 2018, some legislatures are still trying to intimidate and silence teachers (Flaherty, 2019).

But teachers are fed up. In the past they had abdicated their responsibilities to be engaged and allowed largely White, largely male legislators to crush unions, demonize the mostly female teachers, and bury them with mountains of tests and accountability measures. Now teachers are fighting back. They are running for legislatures at the state and national level. They are protesting and demanding change from their state and federal representatives.

While these striking teachers are not specifically talking about race, this spirit of activism is a fire that teachers who seek to be caring solidarity accomplices will catch and spread. To be an accomplice in solidarity includes all that has thus far been discussed and also the willingness to go the next step. White accomplices put their bodies, their money, their jobs, and their whiteness on the line, not to request but to make demands of other White people (Harden & Harden-Moore, 2019; Love, 2019c; Nieto, 2006).

Powell and Kelly (2017) argued that "the core idea that separates white allies from white accomplices is risk" (p. 43). In order to be in caring solidarity with communities, the teacher who seeks to be an accomplice will be more than an ally in the classroom and an advocate in the school and community. They must use their privilege to shield those who are most at risk of losing their lives, their freedom, and their humanity in confrontations with police and others who would force compliance.

This means that people show up when Nazis parade in their streets, and it means they show up in the streets when Black people are shot down by police. Accomplices shield demonstrators from tear gas; they put their arms into the wheel wells of the vehicles of ICE agents stealing the parents of students. Accomplices are people who care enough to be led by Black people, directed by Black people, and stay when the canisters fly.

Besides their bodies, accomplices use their resources to support full equality for Black people. Powell and Kelly (2017) stated,

> An important distinction between an ally and an accomplice is the intentional manipulation of resources to support racial justice. . . . Accomplices notice and share what resources might be available as an academic [or educator] that are not available to communities who are actively working to challenge unjust and white supremacist systems. This may be access to grant bodies, office supplies, printing, meeting space, library and research resources, and otherwise. This may also include leveraging "service learning" opportunities for students to be a part of canvassing for ongoing social movements. (p. 60)

The only way to heal the hole that White supremacy creates in individuals and communities is to fill it with active love, the kind that is discussed in chapter 5. That love will allow White people who have transferred their solidarity to be directly involved in battles for justice and for basic humanity. The *Washington Post* (2018) is finally counting the numbers of people killed by police officers. In 2018, the *Post* counted 992 people shot and killed by police in the United States. Of those, 229 (23 percent) were Black.

Teachers in caring solidarity with communities will be there, working to stop this violence against communities and also to prevent future incidents. The Movement for Black Lives released their platform which includes ending the war on Black people, reparations, investment in education and divestment from prisons and other methods of oppressing Black people, economic justice, community control, and political power (Movement for Black Lives, 2016; Newkirk, 2016).

These are the parts of the mission statement that are frequently left out in schools that say they teach in a culturally relevant manner. To be culturally relevant, schools must take direction from the people of the culture. Too many people think that cultural relevance means only to uplift the icons of the past. It certainly does include that, but the current generation of leaders in Black Lives Matter are here now and accessible. To be in solidarity means to be part of the generation that is fighting for equality now.

Beyond direct action at protests and other ways of getting in the way of White supremacy, White teachers should get in the way at official functions. Leveraging White privilege in the service of people who do not have it is absolutely necessary if White supremacist structures are to be dismantled. School board meetings are often a place where Black parents are patronized, drowned out, or dismissed, even though these are supposed to be places where the people are there to hold the powerful accountable.

Yull and Wilson (2018) described a school board meeting where the Black researcher (Yull) was accused of "race baiting" and "wanting a race war" while the White researcher (Wilson) used racially conscious language to describe the district's participation in the school-to-prison pipeline with no condemnation:

> Wilson had the privilege to speak freely about the racialized dimensions of the district's disciplinary practices and remain invisible and immune to these critiques. At one school board meeting . . . Wilson introduced herself as a University professor, and directly named the "school-to-prison pipeline" as "one of the most important problems facing our schools today." Within the [district] context, even the mention of "race" is automatically assumed to be racist, and yet Wilson escaped scrutiny for using such language publicly. Clearly, anti-Blackness creates a situation where the race of the speaker determines the consequences they face. (p. 12)

White accomplices put themselves at risk, but to be clear, they do not face the same or, some would argue, even similar consequences as Black people do at the hands of police or the justice system.

That is the power of whiteness turned against the system (Clemens, 2019). While there is certainly no guarantee that this will always be the case, White people can count on a certain degree of decorum as to how that are treated when participating in actions. Thus, there is no reason not to be bold. There is no reason not to be strident, uncompromising, angry, and all of the other words that misogyny and White supremacy will throw at those who stand for justice.

The leveraging of resources and the position of a school can attract the right kinds of enemiesm as teachers are more powerful than many think. For example, the 2016 school year started with teachers at John Muir Elementary in Seattle, Washington, working with a local organization, Black Men Uniting to Change the Narrative, dedicated to empowering students in schools. In solidarity with their students, White and Black teachers wore shirts emblazoned with "#BlackLivesMatter" (Au & Hagopian, 2017). The result was predictable yet still shock the conscience:

> A local TV station reported on the teachers wearing #BlackLivesMatter t-shirts, and as the story went public political tensions exploded. Soon the white supremacist, hate group–fueled news source Breitbart picked up the story, and the right-wing police support group Blue Lives Matter publicly denounced the effort. Hateful emails and phone calls began to flood the John Muir administration and the Seattle school board, and then the horrifying happened—someone made a bomb threat against the school. Even though the threat was deemed not credible by authorities, Seattle schools officially canceled the Black Men Uniting to Change the Narrative event at Muir out of extreme caution." (Au & Hagopian, 2017)

As a result of that difficult day, school representatives became more emboldened rather than frightened, and schools across the district took part in a "Black Lives Matter at School" day in October of that same year.

> Some schools changed their reader boards to declare "Black Lives Matter." Parents at some elementary schools set up tables by the front entrance with books and resources to help other parents talk to their kids about racism. Many schools coordinated plans for teaching about Black lives, including lessons about movements for racial justice and the way racism impacts the school system today. (Au & Hagopian, 2017)

Teachers, administrators, and staff who go through an experience like this will have a sense of power and purpose that comes out only through struggle. In this case, the teachers did not give into the intimidation but instead put themselves on the line and faced a real danger, declaring that Black lives matter. Consider the impact such a statement would have on all the people involved in that school. The teachers would become more invested than ever in student lives now that they have gone through that experience. The students would feel valued and see that teachers are not just paying lip service to their solidarity claims.

What to Do

Moving from ally or advocate to accomplice means finding opportunities to get in the way of White supremacy. Educator and writer Jonathan Osler described ways that White people can become an impediment to whiteness and work to dismantle structures of White supremacy.

According to Paul (2017), an accomplice does more than empathize: "Being an accomplice is more than just listening to others talk about the struggle. It is about solidifying a course of action that helps you commit to undoing it."

- It is about vocally calling out the family members you know who voted for Trump or other anti-Brown or anti-Black politicians.
- It is about holding people accountable for their racist and anti-Black/Brown antics.
- It is about holding folks in privileged positions accountable for their passivity on anti-queer rhetoric.
- It is about calling out toxic masculinity and misogyny when it comes up in conversation.
- It is about doing your own research on topics you don't understand but want to help support.

Osler (2016) also described the work of accomplices. Here are the categories with interpretations for White teachers:

Protesting

Being conscious of how a White person takes up space at protests will mean the difference between success and failure. White people at protests should take direction from the people who are most affected by the issue. The purpose of White people at the protest is to shield the leaders and other protesters against police, counterprotesters, and any other entity that would inhibit the message going out.

White people should not speak to the media during these protests. The media will immediately go to White people first as they are most comfortable getting information from them as presumed authorities. The media will also want the unusual in a protest, and that means White people, especially if there are only a few. The other job of White people during a protest is to check other White people. If a White person is taking the spotlight, move the spotlight to the real leaders.

Money

Accomplices will raise funds and look for ways to support movements that are led and run by Black people and community people. The United Way is great, but your dollars will have a larger impact with smaller, more focused organizations where the CEOs do not make over $1 million per year.

White Communities

Create and coordinate antiracism trainings and book clubs in White spaces. Disrupt White communities and push them to be inclusive. Hold book clubs on *White Fragility* (DiAngelo, 2018) in communities or in schools and school groups. Read *We Want to Do More than Survive* (Love, 2019c). Hold these book clubs during brunch so others will listen to the conversations. Be open and loud while doing it.

Advocacy on Social Media

Join groups that are fighting injustice and teaching others about White supremacy's influence in society. Share those items pointedly to teach your social media circle about racism. Also, diversify and extend beyond your current circle. Find people to friend who will challenge and teach you. Many prominent African American scholars use Facebook and Twitter to communicate with anyone who will follow. It is informative, challenging, and entertaining. As time goes by, feel free to challenge other White people in your posts when necessary. White supremacy thrives in silent agreement or tacit understanding. Disrupt that silence with your voice.

At Work

Beyond the classroom and into the structures of the district and school, White people must be disruptors of White supremacy in hiring decisions. Diverse faculty are needed for students and to democratize schooling in America. The teaching force is too White. Disrupt it by demanding the hiring of diverse teachers and administrators, and support them in their work so they stay in teaching.

Electoral Politics

Be a disruptive force in local politics. Know your representatives well and make sure they see you frequently. When it comes to elected positions in the district, teachers should be the largest voting bloc. These officials are people who literally decide your day-to-day fate. They make funding, staffing, and curricular decisions, and teachers have very little input unless they demand it.

For too long teachers have assumed that their representatives would protect them from draconian cuts and meddling from outsiders. It should be obvious by now that teachers are on their own, and until they vote in large numbers and decide who will be voted on in primaries and caucuses, they will continue to be discounted. Lastly, consider running. No one is better qualified than teachers to run schools, cities, towns, counties, and states.

Teachers are trained and ready. Imagine a country run by compassionate teachers in solidarity with communities. What a change that would be.

Confronting Violence

Violence, intimidation, and microaggressions are everyday occurrences in our schools that should not go unchallenged. Besides demanding that students be kind to one another, teachers must also be ready to not accept jokes, or non-jokes, that oppress marginalized people. That means correcting people in meetings or in emails.

Obviously it means removing Confederate names from schools and replacing racist mascots. It also means teaching people why these things are wrong. Teach them that it is not that standards have changed or that political correctness has run amok but that these things were always wrong. Teach them that White supremacy and White normality kept White people from seeing them as wrong, but they always knew they were racist.

Your Children and Your Students

Accomplices do not hide their work with communities of color. Be bold. Have pictures of your life as an accomplice available for viewing by students. Have scrapbooks out with your work. Have pictures on your desk. Be in the newspaper and on TV as part of movements. Accomplices are public and proud. Also bring children and students along when accomplice work is going on. See your students and celebrate them at protests, events, and meetings. Bring your own children with you to events and meetings. Let them see how change is made (Osler, 2016).

Being an accomplice for students and communities of color will transform teaching, teachers, and their schools and communities (Harden & Harden-Moore, 2019). However, there are choices. Teachers can keep going on as they have, perpetuating White supremacy until the end, but the end will come. Beyond demographic changes, the societal wave that is coming will demand that teachers change. Whiteness is a dead end. White supremacy is unsustainable, immoral, and sinful. To teach well is to change the world. Change it to a world that your Black students will want to live in.

Conclusion

An argument can be made that the school system is doing precisely what it was intended to do. Activists and scholars rightly point to the history of schooling in America and show forthrightly, with numerous, well-cited examples, that American schools were never intended to be egalitarian or to lift up the disenfranchised. They show that it was always intended to sift and deliver the White, wealthy, and well tended to an abundant future. They contend that the purpose of schools is to create workers and to weed out nonconformists.

While I am not blind to the evidence, I believe teachers have the power to disrupt and dismantle this system and rebuild it to reflect a new set of principles. I believe that public schools can be the incubators of democratic thinking and action. All human systems are changeable, the problems solvable, and the benefits abundant when we decide to act together for the betterment of our communities.

Dismantling the school-to-prison pipeline is a moral imperative of the first order. However, the pipeline does not only affect African American students. There are many issues in education, and there are many groups that need solidarity, including gay and lesbian students, transgender students, Latinx students, Asian students, Muslim students, and a host of racial and ethnic groups that have been marginalized and oppressed within our schools.

Latinx people, people with disabilities, and people of all races and gender identities are caught up in a system with one goal: to maintain White, male, straight, Christian supremacy in law, economics, and politics. In order to maintain that system, we have jailed our citizens at an alarming rate, with astronomical costs in economic, democratic, and human terms.

Teachers live at the intersection of all identities and oppressive forces (Crenshaw, 1989). So, while I have worked to shine a light on some, I hope that others will shine the light of solidarity in a thousand different directions. We cannot forget that our acts of solidarity are sometimes the difference between life and death, especially for kids who do not identify as part of the gender binary (Wozolek, Wootton, & Demlow, 2016).

Ladson-Billings (1995) explains that when teachers are working in culturally relevant ways or, in the context of caring solidarity are working in solidarity with their students, they can help them become critically conscious. This ability to question, to act without fear, to make mistakes that lead to growth, and to build a new world is exactly what we say we want from education. The democratic project of education depends on this consciousness, and this critical consciousness is only possible when teachers work in solidarity with learners. Ladson-Billings describes teachers in one school who practice this kind of pedagogy:

> All of the teachers identified strongly with teaching. They were not ashamed or embarrassed about their professions. Each had chosen to teach and, more importantly, had chosen to teach in this low-income, largely African American school district. The teachers saw themselves as a part of the community and teaching as a way to give back to the community. They encouraged their students to do the same. They believed their work was artistry, not a technical task that could be accomplished in a recipe-like fashion. Fundamental to their beliefs about teaching was that all of the students could and must succeed. Consequently, they saw their responsibility as working to guarantee the success of each student. (p. 163)

Ladson-Billings described these teachers as rooted in their communities, visible, and present. They worked inside and outside of their classes to build their communities and strengthen the bonds between themselves and their students. They also encouraged the bond between students to each other and to their community.

The life of a teacher is most rewarding when these bonds are strong and the work of the teacher is meaningful. That meaning springs from solidarity with students and the community. Teaching is very hard work. Teaching well is harder, but teaching well is the most worthwhile way to spend a working life that I can imagine. The rewards are innumerable, the frustrations equally so, but they are far outweighed by the satisfaction of students growing into adults who set the world ablaze with their intellect, drive, energy, and idealism. That is the kind of teaching that caring solidarity creates—a world-changing, life-altering conglomeration of experiences.

One of my former tenth-graders, Greta McLain, studied art in Minneapolis and murals in California. Now, as an adult, she and others are turning the city of Minneapolis into a wonderland of color and vibrant walls that reflect the beauty and diversity of the city that lives under a blanket of snow and cold for almost half the year. Some of her pictures grace the jacket of this book. Her work with communities, kids, adults, and other artists is an example for all of us to follow.

She gathers students to talk about their lives and, in solidarity with them, facilitates the telling of their stories on paper, then on parachute cloth, then on the walls of schools and community centers. In one project, Greta replaced a mural that had faded and been vandalized at South High School where I taught her and her brother. The tagline on the mural both explains who South students are and inspires all of us who see it. Among the colors, people, and symbols that represent the students who designed it are the words

I am not in this world to adapt to it, rather to transform it.

May that be said of all of us.

Epilogue

In March 2020, I turned this book over to the publisher after researching, writing, and editing for six years. As I was making the final edits, a worldwide pandemic hit, challenging all of the structures that hold a social system based in White supremacy in place. White people were asked to sacrifice things they once took for granted for the greater good. The responses to the emergency revealed a great deal about who we are as individuals and as a nation. And as to be expected, a small but vocal contingent revealed that they were not equipped for it.

However, the crisis inspired a new appreciation for *essential* workers like nurses and doctors who were lauded in symbolic messages of care and gratitude like clapping for them at the end of their shift and porch lights illuminated across whole cities in the evenings. Parents on social media expressed their thanks to teachers were called upon to radically change their classroom instruction in both sincere and humorous ways. For retail workers, people acknowledged the contributions of the lowest paid employees at grocery stores, mechanics, gas stations, and fast food restaurants. Through it all, the feelings of appreciation were also met with critical voices who asked if these symbolic gestures would lead to real change in how workers are paid, how benefits are secured, and if healthcare is acknowledged to be a right in the wealthiest country in the world.

For teachers during the pandemic, the sudden shutdown of schools after spring break was traumatic. Teachers were suddenly expected, with a few days' notice, to retool their curriculum and pedagogy to an online format. Teachers worked furiously, sometimes with little resources, often with little sleep, to connect with all of their students. Even teachers with little to no background or knowledge in virtual learning formats spent hours researching new online teaching strategies and tools to provide the most effective instruction they could for their students. This emergency exposed clear disparities in students' access to technology and the internet and presented the glaring inequality of access to information in America often referred to as the *digital divide*. It unveiled the privilege of economic classes when telecommuting parents were able to facilitate lessons at home. America saw the wealth gap as White people complained that they were hunkered down with their children in homes that included every possible comfort. As an observer on several platforms, I witnessed teachers break down as they described their exhaustion, their feelings of inadequacy to the task, and the heartbreaking stories they heard from their students. My own college students told me of their struggles with children, job losses, and emergency living arrangements due to the crisis.

People across the nation from all stations of life worked in solidarity with one another, even though they were separated physically by the need to contain the COVID-19 virus. Time and again I watched teachers build and enact solidarity in small and large ways. They held parades of cars in neighborhoods to bolster their students' spirits, and others were involved in more structural acts of solidarity by fundraising online for computers, servers, and cameras so students could participate in classes. Teachers told stories of extraordinary feats to reach students who had no means of communication at their houses and celebrated their return online. Seniors who missed prom, graduation, and a long list of *lasts*—their last game, the last day of classes, the last time cleaning out their locker—had teachers and administrators create online proms and virtual graduations with teachers recording well wishes for grads as they crossed virtual stages.

While all of this was happening, teachers were advocating for more resources for themselves and their students in order to deliver curriculum and to keep students engaged. They were demanding them from their schools, their districts, and their states. The governmental response to the crisis has been demonstrably ineffective, and teachers have taken up much of the slack. These acts of solidarity mattered a great deal to students and communities, and the relationships that were built and preserved would be needed as the next crisis erupted.

MINNEAPOLIS

My hometown of Minneapolis, as by now you have read, is a wondrous place with a diversity that surprises many who visit. That said, it is also a place of segregation and great violence by the police. The state of Minnesota is #2 in the nation for racial inequality, right behind Wisconsin. While Black people, those who identify as African American, and more recently immigrants make up 19% of the population of Minneapolis, they make up two thirds of those who are subjects of force by police. I have witnessed the Minneapolis police brutalize students, protesters, and unarmed adults my entire adult life. I have worked to shield all of my students from their wrath, and as a teacher, I advocated for the removal of police from our school and the Minneapolis school district.

On May 25, 2020, businesses were beginning to reopen even though the threat from the COVID-19 virus was still very real. George Floyd stepped into Cup foods on 38th and Chicago Avenue in Minneapolis. It is a neighborhood I know well, as it is only about a mile and a half from South High, where I taught. On that spring day, Mr. Floyd was detained and killed by strangulation by a police officer who knelt on top of his neck while he was face down and handcuffed. This occurred in broad daylight, in front of multiple witnesses, with cell phone cameras recording. The police officer who strangled Mr. Floyd seemed unfazed by the attention during this horrific event, and as Mr. Floyd begged for air and repeated, "I can't breathe," the officer continued to press his knee into his victim. Three other officers, two of them rookies, kept crowds away as Mr. Floyd lay dying.

Mr. Floyd died that day, and the video taken of his death by a seventeen-year-old young woman immediately raced across the globe. Demands for justice rose up just as swiftly. In Minneapolis, people of all races took to rain-soaked streets the next day to protest the brutality of the death and demand the arrests of all four officers involved. They were met by Minneapolis police in riot gear. Police fired tear gas and rubber bullets directly at protesters who were marching peacefully in the streets. They fired gas canisters out of moving vehicles. They fired at journalists covering the protests and generally sought specifically to escalate the tension.

Acts of caring solidarity in this new stage of crisis were on display everywhere in Minneapolis, from the streets to the schools. A few examples are given here, but many, many more were done in private so only those involved will ever know. Beginning on the first day of protests, Minneapolis teachers were out in force, marching with community members, getting gassed by police, and demanding justice for Mr. Floyd and their students who face harassment and potential death at the hands of law enforcement daily. As Lake Street businesses and the 3rd Precinct Police Station burned in an uprising that night, teachers were checking on students online and by phone to make sure they were secure and out of harm's way. The next day, local artists, including Greta McLain, whose murals grace South High and the cover of this book, created a mural of Mr. Floyd on the side of Cup foods that has become a memorial. The day after the burnings, teachers and community members flooded streets to clean up and help businesses board up to prevent further damage. After much of the food distribution infrastructure had broken down due to fires, teachers organized food drives and created bags to distribute to local families. After a week of protests, the Minneapolis school board voted unanimously to break their ties with Minneapolis police. Minneapolis police will no longer patrol the halls of Minneapolis public schools. The schools will take the summer to develop a new plan that will, hopefully, replace school resource officers with councilors, social workers, and educators who can help students deal with conflicts without sending them to juvenile detention. Shortly after, the Minneapolis Parks and Recreation system did the same. And a few days after that, in an absolutely stunning development, the city of Minneapolis voted to disband the entire Minneapolis Police Department. It will be replaced with a new, community-based public service department.

In the days that followed Mr. Floyd's death, national and worldwide protests erupted with people over the globe. People are making the connection between state violence and the ideology of White supremacy and calling for change. To illustrate, after the uprising in Minneapolis, young people have gone after edifices of White supremacy across the country and across the world. As I write this epilogue, events are happening so quickly that readers will have to look back at all of the events to see just how much happened over the course of a few short weeks. Suffice it to say, the symbols of White supremacy such as Confederate monuments and statues are being removed by the day. Players, coaches, and many others are currently apologizing to Collin Kaepernick, the 49ers player who knelt in protest of police brutality four years prior and was blacklisted. Even in other countries, people are pulling down the statues of a slave trader in Bristol, England, and, in Belgium they are pulling down the former king of Belgium, Leopold II, who enslaved the Congo in the 1800s. Back in the United States, cities are painting "BLACK LIVES MATTER" on their roads, even the one that leads to the White House in D.C. The mayor of D.C. changed the name of the square outside the White House to "BLACK LIVES MATTER" square. While the gestures of this week have been symbolic, that does not mean that they are not powerful. Standing in solidarity comes in both symbols and substance. The structural and the personal are equally important. One without the other does not create a more equitable community.

CONCLUSION

Someone should have stopped the first slavers who arrived with enslaved peoples in 1619. Everyone should have stood up and said *no* four hundred years ago, or one hundred years ago, or a month ago to oppression and violence against people of color. In the America that we create in our minds, someone should have demanded that White people act in solidarity with all peoples in the continent. A few did, but the majority did not, and structures of American White supremacy were laid from the first White step on her shores.

If now is the time when people are finally ready to lay down the heartsickness of White supremacy and embrace solidarity, then let us begin.

The events of this spring may have changed some of the structures that were laid on that day in 1619, but the personal project of caring solidarity has not changed, in fact, I would argue it is needed now more than ever. Whites have a unique opportunity right now, as the sea change is happening, to be part of that movement. The personal project of personal interrogation, understanding our history, connecting with communities, demanding transformation, and dismantling the structures of White supremacy has not changed. These acts of caring solidarity are crucial to building a new world, but the work is not done. The commitment is long; the journey is difficult; the work is hard. It will cost, but ultimately it is our most important historical endeavor. We can create the world where all people know that they belong and that they are all valued.

References

Allen, R. L. (2009). "What about poor White people?" In W. Ayers, T. M. Quinn, & D. Stovall (Eds.), *Handbook of social justice in education* (pp. 209–225). New York: Routledge.

Allen, R. L., & Liou, D. D. (2018). Managing whiteness: The call for educational leadership to breach the contractual expectations of White supremacy. *Urban Education, 54*(5), 677–705. doi:10.1177/0042085918783819

Alonso, G., Anderson, N. S., Su, C., & Theoharis, J. (2009). *Our schools suck: Students talk back to a segregated nation on the failures of urban education*. New York: New York University Press.

Anderson, C. (2017). *White rage: The unspoken truth of our racial divide*. New York: Bloomsbury.

Applebaum, B. (2011). *Being white, being good: White complicity, white moral responsibility, and social justice pedagogy*. Lanham, MD: Lexington Books.

Au, W., & Hagopian, J. (2017). How one elementary school sparked a citywide movement to make black students' lives matter. Retrieved October 28, 2018, from https://www.rethinkingschools.org/articles/how-one-elementary-school-sparked-a-citywide-movement-to-make-black-students-lives-matter

Azoulay, K. G. (1997). Experience, empathy and strategic essentialism. *Cultural Studies, 11*(1), 94–116.

Baldwin, J. (1995). *Notes of a native son*. London: Penguin.

Banks, J. A. (1995). Multicultural education: Historical development, dimensions, and practice. In J. A. Banks & C. A. McGee Banks (Eds.), *Handbook of research on multicultural education* (pp. 3–24). New York: Macmillan.

Banks, J. A. (1997). *Educating citizens in a multicultural society*. New York: Teachers College Press.

Bartolomé, L. (1994). Beyond the methods fetish: Toward a humanizing pedagogy. *Harvard educational review, 64*(2), 173–195. doi:10.17763/haer.64.2.58q5m5744t325730

Bayertz, K. (2013). Four uses of "solidarity." In K. Bayertz (Ed.), *Solidarity* (pp. 3–28). Germany: Springer Netherlands.

Berry, T. R. (2018). *States of grace: Counterstories of a black woman in the academy*. New York: Peter Lang.

Bidwell, C. (2010). *Successful White mathematics teachers of African American students* (Unpublished doctoral dissertation, Georgia State University). doi:https://scholarworks.gsu.edu/msit_diss/69/

Blunden, A. (2003). Honneth's "struggle for recognition." Retrieved July 19, 2019, from https://ethicalpolitics.org/ablunden/works/honneth.htm

Bonilla-Silva, E. (2010). *Racism without racists: Color-blind racism and the persistence of racial inequality in America* (3rd ed.). Lanham, MD: Rowman & Littlefield.

Boucher, M. L., Jr. (2013). *"This is how WE roll!": How "successful" white social studies teachers build solidarity with African American students* (Unpublished doctoral dissertation, Indiana University).

Boucher, M. L., Jr. (2016). More than an ally: How a successful White teacher builds solidarity with his African American students. *Urban Education, 51*(1), 82–107. doi:10.1177/0042085914542982

Boucher, M. L., Jr. (2018). Interrogating whiteness: Using photo-elicitation to empower teachers to talk about race. In M. L. Boucher Jr. (Ed.), *Participant empowerment through photo elicitation in ethnographic education research: New research and approaches* (pp. 201–225). Netherlands: Springer. doi:10.1007/978-3-319-64413-4

Boucher, M. L., & Helfenbein, R. J. (2015). The push and the pull: Deficit models, Ruby Payne, and becoming a "warm demander." *Urban Review, 47*(4), 742–758. doi:10.1007/s11256-015-0332-y

Bowditch, C. (1993). Getting rid of troublemakers: High school disciplinary procedures and the production of dropouts. *Social Problems, 40*(4), 493–509.

Bradbury, B., Corak, M., Waldfogel, J., & Washbrook, E. (2015). *Too many children left behind: The U.S. achievement gap in comparative perspective*. New York: Russell Sage Foundation.

Britzman, D. P. (2003). *Practice makes practice: A critical study of learning to teach*. New York: State University of New York Press.

Brown, A. L. (2012). On human kinds and role models: A critical discussion about the African American male teacher. *Educational Studies, 48*(3), 296–315.

Brown-Jeffy, S., & Cooper, J. E. (2011). Toward a conceptual framework of culturally relevant pedagogy: An overview of the conceptual and theoretical literature. *Teacher Education Quarterly, 38*(1), 65–84.

Browne, J. (2007). Rooted in slavery: Prison labor exploitation. *Race, Poverty & the Environment, 14*(1), 42–44.

Bryan, N. (2017). White teachers' role in sustaining the school-to-prison pipeline: Recommendations for teacher education. *Urban Review, 49*(2), 326–345. doi:10.1007/s11256-017-0403-3

Cammarota, J. (2011). Blindsided by the avatar: White saviors and allies out of Hollywood and in education. *Review of Education, Pedagogy, and Cultural Studies, 33*(3), 242–259. doi:10.1080/10714413.2011.585287

Case, K. (2018, December 3). How NOT to be an ally—part 2: "He-peat, re-white, and amplification." Retrieved August 11, 2019, from http://www.drkimcase.com/how-not-to-be-an-ally-part-2-he-peat-re-white-and-amplification/

Casey, Z. A. (2017). *A pedagogy of anticapitalist racism: Whiteness, neoliberalism, and resistance in education*. New York: State University of New York Press.

Cazden, C. B., & Leggett, E. L. (1976). *Culturally responsive education: A discussion of Lau remedies II* (pp. 1–52, Rep.). Washington, DC: U.S. Department of Health, Education, and Welfare. (ERIC Document Reproduction Service No. ED 135 241)

Cherry, M. (2017). Forgiveness, exemplars, and the oppressed. In *The Moral Psychology of Forgiveness* (pp. 55–72). New York, NY: Rowman & Littlefield.

Chong, D., & Druckman, J. N. (2007). Framing theory. *Annual Review of Political Science, 10*(1), 103–126.

Clemens, C. (2019). Ally or accomplice? The language of activism. *Teaching Tolerance*. Retrieved July 18, 2019, from https://www.tolerance.org/magazine/ally-or-accomplice-the-language-of-activism

Coates, T. (2008, May). "This is how we lost to the White man": The audacity of Bill Cosby's Black conservatism. *The Atlantic*. Retrieved August, 2008, from https://www.theatlantic.com/magazine/archive/2008/05/-this-is-how-we-lost-to-the-white-man/306774/

Coates, T. (2015). *Between the world and me*. New York: Random House.

Coates, T. (2017, September 14). The first White president. *The Atlantic*. Retrieved September 14, 2017, from https://www.theatlantic.com/magazine/archive/2017/10/the-first-white-president-ta-nehisi-coates/537909/

Cochran-Smith, M. (2000). Blind vision: Unlearning racism in teacher education. *Harvard Educational Review, 70*(2), 157–190.

Cochran-Smith, M. (2003). Learning and unlearning: The education of teacher educators. *Teaching and Teacher Education, 19*(1), 5–28. doi:10.1016/s0742-051x(02)00091-4

Coleman, B. (2007). *Successful white teachers of black students: Teaching across racial lines in urban middle school science classrooms* (Unpublished doctoral dissertation, University of Massachusetts–Amherst).

Coleman, J. S. (1966). *Equality of educational opportunity* (pp. 1–749, Rep. No. FS 5.238:38001). U.S. Department of Health, Education, and Welfare. (ERIC Document Reproduction Service No. ED012275)

Cooper, P. M. (2003). Teaching within a community. *Journal of Teacher Education, 54*(5), 413–427.

CRDC. (2016, June 7). *Data highlights on education opportunity gaps in our nation's public schools* (Rep.). Retrieved September, 2017, from U.S. Department of Education Office for Civil Rights (CRDC) website: https://www2.ed.gov/about/offices/list/ocr/docs/CRDC2013-14-first-look.pdf

Crenshaw, K. (1989). Demarginalizing the intersection of race and sex: Black feminist critique of antidiscrimination doctrine, feminist theory and antiracist politics. *University of Chicago Legal Forum*, 139–168.

Crocco, M. S., & Costigan, A. T. (2007). The narrowing of curriculum and pedagogy in the age of accountability: Urban educators speak out. *Urban Education, 42*(6), 512–535. doi:10.1177/0042085907304964

Cuellar, A. E., & Markowitz, S. (2015). School suspension and the school-to-prison pipeline. *International Review of Law and Economics, 43*, 98–106. doi:10.1016/j.irle.2015.06.001

Danielewicz, J. (2001). *Teaching selves: Identity, pedagogy, and teacher education*. Albany, NY: State University of New York Press.

Darling-Hammond, L., Friedlaender, D., & Snyder, J. (2014, June). *Student-centered schools: Policy supports for closing the opportunity gap* (Rep.). doi:10.1007/s11256-007-0066-6

De Lissovoy, N. D. (2010). Rethinking education and emancipation: Being, teaching, and power. *Harvard Educational Review, 80*(2), 203–221. doi:10.17763/haer.80.2.h6r65285 tu252448

De Lissovoy, N., & Brown, A. L. (2013). Antiracist solidarity in critical education: Contemporary problems and possibilities. *Urban Review, 45*(5), 1–22.

DeLage, J. (2016, July 20). Police unions blast teachers' Minneapolis Philando Castile protest. Retrieved August 14, 2019, from https://www.twincities.com/2016/07/19/teachers-arrested-in-minneapolis-philando-castile-protest/

Delgado, R. (1996). Rodrigo's eleventh chronicle: Empathy and false empathy. *California Law Review, 84*(1), 61. doi:10.2307/3480903

Delpit, L. (2006). *Other people's children: Cultural conflict in the classroom*. New York: New Press. (Original work published in 1988)

DiAngelo, R. (2011). White fragility. *The International Journal of Critical Pedagogy, 3*(3), 54–70.

DiAngelo, R. (2017, June 30). No, I won't stop saying "White supremacy." Retrieved August 16, 2019, from https://www.yesmagazine.org/people-power/no-i-wont-stop-saying-white-supremacy-20170630?fbclid=IwAR0FPpizqiM7XgjbhUwTDULoMCApRx0rvRrYT2-z_J1UgXLC_G2u0qBetsg

DiAngelo, R. J. (2018). *White fragility: Why it's so hard to talk to white people about racism*. Boston, MA: Beacon Press.

Dixson, A. D. (2018). "What's going on?": A critical race theory perspective on Black Lives Matter and activism in education. *Urban Education, 53*(2), 231–247. doi:10.1177/0042085917747115

Du Bois, W. E. B. (1994). *The souls of Black folk*. New York: Dover. (Original work published 1903)

Duckworth, A. L., Peterson, C., Matthews, M. D., & Kelly, D. R. (2007). Grit: Perseverance and passion for long-term goals. *Journal of Personality and Social Psychology, 92*(6), 1087–1101. doi:10.1037/0022-3514.92.6.1087

Duckworth, A. L., & Quinn, P. D. (2009). Development and validation of the short grit scale (Grit–S). *Journal of Personality Assessment, 91*(2), 166–174. doi:10.1080/00223890802634290

Duncan, K. E. (2018). "They hate on me!" Black teachers interrupting their White colleagues' racism. *Educational Studies, 55*(2), 197–213. doi:10.1080/00131946.2018.1500463

Duncan-Andrade, J. (2007). Gangstas, wankstas, and ridas: Defining, developing, and supporting effective teachers in urban schools. *International Journal of Qualitative Studies in Education, 20*(6), 617–638.

Duncan-Andrade, J. M., & Morrell, E. (2008). *The art of critical pedagogy: Possibilities for moving from theory to practice in urban schools*. New York: Peter Lang.

EdBuild. (2016, August 23). *Fault lines: America's most segregating school district borders* (Rep.). Retrieved from https://s3.amazonaws.com/edbuild-public-data/data/fault+lines/Ed-Build-Fault-Lines-2016.pdf

Edbuild. (2019, February). Nonwhite school districts get $23 billion less than white districts. Retrieved August 31, 2019, from https://edbuild.org/content/23-billion#CA

Eslinger, J. C. (2013). Caring and understanding "as nearly as possible": Towards culturally responsive caring across differences. *Critical Intersections in Education: An OISE/UT Students' Journal, 1*(1), 1–11.

Fallis, R. K., & Opotow, S. (2003). Are students failing school or are schools failing students? *Journal of Social Issues, 58*(1), 103–119.

Fanon, F. (2004). *The wretched of the earth*. New York: Grove. (Original work published in 1961)

Feistritzer, C. E., Griffin, S., & Linnajarvi, A. (2011). *Profile of teachers in the U.S., 2011*. Washington, D.C.: National Center for Education Information.

Flaherty, J. (2019, May 7). Arizona teachers went on strike. Now lawmakers aim to ban politics in classrooms. *Phoenix New Times*. Retrieved August 31, 2019, from https://www.phoenixnewtimes.com/news/arizona-legislators-politics-speech-class-teachers-strike-townsend-11212255

Frankenberg, R. (1993). Growing up White: Feminism, racism and the social geography of childhood. *Feminist Review*, (45), 51. doi:10.2307/1395347

Freire, P. (2014). *Pedagogy of the oppressed: 30th anniversary edition* (M. B. Ramos, Trans.). New York: Bloomsbury Academic & Professional.

Friedersdorf, C. (2019, August 9). Dismantling Tucker Carlson's White-supremacy argument. *The Atlantic*. Retrieved August 11, 2019, from https://www.theatlantic.com/ideas/archive/2019/08/tucker-carlson-white-supremacy/595789/

Fromm, E. (1956). *The art of loving*. New York: Continuum.

Fry, R. (2009). *The rapid growth and changing complexion of suburban public schools* (Rep.). Retrieved 2011, from Pew Research Center website: https://www.pewtrusts.org/en/research-and-analysis/reports/2009/03/31/the-rapid-growth-and-changing-complexion-of-suburban-public-schools

Fuentes, A. (2012). Arresting development: Zero tolerance and the criminalization of children. *Rethinking Schools, 26*(2), 18–23.

Gay, G. (2010). *Culturally responsive teaching: Theory, research, and practice*. New York: Teachers College.

Gaztambide-Fernández, R. A. (2012). Decolonization and the pedagogy of solidarity. *Decolonization: Indigeneity, Education & Society, 1*(1), 41–67.

Gershenson, S., Hart, C. M., Lindsay, C. A., & Papageorge, N. W. (2017). *The long-run impacts of same-race teachers* (pp. 1–61, Rep. No. IZA DP No. 10630). Bonn, Germany: IZA—Institute of IZA—Institute of Labor Economics. Retrieved September 1, 2019, from http://ftp.iza.org/dp10630.pdf

Godley, A. J., Sweetland, J., Wheeler, R. S., Minnici, A., & Carpenter, B. D. (2006). Preparing teachers for dialectally diverse classrooms. *Educational Researcher, 35*(8), 30–37. doi:10.3102/0013189x035008030

Goff, P. A., Jackson, M. C., Leone, B. A., Culotta, C. M., & Ditomasso, N. A. (2014). The essence of innocence: Consequences of dehumanizing Black children. *Journal of Personality and Social Psychology, 106*(4), 526–545. doi:10.1037/a0035663

Goldberg, D. T. (1995). *Multiculturalism: A critical reader*. Cambridge, MA: Blackwell.

Gonyea, D. (2017, October 24). Majority of White Americans say they believe Whites face discrimination. Retrieved from https://www.npr.org/2017/10/24/559604836/majority-of-white-americans-think-theyre-discriminated-against

Gorski, P. (1999, November). A brief history of multicultural education. Retrieved September, 2016, from http://www.edchange.org/multicultural/papers/edchange_history.html

Gorski, P. (2006). The classist underpinnings of Ruby Payne's framework. *TCRecord*, 1–5.

Gregory, A., & Weinstein, R. (2008). The discipline gap and African Americans: Defiance or cooperation in the high school classroom. *Journal of School Psychology, 46*(4), 455–475.

Hackman, R. (2015, June 26). "We need co-conspirators, not allies": How White Americans can fight racism. *The Guardian*. Retrieved July 18, 2019, from https://www.theguardian.com/world/2015/jun/26/how-white-americans-can-fight-racism

Harden, K., & Harden-Moore, T. (2019, March 4). Moving from ally to accomplice: How far are you willing to go to disrupt racism in the workplace? Retrieved July 18, 2019, from https://diverseeducation.com/article/138623/

Harris, A. (2019, May 28). The new secession. *The Atlantic*. Retrieved August 25, 2019, from https://www.theatlantic.com/education/archive/2019/05/resegregation-baton-rouge-public-schools/589381/

Harris, C. I. (1993). Whiteness as property. *Harvard Law Review, 106*(8), 1707. doi:10.2307/1341787

Harvey, D. L., & Reed, M. H. (1996). The culture of poverty: An ideological analysis. *Sociological Perspectives, 39*(4), 465–495. doi:10.2307/1389418

Harvey, J. (2007). Moral solidarity and empathetic understanding: The moral value and scope of the relationship. *Journal of Social Philosophy, 38*(1), 22–37. doi:10.1111/j.1467-9833.2007.00364.x

Haskins, R., & Rouse, C. (2005). *Closing achievement gaps—Policy brief* (Rep.). Retrieved 2017, from the Future of Children website: https://www.brookings.edu/wp-content/uploads/2016/06/20050301foc.pdf

Hayes, C., & Juarez, B. (2012). There is no culturally responsive teaching spoken here: A critical race perspective. *Democracy and Education, 20*(1), 1–14.

Helfenbein, R. J. (2003). Troubling multiculturalism: The new work order, anti anti-essentialism, and a cultural studies approach to education. *Multicultural Perspectives, 5*(4), 10–16. doi:10.1207/s15327892mcp0504_3

Helms, J. E. (1990). *Black and white racial identity: Theory, research, and practice*. Westport, CT: Praeger.

Herman, K. C., Hickmon-Rosa, J., & Reinke, W. M. (2017). Empirically derived profiles of teacher stress, burnout, self-efficacy, and coping and associated student outcomes. *Journal of Positive Behavior Interventions, 20*(2), 90–100. doi:10.1177/1098300717732066

Hermes, M. (2005). White teachers, Native students: Rethinking culture-based education. In J. Phillion, M. F. He, & F. M. Connelly (Eds.), *Narrative and experience in multicultural education* (pp. 95–115). Thousand Oaks, CA: Sage.

Hirschfield, P. J. (2008). Preparing for prison? The criminalization of school discipline in the USA. *Theoretical Criminology, 12*(1), 79–101. doi:10.1177/1362480607085795

Hitchcock, J., & Flint, C. (2015, September). *Decentering whiteness* [Scholarly project]. Center for the Study of White American Culture (CSWAC). Retrieved July 18, 2019, from http://www.euroamerican.org/public/decenteringwhiteness.pdf

Hoffman, D. M. (1996). Culture and self in multicultural education: Reflections on discourse, text, and practice. *American Educational Research Journal, 33*(3), 545–569. doi:10.2307/1163276

Honneth, A. (1995). *The struggle for recognition: The moral grammar of social conflicts*. Cambridge, MA: MIT Press.

hooks, b. (1994). *Teaching to transgress: Education as the practice of freedom*. New York: Routledge.

hooks, b. (2000). *All about love: New visions*. New York: Morrow.

hooks, b. (2013). *Writing beyond race: Living theory and practice*. New York: Routledge.

hooks, b. (2015). *Black looks: Race and representation*. New York: Routledge.

Howard, T. C. (2002). Hearing footsteps in the dark: African American students' descriptions of effective teachers. *Journal of Education for Students Placed at Risk (JESPAR), 7*(4), 425–444. doi:10.1207/s15327671espr0704_4

Howard, T. C. (2010). *Why race and culture matter in schools: Closing the achievement gap in America's classrooms*. New York: Teachers College Press.

Hughey, M. W. (2010). The White savior film and reviewers' reception. *Symbolic Interaction, 33*(3), 475–496. doi:10.1525/si.2010.33.3.475

Ignatiev, N., & Garvey, J. (1996). *Race traitor*. New York: Routledge.

Indigenous Action Media. (2014, May 4). Accomplices not allies: Abolishing the ally industrial complex. Retrieved September, 2015, from http://www.indigenousaction.org/accomplices-not-allies-abolishing-the-ally-industrial-complex/

Ingersoll, R. M., & May, H. (2011, September). *Recruitment, retention and the minority teacher shortage* (Rep. No. Rr-69). Retrieved from http://www.cpre.org/what-national-data-tell-us-about-minority-teacher-turnover (ERIC Document Reproduction Service No. ED526355)

Irving, D. (2014). *Waking up white: And finding myself in the story of race*. Cambridge, MA: Elephant Room Press.

Isensee, L. (2015, October 23). Why calling slaves "workers" is more than an editing error. Retrieved August 30, 2019, from https://www.npr.org/sections/ed/2015/10/23/450826208/why-calling-slaves-workers-is-more-than-an-editing-error

Johnson, W. (2019, August 28). "Extermination and enslavement": The twin horrors of the American dawn. *Washington Post*. Retrieved August 31, 2019, from https://www.washingtonpost.com/education/2019/08/28/historians-slavery-myths/

Jupp, J. C., Berry, T. R., & Lensmire, T. J. (2016). Second-wave white teacher identity studies. *Review of Educational Research, 86*(4), 1151–1191. doi:10.3102/0034654316629798

Kanpol, B., & McLaren, P. (1995). *Critical multiculturalism: Uncommon voices in a common struggle*. Westport, CT: Bergin & Garvey.

Katsarou, E., Picower, B., & Stovall, D. (2010). Acts of solidarity: Developing urban social justice educators in the struggle for quality public education. *Teacher Education Quarterly, 37*(3), 137–153.

Keating, A. (1995). Interrogating "whiteness," (de)constructing "race." *College English, 57*(8), 901. doi:10.2307/378620

Kim, C. Y., & Geronimo, I. (2009). *Policing in schools: Developing a governance document for school resource officers in K–12 schools (ACLU white paper)* (Rep.). Retrieved 2012, from American Civil Liberties Union (ACLU) website: http://www.aclu.org/files/pdfs/racialjustice/whitepaper_policinginschools.pdf

King, J. E. (1991). Dysconscious racism: Ideology, identity, and the miseducation of teachers. *Journal of Negro Education, 60*(2), 133–146. doi:10.2307/2295605

King, M. L., Jr. (2017, May 3). Man's sin and God's grace. Retrieved August 13, 2019, from https://kinginstitute.stanford.edu/king-papers/documents/mans-sin-and-gods-grace

Kleinfeld, J. (1975). Effective teachers of Eskimo and Indian students. *School Review, 83*(2), 301–344. doi:10.1086/443191

Kobayashi, A., & Peake, L. (2000). Racism out of place: Thoughts on whiteness and an antiracist geography in the new millennium. *Annals of the Association of American Geographers, 90*(2), 392–403. doi:10.1111/0004-5608.00202

Kohl, H. R. (1992). *From archetype to zeitgeist: Powerful ideas for powerful thinking*. New York: Little, Brown.

Kolbert, E., & Hammond, R. (2018, April). Skin deep: What is race, exactly? *National Geographic, 233*(4), 29–41.

Kozol, J. (1995). Amazing grace: The lives of children and the conscience of a nation. New York, NY: HarperPerennial.

Krogstad, J. M., & Fry, R. (2014, August 18). Dept. of Ed. projects public schools will be "majority-minority" this fall. Retrieved October 16, 2019, from https://

www.pewresearch.org/fact-tank/2014/08/18/u-s-public-schools-expected-to-be-majority-minority-starting-this-fall/

Kucsera, J. (2014, March 26). *New York State's extreme school segregation: Inequality, inaction and a damaged future* (Rep.). Retrieved https://www.civilrightsproject.ucla.edu/research/k-12-education/integration-and-diversity/ny-norflet-report-placeholder

Ladson-Billings, G. (1994). *The dreamkeepers: Successful teachers of African American children*. San Francisco, CA: Jossey-Bass.

Ladson-Billings, G. (1995a). But that's just good teaching! The case for culturally relevant pedagogy. *Theory into Practice, 34*(3), 159–165. doi:10.1080/00405849509543675

Ladson-Billings, G. (1995b). Toward a theory of culturally relevant pedagogy. *American Educational Research Journal, 32*(3), 465. doi:10.2307/1163320

Ladson-Billings, G. (2006). From the achievement gap to the education debt: Understanding achievement in U.S. schools. *Educational Researcher, 35*(7), 3–12. doi:10.3102/0013189x035007003

Ladson-Billings, G. (2007). Pushing past the achievement gap: An essay on the language of deficit. *Journal of Negro Education, 7*(6), 316–323.

Ladson-Billings, G. (2008). A letter to our next president. *Journal of Teacher Education, 59*(3), 235–239. doi:10.1177/0022487108317466

Ladson-Billings, G., & Tate, W. F. (1995). Toward a critical race theory of education. *Critical Race Theory in Education, 97*(1), 47–68.

Lam, K. (2019, July 21). New Hampshire lawmaker Werner Horn: "Owning slaves doesn't make you racist." *USA Today*. Retrieved August 30, 2019, from https://www.usatoday.com/story/news/nation/2019/07/18/new-hampshire-lawmaker-werner-horn-owning-slaves-racism-economics/1773670001/

Leonardo, Z. (2013). *Race frameworks: A multidimensional theory of racism and education*. New York: Teachers College.

Lester, J., & Barbour, K. (2005). *Let's talk about race*. New York: HarperCollins.

Levine-Rasky, C. (2000). Framing whiteness: Working through the tensions in introducing whiteness to educators. *Race Ethnicity and Education, 3*(3), 271–292. doi:10.1080/713693039

Lipman, P. (2013). *The new political economy of urban education: Neoliberalism, race, and the right to the city*. Florence: Taylor and Francis.

Lipsitz, G. (2006). *The possessive investment in whiteness: How White people profit from identity politics*. Philadelphia, PA: Temple University Press.

Loeb, S., Darling-Hammond, L., & Luczak, J. (2005). How teaching conditions predict teacher turnover in California schools. *Peabody Journal of Education, 80*(3), 44–70. doi:10.1207/s15327930pje8003_4

Loewus, L. (2018, June 20). The nation's teaching force is still mostly white and female. *Education Week*. Retrieved July 12, 2018, from https://www.edweek.org/ew/articles/2017/08/15/the-nations-teaching-force-is-still-mostly.html

Losen, D., & Skiba, R. L. (2010). *Suspended education: Urban middle schools in crisis* (Rep.). Retrieved 2013, from UCLA website: https://escholarship.org/content/qt8fh0s5dv/qt8fh0s5dv.pdf

Love, B. L. (2014). "I see Trayvon Martin": What teachers can learn from the tragic death of a young Black male. *Urban Review, 46*(2), 292–306. doi:10.1007/s11256-013-0260-7

Love, B. L. (2019a, February 12). "Grit is in our DNA": Why teaching grit is inherently anti-Black. *Education Week*. Retrieved April 19, 2019, from https://www.edweek.org/ew/articles/2019/02/13/grit-is-in-our-dna-why-teaching.html

Love, B. L. (2019b, March 18). Dear White teachers: You can't love your Black students if you don't know them. *Education Week*. Retrieved June 22, 2019, from https://www.edweek.org/ew/articles/2019/03/20/dear-white-teachers-you-cant-love-your.html?r=1885209627

Love, B. L. (2019c). *We want to do more than survive: Abolitionist teaching and the pursuit of educational freedom*. Boston, MA: Beacon Press.

Malik, R. (2017, November 6). New data reveal 250 preschoolers are suspended or expelled every day. Retrieved September, 2018, from Center for American Progress website: https://www.americanprogress.org/issues/early-childhood/news/2017/11/06/442280/new-data-reveal-250-preschoolers-suspended-expelled-every-day/

Masoom, S. (2017, January 25). 2016 should mark the end of the "ally." *HuffPost*. Retrieved August 23, 2019, from https://www.huffpost.com/entry/2016-should-mark-the-end_b_9044904

Matias, C. E. (2016a). *Feeling white: Whiteness, emotionality, and education*. Rotterdam: Sense.

Matias, C. E. (2016b). "Why do you make me hate myself?": Re-teaching whiteness, abuse, and love in urban teacher education. *Teaching Education, 27*(2), 194–211. doi:10.1080/10476210.2015.1068749

Matias, C. E., & Allen, R. L. (2013). Loving whiteness to death: Sadomasochism, emotionality, and the possibility of humanizing love. *Berkeley Review of Education, 4*(2), 285–309. doi:10.5070/b84110066

Matias, C. E., & Mackey, J. (2015). Breakin' down whiteness in antiracist teaching: Introducing critical whiteness pedagogy. *Urban Review, 48*(1), 32–50. doi:10.1007/s11256-015-0344-7

Matos, A. (2015, October 4). Despite Minneapolis moratorium, K–1 kids still getting suspended. *Minneapolis Star Tribune*. Retrieved September, 2016, from http://www.startribune.com/despite-minneapolis-moratorium-k-1-schoolkids-still-getting-suspended/330535511/

May, S. (1999). *Critical multiculturalism: Rethinking multicultural and antiracist education*. Abington, UK: Routledge Falmer.

McCarty, T. L., & Lee, T. S. (2014). Critical culturally sustaining/revitalizing pedagogy and indigenous education sovereignty. *Harvard Educational Review, 84*(1), 101–124. doi:10.17763/haer.84.1.q83746nl5pj34216

McCoy, T. (2016, December 31). He was assaulted and called un-American at a Trump rally. Can he forgive the man who did it? Retrieved August 14, 2019, from https://www.washingtonpost.com/national/he-was-assaulted-and-called-un-american-at-a-trump-rally-can-he-forgive-the-man-who-did-it/2016/12/31/ba91e876-c88a-11e6-bf4b-2c064d32a4bf_story.html

McIntosh, P. (2001). White privilege: Unpacking the invisible knapsack. In P. S. Rothenberg (Ed.), *Race, class, and gender in the United States: An integrated study* (pp. 188–192). New York: Freeman.

Melville, H. (1850). Hawthorne and his mosses. Retrieved September 2017 from http://people.virginia.edu/~sfr/enam315/hmmosses.html

Mervosh, S. (2019, February 27). How much wealthier are White school districts than non-white ones? $23 billion, report says. *New York Times*. Retrieved August 31, 2019, from https://www.nytimes.com/2019/02/27/education/school-districts-funding-white-minorities.html?module=inline

Mettler, K. (2016, June 23). "Good trouble": How John Lewis fuses new and old tactics to teach about civil disobedience. *Washington Post*. Retrieved September 3, 2019, from https://www.washingtonpost.com/news/morning-mix/wp/2016/06/23/good-trouble-how-john-lewis-fuses-new-and-old-tactics-to-teach-about-civil-disobedience/

Michael, A. (2015). *Raising race questions: Whiteness and inquiry in education*. New York: Teachers College Press.

Michael, A., Coleman-King, C., Lee, S., Ramirez, C., & Bentley-Edwards, K. (2017). Naming the unnamed: White culture in relief. In C. A. Warren & S. D. Hancock (Eds.), *White women's work: Examining the intersectionality of teaching, identity, and race* (pp. 19–43). Charlotte, NC: Information Age Publishing.

Michie, G. (2007). Seeing, hearing, and talking race: Lessons for White teachers from four teachers of color. *Multicultural Perspectives, 9*(1), 3–9. doi:10.1080/15210960701333633

Milner, H. R. (2006). The promise of black teachers' success with black students. *Education Foundations, 20*(3–4), 89–104.

Milner, H. R. (2010). *Start where you are, but don't stay there: Understanding diversity, opportunity gaps, and teaching in today's classrooms*. Cambridge, MA: Harvard Education Press.

Milstein, C. (2015). *Taking sides: Revolutionary solidarity and the poverty of liberalism.* Oakland, CA: AK Press.

Monroe, C. R. (2005). Why are "bad boys" always Black? Causes of disproportionality in school discipline and recommendations for change. *The Clearing House: A Journal of Educational Strategies, Issues and Ideas, 79*(1), 45–50. doi:10.3200/tchs.79.1.45-50

Morris, E. W., & Perry, B. L. (2016). The punishment gap: School suspension and racial disparities in achievement. *Social Problems, 63*(1), 68–86. doi:10.1093/socpro/spv026

Movement for Black Lives. (2016, August). Platform. Retrieved August 31, 2019, from https://policy.m4bl.org/platform/

Musu-Gillette, L., De Brey, C., McFarland, J., Hussar, W., & Sonnenberg, W. (2017, July). Status and trends in the education of racial and ethnic groups 2017. Retrieved July 12, 2018, from https://nces.ed.gov/programs/raceindicators/indicator_rbb.asp

Nasaw, D. (2016, December). Americans' view of race relations at two-decade low—WSJ/NBC News poll [Web log post]. Retrieved June, 2017, from https://blogs.wsj.com/washwire/2015/12/16/americans-view-of-race-relations-at-two-decade-low-wsjnbc-news-poll/

Nazaryan, A. (2017, July 2). Whites only: School segregation is back, from Birmingham to San Francisco. *Newsweek.* Retrieved from http://www.newsweek.com/race-schools-592637

Newkirk, V. R., II. (2016, August 4). This is why Black Lives Matter is not going away. *The Atlantic.* Retrieved August 31, 2019, from https://www.theatlantic.com/politics/archive/2016/08/movement-black-lives-platform/494309/

Nieto, S. (1999). Multiculturalism, social justice, and critical teaching. In I. Shor & C. Pari (Authors), *Education is politics: Critical teaching across differences, K–12* (pp. 1–20). Portsmouth, NH: Boynton/Cook Heinemann.

Nieto, S. (2006). Solidarity, courage and heart: What teacher educators can learn from a new generation of teachers. *Intercultural Education, 17*(5), 457–473. doi:10.1080/14675980601060443

Noddings, N. (1986). *Caring: A feminine approach to ethics and moral education.* Berkeley, CA: University of California Press.

Okonofua, J. A., & Eberhardt, J. L. (2015). Two strikes: Race and the disciplining of young students. *Psychological Science, 26*(5), 617–624. doi:10.1177/0956797615570365

Orfield, G., Frankenberg, E., Ee, J., & Kuscera, J. (2014, May 15). *Brown at 60: Great progress, a long retreat and an uncertain future* (Rep.). Retrieved August 6, 2017, from the Civil Rights Project website: https://www.civilrightsproject.ucla.edu/research/k-12-education/integration-and-diversity/brown-at-60-great-progress-a-long-retreat-and-an-uncertain-future/Brown-at-60-051814.pdf

Osei-Kofi, N. (2005). Pathologizing the poor: A framework for understanding Ruby Payne's work. *Equity & Excellence in Education, 38,* 367–375.

Osler, J. (Ed.). (2016). Opportunities for White people in the fight for racial justice. Retrieved May 15, 2018, from https://www.whiteaccomplices.org/

Painter, N. I. (2010). *The history of white people.* New York: Norton.

Paley, V. G. (2000). *White teacher.* Cambridge, MA: Harvard University Press.

Paley, V. G., & Paley, V. G. (2009). White teacher, with a new preface. Cambridge, MA: Harvard University Press.

Palos, A. L., & McGinnis, E. I. (Directors). (2012). *Precious Knowledge* [Motion picture on DVD]. USA: Public Broadcasting Service PBS.

Pane, D. M., & Rocco, T. S. (2014). *Transforming the school-to-prison pipeline: Lessons from the classroom.* Rotterdam, Netherlands: Sense.

Paris, D. (2012). Culturally sustaining pedagogy: A needed change in stance, terminology, and practice. *Educational Researcher, 41*(3), 93–97. doi:10.3102/0013189x12441244

Paris, D., & Alim, H. S. (2017). *Culturally sustaining pedagogies: Teaching and learning for justice in a changing world.* New York: Teachers College Press.

Park, M., Levenson, E., & Jorgensen, S. (2018, March 2). West Virginia governor defends role in teachers strike: "I'm not king." Retrieved August 31, 2019, from https://www.cnn.com/2018/03/01/us/west-virginia-teachers-strike/index.html

Parsons, E. C. (2005). From caring as a relation to culturally relevant caring: A white teacher's bridge to black students. *Equity & Excellence in Education, 38*(1), 25–34. doi:10.1080/10665680390907884

Patel, V. S. (2011). Moving toward an inclusive model of allyship for racial justice. *Vermont Connection, 32*, 78–88.

Paul, J. (2017, September 8). I need an accomplice, not an ally. Retrieved July 18, 2019, from http://efniks.com/the-deep-dive-features/2017/9/6/i-need-an-accomplice-not-an-ally

Payne, C. R., & Welsh, B. H. (2000). The progressive development of multicultural education before and after the 1960s: A theoretical framework. *Teacher Educator, 36*(1), 29–48. doi:10.1080/08878730009555249

Payne, R. K. (2013). *A framework for understanding poverty.* Highlands, TX: Aha! Process.

Pew Research Center. (2015, May 12). *America's changing religious landscape* (Rep.). Retrieved July, 2016, from Pew Research Center website: https://www.pewforum.org/2015/05/12/americas-changing-religious-landscape/

Phillippo, K. (2012). "You're trying to know me": Students from nondominant groups respond to teacher personalism. *Urban Review, 44*(4), 441–467. doi:10.1007/s11256-011-0195-9

Powell, J., & Kelly, A. (2017). Accomplices in the academy in the age of Black Lives Matter. *Journal of Critical Thought and Praxis, 6*(2), 42–65.

Reason, R. D., Millar, E. A., & Scales, T. C. (2005). Toward a model of racial justice ally development. *Journal of College Student Development, 46*(5), 530–546. doi:10.1353/csd.2005.0054

Renkle, M. (2018, July 30). How to talk to a racist: White liberals, you're doing it all wrong. *New York Times.* Retrieved July 30, 2018, from https://www.nytimes.com/2018/07/30/opinion/how-to-talk-to-a-racist.html

Ris, E. W. (2015). Grit: A short history of a useful concept. *Journal of Educational Controversy, 10*(1), 1–18. Retrieved March 13, 2019, from https://cedar.wwu.edu/jec/vol10/iss1/3

Rothstein, R. (2013, August 27). *For public schools, segregation then, segregation since: Education and the unfinished march* (Rep.). Retrieved August 12, 2019, from Economic Policy Institute website: https://www.epi.org/files/2013/Unfinished-March-School-Segregation.pdf

Rothstein, R. (2017). *The color of law: A forgotten history of how our government segregated America.* New York: Liveright.

Sawyer, L. (2016, July 20). Arrests follow in Minneapolis as teachers, activists protest Philando Castile's death. *Minneapolis Star Tribune.* Retrieved August 14, 2019, from http://www.startribune.com/teachers-join-activists-to-protest-castile-shooting/387511391/?refresh=true

Scholz, S. J. (2012). *Political solidarity.* State College, PA: Penn State University Press.

Seltzer, K. (2019). Reconceptualizing "home" and "school" language: Taking a critical translingual approach in the English classroom. *TESOL Quarterly*, online first. doi:https://doi.org/10.1002/tesq.530

Shevalier, R., & McKenzie, B. A. (2012). Culturally responsive teaching as an ethics- and care-based approach to urban education. *Urban Education, 47*(6), 1086–1105. doi:10.1177/0042085912441483

Singleton, G. E., & Linton, C. (2006). *Courageous conversations about race: A field guide for achieving equity in schools.* Corwin Press.

Skiba, R. J., Horner, R. H., Chung, C., Rausch, M. K., May, S. L., & Tobin, T. (2011). Race is not neutral: A national investigation of African American and Latino disproportionality in school discipline. *School Psychology Review, 40*(1), 85–107.

Skiba, R. J., Michael, R. S., Nardo, A. C., & Peterson, R. L. (2002). The color of discipline: Sources of racial and gender disproportionality in school punishment. *Urban Review, 34*(4), 317–342.

Skiba, R. J., Peterson, R. L., & Williams, T. (1997). Office referrals and suspension: Disciplinary intervention in middle schools. *Education and Treatment of Children, 20*(3), 295–315.

Sleeter, C. E. (2001a). An analysis of the critiques of multicultural education. In J. A. Banks & C. A. Banks (Eds.), *Handbook of research on multicultural education* (pp. 81–94). San Francisco, CA: Jossey-Bass.

Sleeter, C. E. (2001b). Preparing teachers for culturally diverse schools. *Journal of Teacher Education, 52*(2), 94–106. doi:10.1177/0022487101052002002

Sleeter, C. E. (2005). How teachers construct race. In C. McCarthy, W. Crichlow, G. Dimitriadis, & N. Dolby (Eds.), *Race, identity, and representation in education* (2nd ed., pp. 243–256). New York: Routledge.

Sleeter, C. E., & Soriano, E. (Eds.). (2012). [Introduction]. In *Creating solidarity across diverse communities: International perspectives in education* (pp. 1–19). New York: Teachers College Press.

Smiley, A. D., & Helfenbein, R. J. (2011). Becoming teachers: The Payne effect. *Multicultural Perspectives, 13*(1), 5–15. doi:10.1080/15210960.2011.548177

Solomon, D., Maxwell, C., & Castro, A. (2019, August 7). Systemic inequality: Displacement, exclusion, and segregation. Retrieved October 14, 2019, from Center for American Progress website: https://www.americanprogress.org/issues/race/reports/2019/08/07/472617/systemic-inequality-displacement-exclusion-segregation/

Solomona, R. P., Portelli, J. P., Daniel, B., & Campbell, A. (2005). The discourse of denial: How white teacher candidates construct race, racism and "white privilege." *Race, Ethnicity, and Education, 8*(2), 147–169. doi:10.1080/13613320500110519

Solorzano, D. (1997). Images and words that wound: Critical race theory, racial stereotyping, and teacher education. *Teacher Education Quarterly, 24*(3), 5–19.

Solorzano, D. G., & Yosso, T. J. (2002). Critical race methodology: Counter-storytelling as an analytical framework for education research. *Qualitative Inquiry, 8*(1), 23–44. doi:10.1177/1077800402008001003

Sondel, B., Baggett, H. C., & Dunn, A. H. (2018). "For millions of people, this is real trauma": A pedagogy of political trauma in the wake of the 2016 U.S. presidential election. *Teaching and Teacher Education, 70*, 175–185. doi:10.1016/j.tate.2017.11.017

Southern Poverty Law Center. (2017). Hate groups increase for second consecutive year as Trump electrifies radical right. Retrieved 2017, from https://www.splcenter.org/news/2017/02/15/hate-groups-increase-second-consecutive-year-trump-electrifies-radical-right

Souto-Manning, M. (2013). Competence as linguistic alignment: Linguistic diversities, affinity groups, and the politics of educational success. *Linguistics and Education, 24*(3), 305–315. doi:10.1016/j.linged.2012.12.009

Stokas, A. G. (2015). A genealogy of grit: Education in the new gilded age. *Educational Theory, 65*(5), 513–528. doi:10.1111/edth.12130

Stotko, E. M., Ingram, R., & Beaty-O'Ferrall, M. E. (2007). Promising strategies for attracting and retaining successful urban teachers. *Urban Education, 42*(1), 30–51. doi:10.1177/0042085906293927

Stovall, D. (2006). We can relate: Hip-hop culture, critical pedagogy, and the secondary classroom. *Urban Education, 41*(6), 585–602. doi:10.1177/0042085906292513

Straubhaar, R. (2014). The stark reality of the "White saviour" complex and the need for critical consciousness: A document analysis of the early journals of a Freirean educator. *Compare: A Journal of Comparative and International Education, 45*(3), 381–400. doi:10.1080/03057925.2013.876306

Sullivan, S. (2014). *Good White people: The problem with middle-class white anti-racism.* Albany, NY: State University of New York Press.

Taie, S., & Goldring, R. (2017, August 22). Characteristics of public elementary and secondary school teachers in the United States: Results from the 2015–16 National Teacher and Principal Survey (NCES 2017-072). Retrieved July 12, 2018, from https://nces.ed.gov/pubsearch/pubsinfo.asp?pubid=2017071

Tatum, B. D. (1992). Talking about race, learning about racism: The application of racial identity development theory in the classroom. *Harvard Educational Review, 62*(1), 1–24. doi:10.17763/haer.62.1.146k5v980r703023

#Teachers4BlackLives hashtag on Twitter. (2016, July 19). Retrieved August 14, 2019, from https://twitter.com/hashtag/teachers4blacklives

Ullucci, K. (2012). Knowing we are White: Narrative as critical praxis. *Teaching Education, 23*(1), 89–107. doi:10.1080/10476210.2011.622747

Utt, J. (2013, July 1). So, you call yourself an ally: 10 things all "allies" need to know. Retrieved August 23, 2019, from https://everydayfeminism.com/2013/11/things-allies-need-to-know/

Utt, J., & Tochluk, S. (2020). White teacher, know thyself. *Urban Education,* January 1, 2020. doi:10.1177/0042085916648741

Valencia, R. R. (2010). *Dismantling contemporary deficit thinking: Educational thought and practice.* New York: Routledge.

Villegas, A. M., Strom, K., & Lucas, T. (2012). Closing the racial/ethnic gap between students of color and their teachers: An elusive goal. *Equity & Excellence in Education, 45*(2), 283–301. doi:10.1080/10665684.2012.656541

Wacquant, L. (2001). Deadly symbiosis. *Punishment & Society, 3*(1), 95–133. doi:10.1177/14624740122228276

Wald, J., & Losen, D. J. (2003). Defining and redirecting a school-to-prison pipeline. *New Directions for Youth Development, 2003*(99), 9–15. doi:10.1002/yd.51

Ware, F. (2006). Warm demander pedagogy: Culturally responsive teaching that supports a culture of achievements for African American students. *Urban Education, 41*(4), 427–456.

Warren, C. A. (2013). Towards a pedagogy for the application of empathy in culturally diverse classrooms. *Urban Review, 46*(3), 395–419. doi:10.1007/s11256-013-0262-5

Warren, C. A. (2018). Empathy, teacher dispositions, and preparation for culturally responsive pedagogy. *Journal of Teacher Education, 69*(2), 169–183. doi:10.1177/0022487117712487

Warren, C. A., & Hotchkins, B. K. (2014). Teacher education and the enduring significance of "false empathy." *Urban Review, 47*(2), 266–292. doi:10.1007/s11256-014-0292-7

Warren, C. A., & Talley, L. M. (2017). "Nice white ladies": Race, whiteness, and the preparation of a more culturally responsive teacher workforce. In C. A. Warren & S. A. Hancock (Eds.), *White women's work: Examining the intersectionality of teaching, identity, and race* (pp. 147–175). Charlotte, NC: Information Age Publishing.

Washington Post. (2018). Fatal force: 2018 police shootings database. *Washington Post.* Retrieved August 31, 2019, from https://www.washingtonpost.com/graphics/2018/national/police-shootings-2018/

Waters, R. (2010). Understanding allyhood as a developmental process. *About Campus, 15*(5), 2–8. doi:10.1002/abc.20035

West, L. (2013, June 19). A complete guide to "hipster racism." Retrieved from https://jezebel.com/a-complete-guide-to-hipster-racism-5905291

Whitaker, A., Torres-Guillén, S., Morton, M., Jordan, H., Coyle, S., Mann, A., & Sun, W. (2017). *Cops and no counselors: How the lack of school mental health staff is harming students* (Rep.). Retrieved from https://www.aclu.org/report/cops-and-no-counselors

White, K., & Ruelas, R. (2016, January 27). Desert Vista High School girl apologizes for n-word incident. Retrieved September, 2017, from https://www.azcentral.com/story/news/local/ahwatukee/2016/01/25/desert-vista-high-school-protest-petition-shirts/79309158/

Wilde, L. (2007). The concept of solidarity: Emerging from the theoretical shadows? *British Journal of Politics and International Relations, 9*(1), 171–181. doi:10.1111/j.1467-856x.2007.00275.x

Williamson, L. A. (2011, March 1). Getting more black men into the classroom. Retrieved October 11, 2012, from http://www.tolerance.org/blog/getting-more-black-men-classroom

Woodson, C. G. (1933). *History is a weapon.* New York: Associated. Retrieved 2016, from https://historyisaweapon.com/defcon1/misedne.html

Wozolek, B., Wootton, L., & Demlow, A. (2016). The school-to-coffin pipeline: Queer youth, suicide, and living the in-between. *Cultural Studies ↔ Critical Methodologies, 17*(5), 392–398. doi:10.1177/1532708616673659

Wu, N. (2019, August 22). Newt Gingrich says slavery needs to be put "in context," calls 1619 Project a "lie." Retrieved August 30, 2019, from https://www.usatoday.com/story/news/politics/2019/08/19/newt-gingrich-calls-new-york-times-1619-project-a-lie/2049622001/

Wyly, E. K., & Hammel, D. J. (2004). Gentrification, segregation, and discrimination in the American urban system. *Environment and Planning A: Economy and Space, 36*(7), 1215–1241. doi:10.1068/a3610

Xiong, C., & Stahl, B. (2017, June 22). Video: "I don't want you to get shooted," daughter pleads to mother moments after Castile shooting. *Minneapolis Star Tribune*. Retrieved August 15, 2019, from http://www.startribune.com/video-i-don-t-want-you-to-get-shooted-daughter-pleads-to-mother-moments-after-castile-shooting/429948923/

Yosso, T. J. (2005). Whose culture has capital? A critical race theory discussion of community cultural wealth. *Race Ethnicity and Education, 8*(1), 69–91. doi:10.1080/1361332052000341006

Yull, D. G., & Wilson, M. A. (2018). Allies, accomplices, or troublemakers: Black families and scholar activists working for social justice in a race-conscious parent engagement program. *Critical Education, 9*(8), 1–18. Retrieved July 18, 2019, from http://ojs.library.ubc.ca/index.php/criticaled/article/view/186343

Index

About the Author

Michael L. Boucher Jr. is an assistant professor of curriculum and instruction at Texas A&M University–San Antonio. He completed his PhD in curriculum and instruction at Indiana University. His research examines the relationships of solidarity between successful White teachers and their students of color in de facto segregated schools. Dr. Boucher studies the interplay between race, power, and curriculum through his varied work, which explores the racialization of historical understanding, the impact on White teacher candidates of student teaching experiences abroad, and the cultural aspect of deficit models in education. Dr. Boucher's studies have been published in *Urban Education*, *The Urban Review*, *Action in Teacher Education*, and edited volumes. His methodological work, focusing on empowering individuals and communities as participants in ethnographic education research, has been published in the *International Journal of Adult Vocational Education and Technology*, *Scholarly Publishing and Research Methods across Disciplines*, the *Handbook of Research on Innovative Techniques, Trends, and Analysis for Optimized Research Methods*, and his edited volume, *Participant Empowerment through Photo Elicitation in Ethnographic Education Research: New Research and Approaches*.